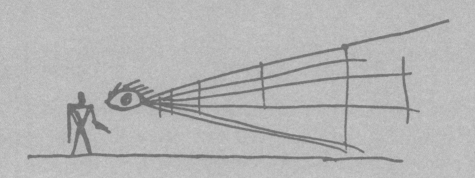

Le Corbusier
and the Continual Revolution
in Architecture

LE CORBUSIER

and the Continual Revolution in Architecture

CHARLES JENCKS

THE MONACELLI PRESS

FIRST PUBLISHED IN
THE UNITED STATES OF AMERICA
IN 2000 BY

The Monacelli Press, Inc.
10 East 92nd Street
New York, New York 10128

DESIGNED BY

Anthony McCall Associates

Printed and bound in Italy

Library of Congress Catalog Card Number: 00-106881

ISBN: 1-58093-077-8

Endpapers: Image is from page 184 of *The Modulor 1 and 2*, by Le Corbusier, accompanying the quote: "I have concerned myself only with objects falling under the jurisdiction of the eye."

Frontispiece: Ronchamp, interior south wall. Light wedges are cut into the thick wall, allowing diffused light to reflect on the sides. A thin shaft of horizontal light separates the wall and the dark ceiling that looms over the viewer. LC conceived the chapel "without windows," and in this sense the interior can be seen as an underground structure with three up-periscopes and twenty-odd side-periscopes. He often made a drama of the witheld view, and here you are meant to peer through deep splays to find exterior nature framed by white walls, and an occasional colored pane of glass, with a moon, star, sun, or virgin. Thus the temple to nature worship, to pantheism, is given a primitive iconography.

Contents

1. Jeanneret, 1921. He lost the use of his
left eye when painting his first picture,
The Chimney-Piece, in November 1918.

The Revolutionary Personality

HOW DO YOU MEASURE the worth of an architect? The architect Peter Smithson once wrote, apropos the Heroic Period of Early Modernism, "Mies is great, but Corb communicates." Mies could teach you good architecture, but "Corb could make you leave home."

That is a bizarre but interesting definition of greatness: someone who persuades you to change your life and embark on a new adventure. This Le Corbusier did to me, as to so many others, through his buildings, paintings, and, above all, writings on architecture. The passion for his field, once he had been weaned from engraving watches, was so strongly felt and transmitted through words and images as to convince several generations of students to become architects. Indeed, Smithson's words are something of an understatement since Le Corbusier wrote some fifty-seven books (depending on what one calls a book), including the widely read classic *Vers une architecture.* He was a consummate journalist, autobiographer, pamphleteer, and travel and architectural writer.

It is enjoyable to follow his letters, journals, and sketchbooks because they are so revealing. Week by week, he would tell us what he was thinking and feeling, and thus there is a dramatic record of his unfolding life, much of which he predicted with uncanny insight. An extraordinary letter of his, written at twenty-one years of age, foretells much of what he wants to do, and will in fact achieve, for the next fifty years. This strong sense of destiny gives a shape to his life, makes it a work of art with its own hidden patterns and, coupled with the paper trail of introspection, an enticing puzzle to be deciphered. What a delight it is to tease out some of his "secrets" and hidden patterns, the meanings that his biography creates.

As a result of his introspection and creativity, he has elicited some of the best scholarship and architectural analysis of the last century. This critical appreciation is a good mark of his enduring worth. The reader will find I draw on it continuously and, because it is such a pleasure to follow others in the hunt for Le Corbusier, I thought it right to single out those from whom I have learned the most.

The writings of Geoffrey Baker, Tim Benton, Allen Brooks, William Curtis, Robert Fishman, Kenneth Frampton, Christopher Green, Richard A. Moore, Colin Rowe, Patricia Sekler, Eduard F. Sekler, Peter Serenyi, Russell Walden, Stanislaus von Moos, Adolf Max Vogt, and Ivan Zaknic are a few of those whose important studies are continually referred to in the endnotes. These authors constitute an unnamed symposium in continuous session, not always in harmonious agreement. Also very helpful to the search is the Fondation Le Corbusier (FLC) in Paris led by Evelyne Tréhin. Its preservation and publication of the archives has made a detailed understanding of LC's life and work possible. Another institute, Heidi Weber's Le Corbusier Center in Zurich, has also helped me and other scholars gain a sharper picture of their subject.

But it is Le Corbusier's own words, and communication, that have most attracted me for more than forty years, and it is those I have concentrated on. If my book is different from others, it is not only in two or three interpretations, but in this focus. His writing counts, demands to be reproduced and analyzed in depth. There is no way to understand him fully other than reading his words, and agreeing and disagreeing with them.

This is one of the secrets to which he referred. There are other fascinating ones that make him "a strange bird" asking to be seen in a new light, but there is this little-known self-definition: when asked in 1930, by the French government, to declare what he was, what profession he practiced, he did not say "architect," "designer," or "painter." He wrote in his passport, on becoming a citizen, "Man of Letters." Perhaps, as sometimes, this was a sly joke aimed at a small coterie; perhaps it was because he never went to the Ecole des Beaux Arts and therefore could not write D.P.L.G. (*diplomé par le gouvernment*) after his name. Perhaps he was boasting, or mocking authority. But there it is, "Man of Letters"—a writer of fifty-seven "books" (some *are* pamphlets, or illustrated booklets). The motive for this self-definition comes, I hope to show, from the "accident" of literary fame, that the nom de plume and prophet Le Corbusier swallowed his other identities, the painter Jeanneret and even his role as a builder.

I first decided to study architecture at Harvard after hearing Eduard Sekler give a talk on Ronchamp, the famous chapel in eastern France. This was in 1959; and for the next forty years, to use one of the architect's phrases, "I gabbled Corbu"—read, drew, and talked about him. My interest lessened somewhat after I wrote an early version of this book in 1972 and felt I understood the richness and depth of his work. But he has remained for me the touchstone of a great architect and, in spite of his undeniable faults, the standard. Because of the way he combined different professions and passions—architecture, writing, painting to be sure, but also cosmology, sexuality, and his curious type of friendship—I have found him broader and more complete than other architects, indeed other creative characters such as Picasso. Again, this is in spite of some notable shortcomings. Even with these, he fulfills the well-rounded paragon of Marx's Renaissance Man of the future: the person who is at least three different things every day—and Le Corbusier *did* carry on at least three different professions. Painter, most mornings until 1:00; architect most afternoons until about 6:00; and, in the evenings, writer, sometime conversationalist, and *bon viveur* (he was not altogether a good husband). A complete man even if, as Lewis Mumford put it, he could be one-sided and arrogant. As the reader will find, while I continue to admire Le Corbusier, I will not gloss over his shortcomings or the difficulty of his character. His own honesty demands it, and while his failings make unconditional love impossible they do not cease making it conditional. The major question marks hanging over his life include one or two professional indiscretions, occasional infidelity, his fallacious planning theories, and his collaboration with Vichy. I do not claim to have said the final word on these questions so much as to have raised them, in the first edition, and examined them more closely here. They present deep puzzles that may reflect Le Corbusier's character or, perhaps more, the time and ethics in which he tried to build.

With all these complexities and his protean character, LC has fascinated me for most of my life. Ronchamp stayed with me, and, in 1975, I understood it as the harbinger of Post-Modernism, a movement that caught on and changed world architecture (sometimes, unfortunately, for the worse). Ronchamp was highly metaphorical and brought together many different languages or codes of architecture. In addition to formal brilliance, it used irony to send complex messages and alluded to historical and symbolic codes—all the things that were proscribed at Modernist academies. LC, like Picasso, stayed well ahead of his followers. Like Michelangelo, who was an Early, High, and Late Renaissance architect, Le Corbusier strode across the categories, often ushering them in. He epitomized at least two periods: the white architecture of the 1920s, the Heroic Period of Modernism, and the Late Modern era, the Brutalist, concrete period of the 1950s. If one counts Ronchamp and Chandigarh as Post-Modern, as I argue, then his parallel with Michelangelo is all the greater. Three periods brought into being: one Minimalist, one Mannerist, one Baroque, and this is not to mention his books, paintings, and other contributions to such things as an emergent High-Tech movement. The powerful god Proteus is invoked in this outburst of demonic creativity, this continual revolution.

So he overcame the categories, he kept creating new ones, he practiced many professions, yet remained an amateur in the best sense of the word. And feeding his genius were various paradoxes. He could be dogmatic, tyrannical, and ridiculous at times, a man who, in spite of his worldly success, saw himself, at the end, as a partial failure, as a Don Quixote tilting at windmills. As his sometime friend Auguste Perret said, "he's a very curious bird, but he will interest you"—and when you dislike him, that too is interesting, for his failings are also protean.

Le Corbusier occupies the position he does, as *the* architect of the last century, not only for embodying three periods, but for the content of his art, his message. As a prophetic character who faced up to the twentieth century, he engaged its basic forces—mass production, the destruction of cities, the rise of kitsch, the ecological crisis, mass housing—for better or worse. His solutions, far from solving all these problems, exacerbated one or two, but that is often the case with a prophet. Confronting these forces led to what I would call his "tragic stance," an orientation that stemmed from a life-long attempt to reconcile opposites—thinking and feeling, industry and art, science and religion—an attempt founded on a dualistic philosophy. It was this dualism that impressed me the most when I first started writing on his opposing personae. The two parts of his character (the first he used for painting, the second for architecture) became the title of my article in 1967, "Charles Jeanneret—Le Corbusier." I illustrated this opposition with a drawing made in 1945, of the Medusa versus the sun god [fig. 2].

When young and impressionable, Charles-Edouard Jeanneret immersed himself in reading about prophets: Pythagoras, Nietzsche's Zarathustra, and *The Life of Jesus.* There is no doubt he saw himself from the age of twenty as a prophet. But of what? The new architecture, surely, but more than this, the new city, and of bringing about a change in taste, in civilization. In brief, he wanted to bring "harmony to an industrial civilization profoundly out of gear." He wanted to reconcile science and religion. He wanted to bring a cosmic worldview back to a newly secular society. He set himself three unattainable goals, and he was sometimes depressed that he did not achieve them. At other, more lucid moments, he knew that his goals, however desirable, were beyond reach. But in his romantic fever as he kept trying to attain them, he noticed, as Nietzsche had written, that there is a certain joy in the struggle itself. The battle to bring the impossible into being is, for the romantic, a war worth testing one's strength.

It was his worldview, perhaps understood before he read Nietzsche, but certainly afterwards, that became the subject of my *Le Corbusier and the Tragic View of Architecture* (first edition 1973, second 1987). The tragic view I found was expressed several ways: in the dualism, in his philosophy of "joy through struggle," and in the way his buildings, like Greek temples, contrasted with nature, but also celebrated it. The tragic human condition—of being part of the cosmos, but also separate from it and conscious of that separation—is expressed in these buildings, through a cool gravitas and violent set of oppositions.

2. Medusa/Apollo, 1945. Le Corbusier captioned this after the war: "The contemporary disaster or the liberty of space." His Cathar ancestors, of whom he was proud, gave equal weight to good and evil. Reconciling, or confronting, duality was in his nature and became his method of design and painting.

Unkind critics said Le Corbusier's buildings were tragic because they were awful.

In any case, there are other meanings of tragedy that matter, such as the heroic struggle that brings, through a flaw in character, a tragic outcome. The flaw in LC's personality, an overbearing egotism, served the compulsive view that city plans can be imposed through an act of heroic will, through the decision of a great leader, a Colbert, Louis XIV, or, coming down a notch, Mussolini. Le Corbusier was often led astray by his "great man theory" of planning, even when this led him to Nehru. But cities are not artifacts to be molded to the artist's vision, however benign, and it is this truth that continuously leads to conflict, to Le Corbusier tilting at the windmills of authority. Charles-Edouard Jeanneret, partially his alter ego, realizes this and so identifies Le Corbusier with the knight-errant Don Quixote, and his partner in design, Pierre Jeanneret, with Sancho Panza. Cervantes's novel, which stayed in Le Corbusier's pocket for many years, can be read as a comedy— and the architect saw himself occasionally as a trickster—or, as the Russians do, a tragedy. Whatever the genre, it is the case, as I will show, that LC looked to literature for guidance and found it in this tragic-comic, misguided saint.

Also, in considering the manifold meanings of the tragic genre, there is the misfortune of being unable to attain the goal for which one fights, here LC's inability to bring harmony to the second machine age. All these meanings show how relevant the Western notion of tragedy is to Le Corbusier's work and life. They are still central to my interpretation, although I now see how they drove him toward an incessant creativity, toward facing the demon of constant change, the continual revolution in architecture, the very perplexity that faces us today. At any one point in the twentieth century there are usually three or four competing movements in architecture and they mutate every five to ten years. There is as yet no adequate description, or theory, of this continual revolution, but LC at least confronted it.

An odd fact behind this book. An unusual, but gratifying, opportunity has occurred in my life as a writer now that old books can be scanned in, and recast on, the computer. I have rewritten two other books, over several editions, producing "evolvotomes" as a result. They evolve as new facts emerge, my knowledge deepens, and, painfully, I discover mistakes. Le Corbusier used to produce

new versions of old paintings, and double date them—1929–1945—
to indicate that a theme was revived and transformed. This book is
an analogous evolvotome with a triple date 1973, 1987, and 2000.
In print in several languages for twenty-six years, an entirely new
edition and the computer allow me to rewrite every word. It has
also allowed me to redraw and analyze many familiar images to
make a new point or unravel a common thread that goes through
the paintings, drawings, and architecture.

This version adds to the evidence of the first edition, that the
tragic view is a meaningful way of considering his architecture, but
corrects errors and brings in new interpretations. Among these are
the importance of what he called secrets—not only his painting and
method of transposing designs, but his interest in Theosophy, the
occult, cosmogony, and sexuality. It is also new because it brings
up the importance of his work for Post-Modernism and rooting
architecture in a cosmic setting. In an appendix I argue that his
contribution is typical of other geniuses of this century, Einstein
and Picasso, two other protean creators with whom he was keen to
be photographed. So spirituality, women, Post-Modern symbolism, genius, and the relevance of a cosmic architecture are new to
this book, and also to Corb Interpretation (now an industry).

If his double dating and my triple writing have a virtue, they
also pose a problem. Charles-Edouard Jeanneret was always looking forward, predicting what he would do and then, once having
done it, looking back. This gave his life its continuity and unity, but
it also makes the way one tells the story preemptive and circular.
Other writers, as I have, note how an early idea foreshadows a later
solution, or conversely, how his late work in India goes back to his
first work in La Chaux-de-Fonds. Thus the circularity in the way
one writes on Corbu, as the French called him, or Corb as the
Americans and English did, or Jeanneret, or Edouard, or LC, or
Paul Boulard, or any one of his four pseudonyms. Or, better, it is
like a spiral, or barber pole, a metaphor of continual revolution
(and revolution had this contradictory meaning in the past—to
revolve backwards to a better future). As we will see, themes keep
recurring in a new key, perhaps every ten years, so that they generate a revolving, helical structure. Looking straight up the helix one
can see a similar idea transformed four or five times. This also
means that a symbol, or formal motif in painting and sculpture,
can have different meanings at different times. For instance, the

open hand and moon goddess/earth mother recur in transformed ways from the late 1920s onwards. They become what I would call "carryover symbols," that is, transhistorical signs and forms that may have one or two deep meanings, but also several changing ones. As we will see, the architect was obsessed by symbolism from the age of sixteen, and so there are many symbols that carry over from one period to the next, but they do not always mean the same thing across time. One has to be alert to this ambiguity and continuity.

In the sense that he pulled together different traditions and achieved continuity, his attempt to reconcile opposites was successful. His protean, combative character kept him revolutionizing the art of architecture right to the end, in 1965. How many other architects or artists "keep going back to zero" to reinvent their field? What does this imply for architecture and living in cities? Such are the questions posed by this Proteus from Switzerland.

3. Edouard with his parents,
January 1, 1909 (BV).

PART I

Dress Rehearsal in a Small Town

Born to a Proud Family

Charles-Edouard Jeanneret was born on October 6, 1887, in the Swiss watchmaking town of La Chaux-de-Fonds. In part it was a very clannish town, as indicated by the way families swapped and hyphenated their names; but the practice revealed something else. Although an integrated, somewhat closed culture, because of the industrialization of watchmaking it was beginning to open up, and fall apart. Thus personal identity could be conferred by a family's past and its name, but also by choosing to change it.

Charles-Edouard, the son of Georges Edouard Jeanneret-Gris, was always called "Edouard" at home, and the father changed the last, hyphenated, part of his name to "Perret," in order to honor his wife's more illustrious family. Her name was Marie-Charlotte-Amelie Perret, "Marie" for short. When Charles-Edouard took on the pseudonym "Le Corbusier," modifying another ancestor's name, not only was he trying to give his new title an air of nobility with the "Le," but he was also following the time-honored family method of changing a name to fit the new circumstances.

Both parents and their two sons—Albert was two years Edouard's senior—were fiercely proud of their strong-minded, if modest, forebears. The family myth, possibly true, was that the Jeannerets descended from the Cathars and Albigensians, tough revolutionaries and farmers, high-minded and persecuted heretics on the run. Pauline, the maiden aunt that Le Corbusier lived with when young, and spoke about with deep affection, mixed a strong religious temperament with a fondness for Rabelais and Cervantes. How she negotiated between high church and low life we do not know, but this upright spinster often chided Albert and Edouard with words from *Gargantua and Pantagruel* and *Don Quixote*. It is impossible to find today's equivalents for the argot of the time, but the flavor of what she called the boys is: "braggart, gasbag, blowmouth, brave clown, dog-boy, proud as Artaban, proud as a peacock, pretentious popinjay, wind-bag, trickster, robber, cocky boaster, naughty-one, over-the-top, awkward country boy, airhead, skin-and-bones, ridiculous empty pot." Sixteenth-century street slang and Protestant righteousness? Inevitably, Edouard spent much of his life working out the humor and profundity in this unlikely cocktail.

"La Chaux-de-Fonds" means "meadow at the end of the valley," here a valley that stretches to the town of Le Locle, seven kilo-

4. La Chaux-de-Fonds, 1971.
Repetitive burgher housing built on a
gridiron in a small town of artisans
shows the contrast of manmade
geometry with a natural setting of
mountains and valleys.

meters away. La Chaux adopted a gridiron plan in 1835, after a fire
of 1794, both of which left their mark on the inhabitants and the
future Le Corbusier. For the burghers the town had a sad, slightly
boring air because of its no-nonsense layout and single industry of
watchmaking, but for Le Corbusier the grid had an implicit meaning which in certain lights could be extremely positive. When seen
against the voluptuous mountain backdrop of rolling greenery and
fir trees, it could symbolize man's ordering and poetic nature—the
mind at work—versus living nature at work. The absolute contrast
of geometry and nature, grid and growth, was to become his hallmark by the 1920s. Rational and repetitive the town appears, like
the sensible Swiss burghers who toil away in their small home-
base workshops: "La Ville triste" it is sometimes known elsewhere
in the country [fig. 4].

The young Jeanneret, between the ages of eighteen and twenty-
six, helped create a more idyllic version of this fabric on a northern hillside known as the Pouillerel district. On the edge of the
grid, near the Rue de la Montagne, is a clutch of houses that he and
his comrades-in-art constructed for the artistic middle class.
These constitute "another culture," a mini-colony, something like
a tiny and provincial rendition of the then vital art community at
Darmstadt, or the later Bauhaus. Here, overlooking the city, is a
dense wood of fir trees and sturdy Arts and Crafts villas nestled

20

5. Pouillerel Hillside of Villas (after Geoffrey H. Baker). These were designed by Jeanneret, except for L'Eplattenier's, and they could be seen around 1910 as a miniature art colony, a utopian community, or an elite departure from the town.

into them. At a cursory glance they might be average Swiss chalets, but on further inspection they reveal a nobility and personality that go beyond stereotype. The Pouillerel hillside is a peaceful place to contemplate both the surrounding mountains and the everyday world below, the sky and conventional life, a world apart from both [fig. 5]. With strong contrasts, it is a potential breeding ground for those with a dualistic view of life.

To understand Jeanneret's early sensibility, one must understand this mountain landscape. His father was president of the local Swiss Alpine Club and he often took his two sons on hiking trips through the mountains. Here they studied nature, got to know the "unity of its laws" as Le Corbusier later put it, but, most importantly, developed a taste for being alone with the pleasures of outdoor existence. Most striking are the monumental fir and spruce trees, the soft pastures sprinkled with wild crocuses and daffodils, and the contrast of this with the bleak beauty of the mountaintop.

The neighborhood villas that Edouard designed are, in a sense, temples to nature placed as mountain aeries beside the forest. They represent an ideal but dual existence, being both in direct touch with the cosmic pleasures—sun, space, and greenery—and civilized life. This dualism Le Corbusier tried to transform, from 1914 onward, into a low-cost version for everyone, and it makes sense to understand both his later triumphs and failures as successive attempts to remake the Pouillerel villas.

While life in this exclusive area on the edge of town may have been idyllic in some respects, it was very hard going for the father, Edouard Jeanneret-Perret. He continued the family business as a watch engraver and developed a very special technique of enameling the watchface with a perfect, ultra-white sheen. White had for him, as his son, a moral Protestant honesty. It was invested with ethical qualities of beauty, control, and sobriety. Furthermore, handwork at home had a kind of dignity and modest creativity not present in the factory, where shoddy goods, often in questionable taste, were churned out. One could work at home during the winter days when the snow trapped one inside, work at one's own pace, and achieve the integrity of the artistic craftsman. In these senses, the reality of watch production in La Chaux-de-Fonds reflected the English moral view, of Ruskin and Morris, that only the contented craftsman, working at his own speed, could create a healthy, living art [fig. 6]. The problem, and this was the crisis that faced the father then the son, was that handwork did not pay very well. Furthermore, it was vulnerable to changes in taste and, particularly, to innovations in mass production.

The depression of 1893 was a great strain on the family's finances, as were later crises in the watchmaking trade. Jeanneret-Perret, a meticulous and responsible family man, took these upheavals badly. He resigned as president of the mountaineering club, gave up most of his favorite hobbies, and, with further

6. Charles-Edouard Jeanneret, center, with his friends Octave Matthey and Louis Houriet carrying out sgraffito work on the Villa Fallet, 1907. Other craftsmen and friends who worked on the building were the painter André Evard and the scupltor Leon Perrin—happy Ruskinian craftsmen all.

economic troubles in the 1910s, visibly aged, ending up looking thirty years older than he was. Ultimately mass production destroyed his life and sent him to an early grave. If a place is sought for the primary motive behind Le Corbusier's proselytizing on behalf of the new machine age, one will find it here. "Industry, overwhelming us like a flood, rolls on to its predestined ends" was one of his formulations in the 1920s. Like Karl Marx, and other nineteenth-century prophets of cultural change, Le Corbusier believed that history marched inexorably and smashed down people in its way. The demon of change was not one class destroying another, but rather a more advanced system of production killing a less efficient one. He learned this lesson through his father's continual loss of work, and this must have developed in him the notion of creative destruction, or destructive creation.

One of the reasons we can piece together young Jeanneret's mind is that his father kept meticulous journals and many of the postcards and letters his son sent home. The historian Allen Brooks has decoded this material, and from it one gets the impression that a proud and concerned father helped his sons build up a strong sense of self-worth. I will select from a few entries to give a sense of his feelings:

> October 6, 1890—Our son Edouard having his third birthday and in perfect health, as is his brother Albert.

> August 31, 1891—Today our two sons begin school, at Miss Colin's Froebel School.

This was a private kindergarten where Edouard, at the tender age of three and three-quarters, had his first lesson in three-dimensional geometry. The Froebel Blocks, or "Gifts," were basic building blocks that related to three very important ideas to come. First, they were simple, undecorated, primary volumes, nearly the basic Phileban forms of Plato—the sphere, cube, cylinder, and cone. Second, they related to the primary building elements of Egyptian and Western Classicism. And third, there was the influence of Rousseau, prevalent in La Chaux-de-Fonds, on bringing up children and developing their creativity. The Froebel Blocks, as light wooden objects pleasant to handle, were meant to be freely manipulated by the young child, as a form of self-expression and self-creation. Architectural historians have often remarked that Frank Lloyd Wright played with them as a child, and now we know it is also true of his counterpart.

Precocity? Many children were brought up on geometry and Jean-Jacques Rousseau, but to be marked for life by both passions, before the age of four, takes some imprinting. Another consequence of Froebel Blocks, also key for Wright, was their necessary organic unity. Piled together by a four-year-old they miraculously produce consistency and harmony: the construction becomes the structure, volume becomes ornament, and exterior and interior are the same. By using them to build a virtual structure, there is no contradiction between style and substance. What the eye sees, the hand manipulates freely, and the mind comprehends. In effect, the lesson of the Froebel is translated thirty years later by LC into "The Lesson of Rome"—the basic building blocks of architecture—and volume, surface, and the plan as generator.

Further excerpts from Jeanneret-Perret's journal reveal the constant concern for Edouard's health and his academic success, two issues that were on his mind until the boy came fully under the sway of his first great mentor, Charles L'Eplattenier.

February 6, 1893—Went yesterday with my two dear ones to Pouillerel. Wonderful walk and beautiful; view, but very cold. These two children hike well, are robust, especially Albert. Edouard [at five], whose constitution is more frail, is rather thin, but these youngsters have survived the winter without coughs thanks to cod-liver oil that we make them take . . .

July 13, 1895—Our two sons each took first prize in their class; these please us greatly . . .

February 6, 1899— [Edouard at eleven] is usually a good child, intelligent, but has a difficult character, susceptible, quick-tempered, and rebellious; at times he gives us reason for anxiety.

April 10, 1900—Edouard obtained a good third trimester report; 3rd among 35 students and one of the youngest; his enjoyment in drawing increases, and he paints flowers very well; [at twelve] he has begun taking courses at the Ecole d'art.

At primary school Edouard was always first, second, or third in a class of forty or fifty, and, as I point out in an appendix to this book, while academic success is not invariably a sign of later genius, the concern of parents for the seriousness of study seems to be a sine qua non of the twentieth-century genius (it is true of Einstein, Picasso, T. S. Eliot, and others mentioned in the appendix). Also of interest in these journal entries is the first note of the young Jeanneret's quick temper and rebelliousness—his "difficult character." Again, like these protean creators, he was not easy to get on with.

The Contradictions of La Chaux-de-Fonds

If the young Jeanneret's character was rebellious and full of contradictions pulling him in different ways, so too was the city of La Chaux-de-Fonds. It might be maddeningly petty, but also, as he pointed out, it was an idyllic landscape for ideal work in small, self-sufficient groups. He quotes Jean-Jacques Rousseau, a considerable influence on his writing style:

> I remember seeing [La Chaux] in my young days . . . a rather agreeable sight, and one that was possibly unique, a mountainside covered with homesteads, each of which was the center of the land about it . . . These fortunate peasants, all comfortably off, free from tithes and taxes . . . cultivated with the utmost diligence their own holdings, of which they enjoyed the produce, devoting their leisure to making countless objects with their hands . . . I continually admired these people, a remarkable mixture of refinement and simplicity.

This small city has been, for the last four hundred years, one of the most important centers for making clocks and watches in the world. Even in the 1970s it exported annually forty-four million watches (then nearly half the world production). These had a mechanical precision that was unsurpassed. When Le Corbusier wrote *Precisions—The Present State of Architecture and Urbanism*, 1930, he was alluding to the meticulous ingenuity of his watch making ancestors, whose survival depended on their mechanical ability. These people were a persecuted sect of French Huguenots who fled to Switzerland in the sixteenth century to establish watchmaking as the major industry of La Chaux.

Indeed, La Chaux-de-Fonds has always been a haven for political and religious refugees, a fact that bears on the formation of Le Corbusier's character. He continually spoke of his persecuted ancestors, and was fascinated by the fierce, Manichaean religion of the Cathars with which he identified. Not only did La Chaux-de-Fonds attract such utopian refugees as Rousseau, but also the anarchists Bakunin and Kropotkin. Karl Marx wrote about it positively in *Das Kapital*, and even Lenin came to La Chaux and admired its original qualities. Lenin passing through the pastoral sobriety of La Chaux seems as bizarre as Stalin visiting the spas at Bath. What attracted the anarchists, utopians, and cynical revolutionaries were the self-sufficient home workshops. In effect, they embodied the mutual aid and free cooperation of workers' syndicates, goals that anarchists have always seen as the final, liberated state of man in society. These were functioning entities in La Chaux for many years.

In 1933, when Le Corbusier was formulating his ideal society for *The Radiant City*, he drew an anarcho-syndicalist form of organization that had parallels with the watchmaking industry of the Swiss Jura [fig. 7]. Groups of workmen were to form the true power base of a hierarchical structure, where control would be kept decentralized through a representational system. The only way in which this contradicted anarcho-syndicalist theory was in the apex of the hierarchy. Le Corbusier always saw society as being led, if not controlled, by a small group of elite specialists: a prophet or great leader such as Nehru; or perhaps a great artist such as

7. A Regional-Syndicalist system of government, 1933, based on power springing from work organizations, or *métiers*, and delegated to a confederation. "Control" is exerted from below, "information" from above.

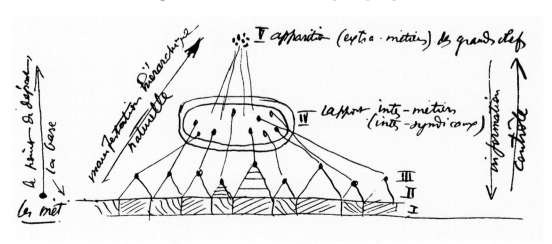

Picasso; or a captain of industry, such as the head of the Citroën or Voisin motor corporations.

In any event, La Chaux was a European place of anarchist thought in the nineteenth century. When Bakunin split with Marx in 1871, and the working-class movement split between libertarian and authoritarian communism, he settled in La Chaux, found a response among the watchmakers, and started a political review called *L'Avant-Garde.* The Jeanneret family was among the supporters of Bakunin. Beyond this, Le Corbusier spoke with pride of his revolutionary grandparents, of whom one died in prison, and one was a leader of the successful revolution of 1848 in La Chaux. The Jeannerets kept alive the tradition of fierce struggle dating back to their original persecution. A typical family motto was "Whatever you do, see that you do it." The phrase comes from Rabelais and was the mother's constant, if somewhat redundant, advice to her son. Yet the meaning was clear: to achieve anything, one had to fight hard and remorselessly for it.

Looking back in the 1940s at this life of struggle, Le Corbusier said:

> Sometimes I despair. Men are so stupid that I'm glad I'm going to die. All my life people have tried to crush me. First they called me a dirty engineer, then a painter who tried to be an architect, then an architect who tried to paint, then a communist, then a Fascist. Luckily, I've always had an iron will. Though timid as a youth, I've forced myself to cross Rubicons. *Je suis un type boxeur.* [fig. 8]

"I am the boxer type." The fact that tennis courts and football fields and stadia always appeared in his city plans implied more than a belief in the healthy effects of physical exercise. Sport was a type of Darwinian competition that sharpened the individual for a combat with life. In fact, Le Corbusier even credited playing basketball in the evenings with giving him the moral security that was reflected in his work! As in ancient Greece, mental harmony and brilliance were to be supported by physical training.

The Abstract Representation of Nature
Edouard accompanied his father on many Sunday walks through

8. Boxing in the hanging gardens of a collective apartment, 1928. The emphasis on physical sport permeated all of Le Corbusier's architecture. Tennis and football were to be played at the foot of every housing block, while running tracks were provided on the roofs.

the Alpine landscapes of La Chaux. These walks were not just feats of physical prowess, but also lessons in seeing, in biological classification, in examining the laws of nature.

That time of adolescence was one of insatiable curiosity. I learned about flowers, both inside and out, the form and color of birds; I knew how a tree grows and how it keeps its equilibrium even in the middle of a storm.

My master (the excellent teacher Charles L'Eplattenier) had proclaimed "Only nature is inspiring and true and should be the basis for human endeavor. But do not treat nature in the manner of landscape painters, who show nothing but its

9. Evergreen fir tree covered with snow, 1906, pencil and india ink, 15 x 17 cm. This study by Jeanneret was made under his teacher Charles L'Eplattenier. Note the ABABAB rhythms, the alternation of equilateral and flat triangles, and the fact that this basic eurhythmy is dramatized by very heavy india ink strokes done freehand. From the start Jeanneret used watercolor studies and thick pencils to design architecture, and that gave his work simple, forceful oppositions—dark/light—volume contrasts, and clear massing. These tree triangles were translated into three architectural motifs: gabled windows, window mullions, and the building volume as a whole.

exterior. Scrutinize its causes, its form and the vital development, and synthesize them in creating *ornaments*." He had an elevated conception of ornament that he conceived of as a microcosm.

The young Jeanneret made many studies from nature at this time—some were analytic sketches which one could find in biology books, with labels and cross sections, while others were more lyrical drawings of natural forms conceived of as ornament, as rhythmical repetitions and transformations of a single theme [fig. 9]. The idea behind these was to find a schematized language of natural form, or *A Grammar of Ornament*, as a book by Owen Jones was called. Jeanneret greatly admired this book, as did so many other Art Nouveau designers, and much of his early work was based on it. Stylize nature was the injunction, a goal common to the Classical tradition, with its acanthus, and Art Nouveau with its whiplash and sunflower. For instance, an engraved watch of 1906, for which Jeanneret won a prize at eighteen, was in part made up of geometrical, overlapping planes that were an abstract representation of rock strata [fig. 10].

The design is extraordinarily sophisticated and powerful for a young man. As Allen Brooks has discovered, Le Corbusier tried to make it seem even more precocious by back-dating it, and misremembering his age as thirteen rather than eighteen, and Brooks even finds in it a subtle transformation of the coat of arms of La Chaux. But, for me, its most striking quality is its cataclysmic confrontation between two formal systems, two languages of design. Here we have a fly searching among dew-drops, represented by diamonds, and moss, in red gold—all in a precious representational language—set off against stylized rock ledges, conceived in an abstract language of cubic planes. Naturalism versus eurhythmy of forms, representation versus abstraction, realism versus idealism—and further oppositions one cares to find. As we will see, this dualism has philosophical roots, and leads to the double coding of his 1950s Post-Modernism in Chandigarh. As often in his long career, there may be a hiatus of thirty or forty years before earlier themes are again picked up and transformed.

On October 2, 1905, Edouard and fourteen other students were admitted to Charles L'Eplattenier's new "Cours Supérior d'art et décoration." The master, at thirty-one years, had the idea of making his provincial school into a version of the leading Art Nouveau powerhouse for students in Darmstadt, and Edouard soon was picked out by the master to be the leader of the group. We can guess this by his father's comments at the time:

> Edouard has just completely renounced engraving despite the fact that he was the best student at the school in this field: he is about to begin architecture, pushed by his teacher L'Eplattenier who speaks glowingly of him and guarantees his success!? (June 12, 1905)

We can also assume his prowess by the fact that at the end of 1905 he was entrusted with the design of the Villa Fallet, at the young age of seventeen and a half, and while still at school. "Learning by doing" was one reason for pushing the prize student so fast, and also the basic idea that architecture amounted to a superior form of three-dimensional decoration—something L'Eplattenier had already taught the precocious engraver extremely well. Furthermore, from reading Ruskin came the idea that architecture and art ought to be based on the love of nature—its high points, such as mountains and rock outcrops studied at source. From reading Henri Provensal, Owen Jones, Eugene Grasset, and Charles Blanc came the ideas of stylization—abstracting nature—and then gridding it into a system of repeat patterns that were varied and symphonic. From reading the art magazines came two specific visual grammars, those of Darmstadt and Antonio Gaudí: the heart shapes, and symbolic forms of the first, and the crystalline finials and stepped corbels of the second.

Edouard was thus visually armed for his first encounter with architecture, but luckily, given his age and inexperience, he had some help. A local architect, René Chapallaz, lent him a draftsman, and the owner of the nascent villa, Louis Fallet, was himself a designer who gave continual advice. Monsieur Fallet wrote about ornament and was a member of the commission of the Ecole d'art: he signed the drawings, lending them authority. No doubt, he also helped work out functional problems.

The extraordinary thing about this villa is not only the age of the architect—like Picasso he *was* precocious—but the way it is an abstract representation of local nature. In a sense, it can be seen as a cross section of the Jura mountainside [fig. 11]. Its base of heavy

10. Watchcase design, 1906. Described later by Le Corbusier: "Watch by my father; case of silver inlaid with steel, copper, brass and yellow gold, all cut with burin and chisel. Small diamonds encrusted . . . Theme: rocks and moss with a fly and drops of dew."

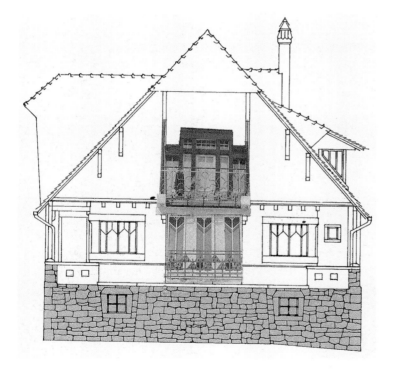

11. Villa Fallet (collage), La Chaux-de-Fonds, 1906–7. The building as a metaphor of the layered earth—geology, tree, cloud, and sky.

12. Villa Fallet, south and east facades. The overhanging eves and gables protect from the sun and snow—*brise-soleil*, *brise-neige*—before the fact.

Le Corbusier: Dress Rehearsal in a Small Town

13, 14. Villa Fallet. This building and the next two show Jeanneret's first attempts to establish a Jura Regionalism based on plant forms and such Swiss details as heavy overhanging eaves, steep roofs, and picturesque massing. The *sapin* (fir or spruce tree) has been stylized four different ways: as a pitched roof, glazing bars, a zigzag, and a triangle. The sgraffito work, in yellow, blue-gray, white, and rust red, is as fine today as it was in 1907.

rusticated limestone blocks represents bedrock. Above this are cut and dressed stone corbels representing rock outcrops—an "unconformity," in geological terms, sitting atop the rustication, in effect the previous layer of the earth's activity. Ruskin would have approved of this poem to rocks. Then above these two layers of geology springs life, above all the pine tree, the *sapin*, to be stylized in jagged timber, sawtoothed edges that symbolize branches and leaves and also stucco ornament, which abstracts the whole outline of the fir tree as well as its Platonic idea—the perfect equilateral triangles. Fir tree triangles and Y-shaped branches also dance around the windows and metal balconies and, at least here on the balcony, billowing clouds in metal surmount the trees. It is one thing to pull off this coding on the back of a watchcase, another to make it into a whole, functioning building. The interior spaces are a bit tight in parts, but some of them flow about a double-height entry hall, the Swiss equivalent of American usage some twenty years previously. Particularly impressive is the way the symbolic program has been carried through in so many details—doors, ceilings, and furniture.

A close reading reveals the attempt to transform a whole building into an icon of nature, a symbol of the cosmos. This is the synthetic imagination for which Le Corbusier is known, put to the use of nature-spirituality. Furthermore, having abstracted and transformed these motifs, Jeanneret discovered a truth that was to become his key: multiple coding and ambiguity. For instance, the decorative triangles refer not only to the local fir trees but also to

15. Villa Fallet. Double-glazing is common in buildings in La Chaux-de-Fonds. Le Corbusier used this principle later in a new way.

16. Villa Fallet. Cubic brackets as rhythmical elements. Jeanneret's brother and mother were musicians greatly interested in eurhythmy and the abstract mathematical nature of music. His early buildings are demonstrations of the old metaphor "architecture is frozen music."

pine cones *and* the local mountains—three meanings in one form, synergy [figs. 12–15].

In terms of relevance, the result, while reminiscent of Olbrich's work at Darmstadt, is actually more sophisticated and relevant, because it is based not on fanciful images, but on real, local nature.

There are germs of other, later ideas in this first building. If one looks at the corbeled, cut stone brackets around the entrance, or near the side windows on the balcony, or in wood throughout the interior, one finds pure forms, particularly the cube, abstracted as such. It may be stretching a point to see here one of his later definitions of Modern Architecture—perhaps the most famous this century: "Architecture is the masterly, correct and magnificent play of masses brought together in light . . . cubes, cones, spheres, cylinders or pyramids are the great primary forms . . . *the most beautiful forms*." We will find this idea expressed later in the 1910s, but its suggestion is here in the brackets [fig. 16].

Froebel Blocks are also behind these cubic forms, but, according to Paul Turner, another influence was a book probably given to Jeanneret by L'Eplattenier: Henry Provensal's *L'Art de demain*, 1904. Provensal put forth the idealist arguments that art follows certain absolute laws, that it evolves more and more toward the general and abstract, and that beauty is "The eternal and the general . . . the splendor of truth, as Plato said—It is the quality of the idea reproduced in a symbolic form (Plotinus)." Jeanneret actually bracketed the latter part of this passage in Provensal's book, and another chapter opens with the underlined definition of architecture as *"l'expression cubique harmonieuse de la pensée."* "Cubic architecture" based on "meditation" was to become a slogan of Le Corbusier.

The other aspect of Jeanneret's design, the representational regionalism, was particularly influenced by Lalique, Gallé, Guimard, and the Nancy School—a form of Art Nouveau he started to reject in his travels in Austria. It was in Vienna, from November 1907 to March 1908, when he started to question the teachings of Charles L'Eplattenier, or "L'Ep" as he called him in letters. This was a creative and confusing period for the young man just turned twenty. He was in one of the great capitals of culture, and spent most of his spare time going to symphonies and operas, or studying to be a sculptor. He *wanted* to get an architectural education especially in statics, mathematics, and practical construction, but instead of going to school, or working with the great architects there, he worked away feverishly, all alone. His good fortune was to have, at his very young age, two more commissions for La Chaux-de-Fonds, two new villas for the brothers-in-law of Louis Fallet. But the bad luck was to have these commitments at the moment he was questioning his roots and trying to deal with his strong affections. He had none more than for his master L'Ep, who, as he wrote to his brother, taught him to know "the History of Art which allows us to benefit from the great laws that guided the masters." Great laws?

We can detect here the mystical tone of a twenty-year-old idealist, a reverence for heroes, the great paragons such as Michelangelo, and the prophets such as Jesus. There is a parallel here that the later Le Corbusier might have seen. Just as Don Quixote was to be inspired to great and tragic-comical heights by romantic literature, Jeanneret was to be inflated by his readings of idealistic literature. But there was another equally important strand to the story. Just visible, under the surface of his letters, was the *spiritual* side of his tie to L'Eplattenier and La Chaux, a belief that the group had some destiny, as a brotherhood, to transform European culture. This spiritual mission, which informed the early Bauhaus fifteen years later, was based on theosophical ideas stemming from Madame Blavatsky, Rudolf Steiner, and others. These were in circulation from New York City to Moscow, from seances in the West to the musings of Kandinsky and Malevich in Russia. Looking back, in a 1925 text given the Rousseauesque title of *Confession*, Le Corbusier recounts the specific mission of their brotherhood:

> So our task was to study passionately our immediate environment; from the bud to the rhythmic repetition of the hills on the horizon, we would build up the most faithful and moving dictionary of speaking forms. Our style would be a style of the country, a poem to our country. [Then answering an attack on his internationalism] You see, Monsieur Léandre Vaillant, quite a long time ago I too was a regionalist.

> So that's how it was.

For ten years we composed a kind of ode to our country. My master had said: "We are going to renew the house and restore the fine crafts that have disappeared." There was a score of us choosing our vocation: sculptor in stone, in wood, worker in ceramics or mosaic, glazier, brazier, engraver, etcher, ironworker, jeweler, fresco-painter, etc. What an army! Magnificent enthusiasm and total commitment.

Sundays often found us together at the top of the highest hill. It had pinnacles as well as grandly sweeping slopes: pastures, herds of large cattle, uninterrupted horizons, flights of rooks. We were preparing the future. "Here," said the master, we will build a monument dedicated to nature and we will make it our lives' purpose. We will leave the town and live under the trees, beside the building, which we will gradually fill with our works. It will incorporate the whole landscape—all the fauna and flora. Once a year there will be great festivals held there, with huge braziers lighted at the four corners of the building . . .

Yearly festivals celebrating nature? Freemasonry and secret brotherhoods have been common to high culture since Mozart celebrated them in *The Magic Flute*, and so perhaps it is no surprise to find the later high priest of rationalism committed, as a young man, to spirituality. He remained committed, throughout his life, and it led directly to work at Chandigarh and the Chapel of Ronchamp. In fact, the "monument to nature" is the latter, and a once-a-year celebration of a cosmic event, a festival of the sun, was contemplated for the former. An idea, once inscribed in Jeanneret's mind, could not be erased, and since he was so committed to his master and the brotherhood back home he could not escape them, even as he tried, in Vienna.

Another tie was their mutual dependency, especially when it came to building total works of art. As Le Corbusier said, they *were* an army. René Chapallaz, the local architect, had constructed L'Ep's design for his own villa in 1902, and overseen the Villa Fallet, and was to supervise building on the next two. Leon Perrin, the traveling companion, would carry out the sculptural decoration, and other students in the *Cours Superior*, such as Andre Evard and Georges Aubert, would carry out the painting and craftsmanship. In effect, L'Eplattenier had turned his students into a build-

17. Villa Jaquemet, preliminary water-color sketch, December 1907 (photo by Tim Benton, Bibliotheque de Ville, La Chaux-de-Fonds).

18. Villa Jaquemet from the south-west. The chimneys have lost their Gaudiesque beehive, but the side projections, in red tile, keep their crystalline forms—V-shaped, diamond, and triangular elements. The crystal was at this time a Theosophical sign of nature's creativity.

ing team and spiritual brotherhood, and it was hard to break from either.

Jeanneret's first designs for these two new villas were like those for Fallet: they had the same sequence of layering, from bottom to top, that Ruskin approved and were poems to nature. First the heavy masonry wall and piers, then a ground floor level of stylized trees and flowers (with more than ornamented shrubs growing on the balcony); then a level with animals, people, and birds represented; finally, a pointed arch, or sheltering roof, crowning this microcosm of the home. The Stotzer Villa and Villa Jaquemet followed such a basic typology. It was both an evolutionary sequence, from mineral to vegetable to human, and a spiritual one, from earth to heaven. Theosophy taught such sequences as a cross between science and religion, and it is possible to see all the villas constructed on the Pouillerel hillside as secret symbols of its secret doctrine.

The early sketches and drawings for Stotzer and Jaquemet end up as highly decorated, romantic watercolors for these "temples to nature" [fig. 17]. Green mossy rooftops (later to be built as Burgundian red tiles) make the whole house a giant tree. Underneath this the windows syncopate in a rhythmical dance—1:2:2:1—to the bar, while again sgraffito pinecones and fir trees trip across the stuccoed pediment (Jeanneret likened this dance "to a polka step").

But reality set in with the cost. The Villa Fallet was over the budget and over the time estimated and, as the historian Tim Benton was to remark of Jeanneret's supposedly functional and economical buildings of the 1920s, "the finished cost would be twice or three times the estimates." Jeanneret's enthusiasm, and desire to make a great work of architecture, was always the first concern, but in the winter of 1907 he was suddenly taken aback when his clients, both brothers-in-law of Fallet, demanded cheaper buildings. The result was a quick loss of confidence, something that beset him constantly throughout his life, however much it was covered up with a facade of composure: "I work at my plans [on the two houses]" he wrote to his parents on December 27, "with an uncertainty in myself that is frightening." Feeling uncertain of his own creative powers, he wrote for photographs of the villas L'Eplattenier and Fallet, made amendments based on these, and simplified his designs considerably, changing all the

Is it too much to say that his idea of economic determinism stems from this crisis, that straight lines and right angles are the necessities of modern production? The idea undoubtedly remained latent for another few years, because he was to attack the grid and its false economies in 1910. Nevertheless, from this transformation of curves into rectangles was born a new kind of minimalist harmony and an appreciation of the horizontal line as a sign of the horizon. In fact, the horizontal band of windows finds a premonition at the Villa Stotzer [fig. 19].

19. Villa Stotzer, La Chaux-de-Fonds, constructed from April to October 1908. In spite of simplifications it was still 19 percent over budget. Rough masonry is below, and two-colored stucco surrounding a heart-shaped window is above. The results recall Behrens at Darmstadt (fig. 21), but here the massing is more forceful and the volumes more sculptural. Clay models were the discipline behind this building and the Villa Jaquemet, giving them both a resolution of lines, solids, and voids. Deep gable hoods, protection from snow, cantilever way out like his later *brise-soleil*, giving the buildings the presence, even the character, of a face. The front gambrel-headed roof sticks out a meter; the side faces address the view over the mountains.

Formation of a Powerful Ego: The Confessional Mode

An extraordinary aspect of the young Jeanneret's protean character is the speed with which his self-consciousness and ego were developed. Partly this was due to his doting parents, who gave him a strong sense of self-worth. Partly it was due to the confidence placed in him by his teacher and mentor, Charles L'Eplattenier, and partly it was due to the good fortune of constructing a house, with his friends, by the young age of eighteen. His sense of identity was also, no doubt, self-constructed, a result of his constant traveling and drawing. Of this last he wrote, toward the end of his life, in 1960:

> When one travels and works with visual things—architecture, painting, sculpture—one uses one's eyes and *draws*, so as to fix deep down in one's experience what is seen. Once the impression has been recorded by the pencil, it stays for good, entered, registered, inscribed. The camera is a tool for idlers, who use a machine to do their *seeing* for them. To draw oneself, to trace the lines, handle the volumes, organize the surface . . . all this means first to look, and then to observe and finally perhaps discover . . . and it is then that inspiration may come. Inventing, creating, one's whole being is drawn into action, and it is action which counts. *Others* stood indifferent—but *you saw*!

This passage is typical of his autobiographical style, with its confusion between the reader "you" and Le Corbusier himself—he is about to describe how *"he* saw." No doubt his constant drawings, and annotations of these, developed a very personal set of impressions and convictions: his notebooks did empower his vision.

His strong sense of identity was also forged through friendships, especially with older men—L'Eplattenier, August Perret, William Ritter, Amédée Ozenfant—all of whom he used as sounding boards. "Though timid as a youth," he said, he was in search of masters until the age of thirty and it was to them he confided his doubts. At the early age of eighteen he developed what I would call his confessional mode, a form of opinionated writing that was to remain a hallmark for sixty years. Because this mode allowed him to personalize history, it made him the most influential architectural writer of the last century.

Where did he find this confessional mode? Through reading Jean-Jacques Rousseau, or John Ruskin's personal travel writing? The latter two we know were strong influences, and perhaps also was the example of his father, keeping his journal. However, as with most of his qualities, the causes are likely to be multiple, and one may have stemmed from writing letters home—to his parents, to his brother Albert, to friends, and to L'Eplattenier.

From September 3, 1907, and for the next four years he traveled, always returning to La Chaux-de-Fonds, testing his poetic impressions on his confidants. In effect, these travels became his university education, taking him to major capitals for extended stays—Vienna, Paris, and Berlin—and throughout the countryside of central Europe, backpacking and living rough. The student in him contrasted the lesson of vernacular or peasant life, "folklore," with sophisticated culture; the Balkans was set against the metropolis, a dying traditional life against modernization. In these oppositions a dialectical frame of mind was born and, at the very outset of his journey of self-education, he tests his own impressions against those of Ruskin, Baedecker, and his masters.

His first test, a letter to his teacher L'Eplattenier on September 21, 1907, we might mark a failure, for he says of Florence, "The city appears to me *not rich* in architecture, isn't that true?" Here he is expressing an opinion, which is then immediately questioned, perhaps because he was checking to see if his own Ruskinian taste was adequate to the city. Ruskin, who was the main inspiration for L'Eplattenier's students, was biased against the Renaissance, and in favor of painting, the decorative arts, and ornament, so naturally the young Jeanneret spent his time drawing mosaics and marble pavements, not the architectural masterpieces of Alberti, Brunelleschi, and Michelangelo. But he continues questioning: "Or are my eyes still dazzled by Pisa [whose white marbles he loved]? As I told you, the Palazzo Vecchio is a great marvel but it is difficult to study; it's an abstract power, isn't it?" His drawings of the Palazzo Vecchio show his first interest in volume and proportional systems, where he measures the floor levels—2 $^{1}/_{2}$, 2, 1, 1, 1. He continues, questioning every opinion of his own: "Mustn't I look *primarily* at painting and sculpture (useless, it seems to me, to copy Raphael or Botticelli) or am I doing the wrong thing, and must I sketch the various palazzi? A word from you will help me greatly."

Three weeks later, in a letter to his parents of October 8–10, we find his opinions changed. He has learned to appreciate the Renaissance a little, or at least one of its buildings, Brunelleschi's cathedral dome: "The cupola of the dome has finally revealed itself to me after four weeks of indifference . . . I descended, stupefied by its grandeur; I retract all the foolish things I thought and per- haps wrote concerning this genius who daringly constructed a thing that is so colossal and so strong." The cataclysmic switch from one opinion to its opposite, from one passion to its reverse, is typical and remains typical to the end of his life. The self- educated pioneer who must stake out the territory and see for him- self—"*Others* stood indifferent, but you *saw*"—he is led by impres- sions that are given the force of truth. The method soon leads to violent contradictions and muddled theory, but it also leads to dialectical thinking and the personal assimilation of architecture. The young pioneer eats up architecture and the past through his drawing and writing; he ingests it so that it is part of his body and memory.

Cataclysm, struggle, elation, doubt, passion, depression, ego- tism, selflessness—such are the swings in mood of the young, made much more intense by a four-year *self*-education.

By the second year, 1908, when Jeanneret settles in Paris, he has started to transform his opinions further, pitting the rational- ism of the French architect Perret against Ruskin, beginning to see that Classicism might be better than Gothic, finding that rein- forced concrete might lead to the "art of tomorrow." He was twenty- one years old and his philosophy of struggle, fighting alone in solitude, had crystallized. The ego has formed; the confessional mode is in place. All this is revealed, characteristically, in a letter home, this one to Charles L'Eplattenier. It contains some major themes of his later life—for instance the "fight with truth itself," as well as the later urgent, passionate tone. Its immediate cause is Jeanneret's discovery that his master has moved his troops too fast, that the fledgling Swiss avant-garde is not yet prepared to conquer new territory, that the new *Cours Superior d'art et décoration* of the art school in La Chaux-de-Fonds will not be the equal of its counterparts in Darmstadt or Nancy. Even worse, that this version of the Bauhaus-to-be is founded on sand, because L'Eplattenier does not know what architecture is all about. It is worth analyzing this explosive letter at length because it is easily the most important early document and it predicts major themes of the future.

Struggle and the Nietzschean Superman

The first theme concerns his conflicted love of his master, the man who started the art movement at La Chaux-de-Fonds, and convinced him to be an architect rather than an engraver (and, even more importantly, the artist he wanted to become):

> I am coming home for a few days; I feel very happy because I shall see you and my good parents again—and also very distressed. Postcards and letters received from Perrin, who is my friend, leave me with an impression of malaise . . . and that leads to a necessity (a difficult task because of my youth) of explaining to you what I am, so that our reunion may be full of joy and encouragement from you to me, and not a misunderstanding.

> You were perhaps not wrong to turn me into something more than an engraver, because I feel capable. I have no need to tell you that my life is not at all amusing, but filled with work, you will understand because from engraving to architecture is an enormous leap. But now that I know where I am going, I can make the effort joyfully.

Second is the idea of the modern metropolis, specifically Paris, as a place of Darwinian struggle where one could sharpen one's wits.

Time spent in Paris is time well spent, to reap a harvest of strength. Paris the immense city of ideas—where you are lost unless you remain severe with yourself. Life is austere and active there. Paris is the crack of the whip at every moment, death for dreamers.

Later in life Le Corbusier was to think of Paris as cruel, ugly, noisy, and chaotic while still being a "selectioner," a place where genius emerges through incessant competition. In his *Precisions*, 1930, he wrote that Paris is a "place of champions and gladiators . . . Paris is paved with corpses. Paris is an assembly of cannibals who establish the dogma of the moment. Paris is a selectioner." Already in 1908, he is seeing the city through the eyes of Darwin, as interpreted by Nietzsche [fig. 20].

The third idea emerges directly from this and concerns the way Paris destroyed his own romantic dreams and substituted in their place a search for truth and logic. In his confessional mode, he emphasizes loneliness and struggle with the ego. The prophetic note is extraordinary, considering his twenty-one years.

But for me, Paris spells loneliness. For the last eight months I have been living alone—alone with this strong spirit which is in every man; and with which I need to and can converse every

20. Sketch of Paris, circa 1908. Dark, turbulent, threatening forms reminiscent of the Fauves and Edvard Munch characterized Jeanneret's sketches of Paris at the time. His landscape watercolors show the riotous use of bizarre colors that Matisse and Kees van Dongen, two artists he admired, applied to the figure. Other sketches show Paris burning, underscoring the Nietzschean metaphor of the city as a selectioner, a crucible that purifies as it burns, a metaphor he returns to again and again. For instance, in 1925, he writes, "happy are those who come [to Paris] to burn themselves amid the general indifference and to clash in the violent skirmishes to which they give themselves over at night."

Le Corbusier: Dress Rehearsal in a Small Town

day. And today I am in touch with my spirits, pregnant hours of solitude, hours when the whip lashes. Why have I not more time to think and learn? Life is petty and devours our liberty.

My concept is now clear—further on I will give you details of its instigation and basis. To draw it up, I lost no time in day-dreaming. It is broad, I am enthusiastic about it, it punishes me, it carries me away on wings, when my inner strength shouts: "You can." I have forty years in front of me to reach what I picture to be great on my horizon, which is still flat at the moment.

I have finished with childish dreams of a success similar to that of one or two schools in Germany, Vienna, or Darmstadt [where Art Nouveau formalism then reigned supreme] [fig. 21]. It's too easy. I want to fight with truth itself. It will surely torment me. But I am not looking for quietude or recognition from the world. I will live in sincerity, happy to undergo abuse.

This prediction of struggle, *before it actually happened*, shows how committed Jeanneret was to a tragic view of the human condition, prior to his own suffering. In fact, the conflict was built into his destructive-constructive method, and it is not surprising that Jeanneret was reading Nietzsche's *Thus Spake Zarathustra* at this time. Aside from the similarities in style—passionate, vigorous, and aphoristic—there are also similar themes: the "superman" struggling among men, and the necessity that he destroy conventional wisdom before he can realize his revolutionary ideas. Jeanneret is about to destroy L'Eplattenier's dreams of the decorative synthesis of the arts.

My inner strength speaks and when I express these ideas, I am not dreaming. Perhaps soon reality will dawn cruelly, because the struggle against those I love is drawing closer, and they must come to my side or we can no longer be friends.

How I wish, ardently, that my friends, our comrades, would abandon their humdrum life of everyday satisfactions and, burning that which they hold most dear, believing those

21. Peter Behrens, Architect's Own House, Darmstadt, Germany, 1901. Behrens was a model for Jeanneret, both in his Jugendstil and Classical periods—note the similarity of roof and heart motifs. The Artists' Colony of Darmstadt, as well as Behrens himself, looked to Nietzsche's idea of a new European culture, led by an elite, overturning the past in a blaze of creativity. Jeanneret knew the painting of Zarathustra's eagle that Behrens had done for this house, and he considered himself a Nietzschean buzzard or condor, as a Christmas card of 1909 shows (fig. 25).

cherished things were good—realize how low they had sunk and how little they had thought.

Burning what he loves, the Nietzschean superman transvalues all values. Jeanneret had also been reading Henry Provensal's *L'Art de demain*, published in 1904, and this book is also behind the passionate, love-hate letter.

It is by today's thought that tomorrow one creates the new art. Thought is uncovered and one must fight with it. And to find it before fighting it, you must seek it in solitude. Paris offers solitude to those who, passionately, look for silence, and a total retreat.

My concept of the art of building is sketched in outline. Since Vienna had killed my purely plastic conception of architecture (research purely for form), I felt, on arriving in Paris, an immense empty feeling and I said to myself: "Poor chap, for the moment you know nothing, you don't even know how much you don't know." Such was my immense anguish. Whom could I ask? Chapallaz [who was supervising construction on the villas] knew even less and increased my confusion; Grasset, Jourdain, Sauvage, Paquet? I saw Perret, but dared not question him. All these men said: "You know enough architecture." My spirit was in revolt, and I went to consult our forefathers. I choose the most zealous fighters, those whom we of the 20th century are ready to be most like, the Romans. And during three months, at night in the library, I studied the Romans. And I went to the Cathedral Notre Dame and I took Magne's Gothic course and then I understood.

It is worth remarking that the architecture of the past—whether Roman, Romanesque, Gothic, Renaissance, or vernacular—will always be used as a touchstone for the architecture of the future, as long as it is transformed, that is, transvalued. Jeanneret continues with his metaphor of suffering, fighting, being whipped, as he brings up another theme—science and statics, the study of the strength of materials.

22. Villa Stotzer, north entrance. As with the Villa Jaquemet, René Chapallaz, who took half the design fees, oversaw this building. As Patricia May Sekler has shown, multiple readings of these forms are possible: the doorway solids can be seen as stepped rock forms and the void as a pine tree. The bare-branch motif is clear at the top, but as with all the symmetrical facades of his buildings the face motif—windows as eyes, door as mouth—is more veiled.

After this, the Perret brothers were like whips to me. These powerful architects chastised me: proclaimed in words and in their works "you know nothing." I began to suspect through the study of the Romans that architecture is not simply an eurthymy of forms but something else; but what? I didn't know. So I studied mechanics, then statics, throughout the whole summer. How often was I wrong. And today, with anger, I questioned the beliefs out of which I created my science of modern architecture. With rage and joy, because I know at last what is good, I studied the strength of materials. They're difficult, but they're beautiful, these mathematics, so logical, so perfect!

Then he uses his typical, dialectical thinking, negating a negation:

At the same time, I followed courses on the Italian Renaissance by Magne and by denial (or negation) there again I learned what architecture is. And Boennelwald's course on Gothic and Romanesque architecture illuminated what architecture is.

On the site, I saw possibilities of concrete, revealed by the revolutionary forms on which Perret insists.

Then the clarion call, the self-dramatization:

These eight months in Paris shouted to me: "Logic, truth, honesty, see behind the dreams of the arts of the past. Paris said raise your eyes, go forward, burn what you love, and love what you burn."

Again the Nietzschean injunction—so it's no surprise that a conflagration follows, the burning of those he has loved. Imagine receiving the following letter from a student disciple, more than ten years your junior.

You, Grasset, Sauvage, Jourdain, Paquet, and others, you are all liars. Grasset, paragon of truth, a liar. Liars because you don't know what architecture is—but all you other architects, liars, all of you. Yes, and worse, assholes. The architect should be a man with a logical mind; an enemy of love of the plastic effect; a man of science, but also with a heart, an artist and a scholar. I know this now, but none of you told me: our ancestors know how to speak to those who understand them.

What these ancestors, Egyptian and Gothic, tell him is that a valid architecture is based on a dualistic mixture of religious and materialistic facts; social belief systems and constructional realism. Thus he can predict the valid art of tomorrow, which will be ushered in by the superman:

> One speaks of an art of tomorrow. This art will be, because humanity has changed its way of living and thinking. The program is new. It is new in a new era: one speaks of an art to come, because this era is that of iron, and iron is partly an innovation. The birth of this art will be overwhelming, because of iron (a material which can be destroyed through rust) we have made reinforced concrete, an unbelievable creation—its results will leave a bold mark in the history of a people, as it is expressed in their monuments.

The next day he continues the letter in even greater turmoil and anguish, realizing that—unable to rewrite the letter, or tear it up—he has burned his bridges. Yet, for all this, he still hopes to convert L'Eplatennier ("liar, asshole") and his student friends to his side, to the idea of struggling in silence to forge a new art of meditation, "based on intellect" (and reinforced concrete):

> You make young students proud and victorious, whereas at twenty they should be modest . . . They have felt no pain, had no setbacks; without troubles you cannot practice art. Art is a cry of the living heart. Their heart has never lived, since they do not yet know if they have a heart. I consider that this small victory [of the *Cours Superior*] is premature; ruin is near, you cannot build on sand. The movement started too soon. Your soldiers are phantoms. When the struggle comes you will be alone; your soldiers are ghosts, because they do not know they are alive—why they are alive, or how they live. Your students have never thought. The art of tomorrow is an art based on intellect.

> Raise up the concept and forge ahead!

There follows a parable of a tree, identified with L'Eplatennier, that kills off its seedlings, the students, by not letting them develop. The metaphor has overtones that are biblical perhaps because Jeanneret was, at this time, also reading Renan's *Vie de Jesus*. Some of the passages Jeanneret underlined in this book show Jesus spurning riches and power, retreating to a mountain in order to meditate and suffer in silence, so that he can perfect his revolutionary message. But also Zarathustra proclaims a doctrine of toughening the soul through individual struggle and uses the metaphor of the tree that shall become great if it will "strike hard roots around hard rocks." His teacher L'Eplattenier, in this Nietzschean parable, becomes just such a noble tree, but one whose very strength squelches that of its offspring.

You alone can see ahead. They see by chance—happy chance sometimes, they proceed tentatively and will fail immediately. You, who have the fortitude, you have known what it is to know oneself; you know what it costs . . . in pain, angry tears and explosions of enthusiasm. And you say—I have suffered. I have prepared the way for them—let them live! But have they the strength? Just as a tree, on a dry rock, which took twenty years to grow its roots generously says: "I have fought; let my offspring reap the harvest!" He lets his seed fall on the few bits of humus which line the rock, a humus which he himself has—once more—made from his dead leaves and his pain. The rock warms up in the sun. The seed opens up and grows small roots with great vivacity. What happiness it is to push up small leaves into the sky! But the sun heats the rock; the plant looks around with fear, made dizzy by the impact of the strong heat. However, the parent tree has taken twenty years to drive its roots through narrow clefts in the stone. Distressed, the small plant accuses the tree that created it. It curses and dies. Dies of not having lived by its own means.

The identification of Jeanneret with Zarathustra and Jesus is plausible, but what a strange inversion the letter implies. Here is a twenty-one-year-old student telling his thirty-four-year-old, beloved master what to do!

That is what I see in the country. There is my anguish. I say: to create at twenty and dare to continue to want to create is aberration, error, terrible blindness, unbelievable pride. Wanting to sing before you have lungs! How can you lack such self-knowledge—how can you be so unaware.

He oscillates with feelings of love and remorse toward his friends and master, then returns to the first theme:

My struggle with you, dear beloved master, will be against this error. Dazzled, subjugated by your own strength, which is extraordinary, you imagine strength to be everywhere . . . I dare not conclude for I am too young to see further ahead. However, that is what I see up to now, based on my personal experience . . . Deep down inside, I shall be sad at heart, because I love [my friends] with a severe affection. The dream of union for a common cause which crumbles, this is what I have seen for some time. Two or three of what we considered the strongest are lost . . .

Then comes the surprising confession, and the goal which he was to aim at for the rest of his life, exploring his ego in solitude, through painting and sculpture.

They did not know what Art is: deep love of one's ego, which one seeks in retreat and solitude, this divine ego which can be a terrestrial ego when it is forced by a struggle to become so. This ego speaks of things embedded deep in the soul; art is born and fleetingly rushes on.

It is in solitude that one can struggle with one's ego, that one punishes and whips oneself.

Our friends must seek solitude. Where? How?

The idea, derived from Nietzsche, supposes the lonely position of the artist, the absolute necessity for solitude, introspection, meditation, and egotistical creation. There are several ways in which these ideas were relevant to the later Le Corbusier. For one thing, his own creative process took place in isolated spots—his

23. *Petit Cabanon*, 1952. The monk's
cell, placed in a direct relation to
nature, was an early idea dating from
Jeanneret's visits to the Charterhouse
of Ema in 1907 and 1911, but it really
springs from his belief in the necessity
of solitary creation, the private struggle with one's ego.

own architectural office, in Paris, where he built a little cell, a nine-foot rectangle with blank walls, where he could initiate a project before passing it on to his draftsmen. Second, was his small cabin in southern France, another cell-like structure where he worked during vacation [fig. 23]. He was to justify isolation, many times, as necessary for supporting a creative elite; for instance, in 1923, in *Vers une architecture*:

> The man of initiative, of action, of thought, the LEADER, demands shelter for his meditations in a quiet and sure spot; a problem which is indispensable to the health of specialized people.

But this need for quietude was also generalized for the whole of society and, citing Pascal, he traced many social ills to the lack of adequate solitude. Hence the relevance of isolation to his large architectural projects. In these we always find provision in the house for the individual to be alone, usually in the form of a bedroom, again a "cellule," or conceptual monk's cell, a place of retreat. The monastery and the ocean liner, both made up of cells, were to become the models for social housing, for the *Unités d'habitation*. As the historian Peter Serenyi has shown, these are strange models for social housing because they entail "a transient habitat for the homeless, rootless, and lonely."

What the young Jeanneret discovered on his travels—in 1907 and then again in 1911 when he visited the Charterhouse of Ema (Galluzo)—was that this monastery had an ideal mixture of isolation and community. He later said there is "a harmony which results from the interplay of the individual and collective life," and this harmonious opposition is very apparent in the juxtaposition of cells and the building as a whole. So struck was he by this marriage of opposites that he wrote home twice, in 1907, to his parents and L'Eplattenier (September 15 and 19) with virtually the same dream:

> I would like to live all my life in what [the monks] call their cells. It is the perfect solution to the working man's house, a unique type or rather an earthly paradise.

One guiding image is the cell with its private garden, later to become the hanging gardens in his *Immeubles Villas*, or Freehold Maisonettes, of 1922 [fig. 74]. But another metaphor behind the ideal monastery is Nietzschean, that of the hero in the cell alone, wrestling with his ego, while he surveys a heroic landscape. This is found in his drawings or the *Unité* he builds in 1952 on the outskirts of Marseilles—in a "landscape worthy of Homer" [fig. 155]. Here he went to extraordinary lengths, and expense, to isolate each cell from the next, to make collective life quiet and bearable.

It raises the question of whether Jeanneret, and then Le Corbusier, conceived society as a collection of isolated individuals, heroic supermen and superwomen—or, as it would be put pejoratively in the United States today, lonesome cowboys. Whatever the case, the Nietzschean metaphor of the struggling individual is forged by 1908, something we can see in this and other letters of the period.

Dualism and the Secret Doctrine

From his letters home and by looking at the books Jeanneret was reading up to 1908 we can build a picture of what was going on in his mind. As Paul Turner and Allen Brooks have shown, there were several key texts that the young Jeanneret annotated or underlined. With Henry Provensal's *L'Art de demain*, 1904, he is oriented in an idealistic direction, toward ideal Platonic and cubic forms, "essential forms," an idea that, in 1918, was to become the keystone of Purism. A future art, reconciling science and feeling, under the universal principles of nature, will have an integrated harmony. This is opposed to the disorder brought about by Positivism and Materialism. Divine, eternal laws will resolve the two necessary parts of life—the spiritual and material—and indeed that resolution is the goal of the artist of tomorrow.

Such a dualistic message was evident in the formal language of Jeanneret's work, with equal emphasis given to form as abstraction (spiritual) and material fact as contingency (structure or, for instance, a represented bee, or flower). This dualism was also evident in another book he was reading at the time, Edouard Schuré's *Les grands initiés*. As he writes in a letter to his parents, January 31, 1908, Schuré makes him very happy because he resolves "my battles between rationalism (which the real, active life and the study of science have strongly impressed on me) and the other part, the inward idea, the intuition of a supreme being which the contemplation of Nature reveals to me . . ."

Ideal Nature versus material, active reality—the opposition becomes the focus for the rest of his life. Schuré argues there is a resolution of this duality that the great prophets show, the great initiates: Rama, Krishna, Hermes, Moses, Orpheus, Plato, and the two that fascinated Jeanneret the most, Pythagoras and Jesus. Like Provensal and Ruskin, Schuré attacks materialism, which he blames on the positivism of Auguste Comte and Herbert Spencer. Again, Ruskin and Nietzsche would have agreed with these sentiments, so something like a consensus is forming in Jeanneret's mind.

Schuré starts off his "Introduction to Esoteric Teaching" with the basic battle of the age. "The greatest evil of our times is the fact that Science and Religion appear as two hostile forces that cannot be reconciled with each other." He shows how Christianity is no longer able to prove her original dogmas against the objections of Science, and that both sides of the grand duality are unable "to gain the victory." "Hence arises profound opposition, a secret war . . . we bear within ourselves these two hostile worlds that are apparently irreconcilable . . ." While conventional religions have failed, a new *comparative esoterism* [his italics] show that underneath them all lies "an interior history . . . the profound science, the secret doctrine, the occult actions of the great initiates, prophets or reformers who established, maintained, and propagated these religions."

Since L'Eplattenier had made a present of this book just before Jeanneret set off on his 1907 voyage, these words must have carried a special meaning, the more so since the chapter on Pythagoras, which he underlined the most, has the Greek prophet setting out on his voyage to discover the secret doctrine, sacred mathematics, divine numbers. These underlie the cosmos, and all growing nature, the spiral growth of a sunflower, the leaves of a tree, or kernels on a pinecone [fig. 24].

Jeanneret was drawing these pinecones, and seeing in them magical numbers, the secret code that later, in 1947, he was to translate into three different modes: his treatise on proportions, *Le Modulor*; some esoteric themes in his painting; and his chapel at Ronchamp. It is fascinating to discover that Le Corbusier is a closet Theosophist and it is Schuré's book that starts him on the way. What begins as esoteric doctrine will culminate as cosmic architecture in Chandigarh. At this time, however, he is still a believing

24. Nature's mathematics: Le Corbusier's studies of tree growth (detail, top left), and buds, circa 1906–7, above spirals of pineapple, 1911, and pinecone, 1939–40. Below, Gyorgy Doczi's mathematical analysis of a sunflower and its Fibonacci growth and, right, a pinecone, with the spirals of a daisy overlaid in plan. LC was continuously fascinated by these harmonies and the way nature's language showed a mathematical ordering principle. Today we understand that the patterns come from the growth order and the ideal close-packing, rather than the maths, as Jeanneret thought. Redrawings: detail from the *Study of Tree Growth*, 1906–7, pencil on heavy paper, 18 x 12 cm (FLC 2517); detail of buds from Petit, *Le Corbusier—Lui Même*, 27; pineapple from *My Work*, 38; pinecone plus my overdrawing from Petit, 90; spirals and maths from Doczi, *The Power of Limits*, 1994, 1, 4, 82.

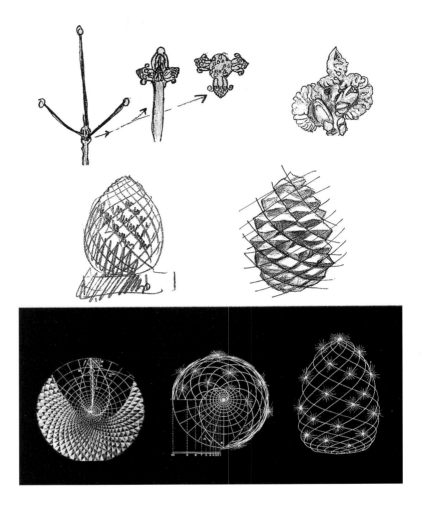

Protestant and he annotates one of the passages on the spirit-matter dualism with a quote from the Gospels. Yet, as a letter of January 31, 1908, reveals, it is the confrontation and resolution of Science and the Supreme Being that really excites him.

Schuré's six hundred pages of secret doctrine, recounting the victories of the initiated, argue that "Spirit is the only reality," "the Ideal is the only Reality." Thus for today's prophets (and Jeanneret must have understood L'Eplattenier, the *Cours Superior*, and himself as the new elite) there was a mission to fight for the hidden truth, the possibility of a new reconciliation between science and religion. Schuré concludes his introduction: "There is only one thing we must resolve to do: affirm this truth as loudly and fearlessly as possible, throw ourselves along with it and for its sake into the arena of action, and rising above the confusion of the fray, endeavor by meditation and individual initiation to enter into the Temple of Immaculate Ideas, there to arm ourselves with Principles that nothing can shatter."

Schuré brought Wagner to the French public, wrote mystical Wagnerian plays, and in his last phrase—"arm ourselves with Principles that nothing can shatter"—we again hear an echo of Zarathustra, who shatters all principles into pieces. As Nietzsche said of his own work, "I philosophize with a hammer."

Thus one begins to get the picture of Jeanneret's growing worldview. It is formed, first of all, by his somewhat difficult character; quotes from his father make clear that he is contrary and dialectical long before he reads Nietzsche. Also, there are endless synonyms for "struggle"—"enter the fray, endeavor by meditation to change the world"—long before he reads Schuré. As for idealism and ideal forms, his letters are peppered with both concepts well after his reading of Provensal. For instance, as Allen Brooks notes, "Jeanneret is tormented by his need for an idea or ideal, words he repeats no less than a dozen times" in just one letter to L'Eplattenier of July 3, 1908. Thus, reading did not determine his worldview so much as articulate an existing frame of mind.

In one sense his emerging philosophy was simply classic dualism, the idea that matter and spirit are both valid and in need of reconciliation. Nietzsche argues that man is composed of both *"bete et tete,"* a formulation Jeanneret liked to quote. The job of the Modern poet, as framed by T. S. Eliot and others, is to resolve the schisms introduced in the nineteenth century between thinking and feeling. For the historian Sigfried Giedion, the job of the Modern architect is the same; for Le Corbusier it would become the reconciliation of reason and emotion, art and technique, head and hand, and a host of other antinomies.

Although this dualism is canonic in the West, the particular way Le Corbusier confronted it led to catastrophes, irony, and, ultimately, the view that joyful conflict is essential, indeed a fundamental fulfillment to life. One can feel the pleasure the young Jeanneret gets from challenging received opinions, from pitting one thought against its opposite, from negating a negation, from attacking conventional wisdom, from the battle of wits. Here there is a precedent from a contemporary theory of the time. Darwin's fundamental principle of evolution, "the struggle for existence," had been transformed by Nietzsche and turned into a positive principle of life, "the *pleasure* of struggle." It is this principle that the young Jeanneret assimilates, both because of his reading and his propensity for conflict.

The Joyful Nietzschean Fighter

This ultimately leads to the persona, the "Nietzschean Corbusier," a concept underlying this book and one that has found some support from other scholars and critics. As well as the many Nietzschean phrases that recur throughout his life ("burn what you love, love what you burn") and his annotated copy of *Thus Spake Zarathustra*, there are also a few drawings. A Christmas card of 1909, for instance, shows a "Grand Condor," perched like a Nietzschean superman on top of a Swiss mountain, looking over the clouds and distanced in wry thought from the affairs of this world [fig. 25]. Zarathustra, like other initiates in esoteric wisdom, came down from the mountaintop, descended to men to bring them gifts and the message that God is dead. In the Christmas card Zarathustra is changed into a rather ironic vulture withdrawing into the wilderness for the quiet contemplation of the human condition, now bereft of a secure religious foundation. Le Corbusier was to portray himself in drawings as a bird, a "corbeau," sometimes a bird of prey or an innocent observer. Here, though, the Grand Condor gives what must have been the strangest Christmas greeting ever received by Swiss parents: "The misery of living makes man! And the disdain of this misery of living is incarnated in the soul of the GRAND CONDOR."

Merry Christmas and Happy New Year. At this time, his father writes in his journal that his son "although possessing a rather 'arty' air . . . was well mannered, agreeably talkative, and with solid morals and opinions (notwithstanding a complete modification of his beliefs and his religious faith)." Signaling that change, Edouard had just grown "a new reddish-blond beard" and, in a photograph on New Year's Day, Jeanneret stares out at the camera like a Grand Initiate, a cross between an underfed student and a prophet to come [fig. 3].

With the aid first of L'Eplattenier, then Perret and then Ritter, he formulates his doctrines, "the transvaluation of all values," and

La misère De vivre
faite homme !
et le DéDain De la misère
De vivre
incarnée en
l'âme Du
GRAND CONDOR

25. LC's Christmas card to his parents, 1909.

prepares to bring a new order to an emerging industrial society. Although it jumps ahead of our story, it is worth mentioning two examples of this struggle to overturn prevailing opinion.

The first is a negation of a negation. In 1910, he starts to write a book on what the new city should become, *La Construction des Villes*, and the transvaluation is completed by 1925, when it becomes an entirely different book on urbanism, with exactly the opposite message!

The second is a more protracted struggle with the local professors. In 1911 Jeanneret sets up, under l'Eplattenier, a *"Nouvelle Section de l'Ecole d'Art"*—along with his cohorts in idealism, Aubert and Perrin. He knows they will be abused and spurned for their message and, indeed, by August 1911, they are attacked in the local press. Intermittent skirmishes follow between the Nouvelle Section and the Ancienne Section, but unfortunately the Ancients outnumber the Moderns, fifteen instructors to four. The war simmers for three more years, with the socialists using the local paper, *La Sentinelle*, to attack the Moderns for elitism. This shocked Jeanneret, for he thought the socialists, believing in collectivity, would support their movement for the future. Yet the socialists were against displacing workers with machinery, against the kind of individualism an art movement implied, against engravers becoming artists. "Artist in La Chaux-de-Fonds," Edouard noted wryly, meant "unemployed and unemployable." From then on Jeanneret, suspicious of political parties, sought a top-down authority for industrialization.

By April 1914, Jeanneret fired off a forty-five-page pamphlet, the first of his many great polemics, called *Un Mouvement d'Art à la Chaux-de-Fonds*. He wrote to some of the famous artists and architects in Europe to enlist their support for this modern movement—Grasset, Behrens, Fischer, and others. At first glance it is hard to see this work as Modern but, on second look, one can see in its geometrical and nature-based properties a tougher and more inventive discipline than the work of those he was fighting, the Ancients [fig. 26].

Apropos the Nietzschean struggle, it is the opening lines of Jeanneret's *Un Mouvement d'Art* that predict the "destruction" of this movement, and indeed, within a month of publication, L'Eplattenier, Aubert, and Jeanneret had resigned from the school. The movement was finished, but Le Corbusier the polemicist was

26. *Sapins en hiver*, 1911 (FLC 2517 and XX, redrawn). Nature's patterns stylized and analyzed.

fully born. Jeanneret identifies with Zarathustra on many points too numerous to elaborate here, but the interested reader will find them in appendix II.

Zigzags between Gothic and Classical

What are the implications of Nietzsche on Jeanneret's character? And what is implied by his intense reading program, of imbibing Provensal, Schuré, and Renan's *The Life of Jesus*? Obviously, as he predicts in 1908, a life of constant revolution and tireless work—the individual truth-teller standing up against the uncomprehending people. Also, as it happens, an intermittent shedding of friends, even the periodic housecleaning of employees. And a constant desire to find the truth behind nature, to discover its laws and build an ideal architecture and city based on them. Finally, a view of himself as a kind of prophet and artistic superman, a man who will make revolutions in four professions—architecture, town planning, painting, and interior furnishings (or five if we count aesthetic theory).

These aspects of his character, and reading, come together in his twentieth year, while he is in Vienna. After seeing and enjoying a production of Puccini's *La Bohème* in the city, Jeanneret leaves for

Paris and, for a while, adopts the persona of this operatic character, becoming, as he says, "the Bohemian of the Boul-Mich." He
finds part-time work with the Perret brothers, intermittently from
the end of June 1908 to November 1909, work that gives him
enough money to read and teach himself design by visiting museums. During this time the artist-student lives in a garret overlooking the Cathedral of Notre-Dame. He fills a whole sketchbook with
drawings and watercolors of the cathedral, and does this in spite of
the fact that he is loosing his faith in Christianity and Gothic architecture: "I have Viollet-le-Duc [*Dictionanaire raisonné de l'architecture du XI au XVI siècle*, he writes L'Eplattenier in July 1908] and I
have Notre-Dame which serves as my laboratory so to speak. In
this marvellous old ramshackle building I verify the words of
Viollet-le-Duc and formulate my own observations. It is there that
I also undertake my design sessions 'after the antique'!" In other
words, he is starting to reject Ruskin's Gothic for the rationalist
Viollet-le-Duc, and take up the antique—that is, Classicism.

But his rejection of Gothic is not complete. The year in
Paris is not only one of turmoil and struggle, but ambiguous transition. From Auguste Perret, who becomes the new father figure
supplanting L'Eplattenier, he learns the revolutionary possibilities
of reinforced concrete and the importance of structural rationalism, but he learns them as a hybrid Gothic-Classicist. That is to
say, the Perret brothers turn out semi-industrial buildings which
accentuate their ribs, structural cage, and mullions as if they were
Gothic cathedrals, but they do this with a grammar that is rectilinear, symmetrical, and often of Classical detail. The mixture of traditions is significant. It carries out the French ideal, started in the
nineteenth century, of synthesizing the two great national traditions under a new technology. From Labrouste to Viollet to the
Perrets is straightline evolution, and for sixteen months Jeanneret
became part of it.

A second point he learns is that reinforced concrete frees up
the plan and space of a building so that the architect has much
more freedom, almost that of an artist. Both lessons are apparent
in the plans of buildings he works on. The Perrets' own office was
located in a reinforced-concrete frame building, and Jeanneret
studied carefully the free plan made possible by point supports.
These Gothic "ribs," or Modern "piers," or Corbusian "pilotis"
took over the supporting role from the walls and that meant, here,

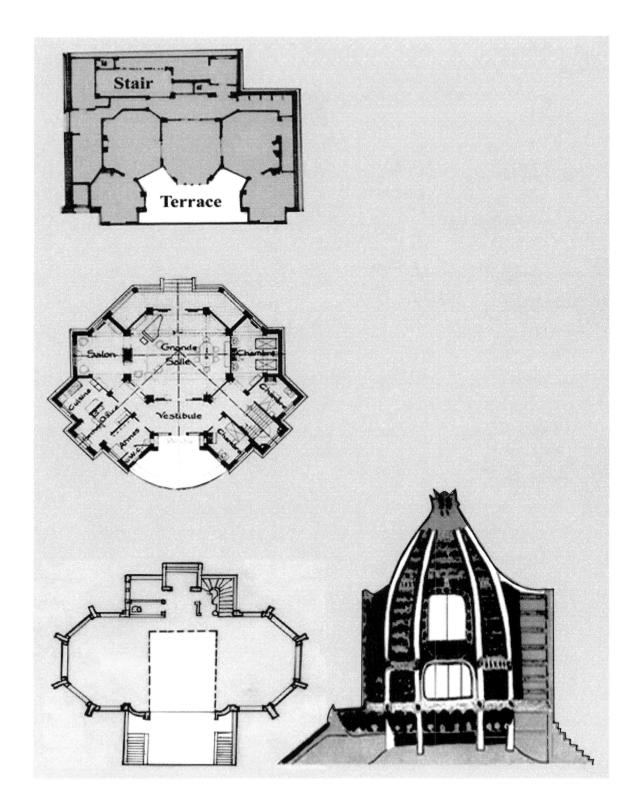

the partitions could create diagonals and acute angles and, further-more, that infill panels could be decorated with smooth or ceramic tiles. In other words, the secret doctrine that Auguste Perret taught was the potential of "loyal concrete" (Corbu's later phrase): it could make the architect an artist, someone who could freely com-pose his plans and elevations according to *compositional*, not *func-tional*, logic. With this flexibility he sees that an artistic revolution is possible. In his exhortations of November 1908: "The art of tomorrow is an art based on meditation. Raise up the concept and forge ahead!" [fig. 27].

While in Perret's office, Edouard worked on the plan and *grand salle* of a hunting lodge and designed a "Maison Bouteille." These schemes also make use of point supports to great effect. The for-mer has a syncopated octagon broken into small and large bays from which spaces and stairs shoot out. The solution has Baroque precedents, and the actual lodge is in an eclectic, Tudor style, but it is the spatial dynamism that is noteworthy. Equally forceful and inventive is the open plan for an unusual "Maison Bouteille": not only a "bottle" as Perret christened it but, as the elevations show, a "bee-hive" and "peaked-hat" [fig. 27]. What the plan shows, how-ever, is a convincing expression of two basic ideas in harmonious juxtaposition: a stretched octagon is countered by a service unit to one side, a double-height space in the center, and, to the other side, the orientation toward Paris and the view. In words Le Corbusier will later use, the architect must understand how the organization of a plan generates the architecture, "from the inside out." The lesson is that organization counts, not style; organiza-tion, not the patterns of Owen Jones. "Burn what you love, love what you burn." First he burns Jones and Ruskin, in the crucible of Paris, only to get them back in a new way, a few years later.

One of the conflagrations leads to a classical cubic design of 1910, the first project he would later illustrate under the moniker "Le Corbusier." When he starts to publish his *Oeuvre Complète*, in the late 1920s, all the regionalist work is suppressed, but he does show a project of stacked cubes reminiscent of the way a child might order Froebel Blocks and the way Jeanneret ordered his many bracket designs of 1906–7 [fig. 28]. The logic of the design is clear and compelling. White cubes, solid and void, shadow and sunlight, green garden and flat roof, alternate as they climb up to a central communal space.

27. Three free plans with structural ribs, or *pilotis*, compared: August Perret, first floor plan, which Jeanneret marked up, 25 bis, rue Franklin, Paris, 1903. La Saulot, Salbris, Loir-et-Cher, 1908 (Auguste Perret and Jeanneret worked on the octagonal, exploding plan of this hunting lodge). Jeanneret, Maison Bouteille project, 1909, plans and side elevation redrawn, not to a common scale: a stretched octagonal open plan, with double-height space (dotted lines) oriented to the view. As Allen Brooks has argued, this is a fore-runner of the later open plans and Villa Schwob. Its resemblance to a cathedral chevet suggests that Jeanneret was attempting a last recon-ciliation between Gothic structural expressionism and his Jura Art Nouveau, rationalism and spirituality.

28. Ateliers d'art, January 24, 1910, axonometric plan redrawn. Eleven artists' workshops and gardens surround a covered, pyramidal, communal space for lectures and exhibits, with offices and salesroom on the second floor.

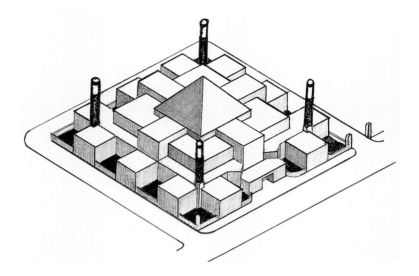

Although they look deceptively simple and ahistorical, the precedents for these stacked cells are many. As well as the Froebel Blocks, obvious influences are the monks' cells of Ema that Edouard so admired, the cubic work of Peter Behrens at Oldenburg, 1905, the Turkish mosques, with their four corner minarets, which Jeanneret was soon to draw, and the prismatic designs of the eighteenth-century revolutionary architect Claude-Nicolas Ledoux—which also have smokestacks at the four corners. So, curiously, the most seminal of all Le Corbusier's early schemes turns out to be highly historical—a fact which he was to acknowledge in 1930 when he was under attack for being a Futurist.

The Ateliers d'art is described polemically by Le Corbusier in 1930 as "the creation of a center of instruction for bringing the building arts up to date, a program similar to that which was to become the Bauhaus at Weimar . . . There, already in 1910, is an example of preoccupation with organization, series, standardization, and future extension." This kind of back-dating of ideas is the equivalent in Modernism of getting the patent in capitalism. Money, power, fame all grow out of establishing precedent; in this case LC is implying that he had grasped the Bauhaus arguments before they did. But there is an irony in his claims, because it brings to attention the fact that he was *not* involved with standardization until four years later, with the Dom-ino system. This minor point could be excused except that it is so typical of him and other Modernists. They have to win the battle, gain the patents, and, by the same token, critics and historians have to catch them stretching the evidence. Allen Brooks has found, in the book that is the definitive study of this early period, five or six examples of Le Corbusier fudging the dates and claiming a little more than he should do.

Still, for all that, the Ateliers d'art is a masterful bit of organizational logic, especially for a twenty-three-year-old, and it also shows where his and L'Eplattenier's idealism were in 1910. They both wanted to set up a commercially viable artistic production system, an outgrowth of the *Cours Superior* that could make good money while making new arts and crafts. Here is the seed of an idea that, in 1919, will turn into one of Jeanneret's many failed attempts to become a capitalist and manufacture inventive building products.

The most extraordinary invention of this transitional period, which again Allen Brooks has unearthed, is a 1910 manuscript of 135 pages entitled *La Construction des Villes*. Rewritten over several years, and with more than 150 drawings, this was a very important mental exercise for Jeanneret for several reasons. First, it gave him the wider picture for architecture, its social and urban concerns, and these were never to leave him. Unlike most architects, who see a vision of the single building, Le Corbusier always tested his individual works at larger scales. Second, it gave him a historical view of the city, largely based on Camillo Sitte's ideas and those of Charles L'Eplattenier, grounded in direct observation. Medieval cities, growing slowly and organically, were preferred to those upstart, mechanistic, and commercial layouts, those gridiron cities of the vulgar Americans that he damns. In effect, the worldview of the idealists and Theosophists was set, very strongly here, against the materialists and pragmatists. The extraordinary thing is that, while keeping many of the same illustrations, words, and examples, Le Corbusier was to change the message entirely, in 1925, when he published *Urbanisme*, or *The City of Tomorrow*. And that is the third benefit this manuscript had. By laying stored in his fertile mind for twelve years, and percolating slowly, it could suddenly emerge, totally reborn, in 1922. Then, working furiously at night, he redesigned the whole of Paris and put it on exhibition. One could call this period "the dress rehearsal for life." The years from 1910 to 1920 were spent simulating ideas that later would be launched on an unsuspecting world, as if they were fully born from his head. In fact they had gestated for a long time.

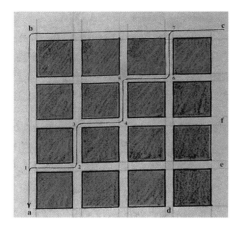

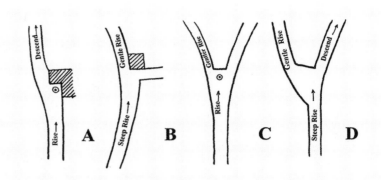

29. *The Mistake of the Grid* from *La Construction des Villes*, 1910, redrawn. To go from c to a, one has to take one of two long routes: c–b–a, or 7–6–5–4–3–2–1. A slightly curved line would be better, more efficient—but not exactly straight: "the straight line, the most noble line in Nature, is justifiably the rarest of all!" We find in such Platonic quotes the Argument from Nature, and this is set dialectically against the Argument from History.

30. *The Lesson of the Curve and Slope*, 1910, redrawn. Streets should curve and slope, views along them should be closed. Symmetrical and geometrical layouts must be avoided, and the pack-donkey's way retained. Specifically, here, Jeanneret says that the beauty of "the solutions a and b surpass the need for commentary" (they recall Neuhauserstrasse in Munich), while "c is too symmetrical and can be improved by becoming less so, d."

31. Neuhauserstrasse, Munich, ink on tracing paper, approximately 7.5 x 20 cm (FLC). The dotted line indicates visual closure by street-forming black boxes in the background, which still allow views of towers above the blocks. Such foreground-background drawings became canonic again with Post-Modern urbanists in the 1970s.

La Construction des Villes is a defense of the street and the square, not the motorcar and airplane, a hymn of praise to the curved road—the pack-donkey's way of zigzagging up a hill—rather than the straight one. It is an ideal city for enjoying the sights, rather than getting around too quickly. *"La lecon de l'ane est a retenir,"* the lesson of the ass must be retained. And this was the man who was to insist in 1925, against the ass, that all cities must be built on straight lines, because "a city built for speed is built for success." Actually, though, the young Jeanneret could use the functional argument, in 1910, the other way around, and he produced one illustration showing the absurdity of designing in a grid, because you could not go straight to your goal [figs. 29–31].

Straight or curved, motorway speed or pedestrian contemplation—the seesaws in taste and dogmatic assertion ricochet back and forth down the century. The switches in Le Corbusier's own opinions highlight a basic problem of the time, when arguments are based on the zeitgeist rather than logic or history. The young Jeanneret could observe, through Camillo Sitte's eyes, some lessons of medieval Germany and generalize from these [fig. 31], then fifteen years later learn lessons of the motorcar and generalize from these. The fact that they are contradictory underscores the rather obvious point that all cities are historical, and its less obvious corollary, that therefore they need opposite solutions at different times and places. One rule book for a growing city is like having one suit for a baby and a man.

German Industrial Classicism

One of the historical periods Jeanneret learned from was the Garden City movement of England. He made direct tracings from journals of the Hampstead Garden suburb, praising it for carrying out the principles he was advocating. He acquainted himself with the social arguments of Ebenezer Howard and their practical realization by Barry Parker and Raymond Unwin. He even designed a Garden City in a picturesque curvilinear layout for La Chaux-de-Fonds. While soon to reject the aesthetic of pitched roofs and curving streets, he kept an interest in the idea of the industrial city in a park. This led to his early essays in prefabrication and workers' housing: the Dom-ino houses of 1914 and the workers' housing for Saint-Nicolas d'Aliermont of 1917. All this work shows a social concern and interest in mass housing which was rare, although not unique, for its time.

In 1910 there was a further consolidation of his turn toward rationalism and a sober, even puritanical aesthetic. Edouard was sent by the school at La Chaux-de-Fonds to study the evolution of the decorative arts in Germany. Jeanneret, and to a certain extent L'Eplattenier, who supported him in getting a grant, realized that there was a need for a new movement, based midway between art and industry, which would train a new type of craftsman. In his first book, *Étude sur le mouvement d'art décoratif en Allemagne,* published in 1912, Jeanneret set the opposition of art and industry in national terms between France and Germany.

> As French [he means French-Swiss], I suffered in Germany; I was overwhelmed in Paris, where they complained of a German invasion [He always gets attacked from opposite sides of a divide] . . . the marvelous Industrial Art of Germany demands to be known . . . Germany is a book of actualities. If Paris is the home of Art, Germany remains the great center of production. Experiences are happening there, the battles are crucial; buildings are raised and the rooms with their historic walls recount the triumph of order and tenacity.

Behind such words, we can feel the Nietzschean, military metaphor and the battle of 1871. Edouard, at twenty-five, had what today some would call politically incorrect views, stereotyping the Germans as efficient mercantilists versus the high-minded French, and one finds such attitudes lasting through the 1910s and, of course, two World Wars. For instance, in *Sketchbook A2,* 1915–16, he recounts how a French department store "routs the Krauts," "offsets the Hun." "For here [in France] there is Life, flexibility, tradition—taste. It's taste and not simply a modern style."

However, being the supreme dialectician, Jeanneret is open to learn from the Krauts and in November 1910 he goes to work for the great German architect Peter Behrens. Behrens was in charge of the first large-scale industrial art venture of the twentieth century—designing a whole spectrum of equipment, or industrial products, for the A.E.G. Company. These revealed what Edouard called "a modest aspect, sober, almost impersonal." What was later to be known as industrial design and the Bauhaus style was being produced for the first time. It is the contrasts between German excellence in the applied arts and French excellence at the traditional high arts—painting and sculpture—that lead to the dialectic, as he sees it, between the genius of the individual creator versus the proficiency of corporate organization. Behrens as an artist and organization man combined both sides. However, there was a downside; for Jeanneret, and other draftsmen in the office, his methods of control were "autocratic and tyrannical." Because Behrens often took trips to get more jobs, when he came back he had to "terrorize" the staff into working hard. These words Jeanneret later applied to himself as he, in turn, commanded things to be done. By 1915, people in La Chaux-de-Fonds, noting this change, were to drop "Edouard" for "Le grand Charles."

Architecture, produced as a cross between a military campaign and a symphony, demands opposite parts of the brain. The conclusion of the *Etude* and his time with Behrens pointed in the same direction: the French love of art and the German love of efficiency, although opposed, were equally important for architecture. Jeanneret, however, soon realized that this two-term dialectic left out an important third position: popular and folk art, a situation he addressed on leaving Germany.

While he was in Behrens's studio for four months, until April 1, 1911, Jeanneret nearly came into contact with the other two pioneers of the Modern Movement, Walter Gropius and Mies van der Rohe. They were there in the beginning of the year, both beginning to forge their versions of a new industrial but, importantly, *Classical* aesthetic. It is interesting that Behrens teaches Jeanneret the significance of proportions, harmony, and moldings, "things that were entirely unknown to me." He picks up "the art of profiles and their harmonious relation" and also the notion of "regulating lines," the way proportional triangles can be drawn over a building to regulate its dimensions, harmoniously.

In this way and others a new dualism was forming in Edouard's mind, the connection between an industrial functionalism and stripped Classicism [figs. 32–34]. The other German architects who conveyed the new spirit of functionalism to Jeanneret were Muthesius and Tessenow.

Yet, although his projects became like Behrens's, carried out in a stripped Classical style, Jeanneret was not altogether taken in by the new German movement and, in a characteristically

32, 33. Villa Favre-Jacot, Le Locle, 1912. Stripped Classical details: the cornice streamlining, horizontal band of windows, arches punched into the wall without moldings, and the separation of colonettes from the wall all derive from the industrial handling of Classical elements—Italianate on one side, Greek on another. The Classical/Industrial style, forged from the German experience, is evident in many projects of Jeanneret during the 1910s.

dialectical way, argued that utility did not necessarily produce beauty, that art was quite independent of it. This dualistic view, that beauty and function each have their own laws, deepened his former set of oppositions, and started to underline his tragic view that the human condition is necessarily divided between things of the mind and imperatives of the body. Most tragic was the split between the demands of the spirit and the will to power; or at its worst, the great divide of the twentieth century between art and money. Like Nietzsche, he accepted that the best art was part intellectual and part lyrical, part Apollonian and part Dionysian. This dualism naturally brought him into continual conflict with other architects because he was acutely aware of the part that might be missing. Hence his attacks on functionalists for lacking poetry and his rejections of Art Nouveau for lacking rigor. Indeed the conflict between these opposed psychological states was becoming sharp enough in his own mind to set him veering off in yet a new direction. By 1908 he had absorbed and rejected Jura Regionalism and by 1910 the Parisian structural rationalism of Perret. In the spring of 1911 he did the same double act with the nascent German functionalism. These zigzags were all rather dizzying and confusing for Jeanneret, as they are for the reader to follow, but a pattern emerges: the return to sources in a new way.

The Useful Voyage

Apparently the inspiration for the next transformation was yet another book. This was Cingria-Vaneyre's *Les Entretiens de la villa du Rouet: Essais dialogués sur les arts plastiques en Suisse romande*, published in 1908 and read by Jeanneret late in 1910 when he was still in Germany. It was recommended to him by his new friend and mentor William Ritter, a man twenty years his senior, because it advocated a different form of Jura Regionalism than that of L'Eplattenier. According to Paul Turner, this book made a new connection for Jeanneret between his area of birth, the Suisse-Romande, and Classical Greek culture. These sets of conjoined ideas were to lead Jeanneret on an extensive trip, what he called a "Voyage to the Orient," to see if he too could tie together Classical culture and that of La Chaux. The argument of Cingria's book seems strange to someone not acquainted with Swiss culture, but evidently it had a profound effect on Jeanneret, for he marked

34. A project for Felix Klipstein, Loubach, November 1914 (BV). A vernacular farmhouse crossed with a Roman verandah and an elevated walkway leading to a raised garden house ("streets in the air"). This villa in an orchard, with its two poplar trees evoking Italy, shows the influence of Tessenow and Behrens, as well as his *Voyage to the Orient*. In 1915, he also produced a design for skyscrapers in a park, another example of the German influence.

it up with very revealing comments: "In a year, at Rome, I will reread it, and, in my sketches, lay the foundations for my own Jura, Neuchatelois discipline."

Cingria argued the necessity for creating a local identity for the Suisse-Romande, that is, the French-speaking part of Switzerland where Edouard grew up, because there the Germans or Italians did not contaminate the racial stock. It was pure Greco-Latin (somehow, Cingria did not notice the irony of being a pure hybrid). This racist theory explains the strange aspect of the argument: that the local identity should be Mediterranean in spirit and Classical, not northern or Gothic. It should be, as Greek temples are, "regular," "calm," white, and made from right angles. Happily for the argument, the Jura mountains were akin to those in Greece, and from this time on Jeanneret was to draw Swiss mountains as if he were in the Mediterranean.

The impact of these meanings is clear in the next few buildings of Jeanneret, such as the villas Favre-Jacot and Schwob, even if they do not strike us as particularly Swiss or regionalist. In any event, Jeanneret was convinced that a local Jura revival of culture could occur and that it would be based on geometry and Mediterranean Classicism. He set off in May 1911 to test these ideas with a young Swiss friend, Auguste Klipstein. This would be his *third* journey of self-education: to Prague, Vienna, Bucharest,

Constantinople, Athens, and Florence—among many other cities [fig. 35].

Jeanneret was twenty-four years old and, like many artists at this time in their life, he had an urge to travel, to move from one city to the next devouring new experiences and knowledge with an insatiable appetite. He started keeping a sketchbook, a pocket-sized writing pad, to jot down ideas, visual impressions, and anecdotes. These sketchbooks, of which there are more than seventy covering the whole of Le Corbusier's life, were in themselves a significant addition to Jeanneret's development, for they became a new medium of expression and source book for later ideas. In terms of expression they forced him to develop a very concise, cinematic presentation, where ideas, buildings, landscapes, and even nude bodies confront each other in rapid succession. As source books, they served for later buildings, polemics, and paintings. In the self-education of Jeanneret they played a paramount role, a subject which is worth considering. He said of his first trip from La Chaux in 1907 that self-education gave him a freedom from stereotype and convention. For this creative freshness, it is worth recalling his emphasis on drawing:

When one travels and works with visual things—architecture,

35. "The Useful Voyage," a map of the 1911 journey classifying the three aspects of civilization that were competing for dominance in Europe and in Jeanneret's mind: culture—mostly French and Mediterranean (c), folk—mostly in the Balkans (f), industrial—mostly Germany (i). The passion for categorization informed Jeanneret's self-education and intensified the conflict between these three areas.

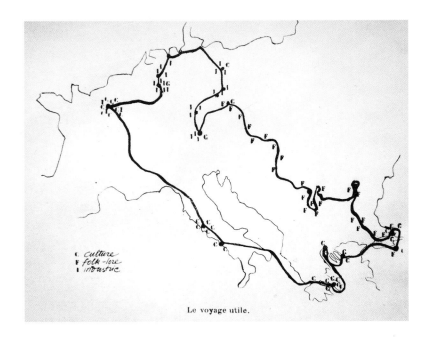

Le voyage utile.

painting, or sculpture—one uses one's eyes and *draws*, so as to fix deep down in one's experience what is seen. Once the impression has been recorded by the pencil, it stays for good, entered, registered, inscribed.

Or, in 1965:

I practiced architecture without professional lectures, without schools, without diplomas. I set out on a road across Europe: Paris, Constantinople, Asia Minor, Athens, Rome. I looked, saw, observed, discovered. Life belongs not to those who *know*, but those who *discover*.

This emphasis on *seeing* what other people only *look* at achieved polemical expression later in *Towards a New Architecture*, with three chapters titled "Eyes Which Do Not See," devoted to the new aesthetic hidden in ocean liners, airplanes, and automobiles. The self-educated man can see what others cannot. Yet the disadvantage to being self-taught, especially in the twentieth century, is that one cannot manipulate ideas very freely, because each one has come through great effort and becomes dogmatically fixed. The self-taught man may become obsessive with his ideas whereas the academic, or the man who has gained knowledge through books and by training, can deal with ideas more easily, discarding them when they become obsolete. This Le Corbusier had trouble doing and, in his late fifties, he even regretted his form of self-education.

I am self-taught in everything, even in sports. And being self-taught, I knew the greatest anguish up to the age of thirty-five. I would not advise anyone to follow the same course.

In particular, Le Corbusier had trouble breaking away from his fundamental architectural concepts such as the city in the park, or the separating of functions, long after their inadequacies were well known. In other respects his method of learning at his own pace and for his own motives made up for a partial inflexibility. What is surprising about the young Jeanneret, as I have mentioned, is his self-awareness and developed sense of personal identity. This obviously came from his self-education and accounts for the

36. *Suleiman Mosque*, 1911, pencil on sketchbook paper (FLC). This sketch, in one of the three styles Jeanneret used at this time, emphasizes both geometrical masses and the great importance of profile or silhouette. Architecture is the play of volumes and the rhythm of light and shadow.

extraordinary feeling of individual destiny which runs through his second book, *Le Voyage d'Orient*, written as a series of letters to his friends in the Ateliers d'art in 1911, although it was not published until 1965. Each chapter has the quality of a confession, a testing of some personally held idea. For instance, Jeanneret and his friend Auguste Klipstein enter into a stormy argument with a Prague student trying to convert him to a new aesthetic based on modern technology.

> We defend beautiful modern technology and say how much all the arts owe to it, in its new plastic expressiveness, its bold realization, and its splendid opportunities which offer the builder, from this time on, the freedom from classical servitude. The Hall of Machines in Paris, the Gare du Nord in Hamburg, the autos, airplanes, ocean liners, and locomotives appear to us as decisive arguments.

Not only are the later arguments for a machine aesthetic here, but also the same pedagogic and persuasive tone which was to characterize his subsequent books. The major lessons of *Le Voyage d'Orient* were the following:

First, the mosques of Constantinople revealed an "elemental geometry which disciplined the masses: the square, the cube, the sphere" [fig. 36]. Litanies to the "sphere" appear so often, in this book and letters of the time, that one could say that of all the Platonic solids, it is this and the cube he favors the most.

37. Turkish house between Murattis and Rodosto (FLC, 4/7/11?, *Voyage*, 80). The white architecture of truth.

A second lesson is that the white, simple peasant houses, which he found throughout his journey, reveal a certain moral rectitude based on a direct harmony with nature. As he was later to put the lesson, in 1925, these whitewashed houses are an "X-ray of beauty . . . an assize court sitting in permanent judgment" on all the objects which are placed against them. Imperfections and visual deceits are quickly exposed by the whitewash [fig. 37]. For instance, he describes visiting a small city on the Danube, Baja, which shows the typical transition from clean folk whiteness to modern commercial decadence. "We visited rooms which everywhere revealed the big city's bad taste in bric-a-brac . . ." Contrasting with this were the old peasant houses whose "white arcades bring comfort, and the three great whitewashed walls, which are repainted each spring, make a screen as decorative as the background of Persian ceramics. The women are most beautiful; the men clean-looking . . ."

The third lesson was Ruskinian, that visual deceits which covered or denied the basic underlying functions were to be found in socially degenerate situations: architecture is a moral thermometer. Thus his judgment of contemporary Vienna. "Invaded by modern buildings the environment is being butchered pitilessly . . . Amid the bad taste that floods the boulevards with bombastic, nouveau riche architecture . . ." The equation of an over-decorated revivalism with disease and crime, which Adolf Loos had made in *Ornament and Crime*, 1908, was formulated by Jeanneret in the same city as a kind of economic and moral law. From now on

Jeanneret was prone to equate useless consumer objects in all the historical styles, save Classicism, with a rapacious form of capitalism.

By contrast, it was the monks on Mount Athos, where he spent eighteen days, who revealed a healthy attitude toward the objects of everyday life. The pleasure they found in basic necessities such as food and drink was manifest in the simplified harmony of the refectory table: the pure forms of wine bottles and dishes conveyed a moral lesson about how little was needed to achieve a relative happiness.

> After the prior has, I suppose, blessed the food, we sit down on the white wooden benches. The monks' hands are rough and callused, swollen from working the fields, and their robustness is at one with the plates and the enameled earthenware common to the country and implying the soil. Before each guest are three earthen bowls containing raw tomatoes, boiled beans, and fish, nothing else. And in front of him is a wine pitcher and a tin goblet, together with round heavy black rye bread, the daily treasure, the meritorious symbol.

It is interesting to note that this moral lesson about the banal objects of everyday use preceded Jeanneret's Purist still lifes incorporating these objects and his philosophy of "equipment" which was to show how they could evolve from the industrial process. In fact, Mount Athos was to epitomize his view of the good life, a life filled with the poetic presence of basic type objects: *the* wine bottle, *the* loaf of bread, *the* salami—as well as sun, space, and greenery. In countless later drawings of the typical urban apartment we find these basic objects, which obviously had a metaphysical presence for Le Corbusier and, in his design for the monastery La Tourette, at least one building where the lesson of Mount Athos was completely realized [figs. 38, 211]. It is also interesting to reflect that this style and set of attitudes became, by the 1960s, a cliché in the West, to become commercially exploited. Terence Conran created his Habitat empire based on the formula, Elisabeth David popularized it for cooking, Peter Mayle brought the pleasures of Provence and simple living to the reading public, and, from then on, the *House and Garden* monthly had to feature the good-summer-life on a white-washed Greek Island. In other

38. Mount Athos, view of Simonos Petras (FLC). One of many monasteries perched "like eagles' eyries." The "most moving sight" that influenced his later La Tourette "was the porch of an ancient fortress, together with smooth bare walls, on top of which perched cellular dwellings high up in the sky with their galleries open to the sea."

words, Jeanneret not only won the century's big style war, at least when it was the noble peasants versus the nouveau riche, but his victory touched off a commercial bonanza—something that might have made him deeply unhappy (the spirit lost to mammon).

The Parthenon as a Dominating Machine

The final and most significant lesson of Jeanneret's 1911 journey was learned in Athens, although he did not write up his notes on this chapter and the one on Athos until 1914. He describes in *Le Voyage d'Orient* how he stalked the Acropolis a whole day before daring to approach it. He arrived at eleven in the morning, but "invented a thousand excuses" for not going up to it with Klipstein. He sat in cafés, drinking and reading the papers; he prowled the streets of old Athens waiting for the sun to set before he launched his direct attack. And when he finally reached it, in the setting sun, when the stone had turned a flaming yellow and orange, he had a strange reaction.

> See what confirms the rectitude of temples, the savagery of the site, their impeccable structure. The spirit of power triumphs. The herald, so terribly lucid, draws to the lips a brazen trumpet and proffers a strident blast. The entablature with a cruel rigidity breaks and terrorizes. The sentiment of an extra human fatality seizes you. The Parthenon, terrible machine, pulverizes and dominates everything for miles around.

The Parthenon was seen, oddly enough, as a "terrible *machine*," a perfected automaton which was cruel and terrifying in its clarity and implacable honesty. His imagination, perhaps inflamed by drinking too much resin wine in order to avoid the cholera that was raging around Athens, projects onto the Parthenon and the Acropolis a variety of powerful metaphors. Twice he calls the hill a "rocky hull," and a "tragic carcass" with "red blood" coagulating in its red earth. Its image in the setting sun calls up all the battles, terror, and "conquered treasures" which clot its history. The shafts of the Parthenon repeat and soar above this carcass, "assuming the appearance of a gigantic armor plate with the guttae of the mutules looking like its rivets." Armor plate, rivets? In other words, the Parthenon and Acropolis, taken together, can be seen as what he calls a "domineering" killing machine, with a front "like a shield"; yet it nevertheless has a calm, magisterial presence in the landscape because of its horizontals. Later, in 1918, his first Purist painting was to capture the calm essence of this landscape, but using, of all things, a table top, books, cube, and shadow to do it [fig. 39].

39. *The Chimney-Piece*, 1918, 58.5 x 48 cm (FLC). What Le Corbusier often called his "first picture" he also said was an abstract portrayal of his weeks on the Acropolis—a mountain land-scape coded as a shadow, and a cube of wood as the Parthenon.

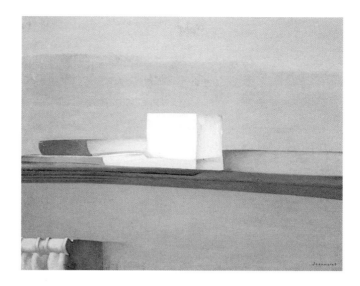

Two images and ideas are fighting it out in Jeanneret's mind: the domineering machine and the ideal of Classical beauty. They are brought into momentary balance by the mathematical rigor of the building blocks, the precise way they are cut, and the harmony that results from their correct proportions. Looking down the length of the Parthenon allows the beholder "to seize at a glance a single block, a gigantic prism of marble cut from bottom to top with a rectitude of clear mathematics and the precision that a machinist brings to his labor."

In other words, this building resolves a lot of the dualities that are plaguing him: the new machine production of Germany and the eternal beauty of Classical geometry; mathematics and har-mony; the landscape and sculptural body. Because of this resolu-tion he twice says it is the ultimate touchstone: "a sacred standard, the basis for all measurement in art" and "the standard for all cre-ation." But because it hits him like a blow to the body—"the vio-lence of combat, I was stupefied"—he is agitated by the implications. It is "the undeniable Master"—in his 1911 original manuscript, he writes this as "the tyrant, the Dictator." And here we begin to get a sense of the dark side of the killing machine and Jeanneret's character, and also his momentary perception of this cruelty. In a letter to William Ritter written while fighting with the Acropolis, he describes forebodingly "the harsh, tyrannical sway of the autocratic tendency, which I feel within me." Partly he is wrestling with the lesson the Parthenon is making on his mind:

that he *must reject* his master L'Eplattenier, the "pope" he calls him in this letter, "my most devoted friend." Why? Because "my faith has left me, because I know success is impossible"—that of the Atelier d'art, the New Movement in La Chaux, and the chance of building big projects there.

Tyranny, dictatorship, an autocratic tendency? By May 1913 he is writing to his older friend Ritter that his large-scale building ambition cannot be realized "in this town . . . and there will be no building in 1913. My ambition prompted me to such work. This profession drives one to support autocracy." To satisfy his grandiose ambitions, he will be searching out captains of industry by 1922; and by 1940, real dictators. Architecture as a cruel art of mutual enslavement is glimpsed first on the Parthenon, and embraced with a tragic ambivalence.

However, it was not until 1923, in *Towards a New Architecture*, that Le Corbusier reworked the idea that the Parthenon was a machine, and turned it into one of the most startling notions of Modern Architecture. First, the same spirit of "imagination and cold reason" that produced automobiles and airplanes produced it, and second, it emerged as a perfected object from technological evolution just as these machines did. It is worth quoting from this later manifesto to clarify ideas which were first formulated in 1911:

> Every sacrifice, every cleansing had already been performed (by mechanical evolution). The moment was reached when nothing more might be taken away, when nothing would be left but these closely-knit and violent elements sounding clear and tragic like brazen trumpets.

We notice the similar metaphors and the reiteration of the Parthenon as a symbol of the tragic view of the human condition, a conclusion Le Corbusier came back to many times, particularly when he was under attack or having inner doubts. The idea of the Parthenon as a machine was elaborated in one more way in 1923.

> We are in the inexorable realm of the mechanical . . . the moldings are tight and firm . . . all this plastic machinery is realized in marble with the rigor that we have learned to apply to the machine. The impression is of naked, polished steel [fig. 40].

40. Photo of the Propylea, taken by Jeanneret ca. 1911 and published in *Towards a New Architecture*, 1923.

Think of the ironies here. The Futurists said "a motorcar is more beautiful than the Victory of Samothrace," a machine is *better* than the Parthenon and something that brings welcome noise, dynamism, fast change, and liberating destruction. For Jeanneret, both the machine and the Parthenon were exactly the opposite: they were beautiful, silent, and eternal. They represented ultimate developments, "sacred standards," even spiritual ones, that one could return to for "certainty," as an absolute check against changing human affairs.

Another 1911 idea that finds expression in *Towards a New Architecture* is developed from Schuré and Nietzsche—that of the great artist, the elite leader.

> It is a question of pure invention, so personal that it may be called that of one man: Phidias made the Parthenon . . . Phidias, Phidias, the great sculptor, made the Parthenon. There has been nothing like it anywhere or at any period. It happened at a moment when things were at their keenest, when a man, stirred by the noblest thoughts, crystallized them in a plastic work of light and shade. The moldings of the Parthenon are infallible and implacable . . . we are riveted by our senses; we are ravished in our minds; we touch the axis of harmony. No question of religious dogma enters in; no symbolical description, no naturalistic representation; there is nothing but pure forms in precise relationships.

While these meanings were not precisely worked out until Le Corbusier was about thirty-four, we can still say that at the age of twenty-four he had understood them in general and formulated a basic attitude toward architecture and life: what could be called the "Parthenon spirit." His later text reworks the earlier one. Indeed, it seems to me that if we are to understand the personal character of Le Corbusier, then we will find it most clearly expressed in the meanings he gives this Greek temple. It stands alone in a beautiful but indifferent universe; as he says, it makes the landscape by standing clear of it. It is a "brazen trumpet blast" of perfected harmony that rings in resonance with our inner axis. It has the qualities he valued of clarity, precision, implacable honesty, severity, and it was the result of an economic competition that produces the perfected machine. Like Greek tragedy it is the expression of the tragic view of the human condition struggling in a hostile universe. Whether he valued its "domineering cruelty" and "tyranny" is for a psychoanalyst to say. But it is the positive meanings which Le Corbusier later introduced into the modern movement and which can be found in his own building—either the reason for their greatness, or the reason for their great failure.

Jeanneret Discovers Sex in a Pot

However, we are in danger here of taking Jeanneret only at the explicit level. There is the humorous, zany, self-mocking side that is just as important in *The Journey to the East.* (After Edward Said's attack on Western "orientalism," and years of political correctness, the "Orient" has had a rechristening by its publishers.) If we read this collection of letters in a way that architectural historians do not, some unsuspected issues pop out. First, like all of his fifty-seven books, it was dashed off in extreme haste as if he did not want to take complete responsibility for what are, in effect, involuntary, confessional expostulations. No less than four times, in his dedicatory preface to his brother, Albert, does he humiliate himself and demean his writing. For instance, he writes of "an audience who really didn't want these lines"; or, "my very poor, sad, incompetent French"; or, "the fluctuating esteem even of our closest friends" who read them. What a way to start a book! It may be a continental literary convention, or his style may have been raw and adolescent; but we *are* dealing, even in 1911, with the most effective architectural communicator of the last century.

Jeanneret had a very sensual side. There are touching photographs of the twenty-four-year-old Edouard, standing by the columns of the Parthenon, dressed in a bow tie, with a wan smile and gawky neck and the eyeglasses of a scholar. What strikes one in this and other photos of the time is that Jeanneret, although a self-confessed ugly crow, could look quite engaging and even beautiful. He may have hidden and suppressed his sexual side, behind the Trappist Monk, as he was to write, but it was always bubbling underneath to boil over in the most remarkable ways.

The start of his letters to his young friends, the first one addressed to "My dear old Perrin," the sculptor, begins with the love they have for form, particularly "the beauty of a sphere." Suddenly this turns into a full-blown paean to the spherical pot,

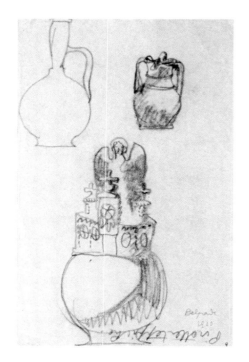

41. Pottery from the Balkans (FLC).

its "contours and my ecstasies." No doubt, Jeanneret is trying to arouse his young audience, sexually, and at the same time mock his metaphor:

> You recognize these joys: to feel the generous belly of a vase, to caress its slender neck, and then to explore the subtleties of its contours. To thrust your hands into the deepest part of your pockets and, with your eyes half closed, to give way slowly to the intoxication of the fantastic glazes, the burst of yellows, the velvet tone of the blue; to be involved with the animated fight between brutal black masses and victorious white elements . . .

He goes on to generalize:

> The art of the peasant is a striking creation of aesthetic sensuality. If art elevates itself above the sciences, it is precisely because, in opposition to them, it stimulates sensuality and awakens profound echoes in the physical being.

And then he extends the generalization to traditional art:

> Thus this traditional art, like a lingering warm caress, embraces the entire land, covering it with the same flowers that unite or mingle races, climates and places. It has spread out without constraint, with the spiritedness of a beautiful animal. The forms are voluminous and swollen with vitality. [fig. 41]

Then he quotes one of the theorists and artists whom he admires, Eugène Grasset, on the definition of beauty as "joy" and ties this to youthful vigor, which is flourishing, beaming, spreading out like aroused pots—"their curves expanding to the bursting point." At this point the sexual metaphor is dropped until the end of the piece, where it fizzles out: "An extraordinary joy gushes from that unique setting. You know how that panel [of small women in a garden] excited me."

Throughout *Le Voyage d'Orient* the attraction of women and the joys of seeing landscapes through the painter's eye are mixed up. A real equation is made that seems to remain throughout Le Corbusier's life, between his own painting, sexuality, and the landscape. Before we examine this in the watercolors and drawings, a few words on Jeanneret's emergent interest in women from the age of nineteen. The first indication is a journal entry of his father, January 5, 1907—"Edouard, all occupied with dancing and with girls, has just bought a pair of skis." The second is a letter to his parents, a year later, where he admits that before arriving in Vienna, "I have passed all my youth without having ever looked at a girl. Now it is a sweet music that penetrates me . . . a jolly harpist . . . who has twenty years and what eyes! . . . I am beginning to know what a woman is." The third is advice from his father, when Edouard is on his journey in Constantinople, that he take care when having sex, and not buy unnecessary things, like pots. Maybe his father is, ironically, turning his son's metaphor on its head, but in any case it implies that father and son have discussed the dangers of unsafe sex and visiting prostitutes. This supposition is given further weight by a letter to William Ritter in the autumn of 1913 when, at twenty-six, Jeanneret gives vent to his anger at his parents' innuendoes.

They wish him to marry, settle down, and have children. But, "I have a horror of marriage, a situation too much like a hole in the ground where any encounter is possible, bad ones before good ones . . ." They also imply that, if he returns late at night after a discussion with friends, on Cézanne, Hodler, Titian, and Tintoretto, then they "imagine that I have turned myself into a whore, where I see several or one slut." Perhaps Edouard is trying to joke with his older, homosexual friend, for he writes about how marriage establishes one socially and, he says, lugubriously, "I'd prefer each time to address myself to my radiator, because it keeps a useful and fecund silence for me."

Often one cannot tell when Le Corbusier is being serious, or quite funny.

The paintings of this period are as colorful as his writings and, as one would guess from his words above, extremely Fauvist. He often speaks about a red or, more often, yellow sky, and many of his landscapes are painted with strange inversions: instead of a blue sky above a green ground, the paintings have citron yellow tops and rusty or blood red bottoms. His favorite artists of this time are the sculptors Maillol and Rodin, and the painters Cézanne, Hodler, Signac, Van Gogh, Van Dongen, and, above all, Matisse—some of whom were associated with Fauvism. Fascinating was the way Matisse could fill a canvas with jagged and voluptuous

42. *Persistantes souvenances du Bosphore*, 1913, charcoal, ink, and gouache on drawing paper, 55.5 x 57.5 cm (FLC 4099). Female symbols (hand, head, leg, foot) and nature symbols (mountain, sea, sky)—all shown in their archetypal generality and disciplined by "rhythm alone," the right-angle diagonals.

43. *Vin d'Athos*, February 1913, pencil and watercolor on drawing paper, 42.5 x 45 cm (FLC 4098). Basic symbols—woman, animal, sky, sea, mountain—again given a rhythmical, diagonal structure. Around this time, Jeanneret was writing about "the pyramid of Athos," and was obsessed with the contrast between this shape and the "horizon."

female forms that wrestled their way to the edges. The freedom with bizarre color contrasts, often graphic and flat, was equally provoking. Fauvism and its primitive energy, not to mention its subject matter of women, boats, and nature, were the impetus for Jeanneret's paintings and watercolors.

There are several works, of 1913, which show the connections he makes between the landscape and the female body. Some are painted from memory, such as *Persistantes souvenances du Bosphore* and *Vin d'Athos* [figs. 42, 43]. The former rotates a right angle on the diagonal and uses the resulting regulating lines to harmonize the angles of the mountains and a woman's upraised leg. Her hands, expressive fingers, and angular head and feet are barely visible. The sky, as often, is a yellow triangle out of which oozes a blood red sunset. Some kind of primary architectural structure, above, contrasts with the green primary forms of her clothes, below. The rest is abstract right-angled triangles. Here is what Le Corbusier will later claim as *"the choice"* of his life, in favor of the square and right angle.

Also evident is his love for abstract symbols, a subject he takes up again in the chapter "Recollections of Athos," written a year later. Note, in the following quote, the shift from an artistic language based on Jura motifs such as the fir tree and pinecone to a more general language. This 1914 Symbolism, not too far from that of Gauguin and the Symbolists of the 1880s, prefigures his Purist theories of communication of 1921, based on *"fixed words"* of a plastic language and "objects evoking a poetic reaction" (see pages 117 and 188).

> The obsession for symbols that lies deep inside me is like a yearning for a language limited to only a few words. My [architectural] vocation may be the reason for this: the organization of stone and timber, of volumes, of solids and voids, has given me, perhaps, a too general understanding of the vertical and horizontal, and of the sense of length, depth and height as well. And I think that such elements, and these very words, which possess infinite meaning, do not need to be clarified, since such a word, in its complete and powerful unity, expresses them all. To go even further, I imagine that color in bands of yellow, reds, blues, violets and greens, with sharp boundaries but otherwise like a rainbow of lines going from the vertical to the horizontal without bisecting the slope. Let rhythm alone arrange this pure graphic expression! I will let my training waste away, with its scruple for details instilled in me by my teacher [L'Eplattenier]. Beholding the Parthenon, its mass, columns, and architraves will satisfy me as does the sea in itself—and nothing else but this word; the same way the Alps, the very symbol of height, of depth, and of disorder, or the cathedral, will be sights important enough to require all my strength . . . To me the entire Orient seemed to be molded into majestic symbols. I recall the vision of a yellow sky, even though it was often blue . . . This same frame of mind makes me think it crazy to seek a shape for a vase other than the millennial form produced all over the world. I would prefer geometric combinations, the square, the circle, and proportions in simple and distinctive ratio. Wouldn't it take me a lifetime of labor to harness these simple and eternal forces, fraught with the uncertainty of ever attaining the proportions, unity and clarity worthy of even a little country cottage built in accordance with the invaluable laws of an age-old tradition?

In effect, Jeanneret has reached the idea that age-old tradition produces symbols that are primitive universals. Such things as *the* sea, *the* sky, *the* Alps are, in their basic abstract form, already symbols for the human that cannot be reduced further. They need no detail, nor improvement, but can be accepted straight from a long vernacular tradition. Basic sexuality would also be an archetypal symbol not capable of further reduction and, like the others, could be called up in the mind's eye. *Vin d'Athos*, another recollection of his trip two years earlier, shows the inebriation he experienced on this island, but also an event that would never occur: a drunken bacchanal on top of a broken-backed mule, by a nude woman [fig. 43].

Women were not allowed on this island of monks, something that inflames Edouard's imagination, both annoys and fascinates him. The woman and mule each seem to be reaching a religious/sexual ecstasy, with mouth opening to the sky as if in orgasm or a death scream, an image-word that continues to fascinate him throughout his life. Her arms flail, legs and back are wrenched apart. The landscape, again, supports this ecstatic fantasy. In the chapter "Recollections of Athos," written in 1914, he describes his sexual longings:

> Sensations, manifold and extreme, virile and languid . . . Our flesh throbbed with resurging blood. Lying motionless late at night, I feigned sleep, so that I could gaze, with eyes open wide, at the stars and listen, with ears fully cocked . . . savoring silence in its glory. These were the happiest hours I have ever experienced, and overwhelming memories of them have been with me for three years now . . . The night was conducive to any emotional contemplation made languid by the warm, moist air, saturated with sea salt, honey and fruit; it was also conducive, beneath the suspended, protective pergola, to the fulfillment of kisses, to wine-filled and amorous raptures.

He comments, later, on the irony of this Dionysian island without women, where the most sensually active of landscapes is inhabited only by Trappists, or by criminals on the run and "filthy, crippled, dissolute monks" who are limited to sex-in-the-head. They have to "intoxicate themselves with liturgical chants," "Byzantine frescoes," "hallucinatory litanies"—and food and wine.

> The table is set with red tomatoes and superabundant wine; we drank the customary resin wines; and here we go on the back of Bacchus's donkey! Night falls, the sky full of stars, the smooth, tender sea filling the entire window frame.

Le Corbusier: Dress Rehearsal in a Small Town

In his aquarelle, he changes the subject from himself to a woman. Can it be that Jeanneret, in these sexual fantasies, is making love not only to a woman, but also to the cosmos—the sea and stars? Le Corbusier's late paintings often collage a nude with a wine bottle and some cosmic sign; perhaps these potent memories of 1911 were fixed in his mind when all alone under the stars?

In any case, a recurrent theme of his painting, first noticeable about 1912, is women on the beach, usually two women engaged in some kind of sexual play or caressing. *Female Nudes on a Beach*, 1912–13, takes up a theme of Matisse and plays it in a very sensual way, with breasts, buttocks, tummies, hair and pudenda, rising and falling like the background sea and mountains. The figures are red-and-blue landscapes in themselves, pushing the real landscape into second place, squeezed at the top. Two women making love or cavorting, often on the beach, becomes a major theme of his painting, part of which is described in a letter to Ritter, of April 6, 1913.

> The Obsession. "The Obsessing" strikes me as stronger. Memories that loom like judges; attractive figures, decadent and intense seductions, moving me, suggesting paintings to me. The sap of life, and this possibly morbid presence of things loved, impose themselves in the form of women to be painted; nude or clothed it is all the masturbation of a bachelor. I have undressed the [statue] of Ariane sleeping in the gardens of Versailles, and I have painted her as a large opulent strawberry, against a background of intense green. And the horizon of Andrinople made me sketch a white and veiled woman with a horizontal and fixed stare—penetration: and a crouching woman, nude and red with a straight head and her body on the same axis: a woman in a scarlet costume with her chin up; heaven and earth are made equivalent in citron yellow.

> I would color the valley of Maritza brown; brown the tiara of the dome and the minarets. The sky always citron. Citron yellow, that's Asia . . . The naked man is for he who can overcome and satisfy his body. It is a complex of rigid and rectangular planes. The naked man is for me architecture. When I don't do architecture, I see everything as woman.

44. *Two Lesbians*, pen and ink with watercolor wash, 33.5 x 26.5 cm (FLC 5163; page 63 in Cahier 10). The body as spherical landscape, sex as wrestling, will emerge later.

Jeanneret's propensity to see every real object as an abstract symbol is heightened by the fact that these works are re-creations of his memories of the East, not painted from living models. He is, of course, here writing to his new master Ritter, who also paints and with whom he would go into the Swiss mountains to paint landscapes. By 1917, as further correspondence and drawings show, he was visiting brothels to study real women making love. The idea of using prostitutes as ready-made models who will take any pose without much self-consciousness, and the brothel as *the* setting for real, urban life, is a traditional one in French Modernism. From Baudelaire to Toulousse-Lautrec, from Degas to Félicien Rops, poets and painters have understood low-life as real modern life and sought to present basic truths. A pen and ink drawing of 1917, *Two Lesbians* [fig. 44], portrays a sophisticated form of double voyeurism. The prostrate woman regards the artist with detached curiosity as if she were studying his drawing. In work of the 1930s, the bodies of the two women will become wrestlers, and then the buttocks and shoulders will become hills and, it has to be said, almost those spherical pots which enflamed Jeanneret's earlier passion.

Jeanneret loved big-bottomed women perhaps because he saw in them some sign of the ancient earth goddesses, those women who dominated prehistoric culture by embodying rebirth and fecundity; or perhaps, like Boucher, he fancied big bottoms?

In any case, they constitute a symbol, a recurring motif one can find running from his *Nude on the Beach*, 1914–15, right into the floor plans of Ronchamp, 1950. This alerts us, again, to the fact that one has to understand all of Le Corbusier's work and life to fully understand any of it. His painting, architecture, urbanism, and sexuality informed each other and, like a poet, he took advantage of the connections between areas. This leads to strange juxtapositions, especially in his sketchbooks. We can be following a nationalistic argument about the French versus the Germans, the "krauts" quoted above, when suddenly he switches gears and brings in the importance of women to modernity:

> Wait 10 years; modernity everywhere: the Vieux Colombier, Perret's theatre, etc. Women take to it. Women feel flattered in that framework. 10 years and modernity has taken over and is victorious. I believe in it, there are so many premises. And then one senses it intuitively.

The text is overlaid by—what else—sketches of big-bottomed women, even fashionable Parisian women who are wearing chic costumes that the artist can see through. It's a strange argument for modernity that can be clinched by a sophisticated tart with a riding crop and high black boots. Several other drawings in sketchbook A2 reveal the unlikely symbolic associations at work. Two drawings show the "nude man" seen from below—acrobat, superman, architecture? Another one is a still life with a hat, flowers, pipe, and a book titled *La Decadence de L'Art Sacré.* "Decadence" was a key word for Jeanneret and he used it to condemn Modern architecture in 1908, Gothic architecture in 1911, and Cubist painting in 1918. But it also had a great attraction for him, as can be seen from his writings on Athos and his constant visits to brothels. One strongly colored drawing from 1916 shows three drunken prostitutes, mutually entwined in an abandoned embrace. Fauvist or Expressionist colors, reds, blues, and yellows, accentuate the voluptuous mood of the place. A black wine bottle is placed below a black-dressed man in a black hat—a client? And the women, having partly finished the bottle, sprawl about exposing their flesh, one opening her legs to the artists' view [fig. 45].

Sexuality is depicted as an impersonal, if exciting, fact of life. As we will see, when Le Corbusier again becomes interested in

45. *Brothel Café,* 1915–16 (FLC, from Sketchbook A2, page 190). Rodin and Matisse are behind the women treated as sexual landscape; Fauvism and Expressionism behind the colors.

women, in the late 1920s, and marries, he takes both a mechanical and spiritual view of sex. He is apt to treat it as an everyday, obvious occurrence, as worthy of comment as a sunny day, and as something having grand, indeed cosmic, implications. These ideas and symbols were formed on his journey of self-discovery through the Balkans, Greece, and Italy. After these discoveries he returns to La Chaux-de-Fonds to try to translate them into architecture.

White Villas in a Green Provincial Land

When Jeanneret was in Athens in 1911 he received a letter from L'Eplattenier calling him back to his hometown. The idea, as we have seen, was to form a "New Section" of the art school which would cover all aspects of design—from the smallest utensil to architecture—and would stand between art and industry. Jeanneret was put in charge of the architectural training while his friends Georges Aubert and Leon Perrin taught the study of form based on nature (animal, vegetable, and mineral objects). Together they formed a team that constructed and decorated such things as small chapels, music rooms, private villas, and even tombs in the cemetery. The intention was to create a harmonious environment in a unified style, an idea not far from that of the Art Nouveau *Gesamtkunstwerk*, but now, because of Jeanneret's *Voyage* and his reading of Cingria-Vaneyre, to be carried out in a white, Mediterranean mode.

Inevitably, Jeanneret and L'Eplattenier fought over questions of style, and the older argument of art versus industrial design, decorative formalism versus a foundation for design in science and mathematics. "It is the ruin of all my teaching, it is you who have killed my work of the last ten years," L'Eplattenier accused Jeanneret. But the bitterness, jealousy, and recrimination were more general than this, and they became a part of Jeanneret's life in La Chaux for the next five years. Once again, in Nietzschean terms, he predicts conflicts and broken friendships *before* they occur, and *as a consequence of* his will to impose his vision of the new truth. In a letter of November 1, 1911, to Ritter, just on his return home, he foresees the battle to come and its reasons.

> Italy is a graveyard, where the dogma of my [former] religion now lies rotting. All the bric-a-brac that was my delight now fills me with horror. I gabble up elementary geometry; I am possessed of the color white, the cube, the sphere, the cylinder, and the pyramid. Prisms rise and balance each other, setting up rhythms . . . in the midday sun the cubes open out into a surface, at nightfall a rainbow seems to rise from the forms. In the morning, they are real, casting light and shadow and sharply outlined as a drawing . . . Straight roads, no ornament. A single color and material for the whole town . . . roads on rooftops midst the trees and flowers . . . and wide-open spaces where one can breathe. We should no longer be *artists*, but rather penetrate the age, fuse with it until we are indistinguishable. Then we should leave behind us Colosseums and Baths, an Acropolis and mosques, and our Jura mountains would provide as beautiful a setting for these as the sea. We too are distinguished, great and worthy of past ages. We shall do better still, *that* is my belief . . . But we need dogma, renewal, a harsh, bracing climate, and to take this whip to those who dissent. I shall return, cut my friends, call insults down upon me . . . and create a void all around me.

This letter, parallel to the one of 1908, once again gets out the lash to whip friends into shape, where possible, or burn them, where not. It is noteworthy for being the first entirely developed notion of the white, cubic architecture and a clear rejection of ornament and curved roads (though he will quickly return to both). It has the first suggestion of streets in the air and roads on rooftops that he had gleaned through reading, and it shows why he did leave La Chaux in the end, because it was not about to allow grand projects, the Colosseum or Acropolis he longed to construct. *Le Voyage d'Orient* is full of references to the "shame and anguish" the stones of the East make him feel "in a sad provincial town." He comes back home to construct the Jura Parthenon, but the commission he gets is a small house for his parents.

"La Petite Maison" as it was first known, or "La Maison Blanche" as he called it after it had expanded in size and cost, virtually bankrupted his parents. His father had predicted this when the project was first mooted in 1907, and notes in his journal, when it is under construction, in August 1912, that it is beginning to do so. In a letter to Ritter of May 9, 1913, Jeanneret laments "the utter blunder of building this house . . . a stupid mistake"; how he "hates [the town] . . . The people also," but does not wish to "abandon one's father and mother in this situation, to let them wither away from anxiety and isolation" while he goes off to "build cities, mansions and palaces." By 1919, after war and a downturn in watchmaking, the family has to sell the house, and they do so at a terrific loss. Jeanneret had almost literally burned what he loved and loved what he burned. When sold, in 1919, the new owners were, characteristically, given an eleven-page lesson in how to occupy the house, a Manual of the Dwelling lest they not "respect... simplicity and severity" in all things.

La Maison Blanche is essentially, like the Parthenon, a white cube, although both have color accents. Both celebrate the circuitous approach that so fascinated Edouard on the Acropolis and thus both lead to the idea of "the architectural promenade," the notion that architectural volumes should be seen in movement, as a drama of discovery with a distinct cosmic climax. In the white house for his parents, this culmination becomes a pure form and a garden porch overlooking the mountains, a place to view the heavens. Both Parthenon and Maison Blanche sit in an enclosure; both are approached from the best vantage point, at an angle and from below; both are also symmetrical structures approached off-axis; both have ceremonial propylaea; both have friezes; and both have a pitched roof. So the Villa Jeanneret-Perret really is a Jura Parthenon [figs. 46 a, b, c].

But the building is also something very different. Influenced by Behrens's German villas, and Balkan houses he admired, it manages to pull into a unity a very diverse set of ideas. The central square space, around which family life pivots, is held together by four point supports, an early version of the reinforced-concrete

46 a, b, c. Villa Jeanneret Père, La Chaux-de-Fonds, 1912. Like most of Jeanneret's villas, this one was designed on the outskirts of town, on the steep slope of a mountain, surrounded by a dense verdure of pine trees—here in sharp contrast to a white Classical structure. Apsidal curves of the dining room, below a bedroom, give the symmetrical garden front the feeling of a church. The later idea of the "ribbon window" is foreshadowed in the strong horizontal frieze made from squat "Doric" piers. A loggia, cut into the center of a flat white plane, is another recurring motif of the later Le Corbusier.

47. *Design for a Meuble-Secretaire*, desk for his parents' house, 1915 (BV). A Revivalist style disciplined by geometry. Geometrical design was the main subject Jeanneret taught in the New Section. The heavy front leg carries a tilt-out section, a curious functional expression crossed with the Biedermeier aesthetic. The *secretaire* is now in the house that Le Corbusier designed for his mother on Lake Geneva.

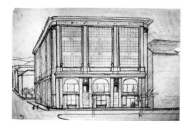

48. Project for the Paul Ditisheim Building, La Chaux-de-Fonds, 1913 (BV). Three-bay industrial Classicism on the American commercial model. Paired pilasters, below, enclose two floors of selling space, while the neutral wall, above, holds the watch factory. Bi-axial symmetry remained a constant theme of Le Corbusier, although he usually modified it with secondary asymmetries.

cage that Jeanneret had learned from Perret. The way space and architectural forms continue to slide around corners and over obstacles recalls the ideas of Frank Lloyd Wright, whose work Jeanneret was beginning to study. And then there is ornament, although very restrained, on the edges, columns, and transition points, that recalls Edouard's longstanding commitment to inventing a Jura language. Many architects in this century have built their first house for their parents, and if one is going to send them to the poorhouse doing so, then at least Jeanneret makes a fine job of it.

Yet the synthesis was not altogether secure, and many inner doubts remained. This can be seen in the lighting fixtures, draperies, French doors, wallpaper, and rugs for the house. If we consider the building as a total work of art, as Edouard would have done, then it has problems of integration. The most convincing parts of the design are the inventive but revivalist furniture which Jeanneret was designing at the time and in the specifications for "Louis XIII" and "Directoire" furniture in his buildings [fig. 47].

When Le Corbusier was later to proclaim, dogmatically, "The 'Styles' are a lie," he was speaking with authority. By 1915, he had already mastered several of them, including the Greek, Italian Renaissance, Louis XIV, XV, and XVI, Biedermeier, and Beaux-Arts Classicism—not to mention all the medieval styles he was then rejecting. Jeanneret's favorites at the time were what Frank Lloyd Wright called "stripped or deflowered classicism," a purgative form of design on its way to minimalism. One of the more ornamented was his design for a watch factory, a cross between a Renaissance palazzo and an industrial building in reinforced concrete, with factory windows [48].

Le Corbusier, as the archetypal Modernist in the tradition of the unappreciated genius, often gives the impression that he was disregarded by society and the power structure, whereas the truth is more interesting than that, as his next commission shows. It was for a self-made industrialist, Georges Favre-Jacot, the sixty-nine-year-old semiretired founder of the Zenith Watch Company, and located in Le Locle, a town next to La Chaux-de-Fonds. It is a grand Italian villa, but very much in the white Jura Classicism that Cingria-Vaneyre had proposed as an appropriate response for the area, and it looks over the valley from where the entrepreneur could see his factory and his six hundred workers churning out 100,000 watches per year.

49. Villa Favre-Jacot. The plan sequence is that of a chateau, accenting the drama of built space that mediates between the city and country. The entrance circle, for the car, is offset from the semicircular steps and the axis through to the garden: most symmetrical forms are disposed asymmetrically, an effective combination Jeanneret noted in Pompeii.

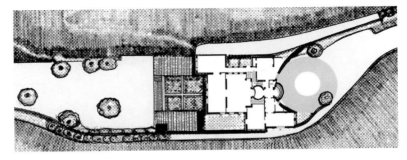

50 a, b. Villa Favre-Jacot (BV). The oval in plan and blind arcade, based on the steering radius of a car, embraces those arriving. This front then leads to two main views: left, over the valley, and straight ahead to the garden. The second drawing (b), which closely resembles the built structure, shows the layering, from right to left, of overlapping symmetrical volumes. "Asymmetrical symmetry," a lesson Jeanneret also learned from the Acropolis, was common to the freestyle Classicism of 1900. This, and early Corbusier, influenced the Post-Modern Classicism of the 1980s.

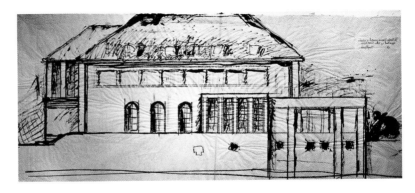

The villa sits on a very long, precipitous terrace, affording spectacular views of itself, the town, and nature. What more could an architect of twenty-four want as a commission? Young Jeanneret lived up to the challenge, mixing thin Schinkelesque bands with flat Italianate arches, offset symmetrical volumes, and a sequence of space worthy of a chateau [figs. 49, 50, 51]. M. Favre-Jacot drives in to the oval forecourt, precisely engineered like a good watch to the steering radius of his car. He marches up the small semicircular stoop that sends out curves to welcome him. He notes the pinecone moldings splayed at the top of the pilasters above his monogram in the iron railing, GFJ; he opens the grand and very strong metal front door to a double entry space, a rectangle followed by a double-height, voided cylinder. This tour de force, whose only fault is that it is closed to the sky, then leads to a

51 a, b. Villa Favre-Jacot. Views from entry side, and hillside and garden. The capital details were executed by Jeanneret's collaborator in the New Section, Leon Perrin.

hall and, the final culmination of the architectural promenade, the salon with its view over the gardens. Louis XIV and his court would have recognized and responded to this sequence; it underlies every great chateau and most Italian villas. The idea is to keep the explosion of nature until the last moment. To hide, to suggest, and lead up to it: architecture as the masterly, correct, and magnificent play of spaces experienced in movement. This Jeanneret fully understands, as well as how to use ornament symbolically, and sparingly, around the key points: the entryway and "la Chambre de Monsieur," M. Favre-Jacot's study and library [fig. 51 b]. Pinecone and tree, pigeon and leaf, are all stylized, by the sculptor Leon Perrin, in flat planes according to the logic that Jeanneret was teaching at the New Section of the art school.

The Diagram of Modern Architecture

From 1914, and throughout the first World War, Jeanneret produced several unbuilt schemes in reinforced concrete which were later to be admitted into the selected *Oeuvre complète* of Le Corbusier because they illustrated several points of a new architecture. The most important was what he called the "Dom-ino system," and it has been seen as the single most significant idea of Modern architecture. Stemming from Auguste Perret's notion of point supports, it is a reinforced concrete frame which allows the plan and elevation of the building to be independent of the structure. This naturally led to new aesthetic principles such as the free plan, the free facade, and movable partitions. Beyond this the Dom-ino system contained properties suggested in its name. Like *domus* (Latin for house) it was intended as housing for postwar reconstruction; like domino blocks it was intended to be mass-produced and assembled in numerous combinations. These were its two great social justifications: mass housing for the poor and quick housing for those whose buildings had been destroyed in the war.

As a visual concept the Dom-ino system exerted a strong impact when it was finally published in the 1920s because it presented these properties with a beautiful, logical clarity, as if it were some idealized, Platonic essence of the new architecture. In fact the ultrasmooth surfaces, architecturally superb, turned out to be costly and inefficient from an engineering viewpoint, which is why it never achieved what Jeanneret wanted: an industrial patent, which would make him a lot of money, so that he could devote his time to painting like a Matisse or a Picasso (this is intimated in later remarks of the early 1920s, when he was experimenting with further prefabricated systems) [fig. 52].

As an ideal diagram, however, it was to exert a hypnotic power over the next five generations of architects, the way Vignola and Palladio did with their formulae—or, even more, the way the Doric order did for Greek temples. The Dom-ino system is to Modern architects what post-and-beam construction is to the Greeks, the arch is to the Romans, and the pointed arch to the Goths—a simplified idea of construction which determines the basic organizational truth behind the system. Insofar as revolutions in architecture are material constraints translated into ideal forms, insofar, therefore, in Mies van der Rohe's famous words, as "you

52. Dom-ino skeleton, 1914–15, redrawn. Called the extensible system because like a domino block it could be added to at the ends or at right angles, thus generating U-shaped urban blocks. Only four elements form a universal system mass-produced on site: footings, square pier, flat slab of hollow tiles, and stairs. Such archetypal drawings created the Doric Order of Modernism, and their logic led to the new International Style: long cantilevered floors, ribbon windows, and flat roofs in a smooth, homogeneous, white aesthetic. This led in the 1990s to the dream of a supermaterial, ultraplastic, the Ultimate Cardboard Model, the dream of many architects that one universal system would do for everything. The cantilever from the six columns makes structural sense because it balances with the internal stresses, and it leads directly to shallow, layered transparency, what Colin Rowe and others see as quintessentially Modern space. The problems with all the smoothness, the flush columns and flat slab, are the increased cost and weight.

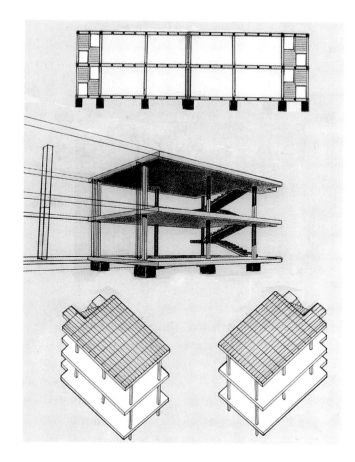

cannot have a new architecture every Monday morning," then the Dom-ino system has to be understood as the last great structural principle of Modernism. It dominated practice until Post-Modern nonlinear structures came on the scene, in the 1990s, and they still have a long way to go before they challenge the repetitive box. Jeanneret did not entirely invent the system. He modified ideas from Perret, his engineering friend Max Du Bois (whom he forgot to credit), reinforced-concrete systems already on the market (such as that of Hennebique), and the visual system of Chicago skyscrapers.

As Colin Rowe has argued, the Chicago frame plus Dom-ino equals Modernism. It is the two-way neutrality of the former, the cagelike expression of the inside structure on the outside skin, which becomes *the* dominant idea for Le Corbusier's major competitor in Modernism—Mies. The two together made the right angle and the dumb box into the most terrifying cliché ever

53. Weston Rise Housing, London, circa 1965. Rent-slab Modernism, a dressed Dom-ino Block, the condition of our time.

perpetrated on an unsuspecting world. Theirs may have been beautifully proportioned and full of transparent ambiguities, but if you want to know why most world architecture today is rent-slabs-on-stilts you do not have to look further than the Dom-ino model, the most influential of the last century [fig. 53].

On a positive note, the system led Jeanneret to develop ideas for mass housing which, while not perfect, at least addressed an important subject consistently, and in depth, a subject to which we shall return. Many writers, above all Stanislaus von Moos, have stressed the synthetic quality of Jeanneret's creativity, the way it fuses disparate material, and in the 1910s he started to consolidate several ideas from different sources, which he would bring together ten years later. For instance, stemming from his work with Perret, the Dom-ino system, and his book on the construction of cities, in 1915 he imagined a city raised on pylons that would establish an artificial level above the ground level, thus separating pedestrians from vehicular traffic. A few years earlier, for a farm-house conversion, he imagined a roof garden placed above massive walls and reached by an exterior stairway [figs. 54, 55]. In these two projects Jeanneret started the logical inversion of customary usage for which he was later to become famous. Reinforced concrete allows one to have gardens on the roof and, where one is used to finding gardens, on the ground, there is green space and vehicular traffic. All of this is synthesized together in the City for Three Million, in 1922 [fig. 87].

54. "Maison du Diable," Le Locle project for Georges Favre-Jacot, 1912 (BV). Decapitating the pitched roof and plastering white the massive stone walls transforms this old "haunted farmhouse" into a base for trees; the roof garden, exterior stairway, and side-wall typology emerge, later synthesized in the Maison Citrohan of 1920.

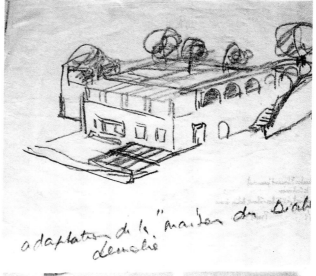

55. Page from *Vers une Architecture*, redrawn to accentuate bridges and U shapes. "Towns built on piles. The ground level is raised from 12 to 16 feet . . . the streets and pavements as it were bridges. Beneath this floor and directly accessible are placed all the main services." This city in the air was made from superblocks that imply a U shape, a form of *redents* that became the basis for subsequent city plans.

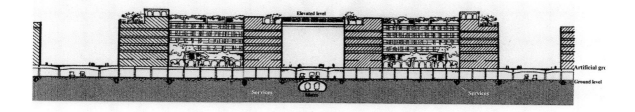

Freestyle Classicism (and a Few Indiscretions)

From 1915 to 1916 Jeanneret hoped to get a patent on the Dom-ino system and settle in Paris, but neither wish came true the way he wanted. Instead he took many small jobs of interior decoration, translating his expertise with architecture, gardening, furniture

98

56, 57. Drawings of interiors, n.d.
(BV). Like the organization of his parents' house, these interiors develop
the theme of a central aedicule
marked off by a strong symmetrical
structure. The size of the space is
greatly exaggerated, as in many per-
spectives, and a freestyle Classical
discipline is played in counterpoint to
the incidents of furniture and painting.

design, and stripped Classicism into a total service [fig. 56, 57].
This did allow him many trips to Paris to buy furnishing for his
clients, the haute bourgeoisie of La Chaux-de-Fonds. As he said in
letters to Ritter, this provincial clientele drove him to distraction,
with its pettiness and lack of commissions worthy of his talent.
They were not building a Colosseum or an Acropolis. Thus when a
developer, Edmond Meyer, planned a cinema and variety theater
for the town, Jeanneret leapt at the opportunity.

His old partner in architecture, René Chapallaz, who had overseen his early villas, actually had the commission already, and
designed plans and elevations. But that did not stop Jeanneret
from entering the fray. On June 20, 1916, he took the plans that
Chapallaz had submitted the day before, redrew them ever so
slightly, keeping essential elements such as a reinforced-concrete
balcony of seven meters. As Allen Brooks has argued, the dimensions and complexity of a very tight and well worked out design
could not all have been developed from scratch in one day.
Jeanneret virtually stole the design from Chapallaz, with the developer's connivance. When Le Corbusier died, in 1965, and newspapers published the designs as his, Chapallaz filed a lawyer's
certified statement. "There seems little doubt," as Brooks summarizes the evidence, "that, except for one or perhaps both facades,
the plans, sections, and the structural system represent Chapallaz's
'intellectual property.'"

Jeanneret's unprofessional behavior is regrettable, but not that
uncommon today, even among the best architects. They appropriate jobs from each other, if the developer or client urges them to
do this, knowing there are no clear ethical guidelines in a capitalist
marketplace. After all, the customer is right, the owner is the final

58. Cinema La Scala, rear facade, La Chaux-de-Fonds, 1916. This striking building contained a 40-foot gallery in reinforced concrete unsupported by columns. This photograph was retouched to restore the center section to its original condition.

arbiter, it is his or her money and choice—why not take away jobs from others, especially if they are not very good designers? This, or something like it, probably went through Jeanneret's mind, as he leveraged the job by August 1916. The local press, the very newspaper in which Jeanneret had published excerpts from *Le Voyage d'Orient*, announced a competition for students from the Ecole d'art to design facades for the cinema. The developer initiated this on July 15 at a stroke, creating a publicity stunt, getting some free design, and letting it be known that Chapallaz was not entirely in control. Architects are easy victims for such exploitation, as Le Corbusier was to find out to his everlasting chagrin—first over the League of Nations, 1927, and then over the design for the United Nations, 1947—when *others* appropriated *his* designs. The first theft was such a crime that, arguably, it led to the formation of the Vatican of the Modern Movement, that is, CIAM, the International Congress of Modern Architecture, with Le Corbusier as its pope (but more of that later).

At least the rear facade of La Scala Cinema and Variety Theater was his [fig. 58]. Here we find a very simplified freestyle Classicism mixing Greek pediments with windows and paneling taken from other Classical styles. To make the facade biaxially symmetrical, Edouard had to create a false front on the right-hand side—a false door and window that open onto nothing. As the drawing makes clear there is also a Mannerist handling of pilasters and moldings, being ghosted in one case and ultrathin in the other. Schinkel's presence can be felt in this minimalist, linear ornament, and also Behrens's, in the case of the proportional

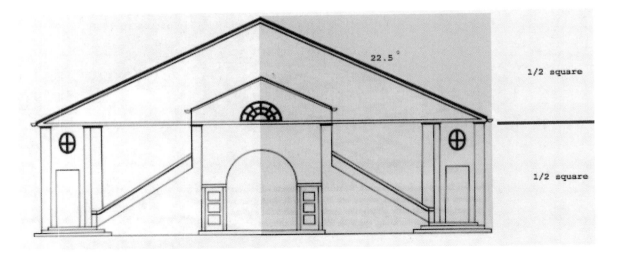

59. Cinema La Scala, redrawn. The harmonious proportions, of 1:1 and 1:2, are reinforced by the very thin moldings. A masterpiece of quiet elegance lampooned by the local socialist newspaper as "a decorated WC."

rectangles that discipline the diagonals. The stair diagonal is slightly steeper than that of the pediments, but they *appear* consonant. Furthermore, simple ratios are used where expedient, for instance the large pediment or pitched roof, at a 22.5-degree slope, constitutes half a square, and the whole facade is a double square, so the ratios 1:2 and 1:1 repeat, like a serene harmony [fig. 59].

This sort of simplicity was praised by the local papers for being in good taste, but the quotes Le Corbusier liked to give, from *La Sentinelle*, the socialist newspaper that hounded him in 1914, show him again persecuted by the Philistines. "It's one of the masterpieces of Cubist architecture," they mocked, probably turning his words against him, "It's a warehouse for potatoes, an ice house, a cellar for cheese"—not for the last time were such remarks fired at him. There is an important pattern here: he would save such epithets to be quoted later, in battle. Sometimes they would be turned against their authors, and shown to be petty and stupid; other times they would be used to show that the prophet of the new, like Jesus, could be crucified for bringing the message. It is not an exaggeration that Le Corbusier sometimes presented these attacks as if to say, "Well, to accomplish anything good you will be attacked, and perhaps justifiably. Struggle and value come as one."

His final building in La Chaux-de-Fonds, the Villa Schwob, summarizes Jeanneret's development just before he left for Paris to take on his new persona, Le Corbusier. The villa was built for Anatole Schwob, an executive of Schwob Frères and Company and the Tavannes Watch Company, between July 1916 and early 1918,

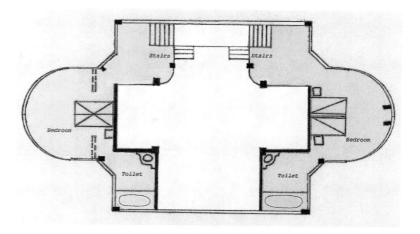

60. Villa Schwob, earliest extant plan, bedroom floor, July 1916, redrawn (FLC 31827). The basic idea consists of a cruciform of space edged by four columns (not independent, as in the Dom-ino Block), the exterior volume a perfect square, and the apsidal bedroom wings with a diameter half the square. As Allen Brooks shows, the plan resembles the Maison Bouteille of 1909 (fig. 27).

while Jeanneret moved to Paris in January 1917. As these dates show, Jeanneret did not oversee the construction or keep control of the building once the costs of the project were discovered to have escalated.

The initial design was a square in plan with two apsidal wings on the cross axis that were half the square in diameter. Thus, like La Scala, simple harmonic proportions dominate, and like his parents' house, which was the initial model that Schwob wanted, the plan recalls that of a church—indeed a centrally planned one [fig. 60]. Proportional triangles were used to determine the secondary elements such as doors and windows, and it is these "nobler proportions," a result of "regulating lines," that led Le Corbusier to illustrate it later as "one of his first constructions." It was the only early work that fit the later canon. Known locally as the "Villa Turque," possibly because of Jeanneret's *Voyage* and its exotic appearance, its massing relates to the mosques of Constantinople, their cubes and half cubes. Here bold, semicircular curves are played against simple cubes, an opposition that was to become standard in Le Corbusier's later work, especially to accentuate functional volumes.

Like so many of his projects of the time, the building is a concrete frame villa, one of the first in Europe. Like his parents' house, it has a central supporting bay of four columns that acts as a kind of aedicule, or little house within a house. Four interior columns of 20 centimeters allow space to flow freely from one room to the next around the central living room. This room, lit from one side by a gigantic vertical window, carries through two

61. Villa Schwob, glass wall, facing south, going up two stories to express the inside on the outside—all hallmarks of later Le Corbusier.

stories and acts as the focus for the house. The dining room is to the right, the games room to the left, the stairway behind, and the garden in front. The living room thus has the kind of open planning that Frank Lloyd Wright initiated ten years earlier, except it is classically symmetrical and framed by moldings that, visually, stop the space from flowing on. This, the most important room, is at the center of a cruciform of space that runs in three dimensions, but, because of the glass wall, always orients one south, to nature [fig. 61]. That combination becomes Le Corbusier's trademark.

It is the way these different, indeed eclectic, interests are synthesized that makes the building an example of freestyle rather than canonic Classicism. The axes and cross axes are symmetrical and, like the functional separation in the Beaux-Arts tradition, the flowing space and flaring concrete moldings of the cornice are new. While the entrance front has a Classical symmetry, the ultrathin columns and massing of horizontals versus verticals are given a Mannerist treatment. For instance, oval windows framed in brick and rectangular doors accentuate the vertical dimension, but this is nullified by the other openings and moldings, which are horizontal. This has caused some scholarly dispute. Colin Rowe has interpreted the blank front panel as an extreme Mannerist gesture, and one that opens Modernism to influence by this period of the 1500s. Many drawings, produced when Jeanneret was attempting to hide the new third story behind the flaring cornices, show this panel as blank [figs. 62, 63]. But other drawings show a set of horizontal and vertical lines, a kind of minimalist ornament, or decorative mosaic, as a surviving draftsman told Allen Brooks. Even if this panel were to take a painting or ornamental pattern, which seems likely, its size, square proportions, and prominence are bizarre in La Chaux.

The "Villa Turque" might have looked like one of the Turkish houses Jeanneret sketched, with their flat roofs overflowing with greenery that spills over a cornice. Originally, as drawings show, it was conceived very much as a villa *and* garden, with planting given equal weight to the house, and with two corner pavilions and a noble square terrace, a projection of the glazed southern wall onto the ground plane.

This was the biggest commission, in size and stature, that Jeanneret had received up to the age of twenty-nine, and had it all worked out and led to further big jobs perhaps he would have

62. Villa Schwob, entrance, with its basically blank facade on the street side. Like a Pompeian villa, this one closes off blind walls to form a street and opens to the garden and the view—public versus private, closed versus open.

63. Villa Schwob, perspective of street and new third story, with its trellis and private penthouse integrated into the volumes but somewhat hidden by the exaggerated flare of the cornice. Not only was this heavy concrete Classicism to hold window boxes, but it kept one from falling off the roof garden. The reinforced-concrete frame also allowed the building to be constructed during the winter, when construction usually stops in La Chaux-de-Fonds.

stayed in the small town. But several unfortunate events led to trouble. First, the agreed budget, 110,000 to 115,000 francs, almost tripled when Schwob asked for more room—about 47 percent more. When the client found that the costs had risen more than the volume had expanded, and found this out from an architect who had moved to Paris, he decided to cut back designs and eliminate the garden pavilions and much else besides. He also refused to pay Jeanneret, for which, on July 5, 1918, he was sued by the architect. A countersuit, and substantial lawyers' fees later, resulted in an out-of-court settlement, but Jeanneret admitted he was wrong: "My fault was of not notifying you in writing of the exact amounts exceeding the original idea of a modest home. I accept this as wrong." Cost overruns and lack of supervision became chronic problems. Le Corbusier, who set himself the job of becoming the greatest architect of the century, and a writer, painter, sculptor, lecturer, and man of the world in the bargain, did not always have the time or desire to see a building to completion. He would work terrifically hard on the idea of the building, but sometimes rush on to another project, leaving the follow-through to Pierre Jeanneret, his partner and cousin, or to no one.

In spite of his relative success—seven completed buildings by the age of thirty—Jeanneret felt more and more that La Chaux-de-Fonds was an impossible city for any architect who wished to innovate and create a new architecture comparable to the Greeks in vision. Hence, when challenged by the best of the past, his feelings of personal inadequacy, even "shame," in his home town:

> It seems to me clear that they don't want me any more, because in the end my utter scrupulousness disgusts the people [of La Chaux-de-Fonds]. One has to be conceited, sanctimonious, sure of oneself, swaggering, and never doubting—or at least not let it show. One has to be like a show salesman. *Merde, alors!*

The Swiss watchmaking town had given Jeanneret several important ideas and commissions, but there was no real opportunity in it for a man bred on Nietzsche and secretly considering himself on a par with Phidias and Michelangelo. In 1917 he was invited by the city of Frankfurt to take part in some municipal building. Just as he received his passport, he decided instead to go to Paris for an indefinite stay.

64, 65. Villa Schwob, details on the garden side. Sometimes Neo-Classical in their simplified geometry: blank, flat rectangles, punctured by oval voids, are set off against half cylinders. A pure sphere, as in Goethe's *Altar of Good Fortune,* is poised here on a solid flat block.* Leon Perrin's small relief can be seen next to a band of clerestory windows; the basement lighting behind gently curving grill-work. Many of these secondary elements are related, in elevation, through a series of "regulating lines," a method of proportional triangles that Jeanneret used in subsequent buildings to achieve simple relationships between parts. In this one can see his preoccupation with the idea of mathematical harmony, the Platonic idea that certain fundamental ratios underlie cosmic order and are a cause, if not a sufficient one, of beauty.

* See Hugh Honour, *Neo-classicism* (Harmondsworth: Penguin, 1968), 129–30, for Goethe's *Altar of Good Fortune,* which like much Neo-classicism seems to have been an inspiration for "modern" architecture.

With ten years of practice under his belt, the protean Le Corbusier was born. Just as he had changed style in 1910, and burned his past, he was to do so in 1918. Friendship with his first master, L'Eplattenier, was finished by 1912; close friendship with Perret ended after the 1920s; Ritter was not seen much after then although he lived until 1955. Amédée Ozenfant became the new mentor, and teacher, a relationship that would last until 1925. Although he kept lifelong companions, and greatly valued them, Le Corbusier also changed friends and styles roughly every ten years, not unique for the "average genius." Having to reinvent oneself is a way of keeping ahead in a capitalist world, and yet rare for an architect. Think of Richard Meier, a late follower of the 1920 version of Le Corbusier; in practice since the 1960s, he is lauded for never having deviated from the Corbu style. By contrast, like Picasso, LC always raced ahead of himself; like Marcel Duchamp, he did not like to repeat an idea for more than five years. Continual overcoming, continual revolution, continual self-reinvention—thus the embodiment of Zarathustra's message for the superman.

66. Four cadets of the New Architecture at Castle La Sarraz, the avant-garde of CIAM: Guevrekian, Le Corbusier, the general secretary Sigfried Giedion, and Pierre Jeanneret. Pompier architecture, the Baroque of Firemen and Statesmen, was always lampooned in such costumes.

PART II

The Hero of the Heroic Period 1917—28

The Darwinian Moment

Imagine what life was like for Jeanneret as he settled in Paris in January 1917. He could have some confidence in the move because he had lived here for months, in 1908, when he was a Bohemian student on the Left Bank, and he had visited the city constantly during the 1910s to buy furniture for clients. His self-assurance would also be bolstered by accomplishments, the buildings completed, and knowing what he wanted to do by way of mass production and the war effort. But, still, he was a provincial arriving in cosmopolitan Paris, a man driven from home by a lawsuit, and someone who had severely dented his parents' finances. His letters tell of his insecurity, a man with a large vision and ego, but out of work.

For the next five years on the work front things got even worse: in spite of vast projects, he built just one water tower and one worker's home and saw four of his enterprises go up in smoke, partly due to the recession of 1921. But, in spite of setbacks that would have broken a lesser spirit, he learned several things that were to complete his self-education: how to become an entrepreneur, how to turn thought into effective polemic, how to produce Purist paintings, and, of course, how to become the leader of Modern Architecture (capitalized, when it signifies a cultural and spiritual movement). Under the name Le Corbusier, adopted in 1920, he was to give the Modern Movement its basic direction and moral force. He, even more than Walter Gropius, Mies van der Rohe, and Frank Lloyd Wright, was to become its polemicist, pope, and maverick leader, until it was undermined, in the 1930s, from within and without.

Jeanneret settled on the Left Bank of Paris in the Saint Germain des Prés area at 20 rue Jacob. He occupied a kitchen and maid's room on the seventh floor of a Louis XIV mansard apartment for the next seventeen years until he constructed his own apartment in 1934. A friend, who he had consulted on Dom-ino and many other projects, Max Du Bois, set him up in business. This Swiss engineer and administrator became his savior. Du Bois not only provided him with an office, a secretary, and a few commissions to go with them, but he made him director of several companies involved with industrialized systems. Thus Jeanneret could call himself a chief executive of SEIE (*Société d'entreprises industrielles et d'études*) and use the acronym SABA (*Société*

67. Maison Monol, 1919. To be pre-fabricated from one of the systems, called *L'Everite-éternit*, that Jeanneret was trying to market. A mixture of asbestos fibers and molded cement sheets, it was used here for one-story workers' housing with shallow barrel-vaulted roofs. This robust, "female," "peasant" prefabrication was to recur in the 1930s in the Weekend House and his own apartment, and in the 1950s in Maisons Jaoul and the Sarabhai House. In this sense it represents the continuation of the "folk" and self-build tradition Jeanneret came to admire in 1911. Although Jeanneret became manager of the Société des Application l'Everite in 1918, it went bust in the crash of 1921.

d'application du béton armé) on his letterhead to give authority to his *"bureau d'architecte."* Under another acronym, SAI, and SABA, he could manage a brick factory, the Briquetterie d'Alfortville, with a labor force of ten. Here he turned waste product—cinders and clinkers—into cheap usable brick and, being an idealist, he started to see the connections between ecology and the economy. Max Du Bois not only facilitated the change of an artist into an entrepreneur, he also introduced him to the rich and influential Swiss community in Paris, above all Raoul La Roche, who was to become his first great patron.

One of Jeanneret's hopes in going to live in Paris was to start some mass-production industry based on a new building system such as Dom-ino, and for the next four years he experimented with a series of new masonry technologies. Obviously Perret's success with reinforced concrete was in the back of his mind because Jeanneret developed one new concrete system after another. The four most important were a poured-concrete method for Troyes in 1919, an asbestos sandwich panel system for the Maison Monol in 1919 [fig. 67], a concrete-plus-rubble system for the Maison

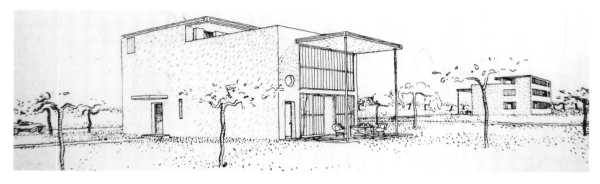

68, 69. Maison Citrohan, 1920, and Legendre Restaurant, Paris. The standard "cell" of an apartment block with two blank walls and a double-height space. This became the basic cell type for all subsequent buildings. Le Corbusier got the idea from, among other places, the restaurant where he ate lunch with Ozenfant; he appended the name Citrohan, as in the automobile, to suggest mass production. Note the outdoor stair as diagonal volume, standard since his La Scala, and glazed south wall, standard since the Villa Schwob. Le Corbusier contrasted the Citrohan and Monol in sexual terms: "in the one, strong objectivity of forms . . . *male* architecture; in the other, limitless subjectivity . . . *female* architecture" (*The Modulor*, 224).

Citrohan, in 1920 [figs. 68, 69], and the small brick manufacturing company already mentioned.

The collapse of all four systems, financially not structurally, the liquidation of all the acronyms, and a growing personal debt of 100,000 francs focused his mind. It sharpened his harsh view of Parisian life and the necessity for discarding romantic conceptions in favor of cold calculation, led by economic and social realities.

A swamp, I found myself in industry. A factory, machines, mass production, "cost-price," date of payment, balance sheets . . . harsh work, in an epoch of economic shipwrecks; shipwrecks everywhere, permanent crises, plunging of statistical curves. It seemed certain that the spirit should be led by a strong discipline . . . a cool reason. Calisthenics of the will. Constitution of a dry judgment. Oh, Bohemian of the Boul-Mich! One does not enter a Bohemian in a stadium of tough competition. It was during these long and serious years that I was keyed up like a tuning fork . . . the why and how of social phenomenon . . . attuned to the [market] forces, the artist has a destination for the products of his work.

The photographs of Jeanneret at this time show this effect: a stern, almost glacial expression verging on cruelty, pursed lips, a physiognomy reminiscent of his Calvinist ancestors, an intense gaze. One does not have to be a Marxist to see that Jeanneret's dire economic condition changed his physical one, made him lose weight, and supported his new philosophy of "Purism"—a doctrine according to which natural selection produces pure forms of elegant simplicity. Many quotes from this period reveal that his catastrophes were interpreted in Darwinian terms, as a form of natural selection where social and economic forces were pointing in one direction:

> A conviction: it is necessary to start again at zero. One must pose the problem. The whirlpool of life. It is not only a question of aesthetics . . .

But it is *also* a question of aesthetics. These two quotes above, taken from a *Confession* in 1925, hark back to the lesson learned in 1911, of a "deadly germ" of "pretentious bric-a-brac," a "cancerous germ" which is coming up against "the fine young vigorous germ, born from do or die"—the "simple, normal, healthy, and natural" will to live. Will to power, will to live, will to establish a new culture after the Great War—the Darwinian imperative and aesthetics, thankfully, pointed exactly in the same direction. The zeitgeist was on the side of Purism—his own bankruptcies proved it!

Ozenfant and Purism

Actually, Purism was an aesthetic philosophy first propounded by the painter Amédée Ozenfant in 1916. Ozenfant, born one year before Le Corbusier, in 1886, was the son of the owner of a construction company which used advanced techniques. Through his father, Ozenfant met Auguste Perret, who in turn introduced him to the young Jeanneret. "He's a very curious bird," Perret said, "but he will interest you." In his *Mémoires*, published in 1968, Ozenfant described, with a slight exaggeration, his influence on this curious Swiss bird, who had the profile of a crow (*corbeau*).

In May 1917 I finally encountered Charles-Edouard Jeanneret and a new life was to begin for him and me, built on understanding and friendship. We admired both of us equally the masterpieces of modern industry and Jeanneret had a good taste in art, especially ancient, although he was still almost blind in front of Cubism, which made him shrug his shoulders. I initiated him . . . and received a long, moving letter which said . . . "All is confusion in me since I started sketching. Throbs of blood push my fingers into arbitrary ways, my reason no longer controls . . . I am disciplined in my actions, but not in my heart and in my ideas. I have let impulses overcome me. In my confusion I think of your clear, quiet willpower. An abyss of time divides us. I am on the threshold of study, you are putting theories into practice . . . Paris, 9th June, 1918."

When the war was over, we returned to Paris, I went through a period of diogenism, sold my furniture, and moved to the center of Paris, near the Madeleine Church. The apartment had these gross moldings with crevices of contorted flowers and ribbons. I wanted to scrape clean these stupidities and whitewash the apartment from top to bottom. This was one of the first signs of the eliminating process in architecture which I called the "Vacuum-cleaning period."

One is reminded in this passage of Jeanneret's earlier letter to his teacher L'Eplattenier. The two aspects of devotion to a master and destruction of the past are present. The desire to start life anew with a clean slate, an archetypal urge of the Modern Movement, was shared by both Ozenfant and Jeanneret. They had a lot in common. Ozenfant had designed the body for a Hispano-Suiza automobile in 1912, in a streamlined classical manner, and the new products of industry such as airplanes and grain silos also fascinated him [fig. 70]. Furthermore, he had also indulged in aesthetic polemics and even run an avant-garde journal, *L'Elan*, from 1915 to 1916. This journal published the Cubo-Futurist artists from Russia as well as the Cubist work from France. It was dedicated to "France and Art" and stood against the militarism of the "Bosche." Aside from a slightly anachronistic nationalism, it was relatively progressive, managing to produce a new typographical

70. Grain elevator, Canada, 1973. LC: "cubes, cones, spheres, cylinders or pyramids are the great primary forms which light reveals to advantage . . . it is for that reason that these are *beautiful forms, the most beautiful forms*" (*Towards a New Architecture*, 1923, 31). This is a photo of the grain elevator that LC illustrates in 1923, taken by the author.

layout which made use of different typefaces and juxtaposed styles. Le Corbusier was shortly to turn this Dadaist typography to his own non-Dadaist ends.

After the First World War, Dadaism and Cubism were the most innovative artistic movements. Purism's authors saw it as the successor to both. They proclaimed that it would be constructive where Dada was just negative, and rigorously intellectual where Cubism had become decorative. Behind Purism was a notion of Darwinian evolution whereby an economic and social competition between products resulted in the natural selection of those that were simple and most pure: the "object types" such as perfect bottles. According to Darwinism, evolution proceeded by decimation, progress depended on it, the killing of nine in ten, so the superior tenth could leave offspring. If it was cruel it was also, as Darwin said, a majestic lesson, and the First World War had "made it necessary to start again at zero." Having stayed on the sidelines during the bitter fighting, they could write about the purification of war with disarming idealism:

> The war is over, everything is organized, everything is clarified and purified; factories rise, nothing is what it was before the war: the great Contest has called everything into question, it has destroyed all the senile methods and put in their place those that the struggle has proved the best . . . Never since the age of Pericles has thought been so lucid.

Jeanneret and Ozenfant started painting and writing at night at a furious pace and in three months, in December 1918, they published the book from which these lines are taken, *Après le Cubisme*, and produced an exhibit of Purist paintings. The book, according to Ozenfant, created a great sensation because it was the first published on a new art right after the war. It appeared only one month after, and therefore it preempted the zeitgeist. Timing in the marketplace of modernity was everything. To clinch victory in the Darwinian struggle of avant-gardes, the authors slipped into a reunion of Cubist painters, where a film on the movement was shown, and surreptitiously inserted at the end of the program their own extension of the spirit of the age —*Après le Cubism*, Post-Cubism—in a bizarre sense the first move of Post-Modernism. This act of psychological warfare had its intended effect—the old-guard Cubists were furious. Among avant-garde manifestos, *Après le Cubisme* was both more polemical and more old-fashioned in its views. It was full of quotations from authors such as Rousseau, Montesquieu, and Voltaire. The opening citation from Voltaire set the tone:

> Decadence is produced by facility in making and by laziness in making well, by the satiety with beauty and the taste for the bizarre.

The authors' main wish was to celebrate the conditions of modern life and persuade both artists and businessmen that they were present at the birth of a positive machine civilization unappreciated by everyone:

> . . . a magnificent epoch, too little understood, often misunderstood, often fought against by artists who ought to root their art in it . . . We have today our Ponts de Gard, we will also have our Parthenon, our epoch is better equipped than that of Pericles to realize the ideal of perfection.

These references to the Parthenon and perfection show how intent Jeanneret was on making the new architecture an equivalent of ancient virtues.

In the second chapter of the book, titled "The Modern Spirit" and clearly written by Jeanneret, we find his recurrent interest in the mathematical beauty found in the machine and the Parthenon, and the obsession with Classical virtues of strictness and severity. In fact, variations on the word *rigor* recur like a litany. The first chapter on Cubism, probably written by Ozenfant, attacks this movement because of its obscurity, its mystical scientism (all the talk about the fourth dimension), and its lack of representation. In the third chapter, on "The Laws," the authors state that Purism will recognize subject matter and thus not degenerate into decorative formalism as did its predecessor. They are also led to subject matter because of economic law: the law of natural selection which inevitably produces the pure forms of standardized objects such as the wine bottle, the flask, the pipe, the column. These are the basic *"objet-types"* found in the Purists' paintings at this time, even those of Fernand Leger and Juan Gris, which celebrate the "heroism of everyday life" [fig. 71]. For the Purists these rather banal objects

71. *Nature morte au Violon*, 1920 (FLC). The geometric profiles of object types are used to set up a formal symphony. The subject matter, while secondary to form, was important for its universality and evocation of the good simple life. Several of these object types were transformed in later paintings. Reading from bottom left in a clockwise direction, we can make out a transparent bottle, stacked plates, a scroll, a violin that echoes it, its silhouette, a faceted glass, two pipes, a fluted flask, an open book, and another faceted glass—which is also a fluted column and a gear wheel. The composition is pulled together by a "marriage of contours" and proportionally divided areas.

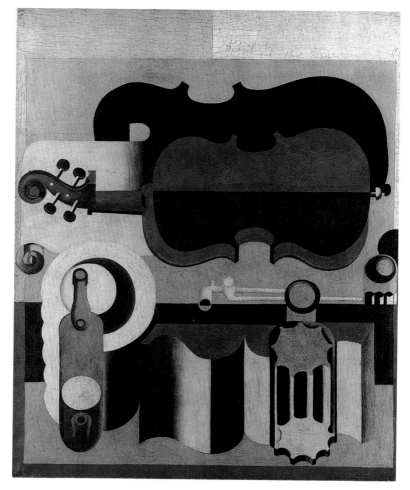

had a "heroic" quality not only because of a certain anonymous dignity and strong restraint, but also because they had been perfected by countless years of reworking. In Paul Valéry's words, "the best efforts of thousands of men converge towards the most economical and certain shape."

One can see how this form of economic determinism would appeal to the Calvinist strain in Le Corbusier, and how he would next try to find a heroic role in identifying his personal destiny with that of vast impersonal forces. He proclaimed a willing subservience to the industrial process in *Towards a New Architecture*, 1923.

A great epoch has begun.

There exists a new spirit.

Industry, overwhelming us like a flood which rolls on towards its destined end, has furnished us with new tools adapted to this new epoch, animated by the new spirit.

Economic law unavoidably governs our acts and our thoughts.

Such sentiments could only be expressed by a man who could turn a machine civilization into something like an ideal, living being. Le Corbusier saw the machine in a spiritual way as evidence of a pure cosmic force uncontaminated by personal interference. In this love of the impersonal he was part of a broad international movement extending across disciplines and countries, from T. S. Eliot in literature to Eisenstein in film. One quality in the "Heroic Period" of the 1920s, in all the arts, was the identification with the impersonal and the universal in civilization. It was this aspect which the doctrine of Purism singled out as its basis.

In "Le Purisme," an article published in 1921, Ozenfant and Jeanneret tried to establish a universal language of form that would appeal directly to the emotions regardless of education or culture, thus embracing all men. They distinguished two types of formal sensation:

1. Primary sensations determined in all human beings by the simple play of forms and primary colors. Example: If I show to

everyone on Earth—a Frenchman, a Negro, a Laplander—a sphere in the form of a billiard ball (one of the most perfect human materializations of the sphere), I release in each of these individuals an identical sensation inherent in the spherical form: *This is the constant primary sensation.*

2. There are secondary associations, varying with the individual because they depend upon his cultural or hereditary capital . . . Primary sensations constitute the bases of the plastic language: these are the *fixed words* of the plastic language . . . it does not seem necessary to expatiate at length on this elementary truth that anything of universal value is worth more than anything of merely individual value. It is the condemnation of "individualistic" art to the benefit of "universal" art [fig. 72].

Jeanneret's attempt to find the "*fixed words*" of an artistic language are surprisingly like his first searches for a Jura Regionalism and his last attempts to establish a formal language based on natural symbols, as at Chandigarh. Throughout his life, Le Corbusier was searching for a type of universal symbolism that would be transhistorical and nonconventional. Like so many sons of the Enlightenment, he never came to terms with the idea that perhaps convention itself might be universal. To him it meant provinciality, subjectivity, and academicism—all the things that the Beaux-Arts convention of Classicism entailed in the 1920s.

L'Esprit Nouveau (or the Accidental Creation of a Revolutionary Identity)

It was against these meanings that the review *L'Esprit Nouveau* was launched by Ozenfant, Jeanneret, and the poet Paul Dermée, in October 1920. If one wants to find the origin of the Modern Movement it is here, in its opening lines and clarion call:

> There is a new spirit: it is a spirit of construction and synthesis guided by a clear conception . . . a GREAT EPOCH HAS BEGUN.

Repeated again and again in different ways for twenty-eight issues, until 1925, like exhortations from an Old Testament

72. "The Lesson of Rome," page illustrating *Purisme* from *L'Esprit Nouveau*. The "*fixed words*" of the plastic language are presented like propositions in a French schoolbook on geometry.

prophet, one might start to believe a new spirit really had come out of old Europe and the war. Basically a call to order in its title (which was borrowed from Apollinaire's writings), this monthly magazine proclaimed the international idealism on every page. This was partly due to the fact that the two editors wrote most of these pages themselves—under various pseudonyms. Ozenfant disguised himself four times, as Julien Caron, Saugnier, Vaucrecy, and de Fayet, while Jeanneret occasionally wrote under the latter two names as well as Le Corbusier, Paul Boulard, and even ****— thus turning two writers into nine. What a zeitgeist. It was like some nineteenth-century revolutionary sect in which everyone had a pseudonym in case the police caught him. Just as "Lenin" and "Stalin" were adopted personae that were invented for practical reasons, and then swallowed the original men, so was "Le Corbusier." Ozenfant described the genesis of this persona one way.

> I wished to keep my real name Ozenfant for articles on painting and aesthetics in general. For architecture I will take the name of my mother: Saugnier. Take that of your mother . . . Impossible, she is a Perret! Like Auguste!
>
> Well then, take that of a cousin . . .
>
> We have the Lecorbésier (or Lecorbézier), who are happily all dead . . .
>
> Good, you will revive the name, you will be Le Corbusier in two parts, which will make it richer!

Le Corbusier, at several times in his life, gives other, more revealing reasons for the pseudonym, some of which explain deep motivations. The immediate motives include the fact that the involvement of his brother Albert and cousin Pierre, who often designed the covers for *L'Esprit Nouveau*, meant that there were too many Jeannerets involved with the magazine. Other less publicized reasons for the persona were his profile, which resembled a crow (*corbeau*, which he used as his insignia in letters and drawings), and the various sexual overtones to the last part of the pseudonym.

But the most significant reason for the pseudonym is given at

the end of his life, during an interview in May 1965. Here we
find that an artist has created a persona at speed, almost accidentally. Sudden success then turns him, somewhat against his will,
into a writer and architect. The invention of a character who
became instantaneously famous around the world changed everything in the author's life, forcing him to live up to his fabrication.
The ironic humor of this transformation by fame is not lost as he
tells the story.

> *L'Esprit Nouveau*, which had such an attractive title, was able to
> justify itself because of the articles that Ozenfant and I wrote
> about painting. And then . . . came the appearance of a gentle-
> man named Le Corbusier . . . who was, you see, all of a sudden
> baptized by Jeanneret . . . Jeanneret, me, Charles-Edouard
> Jeanneret, who announced: "If we must talk about architec-
> ture, I'm willing to do it, but I don't want to do it under the
> name of Jeanneret." I said, "I'll take the name of my maternal
> ancestors, Le Corbesier, and I'll sign my articles about archi-
> tecture 'Le Corbusier.'" So one day I wrote the first article.
> Then I was told, "You must write other articles. You have to go
> on, it's necessary." I had two days to do it. I wrote them in one
> stretch and signed "Le Corbusier" . . . It was published, and
> suddenly this name became venerated . . . a rallying cry,
> throughout the entire world . . . It's really funny isn't it? . . . I
> wrote three consecutive articles, which had the gift of attract-
> ing a vivid interest in countries everywhere among people who
> edited other journals, and among interesting artists who would
> come to Paris and say, "I want to talk to M. Le Corbusier." They
> were told, "There is no such person. It's M. Jeanneret who
> takes care of these things." And after awhile Le Corbusier was
> forced to take the name Le Corbusier even in his everyday life,
> because when he crossed a border his passport read Jeanneret,
> and the customs officials weren't too happy . . . They would
> ask, "Who is this Jeanneret in your passport, your letters are
> all addressed to Le Corbusier?" So I said, "Jeanneret, other-
> wise known as Le Corbusier." And from then on I was
> definitely renamed . . . the signature of Le Corbusier immedi-
> ately gave breadth, an incredible intensity backed up by valu-
> able articles, by valid arguments, or a revolutionary
> nature—unintentionally so, but revolutionary because the

situation was revolutionary, because the age was revolutionary. And this is why Le Corbusier was born and had to put his jacket on . . .

Thus, Jeanneret "was told," "was forced" by success and customs officials, and a "revolutionary situation," to become the revolutionary Le Corbusier, a writer and architect. Of course, the designer in him had sought this outcome ever since his youth, but the painter in him was struggling in a different direction. Fate and success by 1923 tipped the balance to architecture and forced him to paint mostly in secret and devote the rest of his life to building up his fictional persona.

It is significant that the article "Le" preceded the name because it gave a certain objective stature to the persona, as if Le Corbusier were himself some object type or *"homme-type,"* perfected by thousands of years of economic history. Indeed the persona allowed Jeanneret to write about himself in the third person as "he" or "our man did this" as if he were some universal witness suffering the course of twentieth-century history for all men. The pseudonym was at the same time a protective mask and a means of self-dramatization. It had similar overtones to his other inventions such as the Maison Citrohan or *brise-soleil*: something to be accepted as a basic fact of modern life. "Le Style Corbu" became known around the world as a synonym for the new architecture. Today in Marseilles, when one tries to find the *Unité d'Habitation*, one has no luck until one says, "Where is the Le Corbusier?" The persona became a household word conjuring up as many precise meanings as Prada and Microsoft do today.

Most of the articles on architecture appearing in *L'Esprit Nouveau* were signed "Le Corbusier–Saugnier" to signify that Le Corbusier did the writing while Ozenfant supplied the photos and some of the ideas. Their joint articles on painting were signed Ozenfant and Jeanneret, opposed to an alphabetical ordering, to signify who was most responsible for the argument in these cases. Inevitably, however, confusions and jealousy became rampant, and the two parted in bitterness in 1925, the year *L'Esprit Nouveau* stopped publishing. Le Corbusier was furious that Ozenfant should change dates on several paintings to prove that Ozenfant always had an idea a year earlier. Also "Saugnier" was getting too much credit for having written *Towards a New Architecture*, which was published in 1923 under the hybrid name, immediately achieving worldwide fame. So Le Corbusier omitted the name Saugnier from the second edition and dedicated the book to Ozenfant. "The fellow thanked me for the dedication . . . he didn't realize that by printing it I had prevented anyone from thinking he'd written the book." Ozenfant, for his part, complained that the joint signature caused a number of people to believe that he had a mistress called Le Corbusier. He gave a small check to Le Corbusier for his services on the magazine—so paltry a sum that Le Corbusier kept it in his pocket for the rest of his life to pull out whenever he needed to discredit his former friend [fig. 73].

73. Ozenfant and Jeanneret in a balloon, Eiffel Tower, June 26, 1923. Two *hommes-types* in their standard, impersonal dress.

Le Corbusier: The Hero of the Heroic Period 1917–28

74. Freehold Maisonettes, 1922. The classic expression of mass housing as a collective palace that includes nature in its heart. Stemming from Le Corbusier's interest in the Charterhouse of Ema in 1907 and his Citrohan House, this project became a model for the communal houses constructed in Russia in the late 1920s. Communal facilities like kitchens and gymnasiums were provided, while, in the spirit of capitalism, each apartment was owned by an individual and had its private garden, as the monks did at Ema. The "new spirit of synthesis" meant synthesizing opposites.

Yet for seven years the two were inseparable cohorts in their fight for a new sensibility appropriate to the modern age. The similarity and breadth of their outlook allowed them to establish an avant-garde review that was diverse in subject, while unified in attitude. Basically the same message, the heroic potential of modern life, was expounded in articles on music, literature, philosophy, psychology, economics, painting, sculpture, architecture, and politics. The "New Architecture" of Le Corbusier–Saugnier was complemented by an article by Dr. Pierre Winter on "Le Corps Nouveau." A renovation of body and mind was called for, illustrated by Isadora Duncan–like figures leaping across purified objects in Greek garb. Albert Jeanneret, Le Corbusier's brother, wrote articles on eurythmy and advertised his school on it in the magazine. Each issue reiterated the theme: "A great epoch has begun. There is a new spirit . . ."

Issues of *L'Esprit Nouveau* reached the Bauhaus in Weimar, and students immediately called for an alternative to the Expressionism prevailing there: "machines for living in" instead of "glass cathedrals of the future." In Moscow, the emergent Constructivist movement saw Le Corbusier as a herald of their new society, not only because of his slogan emphasizing "a spirit of construction," but also because of his communal housing schemes. Le Corbusier identified mass housing as the primary problem of what he called the Machine Age, and he produced one of the first ideal type solutions to this "problem," the Freehold Maisonettes [fig. 74]. Here were individual villas with their suspended gardens tied into an impersonal collective that looked, and functioned, like an ocean liner. In 1924, the Constructivist architect Moses Ginzburg wrote a book called *Style and Epoch* and sent a dedicated copy to Le Corbusier–Saugnier. The book is not only composed like *Towards a New Architecture*, but also contains the same polemical illustrations of grain silos, airplanes, and ocean liners. Ginzburg was the major creative force behind collectivist housing in Russia and became a close friend of Le Corbusier when he visited there several times in the late 1920s (one of the few Western architects to do so).

The Hero Clears the Field

It would be an exaggeration to claim that Le Corbusier was altogether responsible for the Heroic Period of Modern Architecture. Certainly Theo Van Doesburg and de Stijl in Holland provided much of the impetus, as did Constructivism in Russia and the Bauhaus in Germany. Yet if any one architect is to be singled out, and it would be awkward to have a heroic period without a hero, then it would have to be Le Corbusier, for his self-conscious moral position as much as his buildings. The Classical hero in Western culture is an individual who sees the major problems confronting society, sees them rationally, and then acts directly to change them. Furthermore, he is morally and personally involved in this action in a way which is different from those who are part of a movement or zeitgeist. He takes all mistakes and setbacks as a personal responsibility, thus suffering where others would claim immunity. Perhaps Le Corbusier got some of these ideas from Nietzsche's notion of the superman; at any rate he had a highly developed sense of his own destiny.

> This is a successful achievement, to be able to say to oneself: "I want to attain a certain end, and I shall leave no stone unturned. I shall wait for the proper moment. I shall succeed in what I have decided to do. I shall arrive at the chosen time, at the proper place, calm and smiling, a conqueror and not a casualty." Real heroes are well groomed and absolutely controlled. They are neither unshaven, nor unkept, nor bloodstained. The gods themselves smile.

It is generally understood by Le Corbusier's admirers that he was relatively unbloodstained, or, as they phrase it, he did not bother himself with petty squabbles, attacking other architects and indulging in destructive polemics. This view is profoundly false and fails to take into account the eminently dialectical nature of his argument. For every positive point, there is someone or something which is destroyed. In later life Le Corbusier was partly embarrassed by this fact and apologized for attacks on a sculptor he had admired when very young.

> A thousand excuses for the wickedness done to Rodin . . .
> But "Paul" [the blasphemer] was at the age of revolt and discovery . . . He burned what he loved.

The "Paul" who Le Corbusier is apologizing for here was of course another persona, "Paul Boulard," who had carried out the Nietzschean injunction to burn what he loved in order to create something totally new and superhuman—in this specific case the machine aesthetic.

Before outlining the positive creations of Le Corbusier which established his role in the Heroic Period, it is worthwhile considering his destructive side, not only because it is overlooked, but also because it was so complete, and up-to-date, and it evinces a feeling of joyful struggle, a love of attack. His father, writing in his journal, once again zeroes in on his son's combative character: "He loves to have adversaries, it is in his temperament" (February 4, 1921); and "he is a formidable workhorse who holds his positions without making any concessions" (January 3, 1923). Under his various pseudonyms, such as Paul Boulard, he attacked not only the common enemy of avant-gardes, the Ecole des Beaux-Arts, but also de Stijl, Constructivism, Gropius and the Bauhaus, Expressionism, the Prague Formalists, and Surrealism. Perhaps a reason for all these outbursts was psychological displacement: Did he first have to criticize a competitive movement *before* he could appropriate its lessons?

In *L'Esprit Nouveau* between 1921 and 1924, Le Corbusier condemned modern German architecture for being based on the error of "appearances."

> In architecture such an error is fatal. The systematic use of the vertical, in Germany, is a mysticism, a mysticism of physical

law, the poison of German architecture. The Germans wished
to make their architecture one of the most active armaments of
pangermanism . . . the German Embassy in Saint-Petersburg,
the factories of A.E.G. in Berlin, are conceived to impose, to
crush, to cry out absolute power.

This attack on Peter Behrens, an architect whom the young
Jeanneret had admired and disliked, was not only against the
monumental nationalism, but also against a supposedly false technology, verticality, as opposed to Le Corbusier's technically determined horizontal buildings.

A simple fact condemns everything: in a house one lives floor
by floor, horizontally not vertically. The German palaces are
just lift cages. Here is the aesthetic of caskets.

The argument which Le Corbusier continues to bring against
the Germans is their lack of technical rationality. Gropius and the
Bauhaus are wrong (in 1923) because they teach decorative art and
not architecture or research into standardization, which Le
Corbusier was pursuing.

But what saddens us is the obligation to have to conclude that a
school of art has the absolute incapacity to ameliorate industrial production, to create standards: one cannot invent standards out of the blue. For a long time, in this grave question of
teaching, we have concluded that the schools of applied art
must be closed, because we cannot admit the industrial product removed from the standards, we cannot admit the objects
of decorative art. Now the Bauhaus at Weimar brings nothing
to industry, but just creates decorators who are superfluous
and undesirable quantities . . . we desire exact objects . . .
There thus exist many schools to be closed.

Le Corbusier's, or rather Paul Boulard's, greatest wrath is
directly against German Expressionism, the architecture of Hans
Poelzig, which resembles the ruins of Rome, and of Hermann
Finsterlin, which resembles "viscous ejaculations recalling underwater horrors."

In the depths of our being, larva, toads, and beasts which haunt

126

75. *Expressionist Town Plan*, attacked by Paul Boulard for, among other things, its lack of geometrical order.

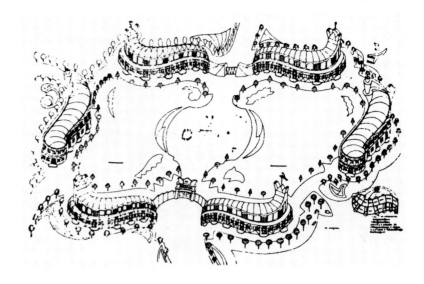

76. Erich Mendelsohn, *Einstein Tower*, Potsdam, 1917–21. Le Corbusier absorbed the lessons of Expressionism and Gaudí and they reemerged transformed in his late work, such as Ronchamp.

the memories of the primordial world reemerge again today . . . we see them in this new crisis of the spirit which followed the war: frightening dreams of Hermann Finsterlin from Bavaria [fig. 75] with their viscous ejaculations recalling underwater horrors, or those viscera, or impure acts of beasts. He was pretending to extract out of this architectural creations . . . Bruno Taut . . . publishes in his review houses where one finds the same distracted neurasthenia. But physical matter is against it. These things can be born in a fevered head and inscribed on paper. Physical facts refuse to let them be built.

This last statement was of course factually untrue, as Le Corbusier himself showed by illustrating Mendelsohn's Einstein Tower, an Expressionist building which influenced his own Ronchamp thirty years later [fig. 76]. Yet in dialectical terms, proving Expressionism unbuildable was necessary in order to prove his own architecture to be generated by constructional laws. The Constructivists, in this dialectic, were the antithesis of Expressionism, but still only one more erroneous solution on the way to true synthesis.

Here is the mirage: *the poetic attitude of truth perceived on the base of geometry is not so easily a plastic truth.* Russian Constructivism makes this jump too quickly, too much without considering pure, plastic facts; things are misunderstood! Still

it's very seductive and incomparably better than the hell of
Finsterlin! It's as much in the truth as the others are in error.
Antipodes. It's at the antipodes of neurasthenia.

Elsewhere Le Corbusier faulted the Constructivists for
thinking that art had nothing more to do than resemble machines,
again forgetting that there were certain aesthetic laws, based on
pure forms, which were eternal. The de Stijl artists who based
their work on these laws still suffered for not taking real objects as
their point of departure. And the Surrealists, who are praised for
having understood that real objects have a natural poetry and
beauty, are nevertheless criticized for thinking that these objects
are either banal or the result of elevated dreams. When they are
beautiful, industrial objects are functional and real (not surreal).
"The realist, useful object is beautiful." This thesis is next countered by an antithesis when Le Corbusier moves to attack the
German functionalists.

Thus, Le Corbusier moves from one attack to the next,
always changing the criticism to suit his ends. It is a game he cannot lose, as is all dialectic wielded by a clever duelist. What's the
point? For one thing, each attack is justified insofar as it goes, and
for another, it crystallized a stage in his own positive development.
The extremes of abstract art led to the Purist insistence on the
industrial object; the monumental German nationalism led to
anonymous, internationalist housing projects. Beyond this
progress through opposition, there were the unique qualities of
relevance and commitment.

Le Corbusier (unlike other architects such as Gropius, Wright,
or Mies van der Rohe) always stayed in touch with and alert to the
contemporary issues. When in 1932 the issue happened to be a
reactionary, rightist nationalism, he wrote a book, *Croisade*, con-
demning it (while the other architects remained silent or indeed
collaborated); when there was a reaction of the younger generation
against the new establishment, including him, he saw its point.
Being always *engagé* with the present situation had its limitations,
but it did serve to keep Le Corbusier creatively acute right up until
his death at the age of seventy-eight in 1965. He never stopped
enjoying a good fight, and the youthful vitality evinced in leveling
all opposing contenders was as much a part of *L'Esprit Nouveau*,
the new, heroic spirit, as anything else. What it brought about,

naturally, was counterattack and a life lived more as a warrior than a gentleman. But this is what is asked of heroes and it helps explain the spartan image of his buildings, their lack of domestic comfort. He enjoyed life as a monk, as a health addict, boxer, overworked student, and nomad on a ship, qualities of living that are well expressed in his architecture. Tough the buildings may be, but they are also exhilarating and heroic gestures.

A Revolution in Four Books

A positive program for a reformation of life was set out in four key books written between 1921 and 1925: *Vers une architecture, Urbanisme, L'Art décoratif d'aujourd'hui,* and, with Ozenfant, *La Peinture Moderne* [fig. 77]. Such creative output was phenomenal considering also the building projects, exhibitions, and paintings

77. Advertisement for 4 Revolutionary Books, in Le Corbusier's *Almanach d'architecture moderne*, 1927 (Éditions Crès).

he produced at the time. Le Corbusier wrote about 10,000 words per month during these crucial five years with *L'Esprit Nouveau*, and like a good journalist turned author, he made every shot count twice by turning all the articles into books of several different languages. The four books, which reproduced articles from *L'Esprit Nouveau* in their original form and size, gave the impression of a total change in life inasmuch as they covered architecture, urbanism, industrial design, and painting. Like his Esprit Nouveau Pavilion [fig. 78], finished in 1925, the same year in which the last three books were published, they covered a spectrum of interests from the doorknob to the regional plan—all from the same attitude. Hence the overpowering feeling they give of the zeitgeist moving through every aspect of modern life. In purely polemical terms the four books were far more persuasive than other architectural manifestos published in the twentieth century and they deserve to be studied in their own right, as contributions to a literary genre which has only recently flourished.

No doubt they owe something to biblical and political tracts, to

78. L'Esprit Nouveau pavilion, 1925. Various views of the revolution proposed for modern living: Purist paintings on the wall; industrial "equipment" instead of interior decoration; a prefabricated cell with "hanging garden"; a collection of cells with communal services forming a superblock. Le Corbusier wrote a book explaining the four different revolutions that would occur as a whole—a modern *Gesamtkunstwerk*.

Nietzsche's aphorisms and Marx's radical thinking, to the artistic manifestos of Apollinaire and the Futurists. But their combination of styles and ideas go beyond all these. In form they consist of short chapters introduced by an "argument," in blank verse, which is reiterated throughout the text so persuasively that one forgets to note both its dubiety and illogicality. The arguments are supported by newspaper cuttings, textbook illustrations of such unlikely subjects as bidets and monkeys playing guitars, photos of astrophysical discoveries, pencil drawings, and sometimes even missing photographs (which the reader is meant to supply with photos of up-to-date equipment). The juxtaposition of typographical styles and subject matter, the argument through poetry, anecdote, statistics, and biblical rhetoric have all had an effect on twentieth-century journalism from *Time* magazine to Tom Wolfe [fig. 79]. The argument conducted through photographs and captions has influenced the former, whereas the baroque, telegraphic, neo-hysterical style has, in some way, come through to the latter. Since the specific arguments of the four books had such a profound effect on Modern architecture and what became known as the International Style, a summary of them is appropriate here, linking them with Le Corbusier's buildings produced at the time.

79. Pages from *L'Art décoratif d'aujourd'hui,* in the chapter on "The Spirit of Truth." Other images of Truth in this chapter include seashells, Santa Sophia, airplanes, fighters, gunboats, cross sections of plants, asteroids, comets, and a dirigible.

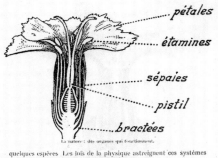

Towards a New Architecture

As already mentioned, by 1911 Le Corbusier had come to several important conclusions, which were to be given final articulation in the 1920s: The first in essence was the Parthenon spirit, the idea that the Parthenon was an absolute in civilization, both a machine which had been perfected through evolution and a symbol of the tragic human condition. His other major conclusion was that architecture is basically an art of geometric volumes or "the masterly, correct, and magnificent play of masses brought together in light." These two ideas were given seminal formulation in *Vers une architecture*, 1923, and supported by various ideas which are basically mechanical, social, and metaphysical.

The mechanical idea concerned first of all "the engineer's aesthetic" and more importantly the engineer's morality of unblinkered truth, as opposed to the deceits of the then current architecture. As usual, the argument proceeds dialectically, with the noble savage engineer pitted against the "obsequious," "peevish" architect.

> A QUESTION of morality; lack of truth is intolerable, we perish in untruth.

One of the truths that the engineer, as opposed to the architect, upholds is that of preserving only useful tools and scrapping all others. The idea of a high rate of technical obsolescence was taken over from the Futurists.

> We throw the out-of-date tool on the scrap heap; . . . this action is a manifestation of health, of moral health, of *morale* also; it is not right that we should produce bad things because of a bad tool; nor is it right that we should waste our energy, our health and our courage because of a bad tool; it must be thrown away and replaced.

Vers une architecture had a great impact, partly because of the breathtaking illustrations of motorcars, boats, airplanes, and industrial objects, all of which had a beauty that was new and ravishing. In chapters called "eyes which do not see," Le Corbusier made his name bringing out this new beauty and becoming its apologist, but he does this from an idealistic and even Platonic viewpoint.

Le Corbusier: The Hero of the Heroic Period 1917–28

132

We claim in the name of the steamship, of the airplane, and of the motor-car the right to health, logic, daring, harmony, perfection.

The qualities of harmony and perfection are those which some engineers may strive after, but only those who have a prior cultural commitment. Next, this supposedly radical functionalism is modified by the introduction of emotional and metaphysical values. Although he expends a considerable amount of energy in this book, and subsequent ones, attacking academic aesthetics—particularly Classical styles and rules—it is essential to realize that he does this in order to substitute better Classical aesthetics, more pure and Pythagorean ones. From this point of view he wants to be more Classical than the Classicists, more aesthetically cogent than the philosophers of art, more academic than the academics! This is very clear when he formulates the tuning-fork theory of cosmic communication, the idea that we resonate naturally with certain forms and laws, an idea with which Pythagoras, Plato, and indeed the French Academy would have all felt perfectly happy.

The purpose of construction is TO MAKE THINGS HOLD TOGETHER: of architecture TO MOVE US. Architectural emotion exists when the work rings within us in tune with a universe whose laws we obey, recognize and respect.

Later on we find, as with Plato, that the language which is common to the universe and us is based on geometry, pure mathematical ratios, and ultimate truths. There is an allusion to God the designer—"a single will behind" the universe—although for the Darwinian LC it probably meant that *Nature* was the architect that designed us to vibrate in accord with the universe. From this time forward, Le Corbusier was to interrogate science and mathematics for their hints of a universal language in accord with our "axis."

This sounding-board which vibrates in us is our criterion of harmony [fig. 8o]. This is indeed the axis on which Man is organized in perfect accord with Nature and probably with the Universe . . . this axis leads us to assume a unity of conduct in the universe and to admit a single will behind it. The laws of physics are thus a corollary to this axis and if we recognize

80. The Parthenon, stylobate and its visual refinements illustrated in *Vers une architecture*. The argument for architectural quality based on the tuning-fork theory of vibration is more subtle than it first appears, since it goes beyond naturalism and nature. LC's "Pure Creation of the Mind," not nature, creates the harmonies with which we vibrate; they may be based on optical refinements, as here, or plastic elements, or masses in light, or the clear statement of an idea or character. Thus the cosmic axis comes from nature but it is the *artistic intention* that crystallizes it.

(and love) science and its works, it is because both one and the other force us to admit they are prescribed by this primal will . . . If the canoe, the musical instrument, the turbine, all results of experiment and calculation, appear to us to be "organized" phenomena, that is to say as having themselves a certain life, it is because they are based upon that axis. From this we get a possible definition of harmony, that is to say a moment of accord with the axis which lies in man, and so with the laws of the universe—a return to universal law.

Not surprisingly the Parthenon is the supreme example of an object which is basically functional and still made up of universal harmonies that are "in accord with the axis which lies in man." If the mechanical and metaphysical arguments have been somewhat Platonic, then the supporting social ideas are even more so. For Plato's elite of philosopher kings we get a modern substitute of enlightened businessmen.

> We are all acquainted with too many big businessmen, bankers and merchants, who tell us: "Ah, but I am merely a man of affairs, I live entirely outside the art world, I am a Philistine." We protest and tell them: "All your energies are directed towards this magnificent end which is the forging of the tools of an epoch, and which is creating throughout the whole world this accumulation of very beautiful things in which economic law reigns supreme, and mathematical exactness is joined to daring and imagination, that is what you do; that, to be exact, is beauty."

"Businessmen of the world unite for beauty, you have nothing to loose but your academic chains and bad taste." The ironies of telling the elite that they were the harbingers of the good, the true, and the beautiful—if only they had eyes to see—was probably lost on the two prophets since they were so zealously trying to convert the rich and powerful. What are the implications? One that can be found later in *Vers une architecture* is an elitism that is developed in Fascist directions (a very good friend of Le Corbusier at this time was the French Fascist Dr. Pierre Winter). Or, one can read this as a return to Zarathustra and Schuré's idea of *les grands initiés*, those initiated into the mysteries of Theosophy and its cosmic truths. Or, one can see this as a form of neo-Saint-Simonianism, where the elite *industriels*, such as Henry Ford, are being exhorted to join the cause. Whether it is the Modern corporation, the Modern state, or the secret society and avant-garde, it is an appeal to leadership, top-down direction, taste being imposed or meant to trickle down, *du haut en bas*. Whichever the case, and it was probably a mixture of all three, this elitism is opposed to populism and the William Morris idea of Modernism—that art should spring from and be for the many.

> The art of our period is performing its proper functions when it addresses itself to the chosen few . . . Art is not an essential pabulum except for the chosen few who have need of meditation in order that they may lead. Art is in its essence arrogant.

Or:

> The social contract which has evolved through the ages fixes standardized classes, functions and needs producing standardized products.

Or:

> Rome's business was to conquer the world and govern it.

Finally in the last chapter, called "Architecture or Revolution," we see a synthesis of these elitist ideas as the enlightened businessman is equated with the great artist and the managerial elite, or perhaps what we would call today the technocrats. The managerial revolution leading to industrialization was just beginning at this time in France, and was seen as an alternative to both Marxism and rule by the rich or powerful. Ernest Mercier, head of a large utilities combine, argued that the big modern corporation, with its technical and economic efficiency, was the only alternative to revolution, and that its managers must take over power within the government. Le Corbusier, with his interest in Taylorization (efficient mass production) could see the future, for the next seven years, precisely in these terms:

> The magnificent flowering of industry in our epoch has created

> a special class of intellectuals so numerous that it constitutes
> the really active stratum of society . . . the engineers, the heads
> of departments, legal representatives, secretaries, editors,
> accountants . . . The modern age is spread before them,
> sparkling and radiant . . .

There was one member of this "special class," reading these lines, both in *L'Esprit Nouveau* and *Vers une architecture*, who must have believed these words were aimed directly at him.

The Perfect Client

Every now and then in architectural history an architect's prayers are answered as an individual or group with the means comes along, reads the message left in the bottle, and says, "I understand, build me a fragment of your utopia." Prince Charles for Leon Krier, the Jewish Museum for Daniel Libeskind, the Guggenheim Museum for Frank Gehry are three recent examples. Le Corbusier finally struck home with Raoul La Roche, a banker in the Swiss-Paris community to whom Max Du Bois introduced him three years previously. He had three advantages that made him the perfect Corb client: first, he was a bachelor who loved to entertain, especially in a gallery setting—hence the necessity for large, uninterrupted, precipitous, flowing spaces, impossible if one has noisy children. Second, he loved avant-garde art and commissioned Ozenfant and Jeanneret to build up the best collection of Cubist and Purist paintings in Europe. He bought Jeanneret's paintings, for such prices as 7,500 francs (when the architect had no work). He also organized support for, and bought shares in, the magazine *L'Esprit Nouveau*. Finally, he had an absolute conviction that Le Corbusier's architecture and paintings, especially when combined, were the best—enough even to displace Picasso's work!

When the La Roche house was completed in March 1925 he wrote words of appreciation that echoed the architect's concern for capturing the best of the past in a new way.

> But what especially moves me are those constant elements
> which are found in all the great works of architecture, but
> which one meets with so rarely in modern constructions. Your
> ability to link our era to preceding ones is particularly great.

You have "overrun the problem" and made a work of
plastic art.

Or, two years later, in answer to Jeanneret's assertions in 1908 of
"what architecture is":

> Ah! Those prisms—one has to believe that you and Pierre have
> the secret of them, because I search in vain elsewhere . . .
> Thanks to you we now know what Architecture is.

Or, when Le Corbusier was hanging the collection in the gallery,
Raoul La Roche asked for the Picassos to be removed, and Purism
to be given pride of place because:

> Your painting is at the level of your architecture and since it
> has come out of it, that it return there is logical.

This hanging, in 1925, was one of the causes of the break
between Ozenfant and Le Corbusier since the latter wanted much
more emphasis given to the architecture's unadorned volumes than
did the painter. The architect won this battle and the display of
Purist paintings led to the fact that part of the house is an "architectural promenade," a concept he had learned as he stalked the
Acropolis in 1911. The idea is that architecture is best appreciated
as a drama that unfolds in movement, where plastic volumes and
mental associations can be enjoyed over time, like a symphony.

Thus the La Roche house, on its very awkward site, sets up a
dramatic if subtle opposition between a slight curve, approached
frontally, and a streamlined white wall that pulls you toward it [fig.
81]. The white wall is the ultimate in aristocratic understatement.
Its windows and doors are proportioned by regulating lines,
brought flush to the surface, and picked out by elegant black lines
[fig. 82]. If you enter by the third door (the first one went to
Albert Jeanneret's part of the house and the second to the
concierge) you step into one of the first great sequences of space
in Modern architecture.

Open the door, go under a bridge, and the tight space explodes
upwards and through punched-out voids that are mysteriously
backlit [figs. 83 a–d]. Go across the triple-height space, look at the
Purist paintings, one of which you now seem to be moving through,

81. La Roche–Jeanneret House, Paris, 1923–25, first and second floors superimposed and redrawn. The plan shows the tight site, facing north, making it necessary to grab light from various small slots of space, and the dramatization of movement along a route, using bridges, balconies, stairs, and ramps.

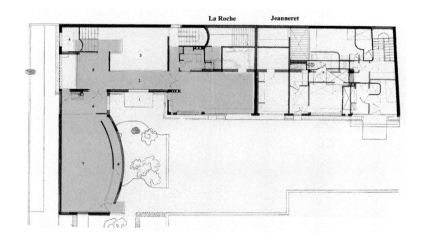

82. Facade analysis, redrawn and edited, showing regulating lines. A, B, and C are proportioned elements, and lines parallel or perpendicular make them so.

83 a, b, c, d. La Roche–Jeanneret House in its present state, now the Fondation Le Corbusier. Various comparative views, 1925 (F. R. Yerbury) and 1971. The curved gallery contained Le Corbusier's first use of the ramp. Note the way a continuation of space is implied by the lighting and layering of punched-out flat surfaces.

turn left up a stair, and survey the pure prisms from a balcony. Catch your breath, turn around, and proceed to the culmination, La Roche's curved gallery. Here you find the paintings hung (or sitting on the floor) and bad lighting (bare lightbulbs—Corbu had not yet solved Purist lighting). Go past some spare Thonet furniture, good Purist *objet-types*, and mount the brown ramp to the left, to Le Roche's little aerie, his top-lit library. The spatial sequence is remarkable and remained a constant preoccupation of Le Corbusier. It also became the stock in trade of subsequent Modern architects.

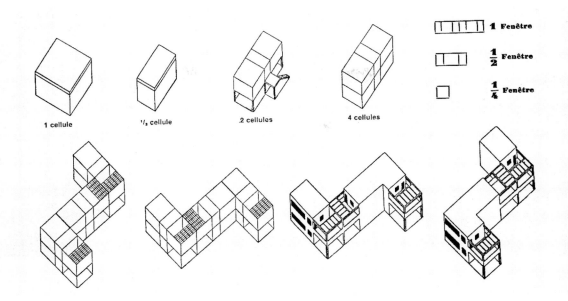

1 cellule   ¹/₂ cellule   2 cellules   4 cellules

1 Fenêtre

½ Fenêtre

¼ Fenêtre

84. Pessac units, 1925. The basic elements of construction consist of the basic cube, or cell, the reinforced-concrete beam of 16 feet 3 inches, and the ribbon window.

In the entrance hall we find overlapping blocks of space which are lit from behind, thus suggesting something beyond. Instead of the eye and mind being abruptly halted by edges and contained surfaces, they are led continuously on in exploration, never quite comprehending the mystery of layered and veiled space. For the most part the surfaces are white, but those in shadow, which Le Corbusier wished to suppress, are blue, while those in direct light are brownish red. This architectural polychromy, in muted earth colors, was next applied to the exterior of buildings—those at Pessac.

The City of Tomorrow

The fifty-one workers' houses built in Pessac [fig. 84], a suburb of Bordeaux, constituted one of the largest schemes Le Corbusier was to build, and hence can be appropriately connected with his next book, *Urbanisme* (or *The City of Tomorrow* as it was somewhat misleadingly titled in English—Le Corbusier always denied being a Futurist and called it *The Contemporary City*). This book develops certain earlier ideas, some forcefully, some to the point of absurdity, and in this mixture we find the origin of his identification with Don Quixote—the epitome of idealism and the ridiculous.

The first three chapters attempt to show that a rectilinear

geometry is not only functional, for speed, and beautiful, because clear, but the basis of the best culture as well. "Culture is an orthogonal state of mind" is one of the absurd epigrams which typifies much of the argument, just as does the opening statement:

> Man walks in a straight line because he has a goal and knows where he is going; he has made up his mind to reach some particular place and he goes straight to it. The pack-donkey meanders along, meditates a little in his scatter-brained and distracted fashion, he zigzags . . .

We recall that his 1910 manuscript, *La Construction des Villes*, had precisely the opposite message: "The lesson of the pack-donkey should be retained," and geometrical layouts must be avoided at all costs. The 1925 chapter ends, equally dogmatically on the other side of the ass, with the conclusion that *because of* winding roads "cities sink to nothing and ruling classes are overthrown." The whole argument culminates in a view of civilization reminiscent of Vitruvius and Vasari: namely the idea that there are contrasting periods of civilization and barbarism. These can be known by the style of urban life, and in some cases, when civilization favors geometry, there can be progressive development. For Le Corbusier, the barbaric disequilibrium of curved lines, jagged surfaces, and unclear decoration is inferior to the Classical equilibrium of rectangles and pure volumes— "One is a symbol of perfection, the other of effort only." Behind these questionable views were two interesting ideas: first, the Purist concept that certain forms constitute a natural language, and second, that Classicism was a natural result of modern industry.

> This modern sentiment is a spirit of geometry, a spirit of construction and synthesis. Exactitude and order are its essential conditions . . . In the place of individualism and its fevered products, we prefer the commonplace, the everyday, the rule to the exception . . . a general beauty draws us in, and the heroically beautiful seems merely theatrical. We prefer Bach to Wagner, and the spirit that inspired the Parthenon to that which created the cathedral.

In part this argument had a certain plausibility inasmuch as most engineering work before Post-Modernism had a Platonic and Classical geometry. Second, the Modern sensibility which emerges from anonymous city life does tend to "prefer Bach to Wagner," or everyday objects to historicist ones. But combined with his social arguments, this leads to the following kind of absurdity:

> Thus a street which had one uniform cornice seen against the sky would be a most important advance toward a noble architecture. If we could insert such an innovation on the agendas of town councils, we should be adding enormously to the happiness of the inhabitants. We must always remember that the fates of cities are decided in the Town Hall; municipal councils decide the destinies of town planning.

The idea that one could change people's lives through architectural form never really left Le Corbusier; but the other idea, that architecture was a political act determined in Town Hall, was dropped by the end of the book.

> My role has been a technical one . . . since the Russian Revolution it has become the charming prerogative of both our own and the Bolshevist revolutionaries to keep the title of revolutionary to themselves alone . . . [my "Contemporary City" project of 1922] was severely criticized [by the Communists] because I had not labeled the finest building on my plan "People's Hall," "Soviet" or "Syndicalist Hall" and so on; and because I did not crown my plan with the slogan "Nationalization of all property." I have been very careful not to depart from the technical side of my problem. I am an architect; no one is going to make a politician of me. "A Contemporary City" has no label, it is not dedicated to our existing Bourgeois-Capitalist society nor to the Third International. It is a Technical work . . . *"Things are not revolutionized by making revolutions.* The real Revolution lies in the solution of existing problems."

Thus Le Corbusier emerges now as the apolitical technocrat, the neutral doctor solving society's problems no matter what the ideology. And yet certain definite social forms *are* favored. The

"Contemporary City" has the business elite at its center. This consists of twenty-four glass skyscrapers containing offices rather than, say, a town hall or cathedral, which occupy the centers of most "ideal" plans [fig. 85]. Throughout *Urbanisme* there are many references to the "Captains of Industry" which show that Le Corbusier was looking to business for the new meritocracy, and there are many appeals for a new town builder to emerge, such as Louis XIV or Colbert, who is capable of making a clear, grand decision to build the city at a stroke.

Le Corbusier found such a patron, on a small scale, in M. Henri Fruges, an enlightened industrialist who had inherited a

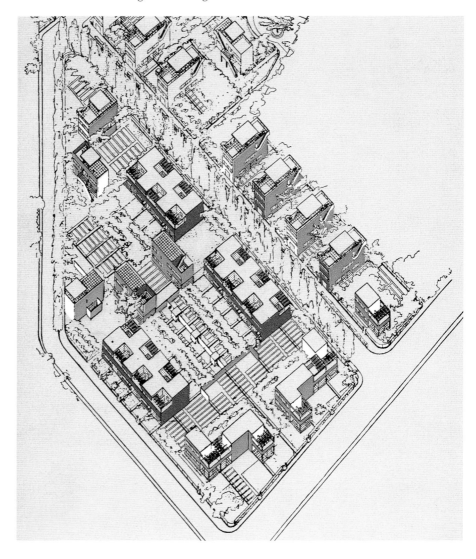

sugar-cube factory from his father. When Fruges commissioned Le Corbusier to build the white, boxlike workers' houses at Pessac, not surprisingly they were compared to sugar cubes. At any rate, Fruges was, like so many of Le Corbusier's clients, an altruistic, creative businessman who had read his writings and been persuaded by the idealism:

> I am going to enable you to realize your theories in practice—right up to their most extreme consequences—Pessac should be a laboratory of standardization and mass production.

Here was a "Captain of Industry" engaging in intelligent, good works, here was a "Louis XIV capable of saying 'We wish it' or 'such is our pleasure'"—the ending words of *Urbanisme*. Fruges was not only a benevolent industrialist but he described himself as an "explorer, multivalent artist, architect . . . painter, sculptor, pianist, and composer, member of S.A.C.E.M. of Paris, writer, art critic, historian, etc. . . ." It probably took such a man to commission Le Corbusier to construct workers' housing as an altruistic experiment.

In any case, it is significant for Le Corbusier's social arguments that such a man took an interest in his idealistic proposals and continued to do so. For these arguments are based on an unusual form of idealistic paternalism or liberal elitism or Fascist benevolence. They all approach the conclusion that a few great men lead society toward its own best interest, or that social liberation and health can only be achieved through the action of the few. It is not surprising that Dr. Pierre Winter, in an article of praise, justified Pessac as the new architecture for Fascism: it combined a new order with cheapness, health, rationality, and clarity. Just as Mussolini's Fascism combined mass social reforms with a new technology, all led by an elite, so did Le Corbusier's Pessac.

In fact, Pessac was built from standardized elements used in ever-changing combinations [figs. 84, 85]. This was not just an economic or technical decision, but also an aesthetic one. As Le Corbusier said in *Urbanisme*, quoting the eighteenth-century French Classicist Abbé Laugier:

> 1. *Chaos, disorder, and a wild variety in the general layout* (i.e. a composition rich in contrapuntal elements like a fugue or

85. Pessac, axonometric view. A mixture of high and low buildings placed at different angles yet all built from similar elements. The greenery that separates these buildings is also dispersed in different ways. All this led the inhabitants to consider the area less monotonous and oppressive than a comparable modern development.

symphony). 2. *Uniformity in detail* (i.e. reticence, decency, "alignment" in detail).

Pessac has this interesting combination of similar details making up ever different ensembles. The elements are intermixed in such an elaborate way that they never become predictable as in most mass housing. Furthermore, they are mixed with greenery to create an ambiguous whole of trees, walls, and columns, "where there is no inside or outside" to the environment—another lesson of *Urbanisme.* Perhaps Le Corbusier's best-known urban idea at this time was the "City in the Park," the idea of achieving high urban densities along with the benefits of nature by building high or with complex setbacks. At Pessac, we find nature introduced by intricate methods such as setbacks, gardens, and treelined axes. This also gives a sense of identity that is rarely found in workers' housing. Indeed, judging by the sociological study which Philippe Boudon has carried out on Pessac, we can see that it comes rather close to Le Corbusier's vision of the Charterhouse at Ema: an ideal resolution of individual initiative and collective well-being.

While such collective elements as windows, staircases, heating equipment, and kitchen were standardized, and thus achieved economies, they were assembled in rather nonrepetitive ways and left with flexible, open space. Hence over forty years the inhabitants have used these "standards" in all sorts of individual ways, walling up ribbon windows, filling out terraces, dividing up the open-plan rooms, and so on [fig. 86]. This, of course, has destroyed the visual consistency of the architecture, turning the Purist aesthetic into a Post-Modern hybrid. At the end of his life, Le Corbusier faced this reality with a paradoxical remark: "You know, it's life that's always right and the architect who's wrong." This was an ironic answer, intended to be so. Just as a "house was a machine for living in," it was also a poetic ruin of crumbling concrete and primitive masonry. Just as Le Corbusier's "standards" were machine-tooled objects of Platonic perfection and precision, they were also rough stones, trees, and a bottle of wine. Starting with the idea of resolving two incompatibilities like the individual and the group, it was not surprising that Le Corbusier could end up, as at Pessac, by admiring the way personalization was destroying his own architecture. All the arguments for a geometrical civilization, put forward in *Urbanisme,* were countered by the

86 a, b. Pessac, 1925 and 1969. The vast alterations that this workers' housing has undergone extend far beyond the visual changes. The open planning of Le Corbusier has allowed for many changes in use and construction. Standardization, because it was not enforced after construction, has resulted in its opposite, a very flexible, personalized architecture. As Brian Brace Taylor has shown, Pessac was beset by all sorts of legal and technical problems, some of which were caused by Le Corbusier's haste and inexperience. He did not get planning permission soon enough and did not provide access roads and sufficient drainage. Thus the water was not turned on by the authorities for several years (P. Boudon).

"barbaric" actions of the inhabitants at Pessac, and yet, according to the supreme dialectician, these barbarians were still "right."

The final ideas which Le Corbusier develops in *Urbanisme* concern the actual functioning of "A Contemporary City," and it is here that he emerges as a neutral technologist. Most of these ideas are connected with transportation around the slogan "A city built for speed is built for success." Basically, he divides up different speeds and types of traffic and arranges them on different levels so that they can cross without interference. We find, in section, a complex Futurist city with all sorts of traffic interpenetrating and even, like the Futurists, a suicidal airport located in the center of office towers. The functional motives behind a "A Contemporary City" are three: to decongest the city center, increase density and circulation, and create more open, green space. The forms that result from these motives are straight lines and right angles interspersed with flowing, irregular greenery [fig. 87]. To characterize the result in a way he would have hated, it is rather like the standard Beaux Arts city plan with radial axes and symmetrical gateways, *Arcs de Triomphes*, surrounded by a green belt and eaten into, on one side, by English landscape gardening (which was to be the area reserved for future expansion). The "brains," the businessmen, were in the center in their cruciform, sixty-story glass and steel towers of omniscience.

To the left were their cultural institutions, to the right their industry. Above and below the business center two different

87. A Contemporary City, 1922–25. Some of the main ideas presented polemically by this plan were the separation of the four basic city functions, the separation of vehicular and pedestrian traffic, the superblock, and the city in the park raised on *pilotis* or stilts.

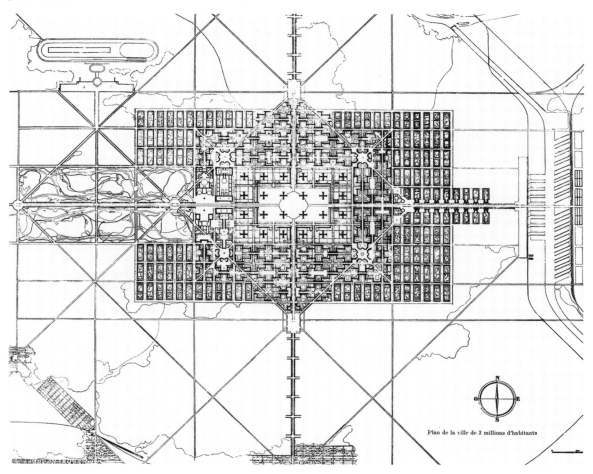

Plan de la ville de 3 millions d'habitants

classes of worker were housed: the elite businessmen in indented blocks of commodious apartments, and the less powerful in lower superblocks of freehold maisonettes [fig. 74]. This built-in class distinction supervised by a managerial elite had certain affinities with corporate Fascism even though Le Corbusier denied any political commitment or ideology. In a sense, it is the apotheosis of an idealized business world where *harmony* was to be achieved through economic competition, not exploitation or conflict. Everybody was to gain, even through the method of finance. Thus the urban land would be redistributed, foreign capital would be attracted for investment in new buildings, and the increase in land values would pay in profits for everyone.

In this benevolent pragmatism we can see Le Corbusier's hope (which he shared with other liberal architects like Gropius and Mies) of escaping from conventional political thinking and alternatives. When CIAM (Congrès Internationaux d'Architecture Moderne) was formed in 1928, it put as one of its main points a theory of land reform which straddled many political positions and was no doubt written by Le Corbusier.

> This redistribution of the land, the indispensable preliminary basis for any town planning, must include the just division between owners and the community of the *unearned increment* resulting from works of joint interest.

In other words, one would redistribute the land (communist), but one would still have owners (capitalist), plus an increase in profit due to larger densities (pragmatic), which would be divided equally between owners and the community (socialist, anarchist). It is not surprising that Le Corbusier and CIAM were accused of every political sin in the book. Their apolitical politics consisted in trying to do all positive things at once, without having bloodshed, class war, or an erosion of freedom—an outcome which if pragmatically difficult was nonetheless desirable.

Judging His Urbanism

Le Corbusier's whole life was affected for better and worse by his "ideal" city plans starting in 1922. He offered them up for the next forty years to many cities, without being commissioned or paid, and he started to believe his own rhetoric that they were the only way to avoid revolution, save a machine civilization, and bring harmony to it. In many ways they predicted and brought into being a rationalized version of massive urban renewal based on the automobile, and have been (mis)used by developers and planners to destroy many historic cities. Apologists have said blaming Le Corbusier for the vulgarized versions of his plans is like blaming Mozart for Muzak. This is not a very apt parallel, but it makes the point that no new city plan ever lived up to his utopian ideals of being completely in a park and being built entirely at a stroke.

Given the importance of the ideal city for Le Corbusier, and the twentieth century, one might point out the unlikely origin of its birth because this explains some of its drawbacks. As Le Corbusier was fond of telling the story, "The Contemporary City for Three Million" was conceived overnight as an accident. The head of the city planning section of the Salon d'Automne asked Le Corbusier to collaborate on an exhibition, no doubt because of his connection to the art world and his writings in *L'Esprit Nouveau*. "What do you mean by urbanism?" asked Le Corbusier. "Well it's a sort of street art—for shops, shop signs, and so on; it includes such things as the glass knobs on the stair ramps of houses." "Fine," said Le Corbusier, "I will design you a monumental fountain and behind it I will put a town of three million inhabitants." For the next several months, working with his cousin Pierre Jeanneret at night, they churned out a 100-square-meter diorama for the Salon d'Automne, giving birth to a city of three million, but carefully subtracted of its monumental fountain.

LC was proud of this joke, turning the request for street furniture into a total urbanism, but on whom does it fall? The hubris of trying to invent a revolution in city planning, overnight, speaks for itself and, of course, no one would have paid it the slightest attention unless it had been beautifully presented, with compelling images and argument. Essentially an abstract diagram for a flat site, it attempted to turn the congested radial city into a decongested concentric city, where the rings are turned into rectangles bisected by high-speed traffic. The analytical and statistical diagrams tell the story and, in retrospect, reveal what was lacking in Modern city planning: an understanding of the real geometry of the city. After the work of Benoit Mandelbrot, on *The Fractal Geometry of Nature*, and several studies that show that growing cities

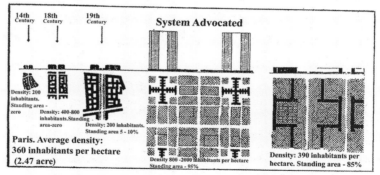

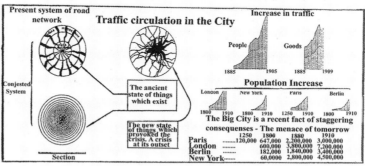

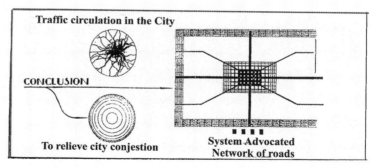

88. Système Préconisé. Old and new, ideal cities contrasted, in scale, traffic, density, growth, and open space. The ideal city of LC, because of its massive tall buildings, will have 85 percent open space; basically it is a gridded landscape, not a continuous urban area. But this revealing drawing is of the existing radial city, growing out in chaotic lines, a black cancerous blot on nature. LC did not have eyes that could see the new fractal geometry of nature, and find this emergent order beautiful and healthy. Rather, he sought to mix (1) the radial tentacles, black cancer, with (2) the concentric circles to produce (3) the synthesis to the right—"irrefutable" logic, as he saw it.

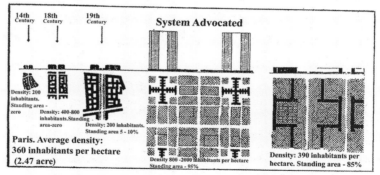

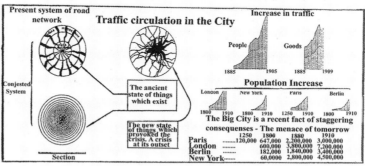

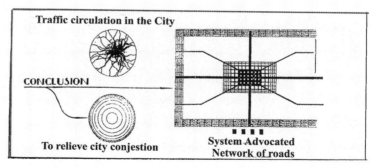

also have a fractal geometry, we now have eyes which can see it was Le Corbusier who was blind to the truth, not his critics [fig. 88].

If one takes a scientific point of view, which LC continually invoked, then it has to be said that the emergent organization of cities, at all scales, shows a subtle fractal order that is much more rich than a Platonic geometry. This truth he never understood, partly because fractal theory and the computer were not around to aid him and partly because he was so committed to the imposition of a simple order. Throughout his life he continued to impose on real historic cities a very coarse pattern, as if he were Louis XIV and Picasso combined [fig. 89]. In order to build his plans, one

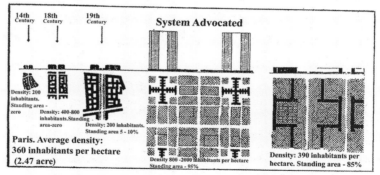

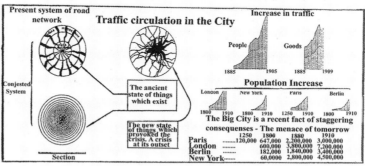

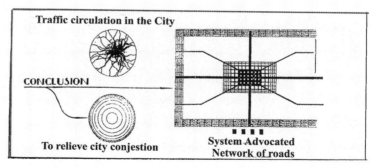

149

Le Corbusier: The Hero of the Heroic Period 1917–28

89. Plan Voisin for the center of Paris, 1925. The application of the Contemporary City to the north bank, just above the Île de la Cité, shows eighteen cruciform skyscrapers, a business center, and surrounding lower housing blocks, taking over an area north of the Louvre and about fourteen times the size of this, the biggest historical structure. A few monuments were preserved, but the city fabric was exploded in scale. As Asian examples have shown, the capital and social control necessary to realize such destruction and rebuilding would have entailed either a superstate or a super-corporation—such as Disney.

part necessitated absolute dictatorship (or at least the Disney Corporation) and the other a great artist. Thankfully cities are not like this. His remark at Pessac, "life is right, the architect wrong," might have been a premonition of a new type of urbanism, one that grows its own kind of order. What would twentieth-century urbanism have been like if he had had more realistic urban theories? The interim judgment has to be that his city planning was based on a beautiful but misconceived idea that the city should be a simple, gridded, landscaped park safe for high-speed travel. It was an aesthetic idea, a noble one, and curiously, as we will see in the case of Chandigarh, not a bad one for the first growth of an entirely new city. But, as Jane Jacobs was to argue, it is not how cities actually work or grow economically.

L'Art Décoratif d'Aujourd'hui

Another book Le Corbusier published in 1925, also constructed from articles dashed off in *L'Esprit Nouveau*, was in many ways more sensible. It proposed a revolution in taste, in daily living, in furniture, clothing, and utensils, and was called, paradoxically, *L'Art décoratif d'aujourd'hui*. The paradox, as our polemicist noted, was that for various reasons decorative art today *must* be undecorated.

His argument, although passionate, circular, and repetitive—as one would expect of missiles fired off from the front line—dealt with key issues that still engage and perplex us. First was the "hurricane" sweeping through folk culture, or what remains of vernacular life, the "virus" of bad taste and commercial kitsch, the mass culture of the West that was killing authentic peasant cultures everywhere, especially in the East, Greece, Serbia, and Turkey. This mass culture could be the result of a neutral invention, as in the cinema and phonograph; or it could be economic, as in the case of peasant vases being replaced by cheap tin cans. The result of both was often kitsch deceit—the decorative bric-a-brac covering most all mass-produced items [fig. 90]. What is inevitable, he says, is that Darwinian competition destroys all folk culture and handicraft in its way.

Secondly, he argued, this machine production was actually producing a new kind of beauty, if only we had eyes and mind to see it. Pushing the ideas of Hermann Muthesius and Adolf Loos to an extreme, Le Corbusier contends that the machine age is creating a geometric beauty that is more precise, elegant, and well

90. A hurricane of decorative kitsch produced by the industrialist, who says that "for an acceptable price I can only produce junk. But decoration will save me: let us cover *everything* with decoration. Let us hide the junk beneath decoration; decoration hides flaws, blemishes, all defects" (*L'Art décoratif d'aujourd'hui*, 55).

91. Educated taste: "the enjoyment of life by a sophisticated clientele. As a result of fashions, the publication of books, and the assiduous efforts of a whole generation of decorators, this clientele has seen its tastes sharply awakened to matters connected with art" (*L'Art décoratif d'aujourd'hui*, 91; photo from 93).

L'ART DÉCORATIF 93

City-National-Bank de Tuscaloosa. U.-S.

de satisfaire aux joies de vivre d'une clientèle cultivée. Par l'effet des modes, des campagnes livresques, des efforts assidus de toute une génération de décorateurs, celle-ci a vu ses goûts fortement éveillés par les choses de l'art. Il existe aujourd'hui un vif intérêt esthétique et le goût d'un art contemporain répondant à des exigences infiniment plus raffinées et à un esprit neuf. Donc une évolution caractéristique vers des tendances d'esprit nouveau;

Saderne, Paris.

proportioned than beauties of the past (except for the Parthenon). This notion of progress in the arts, and a hierarchy of value leading to it, was as shocking to the French public as the first proposition that industry is killing traditional culture. But, even if one did not value precise, abstract shapes such as ship propellers more than decorated utensils, Le Corbusier had a fallback position. There were many good mass-produced products that were anonymous, functional, economic, and in good taste—such as luggage from Hermès, filing cabinets from America, or spats from Saderne, Paris [fig. 91].

In effect, Le Corbusier is dealing with something he usually disparages, the growth of taste, the importance of fashion and learning. The main reason for his accepting taste, in this book and the next one, on painting, is that he believed, following Adolf Loos, that cultural evolution was leading in the right direction—his taste, no ornament. Most importantly, the elite, the arbiters of taste, the captains of art and architecture, as it were, understood the higher languages—those of science, mathematics, and harmonic form.

They were the *grand initiés* of a new scientific/cosmic culture.

These three basic arguments are buttressed with moral ones, such as the idea, beloved by Modernists, that the machine inevitably leads to a more egalitarian society.

> There already exists, and it will increase, the consequences of the crisis which separates the premachinist society from the new machine age society. Culture has taken a step forward and the hierarchical tradition of decoration has collapsed. Gilding is fading out and the slums will not wait to be abolished. Certainly it seems that we are working toward the establishment of a simple and economic *human scale* . . . The palace of the single man no longer exists. Luxury no longer resides with Aubusson carpets, but is elevated now into the mind. The workers' housing already provides a few beautiful and healthy spaces, and the bathroom enters into everyday usage; first class in the metro differs from second only by four sous; the bus stop is a democratic place where men both in bully's cap and topcoat queue up; taking off his cap, the man says with confidence, "Sir, can I have a light please?"

This ideal of social liberation, obtained through the machine, was shared by many artists of the time, for instance those of de Stijl. They saw that the machine's large-scale effect was to realign institutions along functional rather than class lines, and that machine production tended to be antipathetic to conventional decorative forms of hierarchical display. The whole of *Decorative Art Today* (not translated into English until 1987) was devoted to proving that decorative art could not exist today and that designers must search for its contemporary equivalent: "equipment" or standardized, industrial objects, which had their own type of beauty. This beauty resulted from a pure search after function, and, if the search were successful, then objects would emerge which were as clear and aesthetically pleasing as the laws of nature, geometrical bodies, seashells, and all visual manifestations of cosmic truths. Ironically, however, much of Le Corbusier's argument is spent in putting these objects in their place—a position of restraint and discretion *below* that of great art, a place in the background where they will not usurp attention, where they can function unnoticed as silent, dutiful servants.

Decorative art is an imprecise term by which we denote the whole of human *object-members.* These respond with a certain exactitude to clearly established needs which are clearly objective. Need-types, function-types, therefore object-types and furniture-types. The human object-member is a docile servant. A good servant is discreet and self-effacing to leave his master free. Decorative art is equipment, beautiful equipment.

The silent-butler view of functioning objects, the romance of the English, was first proposed by Loos about twenty years earlier, and Le Corbusier has some fun pointing out that it is more moral to treat an *objet-type* as a slave than a living person. In all his four revolutionary tracts he gives countless examples of the new equipment which modern life had created: "its fountain pen, its eversharp pencil, its typewriter, its telephone, its admirable office furniture, its plate-glass and its 'Innovation' trunks, the safety razor and the briar pipe, the bowler hat and the limousine." Aside from a functional beauty which was anonymous, this equipment importantly set a standard based on human scale.

When the typewriter was invented, typing paper was standardized; this standardization had a considerable repercussion on furniture, it established a module, that of the commercial format is not an arbitrary measure. Rather, let us appreciate the wisdom (the anthropocentric mean) that established it. In all objects of universal usage, individual fantasy recedes in front of the human fact.

Le Corbusier backs up his arguments with a list of common, anthropomorphic dimensions which typing paper supposedly introduced into many different areas such as books, photography, magazines, and kitchen tables. Although parts of the argument could be disputed, its overall import was undoubtedly true: utilitarian objects of everyday life introduce a relative anonymity and standardization based on human dimensions. This has found recognition today in the fields of industrial design, ergonomics, anthropometrics, Le Corbusier's own Modulor system, and a host of sciences which study basic human measurements and relative standards.

des minutes précieuses, occupent une place très grande ou même
restreinte dans les vingt-quatre heures de ma journée déjà si
courte. Je prétends au droit d'être sévère pour ces objets qui ne
servent pas, qui sont superflus, qui ne sont pas essentiels.

Section d'un câble.

∗

Dans la nature, dans l'enchaînement des événements, partout
— je le sais bien — se dresse l'inexplicable :
« Tout sert »,
« Tout est émouvant »,
« Tout est inexplicable ». Entendu!

ESPRIT DE VÉRITÉ   177

L'inexplicable des causes. Mais partout, dans la nature comme
dans l'événement, se trouve l'explication de l'enchaînement.
Remontant jusque-là où s'arrête notre prise de conscience, nous

pouvons trouver les raisons. Plus nous remontons haut, plus
nous sommes satisfaits. L'on mesure que tout s'ordonne selon des
principes conformes au général et que tout organisme est un
certain point d'étape de la ligne des variantes autour de l'axe
12

92. The Beauty of Truth—Organization. Industry, a cross section of a
cable, and a patterned fish all show
the tendency of the universe to self-
organize toward a "principle consis-
tent with the whole" (*L'Art décoratif
d'aujourd'hui*, 174–75).

As in *Towards a New Architecture*, another aspect of morality
consists in scrapping objects when they cease to function:

> Useful objects in our lives have liberated more slaves than
> heretofore. They are themselves the slaves, the valets and ser-
> vants. Would you take them as confidants? One sits on them,
> one works on them, one makes use of them, uses them up:
> once used they are replaced.

But again, pure utility is not the only criterion to be considered, and in this first chapter (titled "Iconologie, Iconolatres,
Iconoclastes") Le Corbusier argues for an iconology which is *appropriate* to its subject. The ostrich plumes of Louis XIV were appropriate to his role as a despot, whereas their use today by
courtesans, antiquarians, and, he is delighted to say, professors, is
an anachronism. Contrary to this is appropriate iconology.

> Lenin was seated in the Café La Rotunda on a cane chair;
> he had paid for his coffee twenty centimes, a tip of one
> sou. He drank with a small cup of white porcelain. He wore
> a bowler hat and a brilliant and sleek white collar. He
> wrote away the hours on typewriter paper. His ink-pot was
> sleek and round, made of bottle glass.
>
> He is preparing himself to govern a hundred million men.

The conclusion: that correct iconology, like Lenin, will conquer the world. And yet, given all these moral, economic, and
deterministic arguments, Le Corbusier has to admit to a horrible
paradox: decoration is nevertheless being misused by almost
everyone: to deceive and flatter, to distract people in their loneliness, to impress social snobs, and to camouflage basic mistakes.
Horrible, most horrible, and that is why one must have *iconoclasm*.
His teacher Auguste Perret had said, "Decoration always hides a
mistake in construction." Proceeding dialectically, Le Corbusier
opposes to the camouflaged dandy a wonderful concoction, the
"ALL-NAKED MAN."

> The all-naked man does not wear an embroidered waistcoat;
> he wishes to think. The all-naked man is a person who is

normally constituted, who has no need of trinkets . . . He does not worship fetishes. He is not a collector, he is not a museum conservator. If he likes to instruct himself, it is to arm himself. It's to equip himself to attack the tasks of the day. If he likes, occasionally, to look around and behind himself, it is to seize the "why" of things. And encountering harmony, that which is a creation of his spirit, he receives a shock which is moving, elevating, encouraging, which gives him a support for life.

In Love with Cosmic Evolution

The argument in *L'Art décoratif d'aujourd'hui* is, in one respect, the most radical of Le Corbusier's because it proposes a new iconology and culture based on unfolding truth. His creation, the "all-naked man," obviously the ancestor of Loos's ornamentless intellectual, sustains himself not on the myths and religions of the past that are no longer credible. Instead, there is an emergent industrial folklore of popular science and cosmology that can form the icons for a new culture. Here the argument culminates bringing together mechanical and cultural evolution in the form of the educated consumer and those initiated to the mysteries of the universe.

> We are at the dawn of the machine age. A new consciousness disposes us to look for a different aesthetic satisfaction from that afforded by the bud carved on the capitals in churches. We have learned about such things from science books and have a much more extensive and precise scientific knowledge of them. We are brought face to face with the phenomenon of the cosmos through treatises, documentary pictures, and graphs. We derive the same emotion from it as the shepherd, but our investigations go deeper and introduce us to the mathematical basis of the world.

Besides mathematics, how is our sensibility more advanced, how is it formed?

> Cinema, books [and magazines such as] *Je sais tout, Science et Vie*, have replaced by their documentation all the poetics of yesterday. The mystery of nature, which we attack scientifically and hardly exhaust, always grows deeper and more profound

the more we advance. In fact it becomes our new culture. As for esoteric symbols, we still have them, for those initiates of today, in the curves which represent forces, in the formulae which explain natural phenomena.

A scientific culture, or rather a culture in touch with the cosmos through science, frees us from "cosmic dread" and leads us to the "pure realm of works of art." In passages such as these, Le Corbusier, returning to his youth, Schuré, Theosophy, and the reconciliation of religion and science, finds the spiritual goal of the machine age. The idealistic argument he puts forward, quite unusual for the time, can be found peppered throughout the book, but particularly in chapter eight, "The Lesson of the Machine" [fig. 92]. Curiously, the lesson is, in the end, spiritual! How could he have reached such a strange conclusion?

For most people machinery is opposed to spirituality and freedom, but a small number of prophets have seen it in exactly the opposite terms, as liberating, creative, and representing advanced thought—or the spirit unfolding. From Le Corbusier and the de Stijl artists to Teilhard de Chardin and Marshall McLuhan, there is this other idealistic, evolutionary argument. Here its outgrowth from, and superiority to, humanity is celebrated. In Le Corbusier's parable that follows, one can hear the echo of Zarathustra preaching the superman, the machine as the enabling god.

The machine is conceived within the spiritual framework, which man has constructed for himself and not in the realm of fantasy . . . The machine is all geometry. Geometry is our greatest creation and we are enthralled by it . . . Man has drawn himself up like a giant, he has forged himself a tool. He no longer works with his hands. His spirit gives the order. He has delegated to the machine the work of his clumsy and unskillful hands. Freed, his spirit works freely. On square paper he dreams. Man has learned how to make things work for him . . . "Man's activity," concluded Paul, "is like that of a God—in the realm of perfection."

In this part of "The Lesson of the Machine," Le Corbusier is recounting a parable of Paul, "the Bohemian poet" who discovers the machine. "Paul" is clearly the Charles-Edouard Jeanneret of

1908, and, in biblical and sexual metaphors, we hear of his conversion on the Road to Damascus.

> His enthusiasm overflowed and he knew the beauty of the machine.

> The sensation of pleasure that he received was that of recognizing an organized entity. Organized like living beings, like a powerful or delicate species of animal, that is *never* wrong since its workings are absolute. He pictured the churches abandoned and the lively spirits descended to the place of genesis where beings are remade.

The churches are abandoned—beings are remade. The born-again experience, common to Christianity *and* to Modernism, is framed in terms of "knowing" that machines are making our activity "like that of a God." Le Corbusier has transferred his previous love of nature to the machine: because of its "power, harmony, geometry, and organization," because it is "bringing about a reformation of the spirit across the world." In some respects, it is actually *better* than nature.

> *Ordered!* Let us reflect for a moment on the fact that there is nothing in nature that, as seen objectively by our eyes, approaches the pure perfection of the humblest machine (the moon is not round; the tree trunk is not straight; only very occasionally are the waters smooth as a mirror; the rainbow is a fragment; livings beings, with very few exceptions, do not conform to the simple geometrical shapes, etc.) . . . The machine thus appears to us the goddess of beauty . . . Gods! Geometry and the gods sit side by side (an old human story, truth to tell, the basic and original human story).

Le Corbusier was to regret the phrase he became associated with—"the house is a machine for living in"—and the mechanolotry that this chapter espouses so passionately, but if we interpret the deeper love as that for cosmic evolution, then the argument becomes more plausible. What is really being celebrated is not the machine so much as the evolution toward higher states of organization. That word, coupled with the notion that the machine is "a clear organism," recurs like a litany, and it leads him to attack the fetishism of the machine in Futurism and other movements.

> Art has no business resembling a machine (the error of Constructivism) . . . a new desire: an aesthetic of purity, of precision, of expressive relationships setting in motion the mathematical mechanisms of our spirit: a spectacle and a cosmogony.

It is obviously possible to criticize the naiveté behind much of the argument that mechanical and cultural evolution are both inevitably progressive and related to each other. Yet it is true, within the purposes of culture the goal of production *is* often idealistic (when it is not cynical): to improve quality and performance. This drive is conceived within an evolutionary context and seen as a spiritual truth, and thus *L'Art décoratif d'aujourd'hui* can be seen as a positive step forward in Le Corbusier's development of a cosmic architecture. Furthermore, it proposes a complete revolution in daily living and metaphysics that was to animate *L'Esprit Nouveau* (to make the point clearer, we might translate the magazine as *The New Spirituality*). The modern urban man, the all-naked man, was to nourish himself on a diet befitting both a monk and a scientist, an athlete and scholar. The "equipment" which Le Corbusier designed to fill out this daily life inevitably had overtones of the laboratory, hospital, gymnasium, and monastery. These were the metaphors which counted, the metaphors of truth.

How was all this idealistic philosophy translated into the new decorative undecorated art? Not surprisingly, with the help of a thoroughly modern young woman who worked in the office, an independent spirit who was attracted to new ideas and expressed them forcefully. Charlotte Perriand and Le Corbusier together designed a series of chairs, tables, and built-in cupboards that were meant to furnish the modern apartment. These have an elegance and attention to the contrast of fine materials, such as calf skin with chrome, that show the presence of a feminine sensibility. In fact, Charlotte Perriand remained a very close friend of Le Corbusier for the rest of his life, breaking off intimate contact only in the early 1940s when she and Pierre Jeanneret sided with the Resistance while Le Corbusier worked for Vichy. Except for this break, which was later healed, she remained one of the "*fidèles,*"

93. Salon d'Automne, 1929, designed with Charlotte Perriand. Storage walls of chrome, glass, mirror, and back-lit translucent plastic divide up the space and contain the "clutter" of possessions.

those loyal friends whom Le Corbusier characterized with such key words as *"brave-type," "solide," "costaud"* (his passion for classification knew no bounds).

The work on the "equipment" started in 1927 and culminated in an exhibition room designed for the Salon d'Automne in 1929 [fig. 93].

As in all his work, Le Corbusier starts from basic functional requirements that he takes to be constant and universal. In this case they are the basic postures of the human body and basic, daily activities such as reading, talking, and reclining. From these requirements, or "object-members," he derives the "object-types" or "standards": the easy chair for reading and relaxing; the *"basculant,"* a reworking of the British Officer's chair, for active discussions and "demonstrating a thesis"; and the form-fitting *chaise longue* for reclining [fig. 94]. Not surprisingly, these three chairs are modern versions of older prototypes. Since the intention was to find the standard and perfect it, this was to be expected. It is interesting to see how Perriand and Le Corbusier have extended the inherent metaphors of each prototype.

94 a, b, c. Three chairs, 1927–29, with Charlotte Perriand. *Grand confort, chaise longue,* and *basculant* are still in production.

For instance, the traditional easy chair of the club and the gentleman's library, the *grand confort,* becomes more heavy, plushy, squashy, and rotund. It has five bulging, black, rectangular cushions squeezed up by thin glistening chromium tubes. These tubes embrace, even pinch, the cushions, offering them up to the human bottom as the essence of "grand comfort." The *basculant,* with its pivoting backrest, is as taut as a bow; in fact its leather armrests are strung tightly by springs. The basic division, as in all the chairs, between heavy structure and body support is kept, with the former being articulated in chrome tubes, the latter in calf skin. Visually and conceptually we have a basic separation of functions. The overall feeling is of delicate fur being suspended within a frame of precise machinery, "a chair is a machine for sitting in" being Le Corbusier's explicit metaphor. In fact, this particular machine can be physically painful if one makes the wrong move and activates the pivoting backrest. On the other hand, the *chaise longue* is very comfortable, being molded in shape to the reclining posture. The softened Z shape, a very sculptural form which gives a feeling of embrace, is underlined by the continuous flowing line of the chromium tube, a reworking in metal of effects previously obtained in bentwood. Because this Z shape is further supported at four points by a substructure, the metaphor becomes one of offering up the reclining body for sacrifice or display. It is as if the body is being propped up on fingertips like a precious jewel. The ostensible function of the substructure is to allow for different reclining positions.

In the case of the standard storage wall, the intention has been to provide a thick movable partition which zigzags in section so that it can be used from both sides and so that it can liberate the house from clutter—rather like Japanese storage space built from screens. In the "Manual of the Dwelling," 1923, Le Corbusier states his case for cleanliness and purgation with a pugilistic kind of irony.

> Demand bare walls in your bedroom, your living room and your dining room. Built-in fittings to take the place of much of the furniture which is expensive to buy, takes up much room and needs looking after . . .

> Demand concealed or diffused lighting.

Demand a vacuum cleaner.

Buy only practical furniture and never buy decorative "pieces." If you want to see bad taste, go into the houses of the rich. Put only a few pictures on your walls and none but good ones.

The true collector of pictures arranges them in a cabinet and hangs on the wall the particular painting he wants to look at; but your walls are a riot of all manner of things.

Art Fills the Emptiness Within

This selective attitude toward art brings us to the last of the four related revolutions proposed by 1925, *La Peinture Moderne*, written with Ozenfant and the original name Jeanneret. In this book, many of the previous arguments of Purism are extended and given final formulation. For instance, the idea that mechanical evolution leads at once toward the universal and the geometrical culminates in the slogan that "man is a geometrical animal."

His spirit has created the geometry; the geometry responds to our profound need to order. The works which move us the most are those where geometry is perceptible. [fig. 95]

In this light nature is again seen as a rather imperfect artist, "disorderly in aspect," who realizes greatness only in happy moments when he accidentally produces such perfect bodies as the crystal.

The spirit of man and nature find a factor in common, an area of agreement, in the crystal just as in the cell, where the order is perceptible to the point where it justifies the human laws of explaining nature which the reason has been pleased to impose.

This jumble of ideas, this linking of empiricism and rationalism, is interesting insofar as it shows the authors' intention of basing art on science. An almost scientific determinism is advanced, reminiscent of McLuhan's views, to prove that there can be only one type of modern sensibility conditioned by the new technologies. "Steel has revolutionized society" and created an environ-

95. *Nature morte de L'Esprit Nouveau*, 1924. Numerous objects superimposed in side elevation and plan like an engineering drawing. The rectangular geometry and regulating lines discipline the whole, giving a very static and calm feeling. These are the "higher," more "intellectual" emotions to which the Purists appealed.

ment where everything is based on the right angle; therefore man has to be a geometrical animal. Photography, cinema, and the press have rendered the need for representational art obsolete: stories can now be told better in other media, while art can concentrate on its own ends of being a pure, *emotional* language. Modern life, with its basis in science, measurement, and exactitude, has created a new superior breed of man, whose reason reigns supreme, who is more complex and intelligent, and who achieves the highest state of development—self-knowledge.

> We understand for want of a better word, by *Hieratism*, the state of the mind which a civilization reaches when, leaving the empirical period, it becomes conscious of that which previously it only felt . . . *Hieratism* is the age of knowledge, knowledge of itself, moment of knowledge acquired after a long

period of research. It is thus the moment when man is no longer pushed about by exterior forces or by pure instincts and is in a position to guide himself and choose among the technical means those which permit him to satisfy his spiritual needs of this new intellectual state . . . when Egyptian priests had their hieratic types sculptured they knew that what was being fabricated was a machine to provoke sacred emotions.

The authors insist that this new, Nietzschean man does not look for beauty or pleasure in art, but rather for character and emotion:

> . . . as it was put, the problem of beauty was insoluble. *The error at its basis was to give as a criterion of beauty the idea of pleasure, a final reaction altogether personal and variable . . .* judgment varies with each individual . . . all discussion based on the worth of a work of art was thus vicious . . . the Parthenon is not pleasurable to anyone. Great art is not art of agreement . . . art has the sole duty to move us . . . The Parthenon moves everyone powerfully, even those whom it displeases; what counts is the intensity of the provoked emotion.

Finally, to complete the argument for a determined, modern sensibility, the authors put forward another nineteenth-century idea, which Matthew Arnold and, again, Nietzsche had proposed.

> [Modern man] has need of the ideal certainties which previously religion gave him; doubting it now and metaphysics also, he is driven in on himself where the true world goes on within; the anguishing emptiness which nothing can fill . . . except art . . . Art will have the mission of superior distraction and it will give this exalted contentment without which the calm of the soul is impossible.

Art and culture as the substitutes for religion obviously gave these pursuits a function, or exalted importance, which they could not fulfill, and it was just after this formulation that both Ozenfant and Jeanneret gave up what amounted to their Purist religion and returned to more nourishing subjects. Jeanneret's painting had become academic and rarefied. By 1928 he introduced "objects evoking a poetic reaction" into his painting—specifically the female

form—and, not coincidentally, became more interested in women.
Before turning to this next stage of his life, it is appropriate to conclude the Purist development with a discussion of his two buildings
in which it culminated: the villas at Garches and Poissy near Paris.

Two Ideal Villas—Perfected Modernism

Both villas were constructed for wealthy, enlightened clients who
had connections with art and industry and who hence could be
seen on the one hand as elite "captains of industry" and on the
other hand as those with an acute self-knowledge: collectors of the
most modern art. The villa at Garches, 1926–27, was inhabited by
Gertrude Stein's brother, who built part of the streetcar system of
San Francisco and whose wife was one of the first collectors of
Matisse. The Villa Savoye at Poissy, 1929–31, was built as a luxurious weekend retreat for clients who, according to Le Corbusier,
had no preconception as to what a new architecture could be. It
would be claiming too much to say that these clients would have
subscribed to the philosophy of *Hieratism*, but at least Le Corbusier
could see them as examples of the modern sensibility in its
different aspects. And one can claim that the villas represent this
philosophy since they are culminations of a system which Le
Corbusier, by then, fully understood and had perfected. In this
sense too they are "ideal" examples of high art.

In formal terms, the two villas can be seen as abstract cubes
of space in which various geometric elements are freely disposed
as in a Purist painting. The three-dimensional grid, this Cartesian
coordinate system, exists as an ideal order throughout the buildings even where elements are left out or filled in over the column
and floor grid. The idea, developed from the 1914 Dom-ino system, gave birth to several new principles, which Le Corbusier partially enunciated as the "Five Points of a New Architecture": the
house on stilts or *pilotis*, which frees the ground for circulation;
the roof garden allowed by the flat roof; the free plan and facade
allowed by the independent frame structure; and the ribbon window, which gives more light than that in the load-bearing wall.
In addition to these innovations, there are several characteristic
elements found in these two buildings which Le Corbusier would
often compose in abstract space: the ramp or bridge, the double-
height space, the scissors and spiral staircase, the curved bathroom

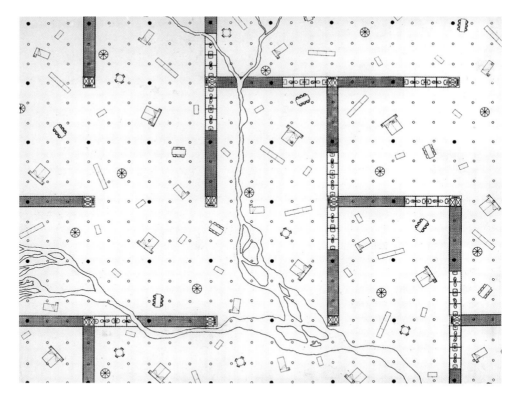

96. Archizoom, *No Stop City, a Climatic Universal City*, 1970. Several elements such as structure and services freely composed in an endless Cartesian space—an extension of Le Corbusier's urban planning of the Ville Radieuse.

or curved solarium (a tertiary space). One might consider these nine elements of a new architecture as comparable to the *objet-types* in a Purist painting. They are invented for both their techno-logical and aesthetic potential and then used as fixed words in an abstract system of Cartesian space. This idea can perhaps best be seen in its most recent, extreme form, the *No Stop City, a Climatic Universal City* by the Archizoom Group in Florence [fig. 96]. These designers have taken Le Corbusier's Platonic approach to its limit and imagined a continuous grid in a space extending everywhere in the world and filled with perfected, beautiful servicing elements. The difference, if there is any, is that Le Corbusier smashes his elements into and through each other to produce what I would call "compaction composition" [fig. 97], whereas Archizoom leaves the elements separate.

Thus in Le Corbusier's architecture, holes of space are cut violently through floors, columns are placed very close to walls, curved partitions jut into rectangular rooms, and so on. Compaction composition is very close, as a method, to collage, inasmuch as the superimposition of elements obscures parts,

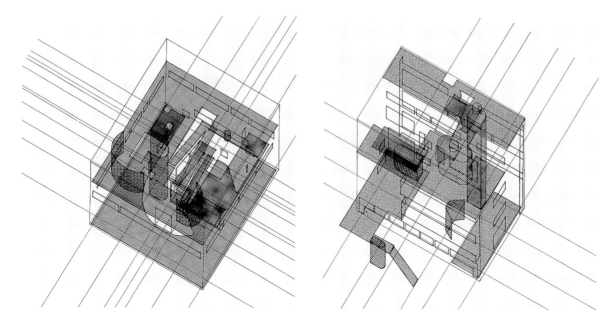

97 a, b. Schematic analysis of the villas at Garches and Poissy, drawn by Ken Yeang. The nine elements referred to on pages 165–66 are juxtaposed in an abstract grid of space, an example of compaction composition. Diagonal lines show the column grid, the structure, projected onto the four horizons as an ideal cosmic orientation—the ideal square in the case of Poissy. On the front and back Garches shows alternating rhythmical bays with harmonious proportions: 2, 1, 2, 1, 2. Poissy has a steady A, A, A rhythm broken in the middle. As Colin Rowe has shown, both villas have Palladian precedents, but as these two drawings show, the basic ideal geometry is countered by secondary incidents. The idea of these contrasts was first learned by Jeanneret visiting Pompeian houses and then in his Purist paintings. The juxtaposition of geometry and overlapping elements creates his method: compaction composition.

instead of allowing them to be seen through (except in the unique case of glass). Hence when one wanders through a Le Corbusier building one finds a succession of elements partly hidden and partly revealed. This accounts for their excitement and suspense. Le Corbusier once remarked that if a building looked out on a beautiful landscape one should sometimes block the general view so as to make its sudden appearance all the more surprising—a revelation. The monks of La Tourette will conduct the visitor through the building on a preferred path showing all the elements overlapping and changing relationship in a symphony of movement. This is most effective when the elements are pure in form and few in number.

Garches was originally designed for the Steins and Madame Gabrielle de Monzie, who was estranged from her husband. The idealism of the villa consists not only in the way it integrates two families into a unity and perfects a Purist system, but also in the way it addresses nature and technology. For instance, the villa was often called "Les Terrasses" by the architect, and the initial schemes showed an elaborate promenade of walkways punching through walls, looking over trees to catch the best views and dramatize movement. A racetrack at the top was proposed (a bit too ideal for Madame Stein, who vowed she would not even climb the outdoor spiral stair). The drawings show the sun and greenery

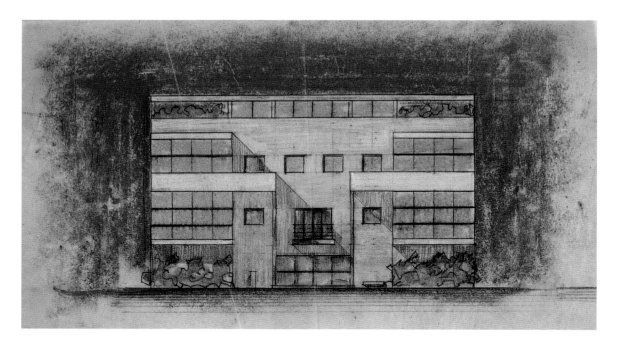

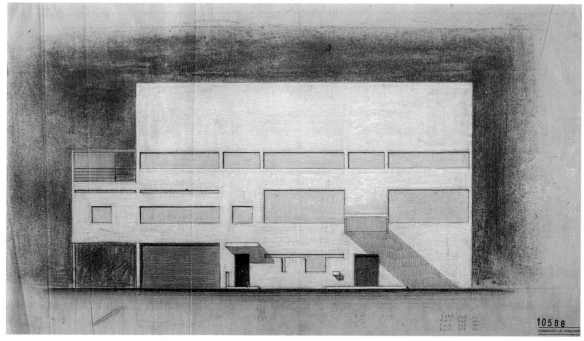

10588
FONDATION LE CORBUSIER

98, 99. Two early studies for the Villa Stein, Garches (actually Vaucresson, next to Garches, but Le Corbusier always called it by its up-market neighbor), 1926 (FLC; photograph by Tim Benton). The earlier one shows the emergence of alternating bay rhythms accentuated by dark glass volumes: A, b, A', b, A. The later, almost final version, shows these rhythms abstracted into the planar wall, cantilevered from the interior columns. In both cases we can infer the column grid and Golden Section proportions from the facades. The later drawing is a much more refined and ideal version of these ideal mathematics.

penetrating everywhere as if the building were an ideal health camp. They also show how Le Corbusier conceptualized an ideal reinforced-concrete technology: seamless, all-over, homogeneous, the perfect sculptural material [figs. 98, 99]. No joints, no details, no drip moldings! Just the perfect material to house people and frame nature with white planes. Here and at Poissy the Dom-ino system becomes an ideal reality to be photographed in black and white and reproduced in the world's press as the essence of Modern Architecture. These two buildings became *the* images of Modernism for exhibitions such as that at the Museum of Modern Art in 1932 on the International Style. In short, Le Corbusier's idealism, enunciated so many times since his letters of 1908, finally brought the greatest of rewards. He established the major code of Modern Architecture: the seamless, Purist abstraction framing nature.

And yet the way he had to do this involved expensive deceit. Because the technology was not generally available to build homogeneous white machines, until Richard Meier came along forty years later, he had to use brick and concrete block construction, cemented, plastered, and painted to look as if it were a continuous material. I mention this not to criticize his idealism, but rather to point up its extremity, the pains he went to. Today architects are again searching for a supermaterial that can curve walls into floors, ceiling, and roof all at once, and much energy will again be expended in the search. One should not underestimate the potency of this idealism: it is one reason Le Corbusier's book was mistranslated from *Vers une architecture* into *Towards a New Architecture*.

One approaches Les Terrasses from the north down a driveway that focuses on the service entrance and balcony above. Photographs invariably show a machine for driving next to the machine for living [fig. 100]. The north and south facades are white planes divided up by proportioned triangles on a 2-1-2-1-2 rhythm, which is also the column grid that disciplines the interior space. The feeling of an abstract rectangular order is further heightened by the blank side walls and the sequence of layered space on the south side, the garden entrance. Here is the classic view of twentieth-century architecture, a gigantic cube of space that is cut into from all sides by terraces, balconies, roof, and wall planes [figs. 101, 102]. This huge loggia looks back to both the

100. Villa Stein, Garches (Vaucresson), 1926–27, north facade. A basic symmetry punctuated by loggia entrance and black openings. Le Corbusier's Voisin automobile was often photographed with his buildings to underline the nature of "a house like a car."

101, 102. Villa Stein, garden terrace and south elevation with space flowing across white planes.

Italian villa and the ocean liner that Le Corbusier often used as sources [fig. 103] and it anticipates the next seventy years of architecture, particularly such multiplications of the genre as the new Getty Museum. The aesthetic of the building is also determined by "the five points of a new architecture": the free facade with its ribbon windows suspended from the floors, the free plan, the roof gardens, the *pilotis*, and the regulating lines.

Although Le Corbusier invariably photographed his buildings unfurnished, to heighten the effect of pure forms in relationship, they still provided a strong background even when filled with objects that are non-Purist. This can be seen in a rare photograph of Les Terrasses when it was inhabited by the Steins [fig. 104]. The photo shows that the Stein family had eclectic taste, indeed they contrasted their collection of antique Italian furniture with Matisses and an aeolian harp. And yet the heterogeneous possessions do not seem overpowered or out of place as they would in much Modern architecture. Compaction composition has provided a rich enough background to accept them more sympathetically.

The villa at Poissy is an even more ideal realization of the "five points." As well as perfecting these, it also demonstrates his other characteristic elements such as the entrance ramp (which cuts

103. *Empress of France* (Canadian Pacific), illustration from *Towards a New Architecture*. Le Corbusier captions this: "An architecture pure, neat, clear, clean and healthy."

104. Villa Stein, 1929, living room (AA). Italian furniture, antique vases that the young Jeanneret admired, and in the distance a sculpture by Matisse; contemporary photo.

Following spread:
105. Villa Savoye, Poissy, northwest of Paris, 1929–31. Classical echoes, a transformed, white entablature above a dark base in shadow, vie with uncanny ones: an alien spaceship, or as Le Corbusier put it, "a box hovering in the air." This summer house for the Savoyes seems to be moving along the flat green meadow like a centipede, a movement suggested visually by the placement of the *pilotis* flush with the sides and set back from the head.

through the middle of the grid), the curving walls of the solarium, and, above all, the *pilotis* and slab construction. In fact, for these last points it was attacked by architects such as Frank Lloyd Wright for being just a "box on stilts" and others for being an alien space capsule that had just touched down on a Virgilian landscape [figs. 105, 106]. It *is* a startling image, especially for the Paris region. A sharp pristine whiteness, a slab of brilliant ice, hovers gently over the ground, the very image of the *machine a habiter*, a manmade artifact in opposition to nature. The effect of a white cube poised above a flat green field is still startling today,

Le Corbusier: The Hero of the Heroic Period 1917–28

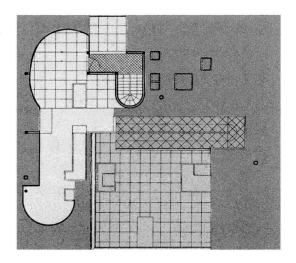

106. Villa Savoye, redrawn. An absolute square plan oriented to the four horizons, an ideal cosmic diagram.

even though the contrast has been partially destroyed by later building.

One approaches the villa by a driveway which circles around and under the first floor and between the *pilotis* in a curve, which was functionally determined by the steering radius of a car. Again the machines for living and driving are equated. Once inside the ground floor, given over to services and servants, one becomes involved in a secular version of a spiritual ascent. As drawings and photographs show, everyday objects such as a wash basin take on a ritualistic presence: one does not only wash one's hands before ascending, but carefully takes off one's coat and gloves and places them against the white canvas of the walls. The feeling is that of a Shaker house, or of entering a Japanese shrine where the removal of clothes and shoes is necessary preparation for the sacred tea ceremony [fig. 107]. Here the ritual is an ascent through metal railings and past ideal, white *pilotis* toward the light and sun, suggesting that this rite might belong to some healing, solar cult. One promenades through a sequence of primary forms and *objet-types* either by a ramp, which penetrates up through the whole building, or a curving staircase.

The first floor, surrounded entirely by a ribbon window, consists of the complete living accommodation wrapped in an L on one side of the open terrace [fig. 108]. Light and air penetrate everywhere. Direct contact with the surrounding landscape is achieved by various openings; views are framed through extra-wide picture windows, or horizontal voids. To underscore the fact that nature is

107. Villa Savoye, entrance hall. The architectural promenade through a Purist still life starts with pure forms and a few evocative elements.

108. Villa Savoye, terrace, inside and outside. The ambiguity of culture being penetrated by nature is increased by framed views of both the architecture and the landscape.

109. Villa Savoye, curves of the solarium, windbreaks for sunbathing, frame for the views, and culmination to the solar promenade.

elevated, greenery spills out of boxes on the terrace. Then one is drawn up to the culminating point, the curved walls, feminine shapes that are a memory trace of the former scheme when they enclosed Madame's bedroom. She had insisted that the living room "should not be strictly rectangular but should have some comfortable corners." However, Le Corbusier disregarded her wishes when it came to the main room and transferred them to the culmination of the route, the place where she might be nude on top of the world, sunbathing, and spiritually in touch with the sun.

If that idea sounds farfetched it nevertheless anticipates his later solar festivals for Chandigarh, those for Man, "son of the sun"; and the curves anticipate his "buttocks motif," a theme of many paintings and also Ronchamp. Le Corbusier was here celebrating the climb to the picture window overlooking nature, the architectural promenade as a ritual celebrating the cosmos. There can be no doubt that everything in this rite culminates on the final view—withheld, suggested, anticipated, and at last delivered [fig. 109].

110. Villa Savoye, bathroom of
Madame Savoye with its chaise longue
in tiles, a voluptuous podium for the
healthy body.

Le Corbusier's rhetoric is again full of tensions. While he cele-
brates the "three essential joys" of man (sun, space, greenery) and
turns them into a drama, he also claims that it is much more
healthy to live above the grass. Thus nature is at once dangerous,
"*malsaine, humide, etc. . . . ,*" and also the focus for his ritual.
Indeed, the feeling of walking through a heroic health camp is
inescapable. The bathroom, with its tiled sunken bath and reclining sofa of tiles, reminds one of Roman gymnastics [fig. 110]. And
it was the first demand of "The Manual of the Dwelling":

> Demand a bathroom looking south, one of the largest rooms in
> the house or the flat, the old drawing room for instance. One
> wall to be entirely glazed, opening if possible onto a balcony for
> sun baths; the most up-to-date fittings with a shower-bath and
> gymnastic appliances.

The rhetorical power of this building illuminates a problem
that has always intrigued me. Why did so many contemporary

architects jump from Expressionism to the International Style, from emphatic statements saying they would never compromise with utility, and the machine, to the complete celebration of both? Walter Gropius's turnabout was only the most spectacular *volte face*; there were countless others. What were the unstated reasons for the shift? The Villa Savoye suggests that it might be made without the hypocrisy that it implies because, when ones considers the villa's spiritual and aesthetic intensity, it is actually an Expressionist building. Its rhetoric and style may be rationalist, but it is really in the end a stunning white box of a new religious faith without God—a perfect receptacle for *Hieratism*. To quote again from Le Corbusier and Ozenfant's manifesto on the new painting: "Modern man has need of the ideal certainties which previously religion gave him . . . Art will have the mission of superior distraction and it will give this exalted contentment without which the calm of the soul is impossible."

A Brief Moment of Victory

With Garches and Poissy, Le Corbusier brought to fruition many of the Purist notions and architectural principles he had been developing for at least ten years. They were immediately recognized around the world as the epitome of the new architecture, and Le Corbusier was asked to give lectures in major capitals such as Moscow, São Paulo, Algiers, Stockholm, Barcelona, Brussels, and Prague. The size of his office jumped, in 1927, from the two Jeannerets, that is, Le Corbusier and his cousin Pierre, to fifteen and more. The young came from around the world to work in the atelier for little or no pay. Why? Because the prophet Corbu could not only proclaim the new religion of Modern Architecture, but build its message and attack the old guard. Here was a crusade worth joining. Students and young designers came in droves to the Paris atelier, 35 rue de Sevres, to an office set up in the corridors of an old Jesuit monastery. How appropriate the setting, how bracing, but how spartan. Here was the prophet and monk, Père Corbu as he sometimes styled himself, ministering over his acolytes in an ascetic space that could, through idealistic glasses, be seen as noble. He creates what he calls his "small army of comrades" (this is the time of collectivism) to bury the old bourgeoisie and usher in the Age of White Protestant Faith (color was permissible only as a secondary accent). Passion, commitment, destiny. It was a replay of L'Eplattenier twenty years earlier: the feeling of brotherhood, common endeavor, conquer the world. But now the new generation was not provincial but cosmopolitan, such leaders-to-be as the Japanese Maekawa and Sakakura, the Hungarian Kepes, and the Spaniard José Luis Sert.

This devoted team—"Rue de Sevres" as it was soon known—helped produce the canonic white buildings of the late 1920s and early 1930s. Spare, truthful, idealistic, and, by intention at least, communal as well as for an elite. Le Corbusier was leading the Heroic Period of Modernism and, to show it publicly, in 1927 he was given pride of place at the Weissenhof Exhibition organized by Mies van der Rohe in Stuttgart at the site's highest point. Here the other "small army" of Modernists also built their "neat, clean, and healthy" white cubes of workers' housing; architects such as Walter Gropius, Hans Scharoun, J. J. P. Oud, and Mart Stam. Collectively this exhibition established a party line, and as clear a break with the past as Alberti and Brunelleschi had made the Renaissance split from the Gothic. But now it was according to doctrine international; part spirit of the age, part conspiracy against the academy, part a social and technological change, even in part good luck.

One has to say, in retrospect, that the Modern Movement might have gone in other directions. Possibly, if the de Stijl architects had more of a say, it could have gone toward Neo-Plasticism; or, in an organic direction of Frank Lloyd Wright and Hugo Haring; or toward Expressionism, or Constructivism, or perhaps even vernacular. But it did not. Rather, the zeitgeist solidified around the International Style, somewhere between the minimalist functionalism of the Germans and Le Corbusier's Five Points. Soon, by 1930, it moved further toward a reductivist program for the *Existenzminimum*, the worker's house produced as the ultimately small cubicle. The goal was to fabricate the mass-produced house with the economy and miniaturization of a Pullman car, and not much bigger than a couple of bunk beds.

At Stuttgart Le Corbusier characteristically designed more than was asked for: apartment units that could expand and contract, for day and night use, flexible boxes of a certain elegance [figs. 111, 112]. The Five Points were enunciated here for the first time, almost as a counterpart to the Five Orders of the Ecole des Beaux-Arts. *Faire école*? They were supposed to be as universal and as teachable as any lesson by Owen Jones or the hated academic bible of Vignola. Le Corbusier showed they could be applied to mass housing as well as villas for the rich—same ribbon windows, independent structure, and gardens in the air. Unlike the German architects, willing to scale down expectations, he provided luxurious open space and architectural quality. He believed, and continued to believe, that mass housing should always be something more than ingenious economic solutions, and this belief led immediately to conflict with those who were challenging him for the leadership of the Modern Movement, its left wing, both the communists and the functionalists. Inevitably, he counterattacked. He wrote *Défense de l'architecture*, 1929, defending geometry, beauty, and the spiritual role of architecture, something he knew would be unpopular with many of his "comrades."

The situation in Europe, particularly Germany, was polarizing quickly. Whereas LC had struggled hard and fought for ten years to build a few, if brilliant, buildings and found himself the world leader of Modernism, he might slip at any moment. In 1927, as we will see, he won and then lost *the* idealistic commission of the century, for the League of Nations, a competition that was exploded apart by opposing ideologies—mostly the Traditionalists versus the Modernists (although there were other schisms). As a result of this fiasco he helped originate CIAM, the International Congress of Modern Architecture, and this soon became the Vatican of Modernism, laying down its own laws for planning and architecture as rigidly as any academy.

But, at the beginning, its idealism and creativity were more apparent: it united, under a single banner, many of the quarrelsome groups of the avant-garde. After Le Corbusier was robbed of the League of Nations competition victory, Hélène de Mandrot came to his aid in 1928 and offered her castle, La Sarraz in Switzerland, for the first meeting of CIAM. Members were invited from all parts of the world to constitute something midway between the Third International, a global communal brotherhood, and a multinational corporation. Its meetings in 1928, 1929, 1930, and 1933 would end with joint proclamations and manifestos. There is no doubt which general was leading this large "small army"; since 1908 the pen had been prepared; since 1914 it was sharpened on its first manifesto; and by 1922 it had perfected the genre. Nietzsche, Marx, and Lenin had nothing on this

111. Weissenhof Settlement, Stuttgart, 1927, collage and photo, redrawn. LC's white cubes were given pride of place at the head of the site, even Mies's apartments, above them in collage, defer to the leader of Modernism.

112. Double Housing slab on steel *pilotis*.

polemicist. That is one meaning of the sardonic smile that beams from a photograph of the four cadets huddled under the ramparts of the Castle La Sarraz [fig. 66]: they spoof, in their demeanor, the very *pompiers* they are about to replace. As he proclaimed in 1908, the struggle is on—"Raise the concept and forge ahead!"

Thus, by a stroke of luck, or misfortune, the hero of the Heroic Period managed to triumph at the very moment when Modernism both won and lost the battle for world domination: at Stuttgart and in Geneva. At the same time, reaction was beginning to set in— regional, nationalist, ideological, and economic. Contemplate the ironies. In his *Oeuvre complète*, as partial justification of the Villa Savoye, Le Corbusier brings up the architectural promenade and refers positively to the Arabs and the way they see architecture on foot, in movement: "Arab architecture gives us a precious example. It is appreciated in perambulation, on foot; it is while walking that one sees things change, that one sees develop the harmonious orders of architecture. This is a principle contrary to Baroque architecture that is conceived on paper, theoretically, around a fixed point. I prefer the teaching of Arab architecture."

At the same time, the upcoming Nazi movement was issuing racist collages of Arabs walking all over the white architecture of Stuttgart, announcing that the new architecture was establishing a beachhead for these aliens in Europe [fig. 113]. The battle was joined. However different in substance, the arguments of both the Modernists and Reactionaries had a few things in common: they both assumed the idea of the zeitgeist and they both believed any arguments could be used to co-opt its beautiful and luxuriant favors. The outcome? Direct, nasty conflict.

113. Nazi collage of the Weissenhof
Settlement, Stuttgart, circa 1930.

114. *Le Corbusier, Pierre Jeanneret, Yvonne Gallis*, 1927. The painting by André Bauchant shows the two Jeannerets, dressed for the city but courting Yvonne in the countryside. Not quite the Surrealist De Chirico, or Magritte, LC admired the naive primitivism of Bauchant.

PART III

Back to Nature
1928–45

Le Corbusier Changes Tack—Five Shifts

The change which Le Corbusier underwent between 1928 and 1945 was somewhat unconscious and escaped notice by the Modern Movement. There was one obvious change in 1928, when he explicitly introduced "objects evoking a poetic reaction" into his paintings—substituted such things as shells, rocks, and people for the Purist bottles, flasks, and pipes. He was deliberate about presenting this new approach to natural subject matter and biological form, as if it represented the noticeable aspect of a much more profound and hidden change. He marked it also by signing his paintings not Jeanneret, but Le Corbusier, thus consolidating his persona as writer, architect, and painter.

His programmatic statements sometimes signal, sometimes betray, a change going on at a deeper level than his philosophy of architecture. There is the turn to worldly pursuits—a renewed interest in women, travel, lecture tours, and friendships. At the same time, because his success makes important commissions seem within his reach, he attempts to build a public realm and architecture based on ideal liberal institutions—world government, global culture. This is accompanied by a shift in his political views, from supporting managerial capitalism to a new form of political engagement, Regional-Syndicalism. Furthermore, the dominating interest becomes city planning, now based on curvilinear forms. And, finally, during this period he becomes increasingly pessimistic about the European cultural situation, which was becoming both politically and artistically reactionary. Even a hostile bitterness becomes discernible in his polemics, as if the fight were not so much fun as it used to be—especially if it is continually lost. After world acclaim in 1928 and 1929 as a leading Modern architect, his commissions throughout the 1930s progressively dry up; by 1936 he loses ownership of his own house-apartment. He has to let Pierre Jeanneret and Charlotte Perriand find work elsewhere; once again he lives off his painting, writing, and wits.

Through all this his architecture starts to shift from the white machine aesthetic toward a hybrid, rough mode that combines crude hand-built masonry and factory-built systems. Like Picasso, he keeps moving ahead of his followers, incessantly revolutionizing his methods and ideas. Partly this is a response to their failures: for instance, the flat, Purist architecture stained and did not protect against strong sunlight so, by the mid-1930s, he developed the sunbreaker, the *brise-soleil*. But partly it comes from the theory of Hieratism and change: when systems are fully understood and perfected, as at the Villa Savoye, "a page turns," it is time to move on. Continual revolution or continual rereading, as Peter Eisenman calls it, is basic to contemporary culture, and any leader who wants to survive at the top must continually reinvent herself every ten years (it was not just women, but the image of Liberty at the barricades which interested LC at this time).

These five shifts pose some interesting questions. Why did the Modern Movement not take notice, but continue to treat Le Corbusier as if he were the spokesman for the white architecture? It was not until the 1950s, with Ronchamp and the Maisons Jaoul, that architects such as James Stirling and historians such as Nikolaus Pevsner recognized, and lamented, the shifts. Was Le Corbusier's 1920s reputation as *the* Modernist and Machine Age architect so forceful that no one could accept a change? Were Modernists in denial? Or was LC unwilling to articulate it with the same sloganeering he had used so effectively in the 1920s? Or was it simply that the 1930s did not want to hear his new slogans? A partial answer must be that Le Corbusier presented the continuities with the machine aesthetic and his large-scale city planning, not the changes. His public image, purveyed through the *Oeuvre complète*, remained the same. But whatever the reason, or combination of reasons, LC does undergo a profound metamorphosis that is not socially registered.

Let me exaggerate and dramatize the changes. Instead of white machines for living, raised on *pilotis*, he produces mud huts with grass roof placed on load-bearing walls. Instead of abstract grids and universal appliances based on ships, he produces curved cities based on the meander of rivers and the thick thighs of fat women. Remember, he had rejected the pack-donkey's way and pronounced that "civilization is a right-angled state of mind." Now, suddenly, both the straight line and the pack-donkey's way are replaced by the curve of the buttock! There were many preoccupations that remained the same—for instance the interest in massproduced steel and glass housing—but fundamentally a new style and approach are forged.

To put it polemically, Le Corbusier becomes a Post-Modernist before the fact, a nascent eco-hippy, building regional and contextual objects that are poems to nature-worship. In effect, he looks

115. *Deux femmes nues*, 1928,
crayon, 21 x 31 cm (Collection
Ahrenberg, *15). Two heroic women
rendered in outline and flowing contour relate to the watercolors of the
period from 1910 to 1920. They symbolize the earth or moon goddess,
fecundity, and above all the landscape.
Indeed, the pun between landscape
and woman's body becomes the insis-
tent idea of the 1930s. The immediate
inspiration was seeing heavyweight
bathers on a summer holiday at Le
Piquey in the Bassin d'Arcachon. Here
Le Corbusier also discovers the nobility
of primitive living; from that time
fishermen's huts become the new
inspiration for housing. All this is
argued in his polemic *Une Maison—
Un Palais* (1929).

back to Charles L'Eplattenier's dream of a symbolic architecture
and city planning based on cosmic elements, but in a new way. This
shift, this return to nature, is inspired by two trips and drawing
during his summer holidays. The journeys are equivalent to those
in 1907 and 1911, one to South America in 1929, the other to
Algiers in 1931; and it is while watching plump women cavort on
the beaches of the Bassin d'Arcachon, in 1928, that he first forges a
new/old style [fig. 115]. This relates to the monumental Classical
experiments of Léger, Picasso, and Braque during the 1920s, so it
is not entirely unique. But LC gives his heroic Earth Goddesses a
particular cosmic and local meaning: that of the Mediterranean
Primitive. With Albert Camus, André Gide, and others a movement
starts, called "Mediterraneanism," a "kind of nationalism of the
sun." Again it is his sketchbook that leads the way; he draws himself into a new architecture, and it is the encounter with life, and
women, that challenges him to do so. Put abstractly this way, it
sounds as if the period from 1928 to 1945, from his great success to
the end of the Second World War, was a fertile and positive development rather like Picasso's during the same time. It was, but it
also revealed, through force of circumstance, the tragic flaw in his

character, or should we say his theory of politics and city planning—or both.

Wordly Pursuits and Friendships

In December 1930, Le Corbusier married Yvonne Gallis, an attractive fashion model born in Monaco. Ozenfant had introduced them in 1922. It took a few years for her to break his monkish habits and establish a stable relationship, but this occurred by 1927, and she stopped seeing other men. By then he was financially and culturally successful, owned a car, painted more, and actually took long summer holidays. Le Corbusier's relationship with Yvonne, as indeed with other women, was never made a matter for public consumption, and the personal evidence which does exist consists in a few scattered remarks, various drawings, and the stories of friends and acquaintances—all of which does not amount to a very accurate or trustworthy account. Nevertheless a rough picture can be sketched which has a certain relevance to Le Corbusier's architecture and city planning.

Apparently, Le Corbusier lived with Yvonne for several years before pressure from his Protestant family, not to mention from Yvonne herself, pushed him into the conventional, legal relationship that, as he said when young, he wished to avoid. Moreover, he was wary of taking on any personal responsibilities that would cut into his time and deflect his primary mission.

> When I was married, I said to my wife "no children" because I feared at that time that my life would be very hard as an architect.

Yvonne, from all accounts, was the kind of woman to which Le Corbusier was occasionally attracted: not an intellectual, a good cook with an "earthy" humor—interested in bawdy jokes and not at all in architecture. She was someone who could be counted on to break up solemn meetings of architectural luminaries, such as those of CIAM, by pointing out some hidden virtues of female anatomy. She had a sharp wit and, like Le Corbusier, loved to shock, even him. "All this light is killing me, driving me crazy," she said about the new apartment Le Corbusier designed for her [fig. 116]. In 1933 he had built in Paris a penthouse at the top of a

116. Yvonne Gallis in the light-filled kitchen of their apartment, Porte Molitor Apartments, rue Nungesser-et-Coli, Paris, 1934. Le Corbusier captioned this photo: "the kitchen has become one of the essential rooms in the house." He saw the housewife directing family affairs from a central point and often gave the kitchen a primary location and significance.

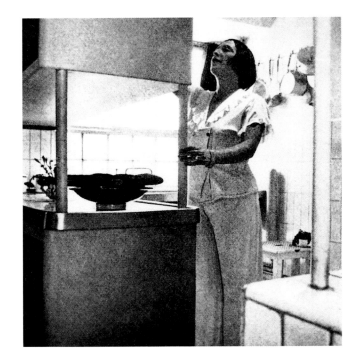

steel and glass apartment block, one of several steel buildings he was developing for mass housing. For her the aesthetic qualities of the glass curtain wall and the attempt to bring light into every nook and cranny of the house was folly, and she never really appreciated what her husband was achieving in architecture. Le Corbusier placed a bidet, that beautifully sculptural "object-type," right next to their bed. She covered it with a tea cozy.

> A great event today: we brought upstairs, with great exertion, a large, homespun couch. All of a sudden everything took on an air of great comfort and calm, "like other people's houses." Yvonne was ravished. In addition, we could also serve ourselves coffee sitting on a sofa. It's like this one acquires by a long journey the rights to enter into bourgeois society.

The sarcasm, even cruelty, of such remarks was underscored by an Indian woman, Taya Zinkin, whom Le Corbusier tried to seduce once or twice, without success, in the 1950s. As she tells it, the following unfortunate conversation took place.

He spent the evening discussing women, prostitution, the

impotence of Indian males and his own wife. "I absolutely fail
to understand her. Of course she is pretty stupid, *mais quand
même*. I give her all the money she wants but that is not enough
for her. No, Madame wants children! I *hate* children. She
already has a little dog, that should be good enough. Take
another dog, have two dogs by all means, but leave me alone is
what I say to her. Children are the curse of society. They make
noise, they are messy, they should be abolished."

As W. C. Fields said, "Anyone who hates children can't be all
bad." One can doubt the full seriousness of these remarks (for
instance Le Corbusier enjoyed the children of his friends, such as
the Nivolas [fig. 162]) and the motive for Taya Zinkin's unflattering
portrayal (which will come out shortly), but still imagine that he
said something like this in a fit of pique, or as a heavy-handed joke.
Le Corbusier's relation with Yvonne was not always idyllic. He told
Jane Drew that while Yvonne was his closest confidant, a friend,
companion, and wife, "he felt he had wronged her" by "keeping her
in a drawer." Perhaps because her taste was the opposite of his, "a
liking for fru-frus," not clear forms seen in sunlight, and because
she could not share his intellectual and architectural life, they lived
in separate cultural spheres. Several French acquaintances have
said that she was more than a woman of easy virtue; others have
said she became an alcoholic and near cripple in later life and that
Le Corbusier looked after her as a nurse. During the Second World
War, she suffered from malnutrition, broke her leg as a result, and
lost much of her previous beauty.

The effects of all this must have been to isolate further a man
who already had difficulty in close personal relationships.
Although Le Corbusier had many extremely devoted friends, he
always remained an enigma to them and would not allow them to
get too close. If they erred, or betrayed him, *finis.* A characteristic
act was his firing the designers at 35 rue de Sèvres when they
became tired, slack, old, or uncreative. Once again he could burn
what he loved, even if this was personal friendship. On the other
hand, in certain respects he was utterly devoted to Yvonne, as he
was to his mother. Marie lived to be 101 and, it was said by Jane
Drew, among others, that his great love for his mother was tinged
with a certain awe and fear of her determination. No doubt,
throughout his life he tried to keep her respect and love. This is

apparent from the letters describing his triumphs on the world stage, words that seem at once justifying and entreating, as if he were trying to convince her he was finally a success. His old rivalry with his brother, Albert, for his parent's affection may explain some of this, and perhaps it may partly explain his insatiable desire to become a great architect.

Yvonne, by contrast, gave him the peace, silence, and service he sought as a creator who often worked at home. According to Walter Gropius and other friends, when Yvonne died in 1957 he suffered something of an extended breakdown, and there are glimpses of a very strong and simple bond in a few photographs, paintings, and scattered remarks.

> Yvonne died yesterday morning at four o'clock, her hand in mine, in silence and complete serenity. I was with her at the clinic for eight hours, watching over her, she was the opposite of a suckling baby, leaving life with spasms and mutterings in a *tête-à-tête*, the whole of the long night. She finally died just before dawn. She was a highly spirited woman with a strong will, integrity and tidiness. Guardian angel of the home, my home, for thirty-six years. Liked by all, adored and loved by the simple and rich, the rich of heart only. She took the measure of people and things in that scale. Queen of a little fervent world. An example for many and yet without any pretence. For my "Poem to the Right Angle," she occupies the central place: character E3. She is on her bed in the guestroom, stretched out, with her masque of magisterial and *Provençal* structure. During that calm day, I discovered that death is not a horror . . . In gratitude to my wife for thirty-five years of wonderful devotion, for surrounding me with the blessings of quiet, affection and happiness.

These were the simple qualities, which he enjoyed, and if he was the mythical French husband whenever he traveled, at least he was faithful and considerate to Yvonne in Paris. Foreign female acquaintances who dared phone him at home received a standard answer: *"Connais pas,"* as he hung up. His later relationships with Marguerite Tjader-Harris and Minnette de Silva were probably unknown to Yvonne. One British female acquaintance with whom I discussed the matter put an interesting construction on his sexual ethics. She described how he said to her "women are good for bed" and made a few rude remarks. After he received the Gold Medal of the Royal Institute of British Architects, in 1953, he and others had a lot to drink when they retired to the home of the British Modernist Wells Coates. Characteristically, LC was elated by the reception, being abroad and of course having received the Gold Medal, and he produced lots of sketches showing himself as a cab donkey, genius, and ass, which he dashed off for the women present. It was all very intoxicating, and by the end of the evening he was under the table with a famous British beauty, enjoying an amorous bout. But, my friend continued, in spite of such indiscretions "he was not unfaithful to his wife." "How do you mean that," I inquired, "in the French sense?" "No, these were just one-night stands, sleeping with other women is not being unfaithful." Although the period was much less promiscuous than today, the implication was that morality was also quite different among the creative elite. As long as LC protected Yvonne from speculation and was faithful at home, it was perfectly all right for him to have an affair when he traveled. Perhaps this is one reason he wrote such passionate paeans of praise to the ocean liner and airplane?

The important aspect of Le Corbusier's relation to women and his friendships was the intense and even moral excitement they generated. This was recognized and underlined in the key words which he used to describe friends. A *"brave-type"* signified those such as Léger and Picasso who, by creating beauty, were actively doing good. *"Fidèle"* and *"sérieux"* were applied to reliable friends and pupils and to those who had the courage of their convictions. Le Corbusier could even find spiritual and moral qualities in music, particularly in the hot jazz of Louis Armstrong. He refers to its "implacable exactitude," "mathematics, equilibrium on a tightrope," and describes it with the masculine virtues of the machine.

Josephine—Goddess of Dance

Such sentiments came together and focused on the person of Josephine Baker, whom he met while traveling to South America in 1929, on board the ocean liner *Giulio Cesare*. She was already a glamorous figure in French café society and art circles, especially among intellectuals such as Adolf Loos, who designed a fancy

117. Nude woman singing, possibly Josephine Baker, 1929, crayon, 29.6 x 21 cm (Collection Ahrenberg, *21). Many sketches were made of Josephine, usually looking slimmer, in action. The goddess with upraised arms becomes an idea motif to be merged with bull's horns as a sign of cosmic regeneration.

striped villa for her in 1928. Traveling with her, and sketching her, opened up in LC a new tenderness toward women that had been repressed by his fanatical work schedule. It might be said that she, even more than the bathers of Arcachon, inspired his renewed interest in the female body as a cosmic force. He drew her with a very fine pencil line, at rest, sleeping; or, with quick strokes, crouching, leaping, singing, and dancing—a kind of Amazonian animal [fig. 117].

In a stupid variety show, Josephine Baker sang "Baby" with

such an intense and dramatic sensibility that I was moved to tears. There is in this American Negro music a lyrical "contemporary" mass so invincible that I could see the foundation of a new sentiment of music capable of being the expression of the new epoch and also capable of classifying its European origins as stone-age—just as has happened with the new architecture. A page turns. A new exploitation arises. Pure music. In the cabin of the ocean liner, Josephine grabbed a little guitar—a child's plaything—and she sang Negro songs. They were fantastically beautiful, touching, rich, inventive, generous and decent! . . . "I am a little black bird who looks for a little white bird; I want a little nest to put us both together in," and "You are the wings of the angel who is come, you are the sails of my ship, I could not let you get away; you are the stitch of the cloth and I will place all of you into the cloth, roll it up, and carry it around so that you can never get away from me" . . . Josephine Baker, known around the world, is a small child pure, simple, and limpid. She glides over the roughness of life. She has a good little heart. She is an admirable artist when she sings, and out of this world when she dances.

The realistic portraits which Le Corbusier sketched of her singing and dancing brought out her simplicity and vitality. Being on board an ocean liner with Baker was not only pure pleasure, it was metaphysical bliss. Here, brought together in one place was everything he wanted: a moving home for sixteen hundred people (later to be an *Unité*). Each individual or family had their cell, but there were collective facilities for all, and, most important, "the three essential joys of life: sun, space, and greenery" (or at least its equivalent on the sea). Here was personal freedom and adventure, the excitement of travel and new experiences—but also control, the machine, and geometry. No wonder Le Corbusier was reborn by this visit to Brazil. In one sketch, on the back of an invitation to a party on board ship, LC draws Josephine and himself dressed—he looking awkward as usual, she looking graceful. In the distance is the curved bay of Rio and its bulbous loaf of a mountain—at once breast, phallus, and shoulder. The curves of the landscape interest him as much as those of Josephine, and no doubt they are equated as signs of vitality, and spurs for a new urbanism [fig. 118].

Le Corbusier left behind a paper trail of comments and

118. *View of Rio de Janeiro*, 1929, watercolor and crayon, 25.5 x 42.5 cm (Collection Ahrenberg, *30). LC paints quick watercolors of favellas, landscapes, and women, sometimes together and sometimes separate. The rounded mountains of Rio and Santos particularly fascinated him and are painted as body parts pushing through the skin of the ground.

sketches suggesting his passion. On the face of it this might be considered unkind, or unfaithful, to Yvonne, to the woman he was to marry the next year, and who is to say it was not both. But considered from his point of view there is a truth to be told, the discovery, rather late in life, of sexual delight seen as a cosmic pleasure, something to be celebrated in poetry, drawing, and architecture. In Josephine he discovers in the human animal "the gods," that vitality which, if transformed through a poetic expression, becomes empowering and innocent.

Sketchbook B4 has a description of a ballet he designs for Josephine:

> 1. Entrance, 2. Show girls made up with tattoos, sound: one step or pure negro <u>tam tam</u> without music, only one negro on stage // 1 negro wearing a banana tree // 3. A modern man and woman x New York dancing, only 1 step, holding each other and slowly, 4. The cylinder is lowered, Josephine descends dressed as a monkey, 5. She puts on a modern dress, she sits down, 6. She goes forward onto a podium and sings, 7. She steps off the podium and sings, 8. Last solemn song: the gods rise // in the background the meandering Sea of Santos, and at the end a big ocean liner.

"The gods rise"—they all come together in this ballet of the ocean liner. Josephine was to remain, like the women of Algiers, a spur and muse, a banner of the new activity. Action, direct action, the Syndicalist philosophy of 1930, becomes Le Corbusier's philosophy. Act first, is their message, and see what happens next, where it leads, organically, naturally. What a contrast for the total planner and control-fanatic in him; but, of course, the contradiction becomes just one more example of his internalizing opposites.

There are countless sketches of a Josephine figure in the nude, and a few paintings during the 1930s that monumentalize and turn her into an animal goddess, a mythic figure that may, as some historians have argued, relate to the prehistoric fertility figures of the Neolithic, perhaps a Moon Goddess. We find several types of woman portrayed: a large figure of the Earth Goddess, or a thin tall figure of the she-goat (*la Licorne*), the fat Arcachon fisherwoman, and the wrestling woman. These are the major characters he portrays, and often they seem to have the hairstyle of Josephine, or her mouth or gesture. Many are sketched or painted from memory, and perhaps in this way he builds up a collective archetype of the feminine symbol.

The Ahrenberg Collection of drawings and graphic work, published as *Le Corbusier Secret*, contains most of the types, and because they are drawn *al vif* they have a liveliness the paintings of women lack. Some, of men and women wrestling, seem to have been sketched from underground Parisian nightlife: the muscular figures are dressed only in boots and anklets. Others show women pleasuring each other [fig. 119]. The face, if not the fact, of Josephine seems present here, and one cannot help but see the rolling bodies in a cosmic setting, as miniatures of the meandering

119. *Two Women*, circa 1930, ink, 27 x 21.3 cm (Collection Ahrenberg, *51). This and other sketches of the same subject incorporate elements of Josephine and the hills of Rio and Santos.

rivers of Santos and the mountains of Rio. Punning, rhyming, transformation of forms becomes LC's method both of painting and design at this time. It is as if he were searching for a new cosmic language of symbols, something that obsessed him in 1907, 1911, 1921, and now again in the early 1930s.

The motive behind these drawings is part sexual, part sculptural. What starts off as fairly representational, the thighs, shoulders, and bottom, ends up as stylized and distorted. The shape grammar is led by the flowing outline, "the marriage of contours," as it was with his Purist bottles and guitars. But then the rounded breasts and buttocks are given shading, as if they were his definition of architecture in 1923, "the masterly, correct and magnificent play of forms in sunlight." As we can see from sketches of the time, this synthesis is reached when he goes to Algiers, in the spring of 1931, and has his long romance with that North African city [fig. 120]. He was invited by a group, "Amis d'Alger," to give lectures on urbanism and, to everyone's surprise, fifteen hundred people turned up to hear what he had to say. This response established his long-term bond with the Mediterranean port, something that was deepened by several visits to its Casbah, where he rediscovered the beauties of vernacular living. As a young architect of nineteen tells it, he also rediscovered the beauties of the joint nude:

> Our wanderings through the side streets led us at the end of the day to the Rue Kataroudji where Le Corbusier was fascinated by the beauty of two young girls, one Spanish and the other one Algerian. They brought us up a narrow stairway to their room: there he sketched some nudes on—to my amazement—some schoolbook graph paper with colored pencils; the sketches of the Spanish girl lying both alone on the bed and beautifully grouped together with the Algerian turned out accurate and realistic; but he said that they were very bad and refused to show them.

As Stanislaus von Moos has shown, these figures led via Delacroix's *Les Femmes d'Alger* and Picasso's *Guernica* to a series of linear, monochrome sketches and a mural. They also led to a shape grammar of rounded U-forms and broken ellipses that, when considered from an architectural viewpoint, are relatively inexpensive.

120. A woman lying
with curtains, circa 1930,
enhanced black lead.

121. Plan Obus A for
Algiers, 1932. The long curvilinear form consists of
dwellings for 180,000 people
below a roadway. The
rounded U slabs are residential blocks, while the rectilinear slab is the business
center uniting both European
and Muslim cultures in an
idealistic synthesis.

The grammar of the straight line and U-curve, a heavy, bulbous
curve, allows the repetition of cellular units. Perhaps this is why
his nudes look a bit like buildings. In any case, these forms are
incorporated into city plans, particularly for Algiers, where the setback blocks of 1922 are turned into undulating U-shapes on the
hill, twenty-three stories of housing for the wealthy, and a lower
snaking curve fourteen stories high for the working class [fig. 121].
This plan, known as Obus ("shell") A, was the first one of six, and
by far the most idealistic. In spite of a rather stark class division, it

attempts to unify Muslim and European cultures while keeping a parity between them. It preserves the past, the Casbah, unlike the Voisin Plan of 1925, which rips to shreds the urban fabric. It is as if the human and organic metaphor behind the female curves has led to a new respect for what actually exists.

If one looks at the plans for such later buildings as Ronchamp [fig. 166] and the Carpenter Center at Harvard, one can also find the U-curves of buttocks and shoulder arches. Again, it is quite a U-turn for a man who had been damning the curve as "the pack-donkey's way" and proclaiming that "culture is an orthogonal state of mind." No doubt a renewed contact with women changed his mind on that score and, when it came to curved roads, took him back to the injunctions of 1910. "The lesson of the Ass must be retained," he then proclaimed, a demand that now becomes a nice double entendre in English, if not in French.

Most of the pencil sketches of the 1930s are of elaborately distorted and heavy women. They are not pudgy or voluptuous like a Rubens, nor quite as calm and statuesque as Picasso's Neoclassical nudes of the 1920s. Rather, they are gargantuan, muscular, and peasantlike: the women of Algiers, athletic bathers, who are encompassed in flowing contours and strongly modeled muscles [fig. 122]. The priority of contour and profile over color and shading remained from the Purist days even though the subject matter had changed from machinery to heavy women. Taya Zinkin, mentioned above, was apparently the victim of this change.

> As we were getting off the plane he asked me what I was doing that evening: "Catching a train, I am afraid," I said. "Pity. You are fat and I like my women fat. We could have spent a pleasant night together." He said this quite casually. He was not being offensive, he was being factual. He took such a functional view of sex that it never occurred to him that the act would not carry its own reward for both of us . . . By the time he had had a few drinks he was paying me the sort of compliments Rubens must have paid to Hélène Fourmont when she was far gone with child. Had I not studied medicine I would have found his anatomical precision embarrassing. I had always known that I was fat, but I had not realized before that I looked as fat as all that.

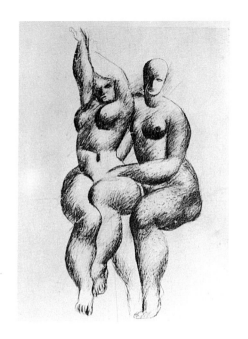

122. Sketch of two nudes, 1931. The theme of two women conceived as voluptuous architecture or landscape preoccupied LC from an early age and, as often, he intertwines them and exaggerates the curves of their hips, thighs, shoulders, and breasts.

A Surrealist Interlude

The situation that Taya Zinkin describes was basically ambiguous from the start. She as a journalist was trying to get a good scoop from Le Corbusier—a fact that no doubt annoyed him as he was always disgruntled by journalists. The crude, functional, and, in the end, unsuccessful seduction scene which she describes reflects as much on her own unsubtle tactics as on Le Corbusier's egoism, which she makes part of her scoop. And while he did take a functional view of sex, just as he classified all human activities in an objective light, there are contrary stories showing a profound consideration for women. One of the more humorous accounts is given by Le Corbusier in *When the Cathedrals Were White*, a book written about his first trip to the United States in 1935 and subtitled, ominously, "A Journey to the Country of Timid People." The timidness was found in the architecture and sex of the Americans.

A small section titled "Everyone an Athlete" starts off with a positive view of the Vassar girl.

> I made a trip to Vassar, a college for girls from well-to-do families. From New York the car plunges north into Westchester; when the slums of New York have been left behind . . . we arrive at the college "within a budding grove" . . . a dozen girls are taking down the sets of a play put on the evening before . . . They are in overalls or in bathing suits. I enjoy looking at these beautiful bodies, made healthy and trim by physical training.

> The buildings have the atmosphere of luxurious clubs. The girls are in a convent for four years. A joyous convent.

Everything works out spectacularly well. Le Corbusier gives a talk, illustrated by drawings, to six hundred girls. After the lecture they swarm the platform, seize the drawings, and rip them up for autographs.

> A piece for each Amazon. Pens in hand, they cry: "Sign, sign!" The drawings at Vassar had a particular verve. The Amazons reduced them to confetti.

But afterwards another aspect of these beautiful athletes begins to emerge. A taste for the Mannerist painter Caravaggio.

"You women are also interested in Caravaggio? Why
Caravaggio? Because of the psychological turmoil in that equiv-
ocal personality. Do you also feel a kind of frustration?" . . .
Caravaggio, an Italian painter of the sixteenth century,
"worked in a studio which was painted black; light came in
only through a small overhead opening." Stop! Through him
we discover a corner of the American soul. If we connect
Caravaggio with contemporary surrealism, which is well represented in American collections, our diagnosis will be
confirmed . . . Caravaggio in university studies, surrealism in
collections and museums, the inferiority complex which
obsesses those who wish to break away from the simple arith-
metic of numbers, the principle of family disturbances, the
funereal spirit . . . [this] reveals, under well-bred external
appearances, a complex disturbance and the anxieties of
sexual life.

Thereafter follows a series of antitheses between Cubism and
Surrealism, health and depravity, functional, cosmic love and fear-
ful desire.

The perpetuation of the species is a cosmic law; love, human
creation, is the luminous joining together of sensuality and
aesthetics . . . is it in the name of art, Vassar student, that you
enter that sewer [of Caravaggio]? I believe that you were
impelled by an unsatisfied heart.

Before continuing this account, we should note in passing that
Le Corbusier had designed, four years earlier, a fantasy apartment
for a collector of Surrealist objects—really a Surrealist apartment
itself, designed with a Purist background [figs. 123, 124]. Designed
for Charles de Beistegui, a South American millionaire with a passion for parties and shocking behavior, the apartment was strewn
with precisely the expensive bad taste that Jeanneret had been
attacking since 1907: Baroque/Rococola made out of the wrong
materials, blackamoors dancing below lighting standards, kitsch of
every kind. Yet so excessive was the commission, with its miles of
electronic cable to move hedges about, that LC must have not only
swallowed his distaste for pretension *and* Surrealism—but, by
combining them together within a Purist still life, satisfied himself

123. Beistegui salon, 1930–31.
Electricity moves walls and even sliding
hedges, but the room is entirely lit by
reflected candle power, a candelabra
skewered on mirrors! At the press of a
button projection equipment emerges
from behind a mirror; a rotating
periscope allows one to peep at passing Parisians.

124. Beistegui roof garden with imitation stone furniture, grass carpet, and
daisies. The position of the mirror
accentuates further the ambiguity
between indoors and outdoors. Visible
landmarks are turned into *objets trou-
vés*, such as the Eiffel Tower or the Arc
de Triomphe, but cut in half by the
high parapet. Here, before its time, is
the installation art of the 1980s.

that he was managing to kill both enemies at once. (One should point out he never published the interiors, except bare, and continued to attack the Surrealists, while being influenced by their "objects evoking a poetic reaction"). Once again one sees LC appropriate another position through attack and transformation, criticism and juxtaposition. Is this hypocrisy, or the poetic license granted to the creative?

Perhaps the rejection of the Surrealist position was caused by its uncomfortable closeness, the way it almost but did not quite convince LC. Such is his reaction to the "Quat'z' Arts Ball" held in the Waldorf-Astoria Hotel in New York City—a continuation of his amateur psychoanalysis of the timid Americans. He contrasts again a healthy, creative nudity, the nudity of artists at the Quat'z' Arts celebration in Paris, with the self-conscious display and rented costumes of the ball in New York.

> As the painting is, so are the architecture, the decoration, and the ball. The little nude women brighten up the affair, of course, and that is what makes it go. At the Waldorf-Astoria there will be no little nude women, oh, never!
>
> The costume man wants to rig me out with a turban and a brocaded robe; this evening, for the same amount of money, I can be a rajah or a khan.
>
> No usurped title, thank you! Not being a handsome fellow, I keep my anatomy out of sight. In spite of more protests, I insist on white and blue striped convict's trousers and an Indian army guard's vermilion coat (he would have loved to see me in a high-ranking officer's coat!); I find an enormous gold epaulette which I fasten on the left side. No military cap, sir, a white, pointed clown's hat, please . . . to finish off, three differently shaped spots of white in my cheeks and forehead, to perplex the curious. If everyone does likewise, there will perhaps be some amusing sights!

Needless to say everyone does otherwise, dresses according to the conventional rules of a costume ball, and the party is respectable, solemn and stiff. Le Corbusier is rejected.

125. Le Corbusier, Josephine Baker, and others at a costume party on board the *Giulio Cesare,* 1929. Le Corbusier was often dressed up as a clown or convict at such parties.

I was neither mad nor clownish, I was a sore thumb. I was out of place . . . Lost, poor fellow, I was the only one of my type, disagreeable, disapproved, rejected. I left ingloriously, thrust aside by respectability.

The moral once again for Le Corbusier is the timidness of Americans, too insecure to create their own style, too conventional to invent their own fancy dress. It is in this light that Le Corbusier's rejection of cosmopolitan life and urbane sophistication is relevant.

The Primitive and the Sexual

He opens *La Ville Radieuse* with the confession of a Rousseauesque kind. He returns to nature for its truth and primitive societies for their wisdom; his words of 1935 echo those of 1910.

> . . . I am attracted to a natural order of things. I don't like parties and it is years since I set foot in one. And I have noticed that in my flight from city living I end up in places

where society is in the process of organization. I look for primitive men, not for their barbarity but for their wisdom.

Out of this interest in primitive societies sprang a series of buildings constructed in a modern folk vernacular—what would be called the "New Brutalism" twenty years later because of its straightforward use of *béton brut*, raw concrete, and various coarse materials "as found." In the 1950s, two of Le Corbusier's buildings, the *Unité* at Marseilles and the Ronchamp church, were interpreted almost universally as a dramatic rejection of the sleek, white machine aesthetic, but in retrospect it is now clear that Le Corbusier had already evolved his own form of Brutalism by the 1930s. This is apparent in several projects and buildings constructed from primitive materials: the Errazuris House, 1930 [fig. 126], the house for the patroness of CIAM, Madame Hélène de Mandrot, 1931 [fig. 127], the Weekend House [fig. 128], the house at Mathes, 1935, and finally the self-built "Murondins," 1940, envisaged for the uprooted population of a Europe at war.

126. Rough copy of Le Corbusier's design for Errazuris House, Chile, 1930, erected in Japan in 1933 by Antonin Raymond. The familiar planning elements such as the double-height living room and ramp are translated into a totally new aesthetic of rough timber and broken stone. Raymond may have derived his Brutalist aesthetic from Le Corbusier's design, or alternatively from traditional Japanese aesthetics.

127. Maison de Mandrot, Le Pradet, near Toulon, 1929–32. Corbusian oppositions of steel versus low-cost rubble, ready-made elements versus local stone, an architectural promenade versus the landscape—an ironic house for a rich hostess of CIAM. She left the house because of leaking windows, damp walls, and the blinds that did not work. He replied to her complaints: "Your house is one of our best. . . . It seemed that Madame de Mandrot, after the act of La Sarraz, which made her enter by the gate of honor into the world of modern architecture, would have been ready to live in a modern house. You have told us you cannot. What the hell, then!"

128. Petite Maison de Weekend, Celle-St-Cloud, 1935. Concrete, glass bricks, curved plywood vaults, and roughcast brickwork became the formula for Brutalism in the 1950s. Beyond this combination was the opposition between the ready-made—photographs on the wall, Thonet furniture—and the primitive—the pots, the bear-skin rug. The concrete vaults were initially more freeform, influenced by Gaudí's work and the flat Catalan vault.

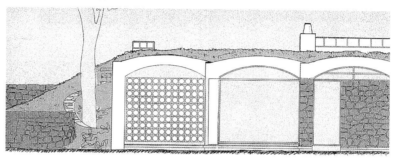

129. Swiss Pavilion, City University, Paris, 1930–32. Heavily modeled *pilotis* support the slab block as "legs" appropriate to their visual and anthropomorphic function. The figure-eight shape was also invented to provide more structural stability, after slender supports had been criticized, and they were known not only as "thighs" but "dog bones." While these organic and sexual metaphors were becoming more conscious by 1930, LC said they should come *after* functional considerations had been decided, not before.

130. Swiss Pavilion, entrance side. The old and new Corbu in juxtaposition: the Purist slab in back, accommodation for the students, is contrasted with roughcast masonry and a curve, themes of the 1930s, even though they are so understated as to escape notice by the Modernists.

All these houses make use of very simple materials ready to hand or found on the site: rough stone, fair-faced brick, raw concrete, unfinished timber, and so on. And the intention is to create a very simple poetry from these materials: "objects evoking a poetic reaction" or the definition of architecture made in 1923 ("the business of Architecture is to establish emotional relationships by means of brutal materials"). Hence one may conclude that by the mid-1930s Le Corbusier had already made his move to Brutalism, a move that was prompted in the deepest sense by a rediscovery of natural orders, primitive societies, and a sexual relation with women unconstrained by conventional etiquette, sophistication, or snobbism. Several formal innovations in addition to Brutalism resulted from this change. Le Corbusier remarked to one of his designers in the atelier: "The columns of a building should be like the strong curvaceous thighs of a woman"—and they were so designed in one or two cases [figs. 129, 130].

During the 1930s Le Corbusier became very close to Marguerite Tjader-Harris, who helped work on his book *When the Cathedrals Were White*, sometimes when they both happened to be in America. Marguerite, a friend of his mother, wanted him to design a house for her near Vevey, a simple one like that for his parents on the lake, and this request started to engender a long-term relationship that lasted into the 1960s. He visited her house by the sea in the United States, and his letters show a great affection for her and her son, Toutou. They also speak of many encounters, and an intense emotional friendship, nurtured on the run between architectural meetings and, for instance, his lectures at Vassar. Marguerite gave him an intellectual stimulation and companionship different from that of Yvonne, but in the interests of his marriage and reputation, he asked her not to write to his architectural office (nor, it was understood, to telephone at home). From 1932 to 1937 women, particularly the subject of two women, dominate his paintings. It would be simplistic to see these as Yvonne and Marguerite, especially since the presence of Josephine can be felt in many of the drawings and the theme of two women making love was an old one for him. But there is no doubt that the feminine presence was abstracted as such during this time, perhaps becoming an earth goddess, mother figure, and object of sexual desire. In Marguerite he might have found all three, but especially the confidant.

That she gave him spiritual and moral support, when he was down and without work, or despondent about his hot and cold love affair with America, is obvious from the number of private meetings they had over the years, and a few scattered remarks—"you are open not closed," "America is a desert without you," and a quote from Lucretius to the effect that life only grows where physical and sensual reality flourish. He speaks of making love to "negresses" in Rio, and writes how much he misses her. Why doesn't she write him more often?—a complaint he makes, later, to Pierre Jeanneret—he seemed to like writing letters sometimes more than his correspondents. These letters, to be published by Mrs. Madges Bacon in *Le Corbusier in America*, imply a strong emotional relationship lasting five or six years and, intellectually, into the 1950s. Marguerite Tjader-Harris wrote me in the early 1970s that Le Corbusier was "very much in favor of the Popular Front under Leon Blum" and that she did not agree with my view that he was influenced by Rousseau—it was, she said, "the simple, humanitarian love for people that motivated him." This abstract love was expressed often, but it did not extend to the Americans after the UN fiasco and other disappointments, as one can see in a letter where he politely refuses to take up a commission for public housing that Marguerite's daughter initiated in the early 1960s. He says he is too old and, besides, the French and Americans have different views on how these matters should be handled. "The land of the timid people" was to become, in his mythic imagination, the land of mammon, and a key opposition between the major battle of our time, the war between money and culture. Marguerite, for a time, was his spiritual guide, his Beatrice, in navigating this battlefield. Yet in the early 1930s his idealism and hope still dominated his growing despair and bitterness.

Ideal Liberal Institutions

While Le Corbusier was retreating from city life to the simplicity of the country he was at the same time becoming interested in the possibilities of a viable public realm. In the 1920s, his city plans culminate ironically in an empty space in the center: an airport, or business center, that is a purely utilitarian institution. Partially this resulted from Le Corbusier's suspicion of the traditional church and state. Like so many Modern architects, he had nothing but contempt for party politics and little respect for all the going political options, whether Republicanism, Communism, Fascism, Anarchism, or National Socialism. The only ideology he could accept was that of his own construction, what might be called idealist liberalism. Like a son of the Enlightenment he would accept only ideals as his guide, ideals based on reason. This allowed him, like Walter Gropius, to remain free from partisan involvements in a sort of apolitical politicism, sailing between the Scylla of Fascism and the Charybdis of Communism, a polarization which compromised many architects in the 1930s. Yet if this position had an intuitive, pragmatic sense, it also brought problems. All the clients had to be persuaded by idealist arguments (instead of party sentiments) and had to be enlightened paternalists on the order of Colbert or, at least, M. Fruges, the commissioner of Pessac.

Le Corbusier faced the ambiguity involved in this directly. He designed "ideal workers' houses" in steel for the ministry in charge of mass-producing houses. Five hundred thousand were to be built under an act formulated by M. Loucheur. But just as Le Corbusier produced design after design—mixing prefabrication and rough masonry—he would accompany them with the disclaimer "The right state of mind does not exist," "There is no point of contact between the two sides involved: my plan (which is a way of life) and those for whom the law is made (the potential clients who have not been educated)." In short, he would pursue enlightened and liberal ideals and then claim that the masses of people were incapable of living up to them. This paralleled the paternalistic idea that only a few great men were capable of initiating significant projects that would educate and transform the masses. He was supported in this idea by the emergence of several liberal institutions, such as the League of Nations, 1927, and by contact with utopian individualists such as Paul Otlet, the client for the "Mundaneum" and World City, 1929.

Both projects for the League of Nations and World City represented a form of internationalism popular to liberals after the First World War. These gigantic projects would contain respectively a rational world government and world culture, an assembly of all nations, and a superanthropology, a scientific collection of all customs, cities, and tongues. In hindsight, it is too easy to laugh at their naiveté. One has to imagine the idealism of the time, prior to the later failures of the United Nations, UNESCO, and other forms of internationalism. For Le Corbusier this internationalism was the basis for an emergent public realm.

The League of Nations [fig. 131] was laid out in many ways like a Renaissance palace with a series of perpendicular axes crossing a *cour d'honneur* which culminated in the *res publica*, the wedge-shaped Assembly Hall.

131. League of Nations, 1927, enhanced and redrawn. This "Palace" is raised on *pilotis* and surrounded by English landscape gardening. Although this scheme was thrown out by the academics, it is interesting to note that the layout is quite classical. The Assembly Hall, symmetrical about an entrance portico, had a sculptural group—a quadriga—placed against the large blank wall facing the lake. The symbolic articulation of important points, of arrival and view, typified LC's approach and distinguished it from that of other Modernists.

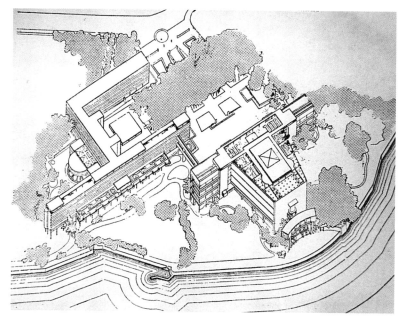

A very clear hierarchy of elements is established, leading from the more utilitarian, the secretariat, to the symbolic, the agora or place of meeting. Not only does the Assembly Hall occupy the supreme position next to Lake Geneva, but its wedge shape and sculptural additions announce its priority over the rectilinear forms. A considerable amount of effort went into determining adequate sight and acoustic lines so that the 2,600 participants in world government could speak and be seen. In fact the wedge form and parabolic section were innovations at the time which later became common to assembly halls, even becoming their conventional and symbolic shape. But the project was excluded from a competition for the building on a technicality, because it was not presented in india ink. At the same time a small newspaper from the city next to La Chaux-de-Fonds started publishing a series of attacks on Le Corbusier by a Herr von Senger. These attacks were also instrumental in the failure of the project and they were later collected to be used by the Nazis to discredit Modern architecture as well as Le Corbusier, who was featured in the title as *The Trojan Horse of Bolshevism.*

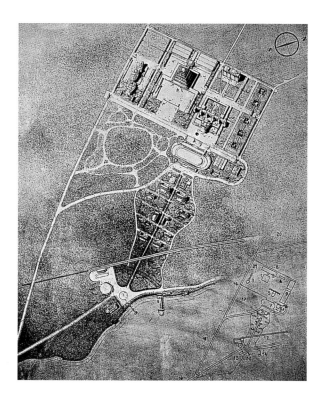

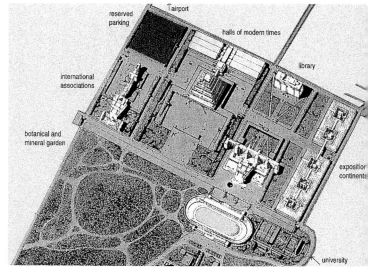

132. Mundaneum Project, 1929, enhanced and redrawn. The hierarchy of spaces culminates in a pyramid containing the world museum; the world library and university are on either side of the axis while the stadium is the terminal point of another. For these shapes and axes Le Corbusier was attacked by the functionalist wing of the Modern Movement.

After this debacle, Le Corbusier came back with another internationalist project to be situated right next to the League of
Nations, the Mundaneum or the "Center of Centers" [fig. 132]. The
program for this was developed by a Belgian industrialist, Paul
Otlet, baptized "Saint Paul" by Le Corbusier for his efforts in
spreading the message. In fact, the two prophets wasted a good deal
of time and money giving lectures and putting on exhibitions trying to interest the Genevans in the World by the City. An extract
from Otlet's manifesto gives an idea of their grand intentions.

> The goal of the Mundaneum is to expose and make known by
> literature, objects and words: How Men, from their humble
> origins, have elevated themselves to the splendour of their
> Geniuses, their Heroes and their Saints;—How the World was
> discovered and, its Forces being brought under control, was
> almost entirely settled;—How the Cities, Nations and
> Civilizations grew up . . .

For Le Corbusier the most exciting part of the project was
the World Museum, a spiral in plan and stepped pyramid in section, which would show the various stages of civilization in continuous development. One would take an elevator to the top and
middle of the pyramid (the beginning of civilization) and walk
down in ever descending ramps until one reached the bottom (or
the present day). A triple nave containing three kinds of information (the objects, where they were created, and a description of
the culture) classified man's knowledge in a typically French way.
One is reminded of the *Encyclopedie* of the Enlightenment, or
the French pursuit of Structuralism, where the same synchronic
and diachronic analyses are attempted. Yet the World Museum
had two obvious faults. Being a hollow pyramid, it was terribly
wasteful of interior space, and starting off with the beginning of
man at the top, not only would it imply devolution rather than
evolution to the present, but worse—have to burrow below the
ground in the future! Thus in his next project for the Endless
Museum, Le Corbusier flattened the spiral and allowed for unlim-
ited, nonhierarchical growth. The idea of the World Museum
did not stop here. In a sense, it was turned inside out and upside
down by Frank Lloyd Wright and built as the Guggenheim Museum
in New York. Le Corbusier himself constructed two Endless

133. Salvation Army, City of Refuge, Paris, 1929–33. The first glass curtain wall hermetically sealed with no window openings, but "conditioned air" instead. Note Le Corbusier's car, once again photographed outside to make the point that it was "a building like a motorcar."

Museums, in Japan and India, none quite as spatially exciting as Wright's.

Late in 1929, Le Corbusier finally met an enlightened client who could realize one of his liberal ideals: providing healthy, even salubrious, habitation for refugees and the destitute. Mme la Princesse Singer-de Polignac was instrumental in commissioning the Salvation Army Refuge in Paris and seeing this revolutionary building through to completion [fig. 133]. Like the previous two projects, this monumental building was a modern version of Beaux-Arts axial planning, with a series of elements disposed hierarchically in an architectural promenade. Because of the tight site, Le Corbusier was forced to push the elements together, laterally, in a very exciting way. A gigantic doorway leads next to a cantilevered canopy and thence to a curved entrance portico followed by a grand hall. The promenade culminates in the glass dormitory slab, which contained two technical innovations: the "neutralizing wall" and "exact respiration." Ideally, these inventions should have provided the inhabitants with pure, clean air at a constant temperature of eighteen degrees centigrade, but, in the event, they were never completed for financial reasons, and the refugees became rather uncomfortable in the summer. The "neutralizing wall" was to be a form of double glazing with circulating hot and cold air between, while "exact respiration" was to be a form of air-conditioning system, found in large buildings today, which supplies and extracts humidified air from a central system. Since the double glazing was not built, the dormitories overheated in the summer and openings and *brises-soleil* were later provided, thus destroying the effect of the clear curtain wall.

Although Le Corbusier has been criticized by several people, such as Reyner Banham, for wishing to provide a constant environmental solution instead of flexible controls, it seems more to the point to commend him for trying to innovate in an area where few other architects were trying. One of these, Pierre Chareau, was constructing the Maison de Verre in Paris at the same time—a building which made use of different types of glass and climate controls in a uniquely functional and poetic way. A strange figure with briar pipe, dark heavy-rimmed glasses, and bowler hat was seen prowling the site early in the morning taking down notes and eyeing the glass brick. Le Corbusier was absorbing lessons not only from Chareau but also from the Russian Constructivists, and he produced at least two projects which owed a lot to them. The first was the Nestlé pavilion of 1928 [fig. 134], which used blown-up graphics and chocolate products to create a Constructivist collage of advertisement, and the second, the Palace of the Soviets, 1931,

134. Nestle Pavilion, 1928.

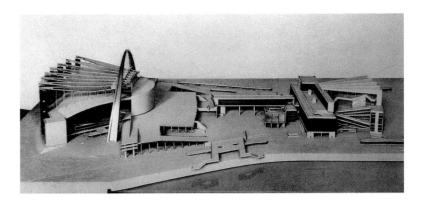

outdid even the Constructivists at their own game of structural gymnastics [fig. 135].

In the latter, two main assembly halls, both wedge-shaped, are slung from giant, bony girders that cut across the sky like so many jagged sawteeth. Below one, the roof of the auditorium zigzags back and forth following acoustic lines, while above the other, a parabola rises holding one half of the girders, which in turn hold the auditorium roof. The dynamic clash of skeletal structures, dark glass, and white volumes, all laid out on a symmetrical base, was appropriately equal to the grandiose nature of this palace. The mania for gigantic spectacle which developed out of the Russian Revolution had found its architectural equivalent. Mass celebrations, the 1920s version of today's pop festivals, find accommodation in a large, open-air platform. Indeed the program and lightweight steel architecture have an obvious parallel with what was produced in the 1960s by such designers as Archigram.

In spite of the sculptural bravado, doubts arise about the nature of the functions. If the public realm depends upon being able to speak and act in public in such a way as both to disclose oneself and to intervene in political decisions, then the size of the assembly halls alone would condemn them to a certain irrelevance. They are at best containers of a mass society and its organized spectacles, at worst organs of a totalitarian state. In part Le Corbusier must have realized this because he spent a great deal of time detailing the lobby spaces, what he called the *forum*, where all sorts of quasi-political activities such as eating, talking, and telephoning were accommodated [fig. 136].

In the event, a jury rejected the project because it looked too much like a factory and, more important, because Stalin had decreed that proletarian architecture must be Greco-Latin in spirit. The Palace of the Soviets was to be built in the Italian Renaissance style. The Stalinists argued that just as the people had taken control of the banks away from the bourgeoisie, so too they would appropriate their Corinthian columns. Le Corbusier's attitude toward this debacle was not his usual fury. Returning to his and Adolf Loos's theories of cultural evolution, he actually agreed with the decision to build in the Renaissance style, arguing that the relative youth of Russian revolutionary culture meant they were at that stage of development. Only a civilization in maturity, at its high point, could have accepted the severe lyricism and technical brilliance of his solution. In fact, Le Corbusier's cultural theories obscured the issue. The rejection and reaction was due to nothing more nor less than the Stalinist party line, a point which many

136. Palace of the Soviets, forum under the assembly hall for 15,000. Le Corbusier finally built such a grand space of columns and walls in the General Assembly at Chandigarh (fig. 183).

PALAIS DES SOVIETS, A MOSCOU 1931

137. Centrosoyus, Moscow, first project, 1929, enhanced and redrawn. A basketball court crowns the central assembly, the public realm. For the second project LC developed unbroken double-skinned walls of glass with air-conditioning between, what he called *respiration exact*, a system that never worked because of extreme thermal gains.

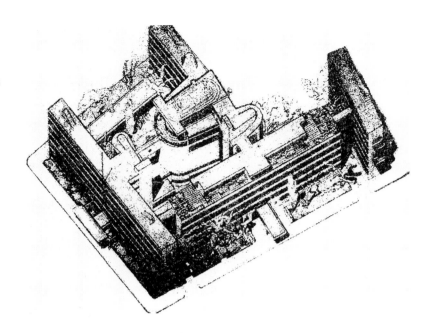

other Western intellectuals also did not understand for a long time, partly because of wishful thinking, partly from ignorance.

The only building that Le Corbusier managed to get built in Russia, the Centrosoyus, 1929–33 [fig. 137], was a caricature of his intentions and the public realm—a monolithic office block gross in scale and without the intended air-conditioning system. It was not until the 1950s and Chandigarh that he had the opportunity to build the public realm for the liberal/authoritarian institutions he imagined in the 1930s.

Participation and the Radiant City

During the 1930s and until the end of the Second World War, Le Corbusier devoted a great deal more time to city planning, partly because he received few architectural commissions and hence had the time to undertake theoretical studies. His output of city plans is remarkable, not only in sheer size, but also in terms of futility. Few were commissioned, fewer still were paid for, and none stood much chance of being adopted. This may account for the new tone that is discernible in Le Corbusier's writings: diffuse, repetitive, sometimes bitter and bombastic, and, invariably, hurried. Books are thrown together so fast from collected articles that their author has to apologize for mistakenly publishing an article twice. But:

In the very first pages of this book I have warned you that this is not a work of serenity, written in the calm study of a man of letters. "Alas! that serenity is not for us!"

Alas indeed, since he had declared himself, in his French passport, a "Man of Letters." The tone becomes hysterical, pathological, and, unfortunately, infectious. Many books on city planning, some written by CIAM members, sound as if they were written in the trenches, and, as a result, all sorts of liberties are taken with the reader which would not be tolerated in a time of peace. The Corbusian planner is at war with a society that will not listen to him, whether he screams or talks sensibly. The metaphors that LC uses concerning a city keep their pathological center: if it is suffering from a "sickness" in 1922, then by 1930 it is "fatally ill" from a "cancer," or "vermin," and, by 1946, it is suffering from a sclerosis of circulation. Paris, London, New York, Rio de Janeiro, and Buenos Aires are now "in a new slavery" and "tentacled." What are the new positive themes that emerge from this period of turmoil?

First of all, the necessity for active participation which is preached in *La Ville Radieuse* and *When the Cathedrals Were White*, both of which were written throughout the early 1930s, but meant to appear in 1935.

> Rome meant enterprise. They invented Roman cement. The Republic, *res publica*, was the object of all their care. The public good was the reason for the city and also for their arrival in the city. Participation in it was their life.

If Le Corbusier is here idealizing the Roman public realm (participation was more a reality under the Greeks) he positively goes overboard about the Age of Faith (perhaps recalling the Ruskinian ideal of the Gothic).

> When the cathedrals were white, participation was unanimous, in everything. There were no pontificating coteries; the people, the country went ahead. The theatre was in the cathedrals, set up on improvised stages in the middle of the nave; they told off the priests and the powerful: the people were grown up and masters of themselves, in the white church—inside and out.

"The house of the people," where they discussed mysteries, morality, religion, civil affairs, or intrigue was entirely white . . . we must get that image into our hearts.

The political method for inducing this participation, pointed out above, was to be a form of anarcho-syndicalism, where workers' unions would form the basic power structure and send representatives to a federal center [fig. 7]. This nineteenth-century ideal of power coming from the bottom of the hierarchy, the trade unions or syndicates, and direction coming from the top, administrators, was a new way of cutting the political cake. It entailed each place of work being the unit of power: workers know what is best for their trade and the local situation. But it is the central authority that determines the master plans for the country as a whole. Liberal/authoritarian, the complex system divides the contradictions facing politics in a way that has never been fully attempted. For that reason, as well as for the way it ensured the complete opposites of individual freedom and collective control, LC preferred it to the reigning approaches: parliamentary democracy, Fascism, and Communism. He found two current examples of participation in action and they are exceedingly odd given the previous models of the forum and medieval commune.

The Van Nelle tobacco factory in Rotterdam, a creation of the modern age, has removed all the former connotation of despair from that word "proletarian." And this deflection of the egotistic property instinct towards a feeling for collective action leads to a most happy result: the phenomenon of *personal participation* in every stage of the human enterprise . . . The Managers, the highest and lowest grades, the workers, male and female, all eat together here in the same great room, which has transparent walls opening onto endless views of meadows. Together, all together . . . Participation! I can truly say that my visit to that factory was one of the most beautiful days of my life.

If this Modern factory of steel and glass designed by the Dutch Constructivist Mart Stam was a current version of the white cathedral, so too was the Ford motor factory in Detroit.

In the Ford factory, everything is collaboration, unity of views, unity of purpose, a perfect convergence of the totality of gestures and ideas. With us, in building, there is nothing but contradictions, hostilities, dispersions, divergence of views, affirmation of opposed purposes, pawing the ground.

What is odd here is that Le Corbusier can so easily confuse a unified communal effort like harmonious factory work with political participation, or the necessary plurality of views in the public realm. It was this confusion of the smooth-running factory with the good state that was one reason he would soon collaborate with the French Fascists. However, in architectural terms his ideas also lead the other way. The large state construction allows individual participation at the small scale. In his viaduct building, for instance, every individual can build a villa in whatever way he or she wants [fig. 138]. Here public ownership of the artificial sites leads to a great deal of personal freedom at the very small scale. The idea again became current in the 1970s with theorists such as Nicolas Habraken and architects such as SITE. In an unofficial form it was also carried out by the authorities in Asia and India, where vast housing structures were built and then allowed to be inhabited in nonstandard (illegal) ways.

It makes economic as well as social sense to separate the public support system from the private dwelling and let the individual have control over the latter. Here participation can result in a much richer and more responsive environment. What is surprising, given Le Corbusier's interest in participation, workers' unions, the public realm, and such liberal institutions as the

138. U-curved, twenty-three-story apartments, Fort–L'Empereur, Plan Obus, 1932. A curvilinear roadway on top of dwellings made by the inhabitants in different styles including Moorish, Louis XVI, Italian Renaissance, and Modern. An attempt to unify different cultures through inclusion of opposite codes became a method of Post-Modernists in the 1970s.

Le Corbusier: Back to Nature 1928–45

League of Nations, is that none of this is adequately translated into the city plans. In his ideal plans for the Contemporary City and the Radiant City there is no forum or public realm, beyond a few cultural institutions. The business center in 1922 and then housing in 1930 occupy the symbolic center and functional place of importance. Perhaps this is because Le Corbusier still equated the captains of industry with the state's leaders, and Ford Motor Company with a public realm. In any case, what he continues to do is to divide the city up into four functions—living, working, circulating, recreating—leaving out the political and public function until the late 1940s.

His general scheme for the Radiant City develops on the biological analogy with the business center as the head of the animal. The housing and institutes are the heart, spine, and sometimes the stomach, while the factories, warehouses, and heavy industry are the entrails [fig. 139]. The biological analogy further justifies the separation into functions, or "organs," in spite of the fact that real life depends on symbiosis and the overlap of functions. But for Le Corbusier it was always a question of studying the statistical nature of cities, adding up all the similar elements, and then purifying them into ideal types. This method of Cartesian analysis comes from the French tradition, and the purification comes from painting and architecture. But this sets a problem. While it makes sense in a building or work of art to essentialize a theme, in a city it makes nonsense. From the 1930s on, LC tried to figure out where cities were evolving. Then, having established the basic forces, he would produce a design based on a single, dominant function. This meant he might predict the future quite well—skyscrapers, highways, and business districts—and present his plans as inevitable trends. But in fact his designs are always Platonic diagrams of purified organs, or ideal types separated from other ideal types, as if mixed use were the cardinal sin. His justification is precisely what will be used to refute it thirty years later: biology.

A plan arranges *organs* in order, thus creating *organism* or *organisms*. BIOLOGY! The great new word in architecture and planning.

The biological analogy extends so deeply into the forms of city planning that when Le Corbusier is flying over the rolling

139. La Ville Radieuse, general scheme, 1935. The city begins to take on the linear form allowing for lateral expansion. Compared to the Contemporary City of 1922, housing rather than offices occupies the center, or heart of the body, administration the head, factories the bottom. The density increases from three hundred to one thousand per hectare—very large skyscrapers of living, *Unités d'habitation*.

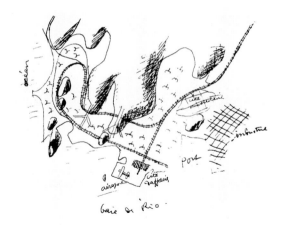

140. Plan for Rio de Janeiro, 1929. The business center is at the culminating point of the curvilinear residential blocks. The Y-shaped office block is introduced in place of the cruciform plan.

landscape of Rio de Janeiro he can suddenly see the topography as a female body and introduce curvilinear forms into his city planning [fig. 140].

One thing that sparked off this link between his interest in women and city organization was the airplane, in praise of which he wrote a book in 1935. The airplane, with its bird's-eye view, reveals a new truth about cities and discloses principles of organization that have previously remained hidden, just as the microscope had done. The airplane thus has the same mixture of implacable truth and lyricism that Le Corbusier admired in science books and statistics. It allowed him to get, literally, above the normal anthropomorphic view and reclassify the accepted urban categories. These became, by 1944, a new book and "The Three Human Establishments." Imagine reducing all contemporary cities to just three ideal types! The dispersed suburban sprawl, which he saw from the airplane, he purified into the cooperative "Radiant Farm." The strip developments along routes he clarified into the

141. Linear Industrial City, 1942. The four functions are arranged side by side in a line. The project is similar to Russian ones of the 1930s and also to the official French policy of decentralization during the war.

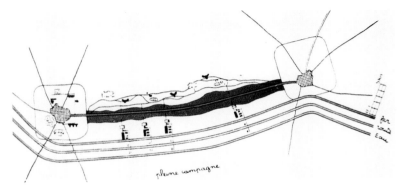

"Linear Industrial City" [fig. 141], and the sprawling city itself was essentialized into the "Radio-Concentric City of Exchange." All of this was quite a departure from his previous ideas, which were against dispersal and very much against concentric rings of city growth. Partly one may attribute this change to the realities that were seen from the plane.

But also one may attribute the shift to the more basic issues I have mentioned, of sexuality, a growing disenchantment with machinery, and a rediscovery of the countryside and syndicalism. The whole idea for the Radiant City came from a quick, intuitive response to a commission. Again the origin of his city plan is oddly ironic.

If in 1922 LC was asked to design a fountain and attached a city of three million to it, then in 1930 he was asked to design a farm—and attached a city of one million to it—*La Ville radieuse*. Is this progress, dropping two million people out of the ideal city? Or should he be applauded for expanding the commission from a farm to the city? The pretext for the 1930 example of mission creep was a farm cooperative, meant for a peasant organization in the Sarthe district. LC's design for this Radiant Farm projects an image that is a very touching mixture of peasant life and industrialization [fig. 142]. The farm is mechanized and prefabricated, but the simple, everyday objects of the farmhand are given an exaggerated importance. Perhaps most important of all is the idea of the Cooperative Center, which distributes communal machinery to the farmers and sells their products as well as provides a new element of village life, the communal club. In this proposal one gets the rare glimpse of Le Corbusier's Regional-Syndicalism and participation actually resulting in an embodiment of the public realm.

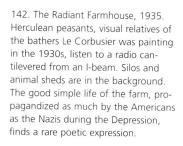

142. The Radiant Farmhouse, 1935. Herculean peasants, visual relatives of the bathers Le Corbusier was painting in the 1930s, listen to a radio cantilevered from an I-beam. Silos and animal sheds are in the background. The good simple life of the farm, propagandized as much by the Americans as the Nazis during the Depression, finds a rare poetic expression.

Counterattack and Defeat

Throughout the 1930s and early 1940s there was a worldwide reaction against the Modern Movement which was directed against its leaders, for example Walter Gropius, Le Corbusier, and Leonidov, and its various avant-garde organizations, such as the Ring, CIAM, and OSA (the Association of Modern Architects in Russia, 1925–32). Le Corbusier, as the best known and most articulate of these leaders, took the brunt of the attack and was, in the event, the only one to mount any sort of counterattack. The other leaders did not write books against reaction. They went underground, into exile, or collaborated with the mounting nationalist movements. Walter Gropius wrote compromising letters to Rosenburg and Goebbels, Mies van der Rohe signed anti-Semitic manifestoes and worked for the Nazis until 1937, Moholy-Nagy fled Germany. In Russia the Constructivist architects mostly just stopped working and were not heard from any more. In Italy, the Fascists compromised virtually all of the Modern architects by adopting a style of stripped Classicism and commissioning such Rationalist designers as Pier Luigi Nervi and Giuseppe Terragni. In America a similar kind of stripped Classicism combined with Hollywood Art Deco became the ruling style. Everywhere a pompous, semihistoricist architecture reigned supreme. To live through this period as a Modern architect was like living through Diocletian's persecutions as an early Christian—a question of compromise and survival. Le Corbusier's record during this period is, like that of so many others, full of ambiguities. It started with the nationalist attacks on his work and the loss of many commissions, such as the League of Nations competition.

M. de Senger published his second book [in 1931]: "The Trojan Horse of Bolshevism." The horse, that's me. The newspapers of Neuchâtel and La Chaux-de-Fonds continued to dredge up this source of clear water and republished these decisive articles. One day, I received from my city of birth, La Chaux-de-Fonds, three editorial articles from its newspaper, consecrated to my collusion with the Soviets, my spurning my country and the beauty of art. My father honorary president of the Swiss Alpine Club, my mother the musician, had left in La Chain-de-Fonds a memory filled with great dignity. The life of my great-aunt, who was for me another mother, was full of devotion, charity, love of God and noble works. The day I received these articles, I cried with the knowledge that she would read such abominations . . .

What stuff for newspaper writers of great and small papers! written to be copied. And Modern architecture born about 1830 in Paris, became Bolshevist in Geneva, Fascist in the Paris *"Humanité,"* and petty bourgeois in Moscow (where gable and column have again come into style), recognized only by Mussolini [see his speech to the young architects in June 1934]. A match is of course a small and unimpressive thing, and yet, it may be the beginning of a catastrophic fire. This campaign of Senger was not without success: two years later the "figaro" in Paris began a series of articles from the talented pen of Camille Mauclair with a sharpness bordering on the ridiculous. These attacks were based on the "heroic" articles that appeared in 1927 in the "heroic" "La Suisse Liberale" of Neuchâtel. The great "figaro" succeeded in discovering this hero and fulfilled its noble mission of saving Fatherland, Beauty, and Art and whatever else was wanted . . . "Is Architecture going to die?" This was the title of the book of Camille Mauclair. He certainly needs to be consoled: "Camille you have lost your head, console yourself, Architecture is far from dying, it enjoys the best of health . . . it only demands that you leave it alone!"

The arguments that Senger, Mauclair, and the Nazis used against Le Corbusier were, in each case, turned on their head and refuted. They were published in various books and magazines and summarized in a book written by Maximilien Gauthier near the end of the war. In a sense, many of the attacks were so degraded that it was humiliating to answer, thereby implying they had some validity. But Le Corbusier, unlike the other Modern architects, was never above polemics or what amounted to architectural street fighting. He fought the worldwide reaction in a series of pamphlets, books, and buildings.

Crusade—or the Twilight of the Academies was published in 1933 to answer Senger and a certain Professor Umbdenstock of the Ecole des Beaux-Arts, who had launched a campaign against Le Corbusier. Here the academies had combined with nationalism

143. Monument to Vaillant-Couturier, 1937. The open hand and expressive mouth of the orator became constant symbols in Le Corbusier's later work. The abstract representation of this work influenced later Post-Modern symbolic buildings and sculpture. Book, hand, mouth are collaged against a cantilevered phallic shape that divides the highway near Fontainbleau.

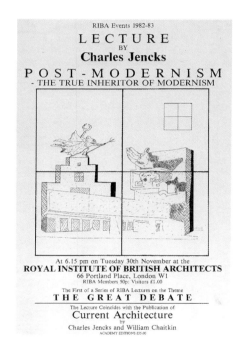

RIBA Events 1982-83

LECTURE
BY
Charles Jencks

POST-MODERNISM
- THE TRUE INHERITOR OF MODERNISM

At 6.15 pm on Tuesday 30th November at the
ROYAL INSTITUTE OF BRITISH ARCHITECTS
66 Portland Place, London W1
RIBA Members 50p: Visitors £1.00

The First of a Series of RIBA Lectures on the Theme
THE GREAT DEBATE

The Lecture Coincides with the Publication of
Current Architecture
by
Charles Jencks and William Chaitkin
ACADEMY EDITIONS £35.00

144. RIBA Great Debate, November 1982 (CJ). My comparison of LC's monument to Michael Graves's Portlandia underscored the importance of abstract representation for his Modernism and later Post-Modernism.

and the traditional building trades to condemn Modern Architecture because it was supplanting the older forms of building and putting many craftsmen out of work. This economic attack was naturally financed by many of the building trades, and, actually, capitalists. It further confirmed Le Corbusier's suspicion of all moneyed interests whether they were capitalist or socialist. Because of this aggressive stance against special interests, the Communist party of France tried to enlist Le Corbusier in the Popular Front against Fascism. The Civil War in Spain, National Socialism in Germany, and the friendship of Communists such as Fernand Léger and Paul Vaillant-Couturier almost persuaded him to join the Popular Front. But, in the event, all he did was go to their meeting and design a monument for Vaillant-Couturier, who died in 1937 [fig. 143]. Characteristically he turned a political platform into a building program.

> From my point of view, there exists only one way for the Popular Front to demonstrate that something new has begun on the scene of social justice; that would be to construct right now in Paris the elements for habitation which reflect at the same time the latest state of modern technique and your wish to put such things in the service of men.

The monument reflects very aptly the qualities of fighting against social injustice which Le Corbusier found in Vaillant-Couturier. It makes use of conventional motifs present in French art of social protest, for instance, the screaming mouth and jutting hand which Delacroix and Picasso also used symbolically. The image of Liberty leading the people and *Guernica* are behind his synthesis, making it one of the first Modern works of public art to be representational and political (and, in that sense, a harbinger of Post-Modernism).

However, if Le Corbusier could see the necessity for a new public art and social justice, he could still be naive about the actual political forces and, because of his commitment to authority and an elite, have a weakness for Fascism.

> In Rome, 1934, my two lectures were authorized after two years of argument by the youth of Rome and the Academy, by an intervention of Mussolini which took place at the beginning of the second lecture: the public reading of a message affirming the necessity of modern ideas concerning architecture. This was in answer to a vote of the Senate, fifteen days previously, declaring modern architecture antifascist. It was by the decree "nulla osta" that Mussolini had authorized my presence in Rome for these two lectures before the unions, on the architectural and urbanistic revolution. He summoned me to an audience, but, as he happened to be then with Hitler in Venice, I returned to Paris . . .

Another story has it that Le Corbusier sent his plans for the Radiant City to Mussolini, saying, "You've made the new state, here's the new architecture and town planning to go with it." Obviously LC held to a certain type of *cultural* elitism which could be compromised, or at least confused, by political elitism. In one diagram he actually puts forward the idea of a cultural pyramid with the avant-garde elite at the top, the romantic and academic group in the middle, and the poor "good people," confused and misdirected, at the bottom. This pyramid was no more than a description of taste as he and many others saw it—led by a small aristocracy—but it suggests how being too realistic might lead to being too reactionary.

And now we confront a tragic episode in his life, tragic in the negative sense: his attempts to work for Marshal Pétain. Understanding Le Corbusier's compromise with Vichy is revealing for the light it casts on a flaw in his character (or is it his theory?), and because it brings up the totalitarian strain in his and in other Modernists' work. As I have pointed out in several books, some Modern architects of the 1930s were attracted by the universalism expressed in Nazi and Fascist rhetoric. For instance, Nikolaus Pevsner could end one of the first books on the new Modernism in 1936, *The Pioneers of the Modern Movement*, with the recommendation that Modernism should be accepted because it was "totalitarian" (the word he uses interchangeably with *universal*). Robert Fishman has clarified many of the issues involved in Le Corbusier's case, and my summary here is partly based on his insights. One has to understand how the magnitude of the Machine Age crisis, as Corbusier called it, was the first step in his undoing.

Consider the size of Le Corbusier's Plan Voisin for Paris [fig. 145]. As he pointed out it would take a modern Colbert, Louis XIV's minister of public works, to command such a destructive and constructive cycle. Even after the building of La Defense in Paris, from the 1960s to 1980s, Le Corbusier's proposal looks grandiose. A

145. Plan Voisin for Paris, 1925, collaged and redrawn. Two square miles of the Right Bank are demolished for luxury gardens and apartments; 85 percent (or 50 percent?) is turned into greenery, and the rest is building and circulation. Monuments and a few urban set pieces are preserved as fragments in a park. The scales of past and future are discontinuous and mutually isolated: with this scheme the architecture of *Noli me tangere* becomes Modernist othodoxy.

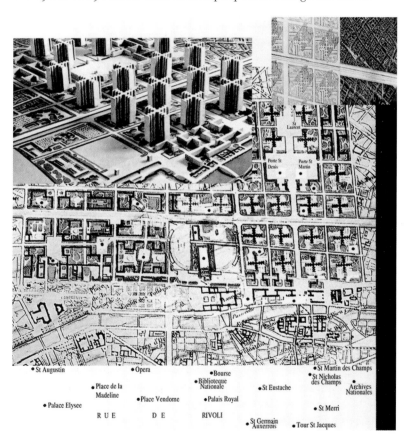

major superhighway bisects the scheme; vast open plazas, five Tiananmen Squares, occupy what used to be the private background tissue. Supposedly 85 percent of the ground space is green although, given the large amount of circulation space, and all the paving (in white), it is more like 50 percent.

What is the attitude toward the past and historical continuity? Monumental set pieces are saved—open spaces such as the Palais Royal and Place de la Madelaine—as are parts of the rue de Rivoli. Churches, the Opera, and the Bibliothèque Nationale are preserved as isolated events decontaminated by new surrounding greenery. But the past, in order to live as preserved monument, must be subtracted of its old urban tissue while a different one is supplied. It parallels Jesus's words to Mary Magdalene, after he has died and before he has ascended to heaven: *Noli me tangere*, do not touch the dead. Or, in architectural doctrine: destroy the virus of past urbanism and do not let the new touch the old monuments because they would be mutually polluting. Here is the Modernist position toward the past: respect, preservation, and dissociating contrast. The past is a fragment to be collaged, as a Surreal *objet-trouvé*, onto a new scale, a future that is discontinuous with it. In other words, Modernism is a cataclysmic rupture with history. According to this doctrine, if the past is over and done with, and negative from a functional and cultural point of view, it can only be honored as a relic. This is how the Plan Voisin and so much subsequent Modernism have treated it.

Thus Le Corbusier saw his role, to find the new Colbert, and with him create massive urban renewal schemes that were violently discontinuous with existing urban reality. Both size and revolutionary change made his search for an absolute power structure something to be expected, not inevitable, but highly likely. Once Monsieur Voisin, Citröen, and other capitalists rejected his megaschemes, he was forced to look elsewhere. In 1928 he wrote a pamphlet, *Towards the Paris of the Machine Era*, and called for a radical "Authority" outside the "established disorder" to impose the common good. Such a new Minister of Public Works would be a technician above politics, outside the polarization of left versus right. He would purchase all the property in central Paris needing renewal, at the going rate, through a type of eminent domain—"land mobilization"—and the subsequent redevelopment at much greater density would make profits for all. "Good urbanism makes money" for the whole community, and thus the General Will and History are resolved together by Authority.

By 1930–31, after the Crash and the failure of parliamentary democracy to do anything effective, Le Corbusier joins the Syndicalists and starts putting his faith in a new authority, what he calls "the Plan." For two years he writes manifestos in a journal of that name, much as he had done for *L'Esprit Nouveau*, and when this magazine fails he starts another one, *Preludes*, which continues to publish his polemics until 1935, when they are collected together as *La Ville Radieuse*. By then, as the Depression becomes chronic, unemployment above 20 percent, productivity half of that of the 1920s, his search for a new authority becomes evermore pronounced: "France needs a Father," he writes in *Preludes*, "it doesn't matter who." Anyone who can impose order is better than the disordered marketplace and wavering opinion. The Machine Era is out of control, democracy does not work. He flirts with Mussolini, who does not take up his offers; he designs megaplans for Stockholm, Antwerp, Zurich, Geneva, and several for Algiers [fig. 146]. All are rejected, unpaid.

After the fall of France in June 1940, and the Armistice, Le Corbusier, Yvonne, and Pierre Jeanneret left for the small town of Ozon, in the south, to contemplate the new situation and their future. Settling into an abandoned farm, much as he had done in 1910, he starts on two books, *The Destiny of Paris* and *Les Murondins*, the latter showing his radical ideas for housing refugees. During this depressing time and throughout the early 1940s he also starts painting a new series of works which he titles the Ubus, after the Ubi Roi of Alfred Jarry. Here he goes against many of his previous ideas, even rules on the necessity of recognizable symbols, and moves into a kind of abstraction. He turns away from the human figure in disgust, even the earth woman he has been drawing in the thousands.

In effect, the crisis of Europe and his personal turmoil forces his imagination onto a new tack. "Thus at the time of defeat" he writes retrospectively in 1948, "driven to the Pyrenees and isolated in the country, I wished to set aside for awhile the figure of a man. Stones and pieces of wood led me on involuntarily to draw beings who became a species of monster or god. The wild rumblings and gesticulations which plunged the poor world into delirium filled the atmosphere with obsessive presences . . . I called them Ubus [after] a powerful and ludicrous person created by Alfred Jarry"

146. Plan Obus A, 1932, enhanced photo. As a close-up reveals, although curvilinear and organic in form, the scale of the imposition is discontinuous with the past, and huge. When LC sent this to the progressive mayor, M. Brunel, he wrote back: "I'm not sure that our present means are capable of realizing [its] goals . . . I would add that for the requisite authorities to declare the complete destruction of an agglomeration of three hundred thousand inhabitants and its reconstruction . . . it would be necessary to have an absolute dictator with the property and even the lives of his subjects at his disposal . . . If my unlucky star were to lead me to this absolute dictator necessary to the execution of your plans, I would not adopt them for the reason that they project the reconstruction of the city on the same site; I would choose another, better, nearby, and it would be easier." In other words, a sympathetic politician could see what LC could not admit and, in effect, predict the compromise nine years later.

147. *Ubu No. 4* , 1947.

[fig. 147]. These hybrids, Christopher Green points out, are similar to the antihuman monsters that Picasso produced under Franco. No doubt war, bestiality, and stupidity were spurs to his move into abstraction and its very opposite, the hermetic iconography of nonsense monsters.

The logic was compelling. If humanity had failed, nature itself could become grotesque, and it is rendered as a series of dismembered body parts—giant ears, combined sexual organs, and sculptural blobs that are almost autonomous. The personal crisis can explain a swerve in the painting during the early 1940s, and that, in turn, can be read as a sublimation of his own decision being worked out at the time to collaborate with Vichy. The significance of this shift into biomorphic, zany, and nonhuman symbolism is extremely important for several reasons. Negatively, it shows the way his private creations and private world compensate for what he is about to do publicly; positively, it shows an imaginative opening that will be worked out in a new language of sculpture and graphic work. I will return to the positive side, and the secret symbolism, when it surfaces to transform his architecture and, with Ronchamp, open a new avenue of architecture.

Publicly he decides by the end of 1940 to jump on the Vichy bandwagon. Why? Because, he implies in one of the few comments on the point, the Vichy Order of Architects granted three designers, who did not have official diplomas, the right to build: Auguste Perret, the engineer Eugène Fressynet, and Le Corbusier. These are three leading Modernists and therefore, the implication is, men of moral scruple. The unstated reason for his collaboration is that he has decided that Marshal Pétain *is* the authority for whom he has been searching for ten years, "Colbert's ghost," "the Father of France." In January 1941, and for the next eighteen months, he lobbies Vichy and attempts to get the levers of architectural power. "I enter into the tumult," he writes, "after six months of doing nothing [in Ozon] and equipped with twenty years of hope." He is appointed head of a study commission for questions relating to housing and building; for the first time in his life, he feels, men in power are taking him seriously. But actually, as Robert Fishman points out, he is a minor member of an embattled faction at Vichy, holed up in a small room, an intellectual and creator trying his best to do the right thing.

The odd thing is that, aside from some grandiose plans of reconstruction, and a few books, this work, "Les Murondins," becomes the most libertarian he ever designed [fig. 148]. Not until the self-build, radical housing proposed by idealist architects in the 1960s is such utopian design attempted again. How ironic and sad that his urban theory should lead him to authoritarianism, while his ideas are going the other way.

In Vichy, LC puts forward a scheme for government planning whereby a few enlightened "Master Builders" are given extraordinary powers. They are to override local codes, plan cities at the proper scale, stop growth if need be, shrink cities from three to one million, keep agricultural cities pure, and control the circulation systems, what he calls the seven kinds of traffic. Here we have not only Fascist authority, but the ghost of Schuré's *les grand initiés*, a reliance on the great man of destiny and a Philosopher King. Le Corbusier's errant thinking on this score parallels the misunderstanding of his own position: he is not yet a Master Builder nor even near the center of power, but marginalized in a garret.

Next he turns the Master Builder into another Nietzschean superman called "the Regulator." This character, who finds an echo in France today with "regulation theory," combines in his

Le chef d'un club de jeunes expo[se] prise

The head of a youth club explai[ns to his] companions

Les constructions «murondins» [use, permettant des groupeme[nts] porte quel terrain

'Murondin' constructions blend [into] picturesque groupings, regardle[ss]

148. "Murondins," 1940–44. Self-build housing for refugees. Load-bearing walls of concrete block and rammed earth or *pisé* on the site mixed with logs and covered with turf—a kind of prehistoric housing brought up-to-date. A reversal of all the Five Points.

idealistic imaginings the objectivity of the scientist with the lyricism of the poet and the power of Colbert. As LC writes in his *Poésie sur Alger*, accompanying his many plans, "the regulator serenely, lucidly, puts the world in order." In early 1942, Le Corbusier spends much of his time trying to get his third plan for Algiers accepted. He begs Marshal Pétain for an interview, he tries to get Vichy to delegate to him powers over the Algerian planners and mayor, and with each rebuff he redoubles his efforts at wresting control. As he tells the early part of the story:

> The minister Peyrouton, who had just arrested Laval, proposed that I go defend my ideas in front of my own *confreres*. I accepted, I went to Vichy, but they refused my entry on the commission. By chance I met, through a common friend, a member of the state council in charge of making building laws. The opportunity was present for the first time in my life, being always rejected by administration and thereby deprived of official data, to be able to know the general data at the national level and thus the power *to think of urbanism on a scale hitherto inaccessible for me*. The twenty-seventh of May 1941, a decree signed by Marshal Pétain gave me a temporary mandate for the creation of a State organization, the Committee for Housing and Real Estate. With François de Pierrefeu and André Boll we attempted to define a doctrine of the built environment for France. I thought I could at last carry out the proposals of the preparatory committee of urbanism

previously worked out with Jean Giraudoux in 1939, but a debacle cut everything short. The director in charge of *equipment general* said: "neither close—nor far—nor under any circumstance, will I work with Le Corbusier and Pierrefeu . . ." [my italics].

Le Corbusier calls this "a decree of death," but he again looks for Pétain's help, which again is not forthcoming. Nevertheless, in April 1942 he is sent by Vichy to Algiers and he brings a skyscraper project which remains, to this day, one of the most radical solutions for a city in the air [fig. 149]. He also brings "The Directive Plan" for the city as a whole, which divides it up into a European section, focused on the skyscraper, and a Muslim section, preserving the Casbah [fig. 150]. The officials, wishing to demolish parts of this and replace them with European housing, again object to his ideas: they are too expensive, too Modernist, and not sufficiently colonialist. But to accommodate the colonialists, he changes his rhetoric. Whereas before, in the previous five plans, the idea is to unite two equals, the Muslims and Europeans, the North Africans and the French, by now the intent is different. As Mary McLeod has shown, he changes *"Alger, Capitale de l'Afrique du Nord"* into *"Alger, Capitale de l'Afrique Française,"* drops his internationalism, and says that Algiers will become "the phoenix of France" insuring "the recognition of the mother country reborn from her ashes." Already he had changed his Syndicalist slogans to nationalist ones: *"Famille, Travail, et Patrie,"* and the new placement of the skyscraper, at the head of the European city, shows he was willing to compromise his planning idealism for realpolitik. But this continual paring away of ideas and ideals is still not enough to gain him success.

His presence is not welcomed either by the CIAM architects, who are embarrassed by his connections with Pétain, or by the local government, which is concerned about his alleged communism, Senger's book *The Trojan Horse of Bolshevism* having just reached Algiers. The mayor of Algiers lets it be known that he will arrest Le Corbusier as a Bolshevik agent. After several more months of his lobbying, the Algiers City Council finally rejects his plans on June 12. On July 1, 1942, Le Corbusier leaves Vichy for good and with disgust. He returns to Paris with the summation—*"Adieux, cher merdeux Vichy!"* He spends the remaining years of the

149. Algiers skyscraper project, 1939–42. The lozenge shape, *brise-soleil*, and complex articulation make this vertical city as comprehensible as the horizontal. A restaurant and hotel are at the top, offices behind the *brise-soleil*, and archives in the three solid bands.

150. Directive Plan for Algiers, spring 1942. The European business and government center is to the left, the preserved Casbah and Muslim center to the right. For the first time, ironically, Le Corbusier is becoming contextual and knitting together past, present, and future. Fascism has turned him into his opposite, a Post-Modern urbanist, but also someone willing to compromise his internationalism. He puts the skyscraper right in the heart of the French colonial sector, a retreat from his and Camus's ideal of reconciling Algerian and French cultures in a new synthesis.

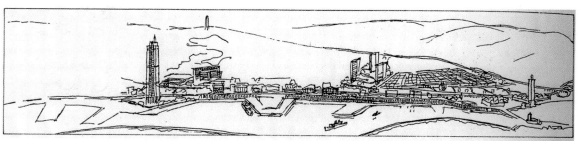

Le Corbusier: Back to Nature 1928–45

war in destitution, painting and organizing plans for a future reconstruction.

His collaboration has ended in disaster, and he expresses this with a bitterness that continues to grow for the rest of his life. He quotes, ironically, the first two lines from his most famous manifesto, *L'Esprit Nouveau*, its doctrine:

Town planning expresses the life of an era.

Architecture reveals its spirit.

Some men have original ideas and are kicked in the ass for their pains.

In other words, the zeitgeist is hell.

This is one conclusion, as he saw it. But another is that he had been trapped by his brand of apolitical politics in a vicious polarization between the Communists and Vichy. There was no room for a man who would collaborate with an authoritarian government, especially in order to set up libertarian reforms. Le Corbusier understood the polarization and, at one time, reversed the normal forms of etiquette in an act which was as humorous as it was naive and arrogant. When the Communist Party asked him to join them during the war, "I told them it was they who ought to join me." This inversion of customary practice is similar to his collaboration with Vichy. If there was opportunism here it was in the service of certain ideals which were held to be independent of politics. His collaboration was different from that of Gropius or Mies van der Rohe because it did not involve the compromising of architectural ideals. His architecture, unlike their proposals for the Nazis, did not become pseudo-Classical, or reactionary, or covered with such emblems as swastikas. It remained as tough, sharp, and brilliant as ever and, in a few respects, went in a more humane direction. One may deplore his ideals and actions, his elitism and search for Colbert at all costs; one may fault the naiveté of his thinking that Vichy would allow libertarian schemes. Like Robert Fishman, one may conclude that the worst thing about this episode is that he never understood its meaning or apologized.

But one cannot doubt the integrity on the level at which he was committed in his deepest being: architectural. Perhaps the artist, who by definition has to go beyond everyday experience, is allowed some political failings, a lack of realpolitik, which other citizens are not allowed. This old idea is at least arguable, as Hannah Arendt has written in an essay on Bertold Brecht. What the artist is not allowed is the compromise of his art for political motives. This Le Corbusier never did. Furthermore, if my reading of the urbanism, housing, and new directions in painting and sculpture is right, there is a surprise. The confrontation with Fascism develops his tragic view, makes him see himself as the tragic-comic Don Quixote, and turns him into a sometime Post-Modernist.

151. Le Corbusier and Walter Gropius, Paris, circa 1955.

PART IV

Monumental and Symbolic Architecture 1946–65

AFTER THE SECOND WORLD WAR, Le Corbusier took up the challenge of reconstruction with a vigor and spirit that were comparable to his efforts after the First World War. He developed the new aesthetic he had forged in the 1930s, particularly based on a sculptural use of the *brise-soleil*. The new plastic language was tough and realistic toward the postwar poverty, the lack of modern materials, and a destroyed industry. In a sense it was a perfect symbol of Le Corbusier's embattled personality and a war-torn Europe. If one likes to interpret architecture as expressing the spirit of the age, as he did, or as underlying iconology, as do Freudians, then it reveals a culture brutalized and made primitive by war, but one willing to face its problems straightforwardly, honestly. This attitude becomes Brutalism twenty years later, and forty years on it becomes another movement, Dirty Realism.

Characteristically, LC faced the social problems directly, the major task being rehousing refugees and those without a home—four million families in the case of France. In his burst of creative strength and commitment he differed from the other leading Modern architects, many of whom, such as Gropius and Mies, had emigrated to the United States and were content to carry through their prewar ideas and settle into commercial practice. When at the beginning of the war it had been offered to him, Le Corbusier spurned emigration. He saw his role as staying in Europe, fighting for his Mediterraneanism, and bringing the promise of Modern Architecture to fruition. What he had not counted on were the paradoxes and contradictions to which this would lead.

First of all, the International Style became officially accepted everywhere, but in a watered-down and sterile form. It became the style for vast schemes of reconstruction and Madison Avenue, every city's downtown and major corporate headquarters. On Park Avenue in New York it led to one glass and steel masterpiece built for Lever—a soap monopoly—another for Seagrams—a whisky giant—and a third (designed by Gropius and a rip-off of the Algiers skyscraper) for Pan Am—a multinational airline. Was the Modern Movement really fought to make the world safe for USA, Inc.? What a travesty of LC's social idealism. But even worse was the mass housing erected in the name of the Modern Movement, indeed Le Corbusier's name: "battery-hatch" living it was termed, among a thousand other epithets. Travesty, betrayal, superficiality—these words soon came to LC's lips as he contemplated the new enemy within, Modernism run amok. The tragic compromise that many predicted, of Modernist idealism with commercialism and quick megaconstruction, became a very Dirty Reality. Hence the popular reaction against Modern Architecture which occurred in the 1950s and 1960s leading ultimately to Post-Modernism and other movements.

In retrospect, the surprising thing about the 1945 liberation is that it did not release the cultural creativity that the end of the previous war had done. There were no movements as strong as Expressionism, Purism, Dada, and Constructivism. Perhaps the exhaustion of war, and its implication as a permanent state, dampened the creative imagination. Destroyed cities were built up on the outlines and styles of the past. The undestroyed sewer systems often served as an argument for keeping to the old road patterns and building plots. Le Corbusier, almost alone, protested against the lost opportunities and offered, once again, a "new spirit of the age" appropriate to the situation as he saw it. In this case, the spirit he proffered through his buildings and paintings was primitive, more realistic toward the aggressive aspects of man, explicitly sensual, and defensive. If the war had undermined his faith in the machine civilization, it liberated a renewed belief in formal gratification and living in a modern "cave." Housing would now shelter the individual as if it were a World War II bunker. Thick, heavy, "loyal" concrete protects the individual from strangers and noise and it frames a natural setting so that the lonely passenger of life can contemplate the cosmos. In a word, Le Corbusier conceived architecture as sculpture in a new plastic language for a new monastic being. The Nietzschean superman was now a monk and nomad on the errant ship of life.

The Archetypal City Center

Le Corbusier's first and most influential plan for reconstruction was for the bombed-out city of Saint-Dié in eastern France. In this scheme he put forward his first crystallization of the public realm [fig. 152]. Unlike his previous city plans, the civic center and marketplace—the agora—now occupy the primary space. It is conceived as a vast pedestrian precinct that would allow the citizens to perambulate around their civic monuments and meet on an informal level in cafés and shops. The value of this informal meeting Le

152. Saint-Dié plan, 1945, enhanced photo. A vast, open piazza containing isolated buildings that can be seen from all sides—sculpture in the round. The piazza is dominated by a government tower, the pie-shaped communal hall, and an L-shaped block of cafés and shops. An industrial green belt is to the south and residential *"unités"* to the north. In its displacement of axes and vistas off center, this project anticipates the Capitol at Chandigarh (fig. 190), though the open space is here not as great.

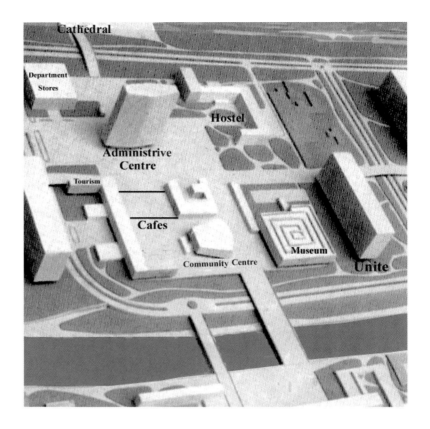

Corbusier understands as necessary to the formation of opinion, of political points of view (he may be imagining the Left Bank and Café Deux Magots).

> A French aperitif is taken when you are seated around a table. There are two, three, four persons. You have chosen your companions. You drink slowly. Conversation is calm, interrupted by the silences of wellbeing: you talk, you discuss, you can even enter into disputes. But the idea is followed through. Thus personal ideas are born, points of view, opinions. It is an agora around a siphon. The aperitif is a social institution and the café terrace is an urban institution.

These words, from *When the Cathedrals Were White*, show that he understood a form of participatory democracy through the very period he was trying to collaborate with Vichy and create an authority which would impose opinions. A typical contradiction. But, by 1945, Le Corbusier sees that civic institutions must be brought to the center of urban life, be made monumental, and replace those building types previously he had put at the heart: the office and mass housing. Western democracy is founded on the agora and the institutions of civic society. If they are not put in the middle of public life, then politics, which depends on debate and social reality, becomes sterile. The plan for Saint-Dié creates a monumental ensemble of giant buildings placed on a flat canvas. It is the forerunner for the capital complex at Chandigarh and it sets the canon of urbanism for the next twenty-five years, for good and bad. As a scheme it was published widely, placed on the cover of *Towards a New Architecture*, and given a traveling exhibition around the United States by the Walker Art Center in Minneapolis.

The focal point of the sculptural composition is the administrative tower to the north. This lozenge shape is set off by an L-shaped block of shops and cafés, a wedge-shaped assembly building, and the square spiral of the museum—objects set in juxtaposition on the grid plan of the canvas. Positively, each volume is a clear and distinct shape, but, negatively, and for the next twenty years of civic centers, space is uncontained and leaks out at the edges. No foreground is set against a background; everything is foreground. The contained urban room of traditional civic space, the *piazza publico*, is intentionally eroded by LC because it is seen as contaminated by the past and irrelevant to the future.

What are we to make of this as a model? The verdict, as usual, is mixed. Positively, the motorcar is kept out of the square, and buildings are treated as if they were Henry Moore sculptures in an open-air sculpture park; but, negatively, the buildings do not relate, except by juxtaposition—they do not form positive space or a street or a figural shape. The influence has not always been benign: most often the tower standing high and majestic in an open space becomes the stained block in a windswept plaza devoid of people. Because too many new town centers started to resemble this model, the criticism of the city center as a sculpture park became widespread with Post-Modernism. Visually this solution erodes urban identity and, economically, it does not provide activity necessary to make a city work. Le Corbusier, for all his polemic in favor of greater densities, never appreciated, in Jane Jacobs's terms, the actual economy of the city. With inadequate theories of how urban enterprises grow in interrelation and piecemeal, he resembled the typical dirigiste. In spite of his constant denials, he even resembled the central planner of the Communist system.

But, if we try to see this and other civic centers he designed, including the United Nations Plaza, through his eyes, then they appear differently. They are heroic landscapes of geometrical abstraction where modern man conducts rational and civic affairs. Their flat, open squares resemble a Greek *temenos*, a sacred space set apart—the stage for a cosmic drama. Or, in his own words: "it is an architectural melody that grows amidst the landscape of mountains of Saint-Dié—a song . . . [The buildings] constitute an opulent symphony . . . [but] an official sitting in his easy chair succeeded in annulling the whole plan! . . ." It was rejected by all sides of the political spectrum—the industrialists, socialists, and Communists—in favor of an academic reconstruction along the lines of the old city. While this rejection was occurring in 1946, Le Corbusier was under way on two more projects which were also to have a great effect on postwar architecture: the United Nations building in New York City and the *Unité d'habitation* in Marseilles.

Brutalism and Its Beauty: The *Unité*

The *Unité*, or Marseillian Block as it is sometimes known, represents the culmination of Le Corbusier's research into housing and communal living. It synthesizes ideas going back to his travels of 1907, particularly the relationship between the individual and collective that he so admired in the monasteries of Ema and Mount Athos. Like these monasteries, the *Unité* provides total individual privacy, something like a monk's cell for each member of the family, and meaningful collective activities—actually twenty-six different social functions—varying from a gymnasium to a shopping center (on the seventh and eighth floors).

Thus the inhabitants, who have formed a collective association, are bound together like a small village (of sixteen hundred people) in shared, everyday life. Yet no individuality is sacrificed, as it is in a small town or monastery, because each apartment is acoustically separated and in direct contact with the surrounding mountains and seascape. The contradictions between urbanity and privacy that we seek in a city, and which LC particularly looked for all his life, are for once successfully resolved.

The feeling of protection and individuality is so strong that it is

153. *Unité d'habitation*, Marseille,
1947–52, loggia. Each apartment has
two heavy balconies that have a direct
view of nature.

comparable to standing in a cave [fig. 153]. Yet the overall feeling is
not cave like or even monastic but more of being on a gigantic
ocean liner plowing through the choppy seas of verdure and hap-
hazard suburban sprawl [fig. 154]. The sheer physical presence
of this shiplike monolith is overwhelming. Its power and weight
are crushing. Its sculptural boldness and aggressive outline are so
emphatic that, although it is now actually smaller than some

154. *Unité*, east facade. Complex
articulation, heavyweight push-pull,
the three-dimensional facade—
all radical departures of postwar
architecture—were seen here for
the first time.

155. *Unité*, "The roof and landscape worthy of Homer." Each element is full-blown and given an emphatic gesture. Concrete curves and rocks by the pool refer to the surrounding mountains. The feeling up here is not only heroic, like being on a Greek temple, but also like being on a floating health camp, an ocean liner dedicated to cultivating the body and mind. Note the three-hundred-meter racetrack, the ship's funnel humming away, the pool, sundeck, and gymnasium. This middle-class commune is very successful with mothers, a place to read, sunbathe, and have the children watched. Free from traffic and fumes, it's the perfect lookout for the spectacle of the Mediterranean. Children lobby their parents not to move away; one family has lived here for three generations.

surrounding buildings, it still radiates a presence throughout the landscape. These visual meanings, comparable to those of the Acropolis, were quite intentional on Le Corbusier's part, especially on the roof [fig. 155]. He speaks about this with the same metaphors he found for the Parthenon in 1911:

> The spirit of power triumphs. The herald, so terribly lucid, draws to the lips a brazen trumpet and proffers a strident blast.

> The sentiment of an extra human fatality seizes you. The Parthenon, terrible machine, pulverizes and dominates [everything for miles around] . . .

The *Unité* is in every way as keen, sharp, and terrifying as the Parthenon. In fact the same effects are achieved by similar means. A straightforward functional simplicity, exaggerated in its plastic effect, and—what is not often seen in metaphorical terms—the power of proportion. The whole building is constructed from fifteen basic dimensions, "Modulor" dimensions, which are related to each other in simple, harmonic proportions. These relationships give a semantic strength quite apart from their numerical ratios, and it may well be that the Modulor (Le Corbusier's system of proportion worked out at this time) will be valued for this rather than its particular dimensions. For what it brings to a building is the *fullness*, even dignity, of each constructional element. They are all allowed a plenitude of space and gesture. None is cramped or hesitant or truncated as in so much architecture where one part obscures or denies another. Rather, by giving each part its ratio to another, a relationship is set up which implies a humane and dignified discourse among equals. Why is this dignity found in so much Classical architecture and not in other kinds? Perhaps because the adoption of a proportional system itself leads to particular visual meanings: harmony, restraint, a set of dramatic relationships where no single part is allowed unduly to usurp the presence of the whole. One thinks of the pyramids of Egypt or the Pantheon in Rome or the villas of Palladio, all of which achieve certain effects of grandeur, and one concludes that perhaps the semantic meanings of all proportional systems are the same regardless of their favored ratios and dimensions. Yet while an overall harmony is common to these buildings, individual meanings vary greatly.

Thus the *Unité* is seen, metaphorically, not only as a ship and a monastery, but by the critic Peter Blake "as graceful as Joe Louis on tiptoe." Indeed there is the graceful power of this heavyweight boxer in the taut "legs" of the building [156]. The violent push-pull of elements—heavy volumes punch up into the sky and the sides—are so many staccato jabs. Perhaps the emergence of this three-dimensional architecture actually owes something to Le Corbusier's image of himself as a boxer [fig. 9]. At any rate, a tough anthropomorphism is evident throughout, especially in the "Modulor Man" who is incised in concrete by the entrance, with legs apart and a gigantic fist raised above his head. At the inauguration of the building, Le Corbusier used an anthropomorphic

156. *Unité*. Anthropomorphic elements such as legs and spine carry what LC called "the artificial ground." Inside it is the air-conditioning, sewerage, rainwater, plumbing, and other utilities—all with open access between the concrete "skin."

metaphor to justify the crude aesthetic, the *béton brut*, the raw concrete, which was to become the insignia of the New Brutalism and postwar architecture.

> The defects shout at one from all parts of the structure! Luckily we have no money! . . . Exposed concrete shows the least incidents of the shuttering, the joints of the planks, the fibers and knots of the wood, etc. . . . in men and women do you not see the wrinkles and the birthmarks, the crooked noses, the innumerable peculiarities? . . . Faults are human; they are ourselves, our daily lives. What matters is to go further, to live, to be intense, to aim high, and to be loyal! [fig. 157]

Remember "loyal concrete," a material Le Corbusier invested with all sorts of human qualities, including even "dignity and truth." The interesting aspect of this is that he is also prepared to see it as crude and ugly and therefore as a possible means of contrast.

> . . . I have decided to make beauty by contrast. I will find its complement and establish a play between crudity and finesse, between the dull and the intense, between precision and accident. I will make people think and reflect, this is the reason for the violent, clamorous, triumphant polychromy of the facades. [fig. 158]

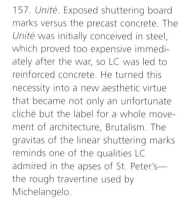

157. *Unité*. Exposed shuttering board marks versus the precast concrete. The *Unité* was initially conceived in steel, which proved too expensive immediately after the war, so LC was led to reinforced concrete. He turned this necessity into a new aesthetic virtue that became not only an unfortunate cliché but the label for a whole movement of architecture, Brutalism. The gravitas of the linear shuttering marks reminds one of the qualities LC admired in the apses of St. Peter's— the rough travertine used by Michelangelo.

158. *Unité*, west facade. The sides of the balconies are painted, thus making the building shimmer like a mosaic. Various rhythms are played at different rates, resulting in architectural polyphony.

These facades are in a sense the antithesis of those of the 1920s. Instead of being an ideal, flat plane, where the glass line and the facade are on the same level with no projections such as a cornice, or mullion, or drip-molding, these facades are violently sculptural in their depths and protrusions. Intense rhythms flow over the surface. Light and dark rectangles alternate at a certain tempo and then are inverted and played at twice the speed. This is the most musical of Le Corbusier's buildings and perhaps the one of which he was most proud. He spent a day with Picasso going through the building very carefully and mentions with obvious satisfaction that Picasso thereafter wanted to come into his atelier "to see how one makes architectural plans." In one sense, Le

159. *Unité*, interlocking section. Interior streets run through on every third floor. The parents' bedroom looks out over the double-height living room.

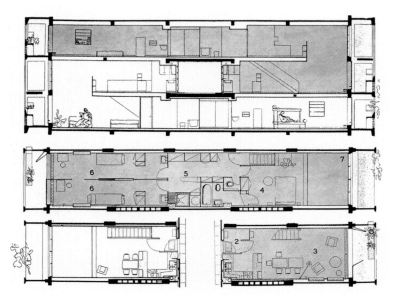

Corbusier valued this artist's opinion above all others, as he considered himself the Picasso of architecture, and both of them as the equals of Phidias and Michelangelo. Yet his other commitment was to the social plane, and it is here that the *Unité* made a great contribution, although one that has been heavily criticized.

The *Unité* is a "temple to family life," to private and domestic life centering around the mother and the daily meal. Each family apartment (there are twenty-three types) has the kitchen as its center, from which the mother can direct domestic affairs [fig. 159]. The children's bedrooms are placed farthest from the parents', thereby allowing a certain psychological and acoustic privacy.

Unfortunately, the children's bedrooms are often little more than six feet wide (unless the partition wall is slid back) and they are more like railroad cars or bowling alleys than places to sleep. Nevertheless, the strong Mediterranean sun lightens their deep interiors, and the exterior loggia provides a feeling of greater space. Indeed, these balconies are designed as extensions of the living space, and on a sunny day, when the large doors are slid back, they create the wonderfully mediated shade of a pergola.

Life inside the apartments varies a great deal and is not at all homogeneous or standardized as many critics have stated. In fact there is the kind of personal transformation of abstract structures that one finds in Pessac and Garches. Postcards on sale at the *Unité*

160. *Unité*, "bar-salon," with partition wall slid back.

161. *Unité*, shopping street. containing fish, meat, fruit, and vegetable stores as well as a bakery, liquor store, and drugstore. A post office, hotel, and restaurant are located nearby. The photograph shows the quieter end of the street with architects' offices, coiffeurs, and so on.

show a "bar salon" placed in the children's bedroom [fig. 160]. The effect is that of a wishing-well or gazebo located in a garden, and while this image may appear kitsch or improbable, it shows the popular transformation which is actually quite prevalent. Why should people personalize this architecture where they might not dare change so much other Modern work—that of Mies van der Rohe for instance? Is it because of the crudity and informal detailing? Television aerials and washing decorate the balconies. The walls of every apartment I saw were filled with bric-a-brac [fig. 153]. Perhaps this is provocative architecture that asks to be modified and territorialized. In any case, it provides a strong frame for variable urban living which is not destroyed when it is taken over and personalized. In providing twenty-three different apartment types, Le Corbusier went much further toward the pluralism of urban life than his detractors would like to admit.

The same is true of the shopping center, which has received much, to my mind misguided, criticism [fig. 161]. Located halfway up the building on the seventh and eighth floors, it has always been faulted for being cut off from the ground, from the connection with the external life of the street. Hence its supposed lack of life and financial viability. Shops remained unoccupied and the center empty for a long time. But this was due, as much as anything, to the maladministration of the center and the state's requirements that shops be bought and not rented—too high a risk for a small proprietor to take. Today all the spaces have been sold and the shopping street really is a marvelous alternative to the hustle and bustle of the marketplace that one can find everywhere else in Marseille. It is very much like the commercial centers on an ocean liner: a calm, urbane space, very close at hand, which the housewife can run to in her curlers and slippers without feeling ill at ease. To think that it should be the only form of shopping would be an obvious mistake, but it does give the inhabitants of the *Unité* a choice, where other comparable developments have none, and a very strong feeling of communal identity. This is further enhanced by the great amount of collective facilities, such as the gymnasium, which bring small groups together around a common activity. One can find children playing on the roof, wading in the pool, not just when supervised by their mothers or the nursery attendant, but at any time—because the roof is quiet and safe, unlike the urban street.

All in all, the *Unité* is what it was intended to be—a radical alternative to suburban sprawl, where groups of sixteen hundred people form a manageably sized association that gives the benefits of both individual privacy and collective participation. If this unity lacks one element, it is the public realm and political space that are implied in an autonomous unit of this nature and which can be found in its utopian predecessors of the nineteenth century. It seems strange that, given the ocean liner, monastery, and *phalanstère* as obvious influences, Le Corbusier has not provided a place for the captain of the ship or general assembly. An odd, perhaps unconscious, reason for this might have been the continuing series of disastrous political events in which he was involved at the time.

Horror and Rejuvenation

The *Unité* was designed and built under nasty pressure, as Le Corbusier remarked in many publications: "Five years of storm, spite and uproar . . . dispicable, ugly. A hue and cry by the press." And a hue and cry by the Communists, hygiene officials, architects, and planners. He had to put up with ten changes of government and seven successive Ministers of Reconstruction, all of which created a stop-go production designed to drive one mad. France itself was in turmoil, a sort of Left/Right meltdown, a catastrophe for those who wanted to get things done. A building team of thirty professionals, ATBAT, dedicated to LC's idealism, produced the incredible amount of 2,785 working drawings, inevitably some of which were contradictory. A suit was brought against Le Corbusier by jealous architects for disfiguring the French landscape. Doctors claimed that the *Unité* would produce lunatics. It was christened by locals *"La Maison du Fada"*—the lunatic asylum. All of this would have broken a weaker man, but not our knight-errant. Meanwhile, Don Quixote was having his United Nations project taken over and watered down by the American architect Wallace Harrison. This little melodrama, for the world's biggest organization, deserved another whole book of justifications and vilification. A lot could be said, and was, on both sides. "The Land of the Timid People," as he characterized America in *When the Cathedrals Were White*, was fighting back. The day before the dreaded Americans made him an Honorary Member of the National Institute of Arts and Letters what did they do? They vetoed his design for the UNESCO building—and right smack in his adopted hometown, Paris. As the saying goes, some paranoids have *real* enemies.

Every contact with the actual world of politics had ended in defeat and bitterness. Why have a public realm, if politics was as petty and nasty as this?

While Le Corbusier was in the United States battling over the United Nations scheme, he spent a lot of time in retreat from the world, staying in the Long Island countryside with his friends, Italian immigrants, the Nivolas. There he relaxed into an almost domestic tranquility, played with the Nivolas' children [fig. 162], took long walks on the beach, and worked on a new form of

162. With Pietro Nivola, 1950.

163. Sand cast, painted sculpture, 1951.

Le Corbusier: Monumental and Symbolic Architecture 1946–65

sculpture developed by Tino Nivola [fig. 163]. Now the other side of his character took over, and he produced different kinds of art. The sculpture consisted in working directly with natural forces and rhythms: waiting until low tide and then working like mad to form the wet sand into a mold, covering it with quick-drying plaster, and then removing the sculpture before the tide had come in again. The results of this "action sculpture" had to be crude and respectful of the simple possibilities of the medium, but clearly conceived, continuous forms could be achieved. They resembled the action painting of Jackson Pollock, who was also working in Long Island at the time—although Le Corbusier felt that this artist and the New York School would be judged, ultimately, second-rate. "Pollock is a hunter who shoots without aiming." This last remark typified Le Corbusier's distrust of the solely intuitive approach, and it should be seen as indicating his preference for a rational, complex approach to art. Hence his programmatic statements on regulating

164. Mural in the Nivolas' living room, Long Island, 1951. From left to right: two interlocked women, a thick wall section in zigzag pattern, a false door, and biomorphic forms from the Ubu series. These last forms were incorporated into Ronchamp (fig. 166).

lines, the function of murals, and "ineffable space." He brought these three preoccupations together in a mural covering two walls of the Nivolas' living room [fig. 164]. The function of a mural was, as he saw it, to create space in cramped areas and break up closed, rectilinear surfaces. "Good walls" were to remain white.

The Nivolas' mural does in a sense break down the protruding cube on which it is painted. This is due partially to the large, flat areas of contrasting colors, which suggest a layered space and also to the strong curving profiles, which contrast with the rectilinear walls and floor. The subject matter itself, Surrealistic in content, also opens up the space: a false door is painted opposite a real opening, giving, for a second, the illusion that one could walk right through the wall.

The quality of *L'Espace indicible*, "ineffable space," which Le Corbusier was developing in his writing, painting, and architecture, can also be found in the mural. In part what he means by this term is the interrelationship of formal elements, their setting up a series of tensions within a proportioned area so that each form can develop fully in relation to the whole. More than other painters of the twentieth century, Le Corbusier composes his paintings so that space can flow evenly through and around forms. They are never cramped. But also "unsayable space" (he noted, proudly, that there was no way to translate this) refers to the action of forms on the surroundings, the way they radiate outward and then respond to shapes nearby. His metaphor translates visual forms into acoustic dishes, or parabolic reflectors, listening to each other. Ineffable forms "take possession of space . . . vibrations, cries or shouts (such as originate from the Parthenon), arrows darting away like rays, as if springing from an explosion." This essay on *L'Espace indicible*, written in 1946, shows how he was beginning to translate his new type of Ubu painting and sculpture into architecture, a very important shift as we will see shortly, but also he was toying with the idea of concentrating more on art, becoming another Picasso.

With every blow suffered, no matter how well deserved, LC thought back to his youth and his preference for being an artist, not an architect. When finally, after five years, the *Unité* was opened (it was scheduled for one) his friend, the *sixth* Minister of Reconstruction, Eugene Claudius-Petit, gave the commemoration address, full of praise for the fortitude of the architect and the brilliance of the building. Uncharacteristically, as an architect who

262

165. Opening of the *Unité*, 1953
(photo by Paul J. Mitarachi). Eugène
Claudius-Petit giving the speech,
LC in tears, Giedion out of photo,
opponent to right. LC commented in
My Work: "1953. Triumphant opening
of the 'Unité de Marseille' by the
Minister, Claudius Petit. The official
photographs of the ceremony show
Le Corbusier's bitter opponent from
the Mayor's offices in Marseille,
wreathed in smiles at L-C's side. The
facts can be verified!"

was there told me, tears came to the eyes of LC and he cried openly
[fig. 165]. He was moved that Authority finally had responded to
his calls, appreciated his suffering and the quality for which he was
fighting. The architect's words at the dedication showed, as
another friend, the historian Sigfried Giedion, noted, a "profound
bitterness": "you realize that imagination is not the strong point
of ministers, or mayors, or municipal councils, or associations of
veterans, or trade unions of all kinds. Imagination is a gift of the
gods to a few, and it earns them innumerable kicks in the ass for
the whole of their life."

Ronchamp—Post-Modernism!

Luckily, through all the debacle of these lean years and while the
Unité was in stop-go mode, some Dominican monks led by Father
Couturier (1898–1954) were plotting a campaign to bring Modern
art into the Catholic Church to revive its somnolent forms and
sleepy liturgy. This campaign, which led to the commissioning of
Matisse, Chagall, and Léger, also led them to Le Corbusier. Father
Couturier, editor of *L'Art Sacré*, made it plain that contemporary

symbolic art need not be entirely representational as long as it had that *"volonté de grandeur"* that could reach the heart of the faithful and bring them back into the Church. He had supported LC against the religious establishment over yet another abortive project, for an underground place of worship at Sainte-Baume. Le Corbusier was bitter enough about this, as all else, so when he was approached by Canon Ledeur of Besancon, another Dominican connected with the program of *L'Art Sacré*, he said he had no time for a "dead institution." He had designed a church in the 1920s, but it never came to anything and, besides, if he was not a complete atheist, he was definitely a nature-worshipper and Nietzschean, more a pagan than a Christian and the kind of intellectual pantheist common since the eighteenth century. And pantheism was a Catholic heresy after the time of Hegel. And if it were not enough to say "no thanks," LC could remember what the Church did to his Albigensian ancestors.

Yet the Dominicans knew their man and how to land him. First Canon Ledeur took him to the site of Ronchamp, a hill above the small village in the Haute-Saône part of France: the rolling hills here could have come from one of his drawings of La Chaux-de-Fonds. Second, the Dominicans told him of their doctrine—spiritual expression through the intense use of abstract and representational forms—and that he would be "given free rein to create what you will." Here was the offer to produce a total work of art, any way he liked, and that meant an answer to Picasso. Third, the commission must have reminded him of the dreams of Charles L'Eplattenier and his dedicated followers of the New Section of Art. To repeat lines from his *Confession* of 1925: "We were preparing the future. 'Here,' [at the top of the highest hill, with uninterrupted horizons] said the master, 'we will build a monument dedicated to nature and we will make it our lives' purpose.'" Here on the Ronchamp hill he was offered the job of creating a new monument to nature, and that is precisely what he did.

Canon Ledeur, who accompanied him walking up the hill, describes how Le Corbusier was "seduced by the site." The first sketches, produced on this visit of June 4, 1950, show that already the architect knew what he wanted to do. His response to the four horizons was instantaneous, as the canon relates: "I can remember so well his immediate reaction to the site: the first line he drew—this south wall (tracing a curve) . . ." Le Corbusier's drawings and

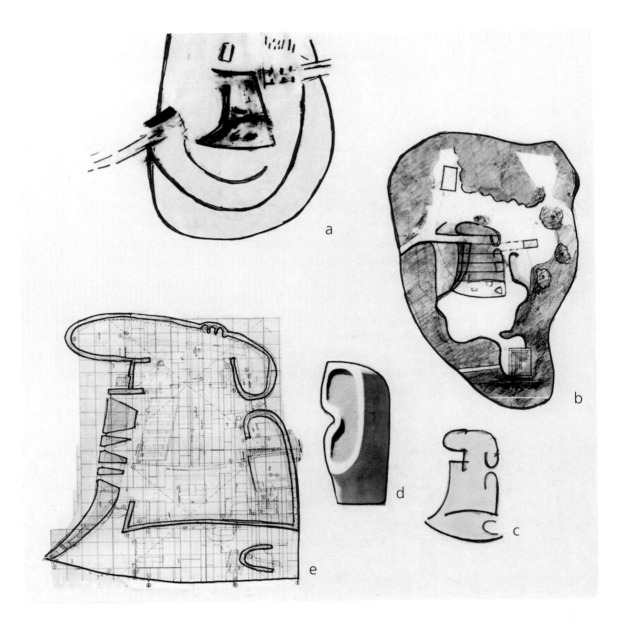

a

b

d

c

e

words confirm this quick creative synthesis, although the first sketches open to only two of the four horizons with curves [fig. 166a]. We find the acoustic forms he mentions in *L'Espace indicible*, the parabolic reflectors; the southeast one in particular, with its outdoor altar, is answered by a curved landform meant to embrace the pilgrims when they come for a large open-air service.

Another early sketch shows a curious echo of the underground

166. Analysis of Le Corbusier's drawings, all redrawn. From top left, clockwise: (a) two main curves, the east with its altar and pulpit, answered by the countercurve of an esplanade for ten thousand pilgrims, and the bent south wall, drawn June 6, 1950 (FLC 7470); (b) site plan showing Ronchamp forming outdoor space conceived as a cave or interior, Maisonnier drawing (FLC 7481); (c) Ronchamp as the character Ubu and a series of eleven fractal, self-similar curves (Sketchbook E18); (d) "Ear" or acoustic form from sculpture of Ubu, *Ozon Opus 1*, 1947 (FLC4); (e) Ronchamp as distorted square. Two plans superimposed and edited, showing conceptual grid and axes with the final lines in the floor and grid of windows (FLC 7455, 7169).

shrine for Sainte-Baume: it conceives the chapel as nestled inside a forest clearing [fig. 166b]. Conceptually it is buried in nature or the ground or, as Le Corbusier wrote, "an outside is always an inside." Here the space inside and outside the church is carved out like a cave, and the blobs of ineffable space pulsate and close off the pyramid to the northeast (built from the remains of the church destroyed by the Nazis). It is not farfetched to see the building, particularly its early plan, as an Ubu itself [fig. 166c]. This is one key to unlock the secret of Ronchamp. We recall that LC christened his wartime paintings "Ubu" after the powerful and crazy king of Alfred Jarry, and he had Joseph Savina make them into abstract sculptures for the next ten years [fig. 166d]. Above all, he was inspired by these acoustic blob forms because they had no human overtones or meaning: his one venture into total abstraction was thus itself a symbol. In his private language the blob signifies the craziness of war, the human species, and perhaps even his working for Vichy, so it was appropriately used to re-create a building that was destroyed by artillery fire in 1944. Or, at least, one may guess this thought flashed through his mind.

What the plans and Ubu sculpture, with their ear forms, make clear is that the acoustic parabola becomes the generator of the whole building. In plan, there are four tight ovoid forms and four more gentle curves, and, in elevation, three tight ovoids—the main chapels. These curves are all in antiphony and oriented either to the four horizons or to each other. When he writes of Ronchamp he mentions that it epitomizes "*espace indicible*" and of this he had written, in 1946 well before Ronchamp, words that recall his reaction to the Parthenon in 1911:

> The work (architecture, statue or painting) acts on its sur-roundings: waves, cries or clamour (the Parthenon on the Acropolis) flashing out like radiating rays . . . both in its immediate vicinity and further afield these shake, dominate or caress the site . . . The surroundings bring their weight to bear on the site of a work of art, the sign of the human will . . . a phenomenon of concordance emerges, as precise as mathe-matics—a veritable manifestation of acoustics in plastic form.

In effect we have a synaesthetic metaphor: acoustics stands for sight, the ear for the eye, hearing is confused with seeing.

167. Ronchamp Chapel, 1950–55, from the east, the outdoor assembly area with the functional elements conceived as gigantic sculpture: the altar, pulpit, chapel hoods or *calottes*, stairway, and so on. The gray concrete roof, which here looks like a boat hull, was conceived by LC when he was visiting the Nivolas and he found a crab's shell on the beach. He imagined its curved strength, two thin shells separated by stiffening, and thus designed the curved roof on this metaphor and structural principle.

Baudelaire, in the famous modern poem *Correspondences*, makes much of a nature temple in the forest where living forms are "symbols" which confuse all the senses together, and no doubt LC knew this poem even if he was not referring to its synaesthesia directly. What he does do, however, is use the three periscope "eyes," the top windows or *"calottes"* of the chapels, as "ears." And he conceives of the site and building sending out rays of light signaling each other, as if they were both acoustic parabolas.

Beyond this deep metaphor, which itself makes the building a harbinger of Post-Modernism, the eleven basic curves form a fractal language. The most significant properties of fractals are that they are made of *self-similar*, not self-same, forms; and their geometries are between the normal one, two, and three dimensions, unlike the Phileban types that have ruled architecture for five thousand years. This shift from Classical and Modern geometries—sphere, cone, cylinder, and so on—to fractal geometry is another reason this chapel is the first Post-Modern building. One only has to compare it to Le Corbusier's *Lesson of Rome* to see the shift, or should we say Post-Modern slide. There are the "pure forms seen in sunlight," to be sure, but not the five Platonic ones that Cézanne and the Classicists said underlay all nature [fig. 72]. Since Benoit Mandelbrot's book *The Fractal Geometry of Nature*, 1977, we now see that nature is mostly curved, crinkly, irregular, fragmented, spiky, grainy—not, as Raphael and Poussin thought, based on the Phileban solids. Ronchamp was the first recent building to open up this tradition of fractal design, one that moves from Saarinen's TWA Terminal to Utzon's Sydney Opera House and, later, to Gehry's Guggenheim Bilbao.

There are other important Post-Modern aspects, but, first of all, the building asks to be seen on its own terms. The pilgrimage church is situated in a rolling landscape, and its white shape against the green hills can be seen from miles around. Its sculptural forms take in the four horizons, sometimes protruding out into space, sometimes embracing it [fig. 167]. The gentle exterior curves have a functional role: they provide an enclosure for large outdoor services at times of pilgrimage and, quite ironically, compress the worshiper in the interior space. Essentially, as with all of Le Corbusier's work, the specific solution is and should be seen as a variant of the generic, orthogonal system—the cube. Here the rectangular volume has been pushed inwards on three sides,

168. Ronchamp, interior south wall. Light wedges are cut into the thick wall, allowing diffused light to reflect on the sides. A thin shaft of horizontal light separates the wall and the dark ceiling that looms over the viewer. LC conceived the chapel "without windows," and in this sense the interior can be seen as an underground structure with three up-periscopes and twenty-odd side-periscopes. He often made a drama of the witheld view, and here you are meant to peer through deep splays to find exterior nature framed by white walls, and an occasional colored pane of glass, with a moon, star, sun, or virgin. Thus the temple to nature worship, to pantheism, is given a primitive iconography.

distorted axially to the south as if by a twist of the rectangular structure, and released downward on the ground by a slight slope [fig. 168]. These distortions give the structure its tense oppositions and make a double reading possible—grid versus curve. They also lead to ironic inversions of religious convention. The walls and roof weigh downward on the worshiper and force his mind in the direction usually thought undesirable by the church—although the weight of the dark ceiling is countered by a sliver of light that also seems to make it float. In fact, Le Corbusier's faith in the established Church and ritual seems quite tenuous, as if it would be strengthened by being denied: "The requirements of religion have had little effect on the design; the form was an answer to a psychophysiology of the feelings."

"Joy and meditation" were the primary religious feelings he

mentions, and the slight opposition of these moods is reflected in

the contrasts. Most obvious is the simple family of forms in counterpoint, the play of light and shadow over the white pebbly plaster, and its contrast to the dark, rough concrete. Another pair of contrasts was achieved by the ambivalent gesture of the roof—exhilarated and deflated at the same time so that the skeptic and believer could worship side by side without compromising their faiths. Indeed they could enter side by side between the towers of the north door. These, as described by a priest who took me around, can be seen in their most reverent light, as two children looking to the morning and evening sun, while the parent watches over them from the south. What he did not point out was the carnal metaphor, present in plan (and a few paintings), the forceful penetration between two muscular curves. Once inside, the ironic double reading continues with the south wall, a piece of sensuous Swiss cheese, blasted away and, at the same time, a religious device. The windows, which one is focused on by the splayed shapes, dramatize the sun and views to nature and aphorisms painted by LC that celebrate cosmic universals. Then the gaze is brought to the cross by the slope and the grid of the floor and the directional marker of the dark center-line. All these markers are remnants of the orthogonal system that is ultimately overpowered, as is the gaze toward the cross. They are completely dominated by the bright window of the Virgin and the streaming morning sun. Thus the cross (intentionally diminished in size) is just another element in the balanced composition, and the chapel becomes a place of worship where the worshipers have to fight the devil in his most sensual forms while standing up on their feet—since seats for only fifty are provided.

All the forms respond to each other, send out a call that is answered. The building is plastically fine-tuned, a "concordance as precise as mathematics." Take away one sculptural element and another will fall flat; exaggerate one too much and another will disappear. This antiphonal balance is so exact that one can call it a rationally perfected piece of sculpture.

Actually it was widely interpreted as a highly irrational building, a retreat from the Modern Movement, and a primitive piece of technology built of sludge (that is, sprayed concrete). Instead of embodying the rectilinear, lightweight steel which Modernism seemed to be all about, it was seen as a private regression. The architect James Stirling and the critic Nikolaus Pevsner, as well as countless others, were highly disturbed by what they took to be an Expressionist building. Indeed, within the politics of the Modern Movement, Ronchamp probably did act as the catalyst for a neo-Expressionism, precisely because it was interpreted as such.

Yet there was nothing really new in the curvilinear forms, as far as Le Corbusier's work was concerned, since they went back to the early 1930s. And they were all rationally determined by the program and internal consistency. They are even variants on the straight line and right angle [fig. 166e]. That is to say, Le Corbusier has taken a rectangular grid, proportioned by the Modulor, and distorted it in various directions as if it were a piece of india rubber. The remnants of this underlying grid can be found everywhere: in the floor lines and wall rectangles, and frontal layering.

Perhaps a reason that so many Modernists found this building disquieting is its elusive metaphorical quality. All sorts of images are suggested—a nun's cowl, a monk's hood, a ship's prow, praying hands [figs. 169, 170]—and denied at the same time. It is as if some specific mystical interpretation existed for every form while the language which would unlock their secrets had been lost. The anxiety of the critics can be compared to that of archaeologists who have discovered a beautifully articulated text they know to be nonsense. Because the forms are plastically exact, they appear to be determined by years of religious ritual and iconography. Yet Le Corbusier, the pantheist and nonconformist, specifically rejected all conventional religious motifs and approached the problem psychologically. As he expressed it emphatically:

169. Ronchamp, south wall. Apparently random fenestration: Swiss-cheese facade, cotton candy, ship, nun's cowl?

170. Ronchamp (drawings by Hillel Schocken). Metaphorical analysis showing multiple codes. Popular and elite, stereotyped and hermetic, a building that cuts across the usual boundaries of taste and culture. Multivalence of meaning became a major goal of Post-Modernists in the 1970s.

Le Corbusier: Monumental and Symbolic Architecture 1946–65

[Journalists at Ronchamp] virtually machine-gunned me with their flash cameras. I told the workmen near me: "If these people don't get out of here immediately take them by the shoulders and . . ." One of these fellows who had pursued me in front of the altar of pilgrimage outside, called to me, "Mister Le Corbusier, in the name of the manager of the Chicago Tribune, answer this question: was it necessary to be a Catholic to build this chapel?" I replied, *"Foutez-moi le camp!"*

In spite of these outbursts and denials, Ronchamp has been interpreted by many as the most religiously convincing building of the twentieth century. Partly this must be due to Le Corbusier's spiritual attitude toward cosmic truth and natural law, which was in every way as serious and profound as the attitudes of conventional religion. Yet it is also due to his powers of imaginative integrity. Like a plausible fiction of Borges, Le Corbusier has constructed an alternative world that is as tantalizingly rich and believable as the real one, having all the coherence one expects except conventional reference. He may call this fiction "ineffable space" or "visual acoustics," as he does in describing Ronchamp, but it is as much "plastic integrity," or imagining new forms and then resolving their interrelationship until they seem necessary and inevitable.

At the same time, he was here experimenting with his private symbolic language and perhaps, as Richard Moore has argued, an older alchemical one. The painted windows and enameled door of Ronchamp are the first notable attempts to make this symbolism more public. Fairly clear on the brilliantly colored panels are the archetypal symbols of open hand, star, pyramid, meandering river (or snake), rain, and clouds [fig. 171]. The eight panels, on both sides of the door, create an ambiguous space that is half perspectival and half flat. The motif at the center is meant to be ambiguous and multivalent: partly it is a window, key, and lock, partly a gear wheel and red and blue series (symbolizing the union of opposites, architect and engineer).

A quandary. The fact that the door pivots on the center, on either side of the two hands giving and receiving, probably indicates that the overall message is dualistic—except that *most* of LC's large doors pivot this way. So, here is the problem, and opportunity, of enigmatic symbolism, that typical Post-Modern genre. We are set off on a game, "Hunt the Symbol," that can be rewarding or

171. Ronchamp, main door (photo by Tim Benton). The square door, which pivots, has a definite dualistic quality. Note the color contrasts and the red and blue interlocks, a kind of key shape that for Le Corbusier symbolized the union of opposites—the joining of architect and engineer, humanism and physical laws. The cosmic symbolism is straightforward, though Surrealist: clouds turn into traditional French loaves of bread flying through the sky. Enameling, his father's profession, is amplified from the size of a watch to fifteen feet, a new method LC invented on steel, and the results are as fresh and clean today as they were in 1955.

maddening depending on how well we play it and whether we are in the mood. That we are *meant* to play it is clear both from the building and LC's writing. As he said on more than one occasion, "in a completely successful work of art there are hidden masses of implications that reveal themselves only to those who care, that is, to those who deserve it."

No doubt all great works of art provoke multiple decodings, and an essential part of their greatness is that they can do this coherently. They continue to live precisely because they spark off continual reinterpretation. So, is Ronchamp a carefully coded alchemical text, as Richard Moore contends and so ably demonstrates? The answer is probably the unsatisfactory one—partly, yes. But, if it had been systematically coded this way, then we can be sure that somewhere its very didactic creator would have left explicit comments and a reader's guide as he did with other such works. What we *can* identify with a certain surety are the formal similarities behind the different symbols.

Take the most emphatic form of Ronchamp, the upturned roof

172. Ronchamp, collage redrawn, clockwise, from top left: (a) south prow, also a horn and breast; (b) the moon goddess in *La femme et le moineau*, detail of tapestry, 1957: her shoulder and left breast with its shadow become the prow; (c) *Alma-Rio*, detail of painting, 1949: the prow/shadow doubles as arm, breast, and part of buttocks; (d) *Taureau 12*, detail of painting, 1956: buttocks and breast merge, are equated with a bull's flared nostrils, and placed above the silhouette of Ronchamp's prow; (e) sketch plan of Ronchamp, 1950–51, showing parallel between nostrils, buttocks, and to the right, the figure-eight of the waterspout (f), also termed a shotgun by LC.

that Moore identifies variously as Capricorn's single horn, the bull's horns of Minos, and the moon goddess's upraised arm [fig. 172]. This surging prow-thrust does pull one upwards, and leads the eye heavenwards; it is the most potent of Ronchamp's forms, especially with its clear shadow line echoing the curves [fig. 172a]. If we follow this motif in my diagrammatic analysis—horn and shadow—we can find Le Corbusier reusing it in many paintings and combining it with other figures. Sometimes the prow motif signifies the breast, and the breast's voluptuous shadow, of his moon goddess, or one of two breasts [fig. 172b]. The painting *Alma Rio 36*, a key work that hung in his living room, shows two figures interlocking, man and woman, the bull and Pasiphaë, and here it is clearly part of two breasts [fig. 172c]. Yet, in a transposition of signs, and another painting, *Taureau 12*, 1956, the prow of Ronchamp is now seen in silhouette, the breasts are a figure-eight and they are equated with the nostrils of the bull, and also with buttocks [fig. 172d]. Breasts and buttocks, we have seen, occur in city plans for Algiers, and they can be found in the plan of Ronchamp [fig. 172e]. But we know from other contexts that this figure-eight is also for Corbu the barrel of a shotgun *and* bull's nostrils. These overtones are quite clear in the spout of Ronchamp's gargoyle [fig. 172f]. In other words, the transposition and multivalence of signs we found in the building as a whole can be found in just one motif. Many overtones, alchemical and formal, are obviously intended, and it would be misguided to think there was just one key that would unlock the secret of Ronchamp's meaning.

The basic insight of Post-Modernism, that multimeaning is an end in itself but also one that allows different groups and individuals from various backgrounds to interpret it, is the relevant point for architecture. As a public symbolic form it must mediate all kinds of opposite tastes and meanings, something that Le Corbusier next attempted on a heroic scale at Chandigarh. Before looking at this, the culmination of his life, we must glance at his growing reputation, because this had a direct effect on subsequent work.

Bittersweet Fame

The architect in a commercial electronic society is in a double bind: he cannot but must advertise himself. LC had already discovered in the 1920s the way to get around this conundrum—by writing incessantly and publicizing a revolutionary position or new theory. Mass culture is more than willing to collude in this charade; it demands nothing less.

Up to the 1950s Le Corbusier nurtured his persona as both the prophet of the new machine age *and* the embattled, misunderstood genius—the quintessential Modernist role that Frank Lloyd Wright also never tired of playing. By the time the Museum of Modern Art was founded in New York City, in the late 1920s, Modernism was both inside and outside the Establishment. The Rockefellers, Blisses, Whitneys, as much as foreign heads of state, started to collect and support Modern Art (again, capitalized when it is a spiritual movement). Guggenheim commissioned a Museum of Non-Objective Art from Wright, and by then, 1959, and with the help of the CIA, it became the official style and stance of the Pax Americana. *Time* magazine immortalized one Modernist after another on its cover, including Le Corbusier. Fifteen minutes of media fame, as Warhol was later to put it, became an essential part of the successful architect, and the delicious difficulty was that he had to present—at the very moment of acceptance—a convincing act of misery at being rejected.

The idea behind this view of Modernism, the myth of the heroic fighter for authenticity, is known as the Theory of Van Gogh's Ear. Completely unappreciated in his lifetime, selling only two paintings, and those to his brother, and living close to nature and the common people, he became, after he cut off his ear and committed suicide, *the* symbol of the Modern Artist. Popular writers and Hollywood immortalized his story. Jackson Pollock, in his romantic relationship to society, and whose worldwide fame was celebrated in an issue of *Life* magazine, followed Van Gogh in his rebellious martyrdom and subsequent apotheosis. By this time every savvy Modernist was a Rebel with a Cause.

Managing this tricky act of being very famous and rejected at the same time was easier for "Père Corbu," as he started calling himself in the 1950s (when he was in his middle sixties). For instance, although Ronchamp became the single most famous Modern building in the world, was put on a French stamp, and was visited by millions from around the world, it had been continuously damned. First by the local parishioners, who preferred restoring the old church, second by the traditional religious establishment for being a strange object, and third, most of all, by the popular press: they labeled the building "an ecclesiastical garage," "a slipper," and "a nuclear shelter" (a phrase of abuse Prince Charles was later to adopt against another Corbusian, Denys Lasdun). Predictably enough, they also called it "a concrete heap" and "a bunker."

These populist metaphors may, in some cases, be coded into the forms, just as clearly as the positive ones we have decoded, but they show that LC was a natural Modernist martyr. He became the lightning rod for attracting good and bad electronic comment. The Legion d'Honneur could come his way, 4,500 students could turn up for a lecture at the Sorbonne (1,500 even listened outside), and he publicized pictures of the audiences to prove it. *My Work* has two full pages advertising his triumph. Perhaps victory over the Academy he savored the most: "In 1956 L-C was asked to accept membership of the Institute de France (Académie des Beaux-Arts) in Paris: 'Thank-you, never! . . . My name would serve as a banner to conceal the present evolution of the Ecole des Beaux-Arts towards a superficial modernism' . . . Le Corbusier is a member (against his will) of every academy in the world; one gets nominated in such places without being asked. But Paris is altogether graver, more serious, more involved. There are times when one's moral responsibility to others . . ." He does not finish the sentence partly because he realizes that his moral responsibility cuts several ways. To be sure, he has been against the Academy since 1920, and that is one reason the students always loved him. But at this time, and soon thereafter, he was also courting big business and big government and the very forces of reaction he attacked—so how can one finish the sentence?

His most bittersweet moments came in 1953 and 1956 when there were exhibitions on his total work at the Musée d'art Moderne in Paris, and Lyon. The exhibition, simply titled "Le Corbusier," was just like the other retrospectives called "Léger," "Renoir," "Bonnard," "Courbet," and, best of all, "Picasso," as LC liked to point out. Finally, after fifty years and L'Eplattenier's advice not to, he had made it into the Pantheon of painting. His life's ambition was partially fulfilled. A thought must have gone through his mind: Should I give up architecture, and all this suffering and horrible invective? For the November 1953 opening he invited all the ministers of state, leaders of art, and directors of the Beaux-Arts to his "Expo Corbu." But none of them came, a fact he points out with sardonic emphasis in one of his biographies, *Le Corbusier Lui-Même*.

What he also claims here is that he has been silent for thirty years about his work as an artist. It was the "secret" behind his architecture, but, because of prejudice against architects being artists, he had to keep it that way. Since 1923, he had to create patiently in private. Factually this is not true, since he had exhibitions in Paris, Boston, and New York, in 1936, 1938, and 1948. But it is important that half his brain *thought* it was true, because this fed the martyred Modernist *and*, as he says, gave him the independence to fight for architecture: "It is there [in creating art] that you can find the source of my liberty of spirit, my disinterestedness, the independence, and the loyalty and integrity of my invention." This claim I am sure is true and relevant, for what else would have kept him persevering as an architect through ten changes of government, commissions deservedly his going to others, and every possible media insult?

Bittersweet triumph, and bitter too. Major French art critics such as Frank Elgar, Georges Besson, and Christian Zervos damned his painting ("Should he not keep his production secrets to himself; for to reveal them is to kill them off"). Nevertheless art was the source of his architecture, its laboratory for invention, its storehouse of forms and symbols, and his spiritual exercise for every morning. In the 1950s and early 1960s it becomes freer than before, and like his compaction composition, it is a method for layering line, graphic tone, and space. These multilayered works, preempting the Post-Modern media work of artists such as Sigmar Polke and David Salle, have a great deal of energy and panache [fig. 173]. There is still the "marriage of contours" of Purism, the importance of line and silhouette creating a symphony of echoing forms, but now there is also a counterset of themes in juxtaposi-

173. *La femme et le moineau*. A later version of the moon goddess/earth mother figure was inspired, as Eduard Sekler has shown, by a scene LC witnessed during a storm on board a ship in 1945. While the winds and waves battered the boat, a Catholic woman lit a candle and knelt to pray for deliverance. Other carryover symbols are the interlocking hands, sign of harmony, the small bird, and, to the right, the brown bark and two interlocking trapezoids. The three prongs, often a sign of shoulders and bull's horns, are also a formal motif that travels through Ronchamp—carrying over from one context to the next. See Eduard F. Sekler, "Le Corbusier's Use of a 'Pictorial Word' in His Tapestry *La Femme et le Moineau*" (HGSD, bulletin, 1976), 6–7.

tion. Like the superposition of a city plan that is a palimpsest of different ages, each of which has left its trace, these paintings layer color on top of and counter to line, and silhouettes across subjects. As a result there is always more than one visual and symbolic way of reading the work. The paintings become visual puzzles and puns on similar shapes; flat color is contradicted by shaded depth. This layering and compaction composition then become the method for designing a whole city, Chandigarh.

Small Bird of the Islands

Before he got this commission for Chandigarh, the most important of his life, he met a woman who took on a certain spiritual importance, Minnette De Silva. She was an elegant, petite beauty from Sri Lanka (Ceylon at the time) who settled in London after the war to continue her architectural studies. A young friend, Gillian Howell, who was a student at the Architectural Association at the time, told me the impression that this exotic young woman made. She usually dressed in glittering saris and often tied her hair up and punctuated it with a fresh, perfumed flower. "She was shatteringly beautiful in her multicolored sari, so shatteringly good looking that she would be trailed by men carrying her drawing board and drafting instruments—more than willing to carry out a drawing or design at a moment's notice." She gave the appearance of being full of self-confidence and absorbed in her mission. She intended to be the first woman architect of Asia and to bridge the gap between modern techniques and the indigenous craft culture of Ceylon. Her father and mother, from a well-connected family, gave her the freedom and requisite background to strike out on her own. They had many political and cultural contacts with the then decolonializing world. Tagore, Nehru, Gandhi, and other important Asian leaders were among the acquaintances she and her father would meet at the international conferences they attended.

Thus, right after the Second World War, Minnette was ready to take on the European social scene, prepared to use her exotic charm and outgoing boldness to best advantage. An introduction to the Queen, at a garden party, merited headlines, and later she nourished close friendships with Henri Cartier Bresson, Laurence Olivier, and David Lean, the last with whom she became romantically involved.

Yet in spite of her beauty, Minnette was brought up, with her brothers and sisters, to be independently minded. Indeed she was independent enough as a youth to renounce her father's Buddhism and embrace Christianity. Her free spirit and international connections took her to London and there she immersed herself in Western culture and Modernism. In December 1946, André Bouxin, an editor of *Architecture et Techniques*, took her to Le Corbusier's penthouse studio in the rue Nungesser et Coli and thus started a personal and professional relationship that was to last until LC died. She has described the impact of the first and subsequent meetings in a posthumous autobiography, a book that reveals a very significant confusion, that of Ceylon with India.

> I was, I think, his first encounter with "India," as he then called Ceylon—soon to lead to Chandigarh. My subsequent visits to his studio were always associated with traumatic or important events in his life . . . Le Corbusier was asked how he would talk to me [at the CIAM meeting at Bridgewater in 1947] since he refused to speak in English, as it wasn't good. He said, "She doesn't speak French so I have to in order to converse with her."

This non sequitur, perfectly understandable, is then followed by a revealing truth.

> He was greatly attracted by his first live contact with *L'Inde*. I think he romanticized our meeting. I became the symbolic link with *L'Inde*, the idealized symbol. Since then I have been deeply touched by his sympathy and interest in me and my work.

We will examine this symbolic link shortly, after looking at a few of the remarks from Corbu that she published. These are usually addressed to the "Petite oiseau des Isles" and often signed "with friendship," and the picture of the large *corbeau*. From his large bird to her small bird, their relationship appears to be idealistic and professional, Platonic and sensual, paternalistic and filial. As for the professional contacts, Minnette, and her equally glamorous sister Anil, sent him copies of the art and architecture magazine they helped create in Bombay, *Marg*. From this correspondence and various encounters he built up an idea of her as a symbol of a future ideal, a professional architect and delightful creature to meet when traveling. One business letter contains that strange mixture of idealism and self-promotion that Le Corbusier was happy to confuse. He underlines this unusual mixture with a bit of heavy-handed irony.

> Chère Mademoiselle, I would like to ask you a very unlikely favor . . . I am making a boutique in the center of Paris for the shoe company Bally *tout à fait* up to date . . . and [we want to put a sheath or skin] around a skeleton of plywood. But what sort of leather should we choose? . . . I propose the skin of a grey elephant and it is because of that that I think of you (there are other reasons to think of you, without that) . . . Could you buy the necessary amount in Ceylon . . . ? It would be the first Modern penetration of the Indian continent in the West. And the door, clothed in elephant skin, would be the door of honor opening the future on all the good that I wait for coming soon from your country . . . With deep friendship to you, LC (20 December 1949).

And then he adds a private handwritten postscript that is not seen by the secretary who typed the letter: "Our West is breaking on half a century of torments. The door is opening on the future. You are—you—a clear sign of that future. I cannot tell you all the good things that I think of you in this letter consecrated as it is to the skin of an elephant! But from Bridgewater to London to Paris and one day to Ceylon the furrow is ploughed, the line is traced towards those countries from where you are—where dominates the idea. Good friend! I give you a small drawing, Corbeau."

This ironic flirtation again shows Le Corbusier's old idealistic view of the idea, in this case the idea that India is about to inherit the cultural role of Modernism that the West had lost in fifty years of stupidity and war. The day before he had written her a note saying "I am going to start a great enterprise of art in 1950, in Paris, an exhibition of a synthesis of architecture, sculpture and painting. You see I have thought of you. But you don't write to me anymore." Here is the old complaint, that he was a better correspondent than his friends, a sentiment that is reversed nine months later, in a letter of September 3, 1950, written on news of her father's death.

Here he apologizes, from Bogotá, for not having found the solitude in which to write well:

> Petite Enfant, petite aimè des Iles, How are you? I often think of you, but one needs the solitude of Bogotá to find the time of silence that permits one to write well. I was upset by the unexpected death of your father . . . who was so lively and passionate. Poor friend—well then, what will become of you, bereft of your great support? . . . Your image is always in front of me—you who carry two thousand years of beauty and traditional wisdom in a bearing that really moves me. It all began with those little toes in the sandals and it finished with your face crowned with flowers so beautifully arranged in the blackness of your hair . . . In my difficult life as an architect and urbanist, in this everyday and unceasing effort, you were a miracle. A miracle that appeared at a turning in the road and disappeared—very far away.
>
> I am more and more possessed by a desire for harmony and beauty. And I will willingly accept the most simple and impoverished beauty. But when, out of Ceylon appeared the little statue whose movements and clothes are of silk and with a lively eye, I was ravished after an unexpected natural encounter: the song of a nightingale, a sensational flower. Little friend I have used a huge number of adjectives. See how wise I am to write so seldom. The pen is a dangerous seducer. I hope with all my heart that all goes well with you and that you are happy. Your old Corbu.

Several friends of Minnette De Silva have said that she did not have a sexual relationship with Le Corbusier, and just as many suppose that she did, because she spoke so often and proudly of their relationship. The evidence from her book can be read both ways. He addresses her respectfully as just a deep friend; but then, in one letter, he asks her to write him only at the office—and this in spite of the fact that she says that when in Paris she often visits his studio penthouse. In any case, the significance of their relationship has more to do with what Minnette herself emphasizes, the fact that he romantically links her with an idealized India. On the death of her mother, he writes on December 24, 1961, another letter of condolence that again turns from fatherly advice into cultural panegyric.

Chère amie, "Petite oiseau des Iles" "Small Bird of the Islands" . . . You have lost your mother, and you are in great pain. Courage! Il faut avoir du courage, il faut acquerir du courage! Go see [José Luis] Sert and his wife. They are people of the first class. They are *chic* types and you will find there a beautiful atmosphere: calm in spirit. Go see the USA, so deceiving. You will gain in estimation for Ceylon and your magnificent country: Asia. And you are an Aryan Asian (Salut Adolf!!!) that is to say the parent, that is to say the hearth itself of that which has become Europe.

One meaning of these asides, and attempts to cheer her up, goes beyond their immediate relationship and concerns his personification of India. Not only is it the mother of Europe, and an older culture that may still avoid the disasters of the First Machine Age, but it is a symbol of the eternal feminine. And it is Minnette who also takes on this role in LC's mind. The first drawing he sends to her, after their meeting at Bridgewater, shows his ideal, broad-shouldered and large-breasted earth mother sitting with hands folded in her lap. A year later Minnette came to Paris, went to the city university, and watched while Le Corbusier worked on a large mural that covered a wall of the Swiss Pavilion [fig. 174]. A

174. Moon goddess/earth mother, Swiss Pavilion, City University, Paris, 1948. To the right, the she-goat with a long horn, *licorne*, is cradled by a hand, while the central figure with a crescent-shaped face probably symbolizes, as Richard Moore argues, the moon goddess consorting with the horned bull (the prongs below). Pasiphaë, the moon goddess or earth mother, mates with Minos to produce the Minotaur, a myth of regeneration that fascinated LC. At the same time, Minnette, who was with him when he was painting this mural, might have discussed the moon goddess of Buddhism and her festival in Ceylon. The upturned prongs prefigure recurring shapes of Chandigarh and Ronchamp.

little later he sent her a drawing for the central figure, the "moon goddess," again with broad shoulders and folded hands. Although this figure symbolizes other particular events in LC's life, as we have seen, it is clear from his remarks and such drawings that she, and Minnette, also symbolize the beneficent, maternal, and sexual power of women, the way that beauty can tame ferocity. This image of the moon goddess is constantly set off by, and interpenetrated with, bull's horns. LC was fascinated by the myth of Pasiphaë and the Minotaur. Woman, the beautiful and noble female, might, like an idealized India, lead an old and quarrelsome Europe into a new age of peace and harmony.

This is ultimately what lies behind their romantic attachment. Corbu's passion for his "Little Bird of the Islands" is finally like the Frenchman's love for Liberty at the barricades or Joan of Arc, the idea of a beautiful woman of peace leading Europe into a new future. Not only do his and her words confirm this idealism, but so too do other important drawings he sends her from Chandigarh. Two are made at the foundation moment of the city; both show a woman seen from behind holding a small child in the air but protected by her sari. In the background are the foothills and mountains; in the foreground are the upturned arms and mouth of the child, forms that are to return again and again in the U shapes of the public buildings. The caption says, "birth of a capital." Le Corbusier will attempt to translate mother and child into a concrete symbol for the new India, literally in concrete. He will do the same with the icon of the moon goddess/earth mother. It would be simplifying to say a single meaning, India or Minnette herself, was the referent of this transforming symbol, but for a time they all came together in Le Corbusier's experience.

Symbolism for the Public Realm—Chandigarh

The story of LC's involvement in the capital city of the Punjab is long and needs an entire book to tell it. Several have been written, none of which are definitive because the new city is still, after fifty years, in its first stage of growth. Though it has added 300,000 more than its projected population of 500,000, it is, as is often said of the French Revolution, still too early too judge its merits. At least in this case the adage is true, because a million more Indians are predicted to settle here in the next fifty years. In the nature of ideal cities for a new nation, and ones that grow exponentially, an elastic yardstick is needed. Nonetheless some generalizations can be made, ones that I was fortunate enough to be able to check, at the fiftieth anniversary celebration of its design, in January 1999.

The basic fact one has to note is that Chandigarh was created as the most significant manifestation of the New India. In July 1947 India became independent and a year later split with Pakistan resulting in the need for a new western state—the Punjab, with a capital city to run it, Chandigarh. Hence the logic that a New India equaled a new, modernized version of New Delhi, an answer at once to the British and the traditional past. Pandit Nehru, the leader committed to realizing Chandigarh, emphasized this point at the inauguration of building in 1953. "The city," he said, "is the first large expression of our creative genius, flowering on our newly earned freedom . . . unfettered by traditions of the past . . . reaching beyond the existing encumbrances of old towns and old traditions . . . a temple of a new India."

Le Corbusier would have seen eye to eye with him, as Stanislaus von Moos has shown, on several points. First is the notion of being a new city unfettered by traditions, and one that had to modernize quickly, but in a new, non-European way. Both men shared the hope that India could be an example to the world of "the Second Machine Age." By this LC meant not only the new electronic age, but the period after the first hundred years—1830 to 1930—when mechanization had destroyed cities and cultures. Ideologically the two were committed to forging a unique synthesis between ancient and modern cultures, a new hybrid or doubly coded reality, part progressive and part five thousand years old— again a Post-Modern mixture.

Secondly, LC would have leapt at the words *genius* and *temple*, especially coming from the mouth of a cultivated leader, an Authority with culture, the Ghost of Colbert, for whom he had always been searching. Here in the poorest part of the world, LC reflected ironically, he found the Great Initiate and the Great Power in one person, and one who was asking him to build the Radiant City. The backing of central power was real. If Nehru had not supported him on countless occasions when he complained of sabotage, and if both he and Nehru were not authoritarian figures demanding respect, then Chandigarh would never have been built. In the nature of Indian politics, and the ethnic divisions of the

175. Plan of Chandigarh, and commemorative plaque, issued January 1999 at a conference, "Celebrating Chandigarh—50 Years" (City of Chandigarh). Waterways, sewers, and lakes.

Punjab, it took a mixture of power from Delhi and Paris to focus the energies of the civil servants and administrators. The fact that stalemate has beset the city since their deaths makes this point.

Both men liked the heroic sweep, the grand generalization, the big view of history, and often delegated realization to others—LC particularly, after he came here in spring 1951, and then only visited twice a month for a year. His cousin Pierre Jeanneret, and to a less extent Jane Drew and Max Fry, carried out a lot of day-to-day work. If there are some heroic and good decisions that are evident today, they may be a bit of a surprise. Chandigarh, in a dry plain, has a very good sewer and water system and a couple of wonderful, artificial lakes [fig. 175]. The cosmic symbolism that drove the artist in Le Corbusier was also supported by some very real ecological thinking. What strikes the visitor is finding, in the middle of a semiarid landscape and in a country where too many people live close and in squalor, that Chandigarh is spread out like a low-density garden city and is full of flowers. LC did not like the sprawl, and he made characteristic jibes about the officials being too "Oxfordish." Indeed the city does suffer from being too much of an English colonial new town; but, it has to be said, it is unique here, and much loved, for having more greenery and shade than any comparable oasis. The irony of this popular success is that the rich and powerful administrators do not want anything to change, for their way of life in this Beverly Hills of the Punjab to be threatened. With a million more people to come, this conservative stance is not likely to conserve their peace. To preserve value one has to adapt the plan.

Besides the benign ecology, another benefit of the plan, whipped out in a month on the basis of Albert Mayer's previous one, is the layering of roads, open green spaces, homes, and work spaces. They weave through each other like a tartan. This palimpsest, like a Corb painting of the time, incorporates diversity and difference, if hardly enough. Indeed, at the conference "Celebrating Chandigarh—50 Years," virtually every speaker agreed on this point. The basic structure is a good one, but it definitely needs more mixed uses, diversity of building type, various styles of architecture, and the interpenetration of sectors. That is to say, it needs to be Post-Modernized, along the lines that Jane Jacobs and others were advocating in the 1960s. To say the city suffers from the functional separation of Modernism is to repeat a truism. What might be mentioned in this context is that the city's basic layout is like the first growth of an ecology, a very good basis for successive growths—second, third, fourth, and so on—if only the administrators would allow it. Like a thirteenth-century *bastide* or a military camp laid out at a stroke, its structure will benefit many future developments, especially those in traffic. Indeed, with its seven types of circulation, carefully dimensioned, it might become the first coherent and safe motorway city of the next century.

Much could be done by way of public transport and improving the lot of the very poor, who are now herded into unofficial areas. Indeed, to take a technocratic line that LC might have followed, and several delegates mentioned, a few innovations in the infrastructure would be of the greatest help to the destitute. For instance, new cheap transport systems and a sewer system for the slums. As in the new city of Curitiba in Brazil, one can turn garbage into money and clean up the city in the bargain, if the right measures are put in place.

Instead of dwelling on the way Chandigarh could become the second growth city of the future, and its other potentials, I want to highlight the way Le Corbusier used the capitol area to test a new public symbolism, because, after the general layout, it was this to which he was committed. No architect in the last fifty years has taken on this task, and the successes and failures of the city's acropolis, for that is what it is, remain the most instructive of our time. In the past, in traditional cultures, providing public symbols for civic structures was an accepted part of the architect's role, and this obligation gave architecture aesthetic as well as ceremonial power. But, with the decline of religion and belief in social movements, public symbolism has all but disappeared, except with authoritarian regimes such as that under Saddam Hussein. Thus the neutral public space has become the norm of our time, enlivened with some sculpture brought in at the last moment, much to its embarrassment. Le Corbusier's capitol is the last *big* attempt to make something more than agnostic blankness.

The symbolic program he worked out developed from his painting, Ronchamp, and previous city planning. It even developed from his first building at age seventeen and a half, the Villa Fallet. Inevitably it was centered on nature, particularly the sun and monsoon rain, both of which are fearsome in Chandigarh, and also the presence of the surrounding mountains, the people, and animals such as the Indian buffalo and sacred cow. Mankind, society, and the cosmos composed the trinity he mentioned as guide, and one finds symbols of them incorporated in the concrete and tapestries. As usual, he generated the icons through a series of descriptive sketches on the site, an empirical method for creation that was often a lot more realistic than his plans for the city, some of which were thought out as a version of Paris. For instance, he used the distance from the Etoile to the Louvre as the measuring stick but, according to one conference speaker, got the dimensions wrong: Maybe that is why the capitol is too spread out?

At any rate, the major emblems LC fashioned, mostly from the site, were the sun, moon, stars, lightning, and clouds; the mango tree, snakes, cows, and crow; the standing man; and the open hand and footprint (both also Indian symbols); the carriage wheel, borrowed from the national arms of India, scales—the symbol of justice—and the cross section of the *Unité*, or signs of shelter [176].

These signs and symbols do liven up dead places and are relevant to everyday realities. Some critics see them as overblown trademarks, or as kitsch religious symbols without a state religion, but I find these judgments too harsh, at least when it comes to the

176. Chandigarh, Council Chamber, General Assembly, 1953–61. Tapestry and symbols: wheel, mango tree, footprints, rain, clouds, and meander or snake are under the basic cosmic sign that rules the twenty-four-hour cycle of the sun. LC came to this last symbol in 1925 when he realized that this cycle of time limited possibilities. By now it is the basic law to which all life is subject. At Chandigarh, in 100-degree heat, it is all-powerful, and Le Corbusier designed a lot of shade and several rituals meant to acknowledge this truth. The pyramid over the space, symbol of sun, is splayed to receive northern light.

177. Chandigarh, view from Assembly roof across to High Court. Pyramid Council Chamber in the foreground, Tower of Shade with *brise-soleil* in midground, and to left the Martyr's Hill. Admittedly these piles suffer from the fact that access is denied to citizens, but even so, would they be connected to everyday life?

178. Chandigarh, Assembly entrance and pivoting door. A sculptural symbol of bull's horns and the upraised U shape of the mother's and child's arms is apparent in the giant gutter. Functionally this picks up the monsoon rains and provides welcome shade to the ceremonial door below. On it can be seen the summer and winter paths of the sun above other symbols.

179. Chandigarh, detail of the open door, with local signs including a red man, the sun, and a bird that actually still alights on these buildings.

small scale of a door, wall, or tapestry. The Tower of Shade and Martyr's Monument, clumsy in the flat open space, deserve this censure, but not the enameled doors and concrete reliefs [fig. 177]. Most convincing is the great door that opens into the cool shade of the Parliament, or the General Assembly, for state occasions [fig. 178]. Here we find, under a giant, upturned portico—what must be the largest gutter in the world (and one symbolizing bull's horns and mother and child on its ends)—a brilliantly colored homage to the universe [fig. 179]. On the entry side, the summer and winter sun dominate the top register and this sets the basic theme for the whole building, indeed the whole of Chandigarh.

Le Corbusier imagined a solar ritual to occur once a year in this building. The central assembly space, a parabolic "cooling tower" in form, would be the focus. Above it a giant oculus, like that of the Pantheon in Rome, would open up and allow sunlight to descend onto the parliament, perhaps the speaker's rostrum. Apparently he had other examples in mind—the light streaming through the dome of Hagia Sophia, and Hindu precedents, such as when a shaft of light, at key points of the year, comes through a temple opening and hits an upright altar stone. Even "nocturnal festivals" were contemplated, and outdoor celebrations on the roofscape, which is equipped with an auditorium. From here one could follow cosmic events, like the recent solar eclipse that captivated over a billion viewers.

Symbols of summer and winter sun dominate the "cap" of the cooling tower, symbols that relate to the Jantar Mantar and other cosmological observatories in India [figs. 180, 181]. At first this tilted oval was meant to slide open, as well as display the facts of the universe: "This 'cap' . . . will become a true physics laboratory," he said, "equipped to ensure the play of light . . . Furthermore, the 'cork' will lend itself to possible solar festivals, reminding man once every year that he is a son of the sun." Son of the sun? One can agree with the diagnosis and applaud the idea of a solar festi-

180. Chandigarh, cooling tower "cap," with its signs of summer and winter sun, surmounts the assembly, a reference to reality and Indian cosmology. The use of the crescent symbolizes both the phases of the moon and the paths of the heavenly bodies.

181. Jantar Mantar, New Delhi, 1724. One of several monumental solar observatories in India that served as a model for the sculptural symbolism. LC noted: "The astronomical instruments of Delhi . . . point the way: relink men to the cosmos . . . Exact adaptation of forms and organisms to the sun, to the rains, to the air, etc. this buries Vignola." Burying Vignola meant the end of Classical ornament and the birth of a new iconography based on cosmic symbolism—a foundation statement of the Post-Modern agenda.

val, but it has yet to happen. As a cosmic symbol for this part of India, the sun is particularly apt. It sustains life for all of us, of course, providing the energy that is photosynthesized, and without it for a day the earth would simply freeze. But for Chandigarh, most of the year, it is pulverizing, searing, killing—a flaming sword. The potency of this symbol here comes from mediating everyday reality and the universal.

Inside the Assembly the sun symbolism is continued by emphasizing its opposite: the large concrete spaces are cool, dark, protected by vast bastions of concrete sunshades. These are sus- pended away from the building, creating air circulation. Here is the cave space, antithesis of the sun. The two main legislative halls are suspended in a grid of triple-height space while they also slam through the horizontal roof line as a hyperbola and pyramid, a dramatic version of compaction composition [figs. 182, 183]. Columns, ramps, lifts, and lighting troughs interpenetrate in a way which is Piranesian and can only be described as violent. Yet because the Modulor was used to harmonize the relationships between forms and because there is plenty of free space within which to suspend these forms, none is truncated or compromised.

This open space is devoted to what Le Corbusier again calls the Forum, that informal place of conversation and rest where del- egates can pause and formulate opinion between meetings. This is the only public realm that he was lucky enough to build at this scale. It has a dignity which is appropriate, yet its freedom from convention keeps it from being pompous. Within the main hall of parliament, Le Corbusier has also followed the democratic notion of the forum without falling into conventional notions of

182. Chandigarh, section of General Assembly, redrawn collage. Compaction composition: the layering of *brise-soleil*, pyramidal council chamber, main hall, offices, columns, and ramps. Sometimes the volumes are independent from the building, such as the sunshades; sometimes they visually overlap and are juxta- posed, as in the ramps and Main Assembly. This last was meant to open at key times of the year for solar festi- vals, and they dramatically celebrate with a shaft of light the priority and beauty of cosmic power.

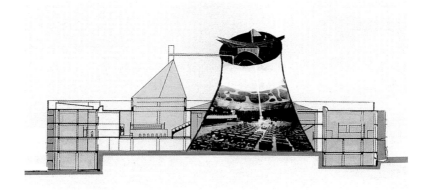

183. Chandigarh, Meeting Hall outside the Main Assembly. Light penetration is dramatized in three different ways: directly in a sun scoop, indirectly bounced off the ceiling, and filtered through the offices. Columns and structural fins syncopate in opposition against a cool black ceiling, creating a Piranesian grandeur and a convincing public space for informal discussion.

184. Chandigarh, General Assembly, 1953–61, in front of the Secretariat. The main assembly hall is under the hyperbolic shell with its symbols of the sun, and the council chamber is under the pyramid. A tilted concrete portico masks the entrance, *brises-soleil* indicate offices, and flat concrete signifies the stairways. Since the Punjab split up further in 1966, becoming half of the State of Haryana, two different parliaments meet in the two council rooms. Open areas are now enclosed by chain-link fencing and patrolled by armed guards—hardly the situation Nehru or the designers foresaw.

a hierarchical organization. It is one of the most welcoming but grand debating halls I have ever been in. Each "orator," as LC called them, has a microphone so that he can be heard and interrupt the course of political events. Acoustic clouds dampen reverberation, and changes of level break up the usual serried banks of politicians. The ambience is like being enveloped in a sensuous vineyard, an uncanny and exciting feeling, especially surprising to find at the center of democratic debate. I cannot think of a better communal space of the *res publica*; it only lacks the oculus of the Pantheon and the movement of the sun to complete the intended symbolism.

Le Corbusier's work at Chandigarh represents the culmination of his new heavyweight aesthetic and enveloping, defensive architecture. This protective and primitive aesthetic does create certain problems—for instance, it re-radiates heat at night—and, at the planning level, the buildings are far too spread out. The capitol complex is removed from the center of civic life, where it should be if democracy is to be a reality, and as an acropolis it is too dispersed, both for the officials to walk from one building to another, in the extreme heat, and to appreciate the juxtaposition of monuments [fig. 184]. While the monuments do, like Ronchamp, send out echoes to each other and the Himalayas, they are dissipated by both the extreme distance and hard, flat, open landscaping.

Even more problematic is the lack of contact between city and political life, and the absence of a relation between figure and ground. Monuments need background tissue, governmental offices need servicing and cafés, flat spaces need animating, and foreground needs background. In a series of amusing sketches and Corbusian plans, Roderigo Perez de Arce has "re-urbanized" Chandigarh and supplied the missing background [fig. 185]. Shops and a proper agora surround the Monument to the Open Hand and its "Ditch of Consideration," where the people were meant to come to debate freely in public. Presently the Open Hand, finally erected in 1985, pivots balefully in the wind all alone, a giant Pop icon of democracy. It was the symbol that obsessed Le Corbusier the most. It looks like a bird, and is based partly on Picasso's and Braque's doves of peace [fig. 186]. When the prairie birds alight on it and sing very loudly, and when one recalls LC's many self-portraits as a *corbeau*, this metaphor of the bird of peace takes on deeper meanings. It also relates to the mountains in the background and, as it spins in the wind, the change in political opinion. So, like any good symbol it mediates local, natural, and social meanings. Particularly relevant for Le Corbusier was the Open Hand as a sign of the Second Machine Age.

185. Roderigo Perez de Arce, "The Re-urbanization of Chandigarh," project, 1978. The Open Hand Monument is given a surrounding urban tissue, as de Arce also gives the other monuments, to provide a background contrast, some welcome shade, and necessary functions. Although the conservatives resist such radical proposals, many urbanists would support such sympathetic transformations of the capitol area and not a few Corbusian enthusiasts believe that the master himself, seeing the problems of the area, would have made them as well.

186. The Open Hand, design 1951, erected 1985. As many paintings of the hand symbol show, starting in the early 1930s, it is meant to capture several key meanings: the bird motif, the distant Himalayas, the hand that creates and commands, and the gesture of giving and receiving. In LC's copy of *Thus Spake Zarathustra* an open hand is drawn in the margin where Zarathustra is described as a "Christlike sacrifice, it also pivots in the wind becoming, in its political context, a sign of a fickle opinion and, perhaps, the necessity to change with it in order to direct it."

Here he was thinking of the way that jet travel, film, television, radio, and telecommunications, even computers in 1960, had revolutionized the globe and created a single culture—"made all things interrelated. The relations are continuous and contiguous around the globe . . ." The hope, and idealism, was that one communicating world would produce a new global order and peace; and the promise of the machine was wealth for everyone. This is the major message behind the Open Hand. As LC must have said and written a thousand times, it is "open to receive newly created wealth, open to distribute it to its people and to others. The 'Open Hand' will assert that the second era of the machine age has begun: the era of harmony." This McLuhanite optimism, the new world brotherhood brought about by technological progress, would have recommended itself greatly to Nehru and a new nation. We know it became the ideology of CNN, MTV, and in India Channels Z, V, and a thousand cable networks, as much as that of Bill Gates. One-world brotherhood did not happen quite the way the idealists predicted. Nationalism, since the mid-1980s, has become more, not less fractious. Moreover, transnational cultures were hybridized, both in the positive way LC designed Chandigarh, and in the negative way multinationals mongrelized and exploited taste. As with Le Corbusier's enthusiasm for the car in the 1920s, his techno-progressivism was naive and self-serving.

But, if part of the symbol is Modernist agitprop, the weather-cock aspect signifies contingency. Shifting this way and that in the wind, it meant for him "humility before the unknown" and the difficulty of life: obviously his life as the errant idealist, Don Quixote. Late in his life, he drew it at several points in his copy of Nietzsche's *Thus Spake Zarathustra*: when Zarathustra becomes "the Christ-like figure, descending to the level of humanity and voluntarily chooses to sacrifice himself in order to bring men the Truth." Or, as Zarathustra says, "This, in fact, is the hardest task of all: to close, out of love, the open hand and maintain, in the act of giving, one's shame." In other words, it is a sign of personal sacrifice, giving as giving up one's life to others, out of love. Hence the deep scars in the palm of the sculpture, apparently modeled on his own hand. Just before he died, in 1965, he urged André Malraux to help realize this "sign of our epoch . . . which marks for 'le père Corbu' a deed, a course traversed." If Father Corbu is invoking a religious meaning then, like Chandigarh as a whole, it is one turned upside down, or at least through ninety degrees. Christ's hand was raised in benediction, Buddha's in welcome and tender peace, but Corb's flies sideways, and points three fingers up. If you'll forgive the

187. Chandigarh, High Court, Courts of Justice, 1956. Nine High Courts are protected by rhythmical *brises-soleil* and a gigantic parasol that keeps out the sun and rain and allows air to circulate over the courts. Reflecting and cooling pools are crossed as at Fatephur Sikri. The symmetrical outline, in effect a megastructure with nonloadbearing arches, is given asymmetrical articulation by the off-center entrance and different colors—green, yellow, red.

188. Chandigarh, shade on poles. This afterthought visually interferes with the graceful curve of the *brise-soleil* and becomes a sad and squalid place for those awaiting trial: the seats do not even face the view!

pun, you have to hand it to him—his reinventing tradition, the transvaluation of all values, and cosmic grandeur verging on megalomania.

It may strain credulity, but as many associates testify, when he was not fighting to realize his ambitions, LC could be modest, humble, and admit his mistakes—even be the first to attack them with good humor. Thus let me invoke his example, and point out one or two of the more unfortunate botches. The High Courts, although noble in outline and dynamic in detail, have suffered a series of alterations due to lack of functional foresight [fig. 187]. Several years after they were completed in 1956, a concrete sun-shade had to be added at ground level because the courts were overheating and—some oversight—there was no adequate place for those awaiting trial to sit. I could not believe that LC himself had designed the tawdry horizontal shelter under which the accused sit in rows of plastic, so many guilty ducks lined up to be shot, but officials assured me that was so, and there are photos of him in front of the addition. Not only does it demean the process of justice, it destroys the voluptuous curve of the ascending sun-shades [fig. 188].

Not enough courts were provided, nor a system of easy expansion, so that when additional courts were built, they had to be suppressed, visually and functionally, at the back of the build-ing. The eminent judges themselves started to disfigure the archi-tecture by parking their cars under the gigantic three-pillared entrance, a practice that has continued for thirty years. They do not like to park with the rest of the people, especially those on trial. Finally, the judges switched the operation of the courts around, placing themselves against the brilliant light. How could you tell if the accused were lying? Because of the glare, you could never see his face.

These functional shortcomings show both Le Corbusier's greater age (he was now in his middle sixties), and the fact that he spent much time in Paris while work was going on. He delegated much of this to Pierre Jeanneret, who undoubtedly deserves some credit when the workmanship is well done and functions have been thought through. Yet even with the faults, and the fact that the con-crete has weathered, turned black in spots, and not been cleaned (how could it, since the capitol is divided politically), the magnificent vision of this acropolis towers over other symbolic

189. Fatephur Sikri, 1569–74. Interlocking courtyards laced by causeways, pools, and sheltered walkways, all carried through in a monochrome rich red sandstone and asymmetrical, shifted axes. This was a model for LC, but in truth its scale and shade are slightly superior.

centers of the last century. Its symbolism and sculptural invention make Brasilia, Canberra, Berlin's Reichstag, and London's Millennium Dome look somewhat flat, gestures without great resonance. Why? Because LC has created a form language and set of specific symbols that relate to local Indian life and the cosmos in complex ways. They are not one-liners, but rather suggestive forms that call on history and hopes for the future with such variety that they provoke continuous reinterpretation.

For instance, the waterways and reflecting pools of the capital relate to another capital city, Fatephur Sikri, built by Akbar in the late sixteenth century [fig. 189]. Here are islands across causeways, monuments in stone placed asymmetrically on a flat landscape, threaded with colonnades. Chandigarh's capitol is a contemporary version of this stone citadel, but in concrete. Like Corbu's plan for Saint-Dié, a flat *temenos* plays the game of monumentality by shifting axes, by a carefully tuned asymmetrical symmetry woven together [fig. 190]. That is, every symmetrical form speaks of monumentality, but it is shifted slightly off axis, and given secondary asymmetries. The General Assembly is a basic temple, but with two skewed forms breaking its entablature; the High Courts, 400 yards opposite, are shifted slightly north. Its entrance is a giant order of pylons, but placed carefully off center. This asymmetrical symmetry gives both monumentality *and* movement beyond; one is pulled toward the entrance *and* shifted toward the landscape. Here is the both/and architecture that Robert Venturi was to make the hallmark of Post-Modernism a few years later, and played with a strength that James Stirling would match at Stuttgart. But to my mind it is more convincing than any public architecture produced

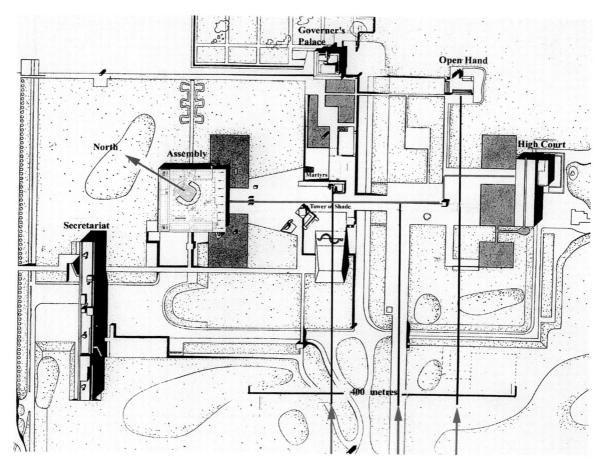

190. Chandigarh, plan of the Capitol, 1952. Shifted and sliding axes, asymmetrical symmetry, monumentality, and openness to the landscape. Four monuments were to carry on a conversation with the main dialogue between the Assembly and the High Court, 400 yards apart. The Governor's Palace and Open Hand, to the north, tighten the focus on the distant Himalayas. The Assembly is rotated to the cardinal points so that all the delegates face north.

since its erection in the late 1950s, the one example of monumental symbolism that remains, with all its faults, the standard to meet.

The Secret Method

That Pierre Jeanneret and local Indian architects could carry out these buildings while the designer was absent brings up the question of Le Corbusier's method of design, one that allowed a certain amount of interpretation and execution by others. Every architect keeps a file of his favorite details. These consist of products on the market and preferred sets of solutions (a prefabricated staircase or a method of joining concrete and glass, for example). The reasons for this filing-cabinet approach are obviously economic, but also aesthetic. Just as one speaks with ready-made words, the architect builds with preexisting elements, and in both cases, language and architecture, this traditional repertoire actually allows invention. The linguist Noam Chomsky has stressed that with fixed language rules and finite grammar, one can generate an infinite number of new sentences.

In like manner, the architect's creativity is dependent on using a preexisting syntax (or structure and technology) and semantics (or the conventional connotations of doors, windows, stairways, and so on). The difference between language and architecture is a matter of degree. The architect can much more easily proffer new elements than an individual can coin, and have accepted, new words. And the architect can change the relation between form and content much more easily than the speaker can alter the conventional associations between sound and sense. In these ways architecture is more flexible, permissive, and changing than language, but at the same time it is less powerful for manipulating ideas (except, of course, purely architectural ideas). Saul Steinberg's cartoons to the contrary notwithstanding, we will continue to speak in words rather than buildings.

If T. S. Eliot said the job of the Modern poet was to reinvent and "purify the language of the tribe," then Le Corbusier also saw this as an obligation of the Modern architect: "It seemed to me that I was at the end of the road of logic. I had touched at the essential principle: The architect dispenses new words—we will see!" We have already seen that he tried, with partial success, to create four or five new languages: a naturalistic, geometric Art Nouveau at eighteen, a Regional Classicism at twenty-five, Purism at thirty-one, heavyweight Brutalism and a metaphorical Post-Modernism in his early sixties. Just at the end of his life he was starting to create a sixth, lightweight, proto-High-Tech language. The continual revolution of architecture is entailed by this restless creativity, and it is well to look at his method of "dispensing new words" and how it related to one of his "secrets," that is, painting and sculpture. It can be illustrated by further Indian work completed in the early 1950s.

Like so many rationalist architects before him, Viollet-le-Duc and August Choisy, for example, Le Corbusier conceived new languages to stem directly from a change in technology. His "Five Points of a New Architecture"—those five new building elements that result, naturally, from the perspicacious use of reinforced

191. Chandigarh, Secretariat, 1958. Almost 800 feet long, this must be one of the longest bureaucracies in the world. Various Corbusian "words," added at the last moment, break up the mass: the central double-height volumes, and the Y-shaped speaker's rostrum. Other words are also collaged onto the roof and surface, such as the upturned canopy and massive ramp. LC spoke of the "words" of painting as "massive and full of meaning."

concrete, are a good example. This technological determinism and rational invention were then supplemented with a formal invention stemming from the past and his travel sketchbooks, and the present and his metaphorical drawings. With a growing repertoire, he could design a whole city in a unified manner with the words he invented—the endless museum, the pie-shaped assembly, the *Unité*, the *brise-soleil*, and so on. How did he create them? Essentially, he would start with the rationalist method, as formulated by the eighteenth-century French functionalist Abbé Laugier, from whom he often quoted: "It is necessary to start at zero. It is necessary to state the problem . . . 'If the problem is well stated, the solution will be indicated.'" In other words, rational analysis first, intuitive and formal invention next.

In creating the new word "*ondulatoires*," which he first used on the Secretariat at Chandigarh [fig. 191], he restated the "problem of the window" as four separate functions: to air, to ventilate, to view from, and to let in light. The four functions, which are somewhat compromised in the traditional sash window, are pulled apart and each satisfied by a new form. The various *brises-soleil* shade the glass wall from the sun; vertical, pivoting ventilators of sheet metal allow fresh air in—otherwise ventilation is achieved by fans; finally, the fixed glass wall, obscured at points for indirect light and open at other points for view, answers the two last "problems of the window."

So far, then, "form follows function," but this was never far enough. It had to be translated into a clear and distinct sculptural shape seen under the strong Indian sun—and handed to a designer in the office. There were several trusted assistants. Balkrishna V. Doshi, who was working in the atelier and supervising work at Chandigarh and at Ahmedabad described a typical situation. He redrew the exceedingly long Secretariat, which was under construction, and realized that the monotonous repetition of the same element would emphasize bureaucracy. LC immediately agreed, and in the middle of the building "completely changed his ideas," adding a middle section of "words" he was using elsewhere: for instance, double-height volumes and a sculptural Y-shape, an echo of the Open Hand and bull's horns. This last-minute change, as Doshi said, characterized Le Corbusier's method, which was based equally on control, accident, and sudden juxtaposition. Thus, in general, he worked out the scheme rationally, left it to ferment, reached a creative synthesis, and then responded with visual solutions that had been stored in his memory. The Y shape and bull's horns were one of the "massive words" that he had researched in his painting, and he credits this activity as being one secret: "I think if one accords some significance to my architecture, it is to this secret labor that one should attribute its profundity."

This method accounts for the freshness and distinctiveness of all his work. A building by Le Corbusier can always be recognized as his own, even though many of his words have become architectural clichés. The reason for this identity is the emphasis placed on each element—forceful, iconic, and memorable—and the way they are juxtaposed by the artist in LC.

Another secret of his method is the way it responds quickly to everyday reality, an aspect we can find in his drawings of daily Indian life, living outdoors, feeding barnyard animals, going into the slums and recording the climate as experienced by the poor, and so forth. This also gave his symbolism at Chandigarh freshness and relevance. But the method is deeper than that and connects with the way he would throw himself into things unprepared. Because LC was self-taught and operated outside the usual professional norms, he would improvise on the spot. He spoke about this improvisation in several contexts:

> I adopted a technique of my own that was rather unique . . .
> I never prepared my lectures . . . I would improvise.
> Improvisation is an amazing thing, but I would draw . . .
> When one draws while speaking, and uses effective words, one
> creates something . . . and all my theory, my introspection,
> and my retrospection on the phenomenon of architecture
> and urbanism come from these improvised and illustrated lec-
> tures . . . the act of improvising, of waging battle, the fact
> of being in a state of intensity—to jump in completely willingly
> and to tell oneself, "one has to fight one's way out"—is an
> extremely important fact in life . . . père Corbu is always
> well received [by audiences], because I speak naturally and
> spontaneously.

This, the spontaneous, Quaker Corbu who creates on the spot, to keep from falling off the tightrope onto which he has jumped, obviously communicates with an audience very effectively. He persuades as does the preacher, the stand-up comedian, and the magician who create something new in public. But the secret method is even more than inspiring improvisation and it relates to something I mentioned at the start of this book, Corbu the Renaissance man, the dialectical creator.

Perhaps this aspect was somewhat hidden to himself, because he does not theorize it per se. There are, however, a few moments when he starts to adumbrate a method of multiple creation, such as the following: ". . . And it turned out later that, not being able to build certain things, I could draw them; but not being able to explain them entirely in drawing, especially when it came to urbanism, I had to explain them, so I wrote. One day Paul Valéry told me I wrote like an angel . . ." Here we have the beginning of a theory of what the cognitive scientist Howard Gardner calls "multiple intelligences." Intelligence, creativity, skill is never just one thing, as IQ tests seem to suggest, but rather, as Gardner has shown, something that is dispersed around the body and brain. Thus a mathematical intelligence may relate to a musical gift, or playing soccer to running the hundred-yard dash, but they are also separate skills. Great intelligence, the secret of a protean creator such as Picasso and LC, consists in an ability to pass a problem *through several different media*. Looking at an architectural problem through the media of drawing, sculpture, modeling, city planning, lecturing, and writing—all of which Corbu did passably well—allows it to be reinvented in many different discourses at once. Here is the real secret of Le Corbusier's method: his multiple intelligences successively applied. As a bit of a monk, he might have not been well rounded in all respects, as much of a Renaissance man as the courtier Raphael, but then no other architect of the twentieth century has operated on all these different levels as thoroughly as LC.

We can see these methods of improvisation and multiple intelligence bearing fruit in other Indian buildings. For the rich merchants of Ahmedabad, the textile and fabric manufacturers, he reworked several of his old ideas and placed them in new combinations. The Millowners Association Building is a typical bricolage of past "words" carried out with freshness and great speed [fig. 192]. Here we find the *brises-soleil* on the approach side, but they are sharply tilted at an angle to shield from the strong western sun and provide a row of interesting diagonal shadows. They are also exploded apart by two more familiar words: the ramp and stair, both put in violent juxtaposition with each other, and a slot of cavernous space. The architectural promenade, first used on the La Roche and Savoye villas, takes over much of the building, literally so. The functional justification was the kind of open-air receptions and parties that the millowners required, an excuse to give over 50 percent of the building to circulation.

Again, the artist pulls all the parts together as a compaction composition. The ascent through the building is dramatized by curved forms and rectangles set on a rectilinear canvas, and this canvas is layered frontally to the approach. Even the diagonal sunshades assert this frontality by having their front edges parallel to the picture plane. But then, the box, whose squareness is also asserted on the sides, is again broken apart on the roof by blocks of concrete set in tense opposition. On the surface here one can still discover a most surprising note drawn in pencil, and circled:

"Stone flooring, same design as other floors, Doshi, 28/6/55."
Working drawings and commands on the building itself! That says
a lot about how sympathetic cohorts could translate the new words,
at speed, into what LC called a new "Indian grammar."

The Shodan House, designed at the same time in Ahmedabad,
has similar themes played differently. At first it was conceived for a
gregarious millowner with a passion for holding large parties, and
so it became another extensive promenade up and around many
roofscapes. The site changed, along with the client, a more retiring
family. But LC, liking the solution, simply rotated it to fit the new
context, as if the whole building were a perfected object-type or
single word of his new language. No functional justification here—
just the sort of a priori solution he had criticized as Beaux-Arts
thinking—except that here it is entirely fresh and dramatic. Sun
and wind, the cosmic determinants, now amplify the *brise-soleil* to

192. Millowners Association Building,
Ahmedabad, 1951–55. Old ideas
partly transformed: the architectural
promenade with a ramp and stairs
dramatically breaking through the box
of *brises-soleil* that are now tilted at
an angle away from the western sun.

193. Shodan House, Ahmedabad, 1951–54. The garden spills right into the living room, to the right, and room-size sunshades, with planting, become suspended gardens.

194. Shodan House, roof terrace on the first floor. Punctuated by cantilevers, stairs, and columns opening on three stories of space.

Herculean proportions [fig. 193]. Each sunshade is the size of a room, pulled away from the facade, as if it were a suspended rectangle of space to be enjoyed for itself. No railing spoils these sculptural shapes, and the sense of vertigo and danger simply heighten the experience of architectural pleasure—free spatial interpenetration.

In terms of his previous grammar here are the basic elements—*brise-soleil*, independent structure, cantilevers, and curled curves—and the older organizational strategy. A ramp goes up the middle, as at Poissy, and the interlocking section of the Citrohan House and Villa at Carthage pulls together the floors. A parasol, or independent roof, shades the whole building and encourages cool air to flow through, as it does at the High Court in Chandigarh. In other words, the Shodan House is a synthesis of previous ideas played at a higher pitch. Nothing is more extreme than the planes of punched-out space [fig. 194]. Here are the hanging gardens of 1925 going up, not two floors, but four. They are split apart by curled lightwells and made even more dramatic by the cantilevers and columns shooting through space. Indian reality, outdoor living in the heat, is exploited for every possible effect. Downstairs, in the more domestic context of the living room, the garden comes right into the house and then is framed by yet another invention, the thick wall of splayed windows, a mini-Ronchamp played as a syncopated grid [fig. 195].

195. Shodan House, living room. Opens to the garden, on the right, and frames trees with the splayed walls of Ronchamp, all dimensioned by the Modulor.

196. Sarabhai House, Ahmedabad, 1951–55. Diagonal pool slide, like a cosmological instrument, connects water, garden, and sky. Heavy, horizontal concrete balconies shade the veranda and hide the flat Catalan arches of the interior.

197. Sarabhai House, interior vaults on the first floor. The Monol solution of rows of vaulted shells placed side by side creates a grammar of walls and voids below, which punctuate domestic space, giving great variety and enclosure.

As Le Corbusier became successful in the 1950s, and Indian commissions flowed in one after another, he might have been overwhelmed by the volume of work to repeat similar solutions. But here his repertoire of opposite models, another "secret" of design, came to his aid. He called this storehouse a "box of miracles," and he could select a separate set of tricks from it for roughly the same commission. Thus the Sarabhai House at Ahmedabad, for a merchant family committed to the arts, has an entirely different feeling than the Shodan House. Instead of standing over nature like a temple, it allows nature to cover it like a landscape [fig. 196]. Pool and dark cave are the abiding images derived, ultimately, from his very first building, the Villa Fallet. A series of primitivist buildings are generated from this first lesson in regionalism—the "female" Maisons Monol with their flat Catalan vaults, the

198. Sarabhai House, section
illustration.

Weekend House of 1935 with its thick turf roof, and the Maisons
Jaoul in Paris designed at the same time as the Sarabhai House,
also with heavy brick vaults and tiles [fig. 197]. Shallow vaults, held
by walls and piers, generate an interesting grammar quite opposite
that of the Citrohan House. In effect, these solutions are all variations on a set of fundamentalist themes of going back to nature and
building with handcrafts. It is true that modern techniques and
Modern art are accepted into this ambience, but it is the greenery,
concrete forms, and voids that dominate.

Conceptually it is another version of a hybrid Indian grammar
since certain traditional features are recognizable: the long diagonal slide that falls into the pool—down which the young Sarabhais
would plummet—recalls the cosmological observatories at Jaipur
and New Delhi, while the water channels that criss-cross the roofs
are clearly derived from Mughal gardens. Yet because these elements are made in thick concrete that harmonizes with the heavy
horizontal bands of balconies, the quotation is disguised or understated. Understatement, except for the thick concrete, comes as
something of a surprise in LC's work. One is so used to seeing his
buildings proclaim their existence as heroic gestures against the
sky, it is hard to believe in this image of the modest, self-effacing
structure that burrows into luxuriant nature and becomes a
part of earth.

Transposition of Meaning

The new words of architecture that Le Corbusier forged throughout
his life became seminal, not only for himself but for others.

199. Youth and Cultural Center, Firminy-Vert, designed 1956, built 1963–66. This inclined linear building was initially meant to shield a stadium on one side. Although the functions and placement changed, the inclined shapes remained and suggested a third form, the suspended, catenary ceiling. This balanced formula, two outward-canting walls plus a hung ceiling, was taken up as a unit of architectural meaning around the world.

200. Eero Saarinen, Dulles Airport, Chantilly, Virginia, 1962–64. The inclined plane and catenary curve holding the roof, a formula adapted from LC, is made more expressive in the slight curve and counterthrust.

Because they had visual strength and were functionally based, they found a world audience and became the morphemes of contemporary architecture, or new units of architectural meaning to be reused and misused. For instance, the forms of Ronchamp appeared on banks in Los Angeles, and *brises-soleil* appeared everywhere, even on the north elevations of solid facades. Both these transpositions show the arbitrary nature of the architectural sign, the fact that the relationship between form and function is partly set by convention. They also raise a fundamental problem for architectural communication in the era of continual revolution.

If meanings can be transposed between functions and between cultures, so that a Los Angeles bank looks like a French church, and if the "form givers," as LC was called in the 1950s, are continually dispensing new words, then how will society ever build up a coherent language? Why won't large cities resemble a World's Fair? The force of fashion, the dissemination of architectural culture through the magazines, the ease with which architectural meaning can be transposed all point to this problem.

We have seen Le Corbusier reusing an industrial cooling tower for the General Assembly at Chandigarh, that is, a utilitarian form for a cultural and communal role [fig. 180]. This equates the factory and machine with politics, at least semantically. At the level of metaphor, he transposes a crab's shell into the roof of Ronchamp, and a bottle rack into the structure of the *Unité*. Much of his invention is of this kind, a displacement of concepts, which are then taken up by others. For instance, at Firminy-Vert, a new town in southeastern France, he invented the inclined building shape for protecting viewers in a stadium. But then, when the program changed, he found new functions for the shape, moved it across the site, and turned the stadium into a cultural center [fig. 199]. Eero Saarinen took up this interesting formal solution for the Dulles Airport [fig. 200], Alphonse Reidy used it on the Museum of Modern Art in São Paulo, it traveled to I. M. Pei's City Hall in Dallas, and soon there was a flood of tilted slabs and even several upside-down pyramids turned into offices. One formal type, six different functions. This runaway meaning is typical of architectural culture in the global city: form givers propose and followers dispose. It was ever thus, except in the past there was no continual revolution: cities and architectural language were more stable.

Le Corbusier did not recognize that his continual invention might cause problems of shared meaning. He consciously promoted the transposition of concepts, of course, but at the same time he sought to stabilize the vocabulary, with recurring elements, such as the *brise-soleil*. This coherence of use allows one, when acquainted with the work, to read off the semantic meanings, much as past ages could decipher their own classical language of architecture. He clearly hoped that a comparable tradition would grow for the twentieth century, based on the poetic use of new technologies. If these *did* evolve, according to plan, then a whole culture might emerge understanding, if not speaking, the same architectural language. Cultural integration, Periclean Athens, the dream of the West. This was an ideal behind his books, the *Oeuvres complète*; they would make public and rational the basis for a new cultural integration. It was also the idea behind the Five Points of a New Architecture: to translate the new techniques into the new lexicon.

There were, inevitably, more than five neologisms, many more. I have found more than fifty (ramps, *ondulatoires*, etc.) which he presented less systematically. If, as he would have liked, these new words became the basis for global architecture, then it might have evolved a coherent language based on function, poetic expression, and semantic meaning. Something like this was on his mind when he and others tried to set the building codes for Vichy France, and then succeeded at Chandigarh, and when, at the end of his life, he worked at Firminy-Vert. In these latter two cases, one can read off specific architectural messages in each building, see how they relate building types, and find what values are being communicated. The problem with these new towns, however, reverses that of the global city: the architectural languages are too limited, too boring—often a problem with designed cities.

Always sensing the paradox within his own position, like Picasso, he raced ahead of his own theory, left his followers behind, and moved on to yet another language of architecture, his sixth.

A Lightweight, Electronic Language

Ever since 1911, Charles-Edouard Jeanneret wanted to create a white Mediterranean architecture based on pure volumes. In the late 1920s, he flirted with the machine aesthetic, an architecture that took its cue from airplanes and the Eiffel Tower—that is, tensile structures without much volume. This minor interest might have become major had steel become cheap and conventionally acceptable. He designed mass-produced steel housing several times, but with the realization that it would not be accepted because "the right spirit does not exist." The only examples built were two apartment blocks, one in Paris, 1934, the other in Geneva, 1931, and these were tentative essays in the new aesthetic, rather dry like so much functionalist work of the 1930s, and built for the middle class. Yet in three later exhibition buildings, Le Corbusier showed the wit and lyricism that could be attained with a lightweight technology. Had these three buildings been accepted as his heavyweight creations were, the mobile, responsive

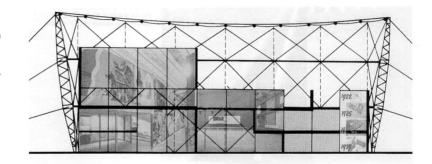

201. Pavillon des Temps Nouveau, Paris International Exposition, 1937, collage. Steel cables and pylons held a translucent tent suspended above an exhibition structure of ramps and demonstration stands. The strong separation of container and contained reappeared in later buildings.

architecture of the late 1960s would have taken off over two decades earlier. They contain the interest in audio-visual techniques combined with flexibility that became so strong with Archigram and then with media architects in the 1990s.

The Pavillon des Temps Nouveau was built in 1937 as a short-term exhibition to propagandize the "lyricism of modern life" and educate the people in his views on redesigning Paris [fig. 201]. As such, the content as well as the form of this exhibition tent were very much of Le Corbusier's own choosing. One followed a clear path of circulation which had a didactic message that unfolded in time. The first set of images, a collage of words, photos, and drawings, proclaimed "the revolution in architecture is accomplished." From there one went on to the ClAM analysis of urbanism, the separation of the four urban functions, various city plans, the Radiant Farm, and finally to the exit—"the understanding of the true programme for a machine civilization." All of this had a heavy, dogmatic tone as the sections indicate, and LC complained that no officials noticed his plans nor even acknowledge his thirty-six-page book that complemented the exposition. Yet some of the images were extraordinarily light and dynamic and became, in a sense, a greater reality than the ephemeral structure that enclosed them. Here the writer, book illustrator, graphic designer, polemicist, and architect all came together. Negatively, for this exposition, one understands why LC called himself a "Man of Letters" rather than an architect since many of the walls are filled with slogans and paragraphs of print; but, positively, they also make striking use of photomontage and airplane models.

This shift in emphasis from form to content or medium to message became stronger in Le Corbusier's next exhibition tent, constructed for Philips at the Brussels World's Fair in 1958 [fig.

202. Philips Pavilion, Brussels, 1958. Hyperbolic-parabolas enclose a circular "stomach." Entrance and exit are marked by the high points. Xenakis worked out the details of this building after sketches and models of Le Corbusier.

202]. LC was asked to design the facade of the building in any way he liked, but instead of concentrating on this he gave it to a fellow designer, Xenakis, and spent his time inventing a new form of light and sound show, the "Electronic Poem." He wrote to one of the directors of Philips:

> I shall not give your pavilion a façade, but I shall compose an Electronic Poem contained in a "bottle" . . . the Poem will be composed of pictures, colored rhythms, music. The Electronic Poem will combine in a coherent whole what films, recorded music, color, words, sound and silence have until now produced independently. The Poem will last ten minutes. It will be performed for 500 spectators at a time: The pavilion will, therefore, be a stomach assimilating 500 listener-spectators, and evacuating them automatically at the end of the performance . . .

The stomach form and the expressive hyperbolic-parabolas that lean away from each other in soaring balance were the main aesthetic decisions taken by Le Corbusier and then delegated to Xenakis. Again it is his painting that informs the upward-tilting

203. Frank Gehry, New Guggenheim, Bilbao, 1992–97. Complexity architecture of the 1990s, generated and cut by computer, develops many similar motives, including fractals, self-similar curves, and biomorphic forms.

shapes—bull's horns, prows, *licorne*, cornucopia, breast, and armpit—all the visual sources that were behind the same forms at Ronchamp. The biomorphic shapes and reference to the stomach underscore the biological metaphor present in Le Corbusier's work from the very beginning. For these reasons the Philips Pavilion can be taken as a harbinger of the Complexity architecture of the 1990s, the work of Frank Gehry, Peter Eisenman, Daniel Libeskind, and those rooting their work in nonlinear dynamics [fig. 203]. Curved buildings, generated and cut by computer, can now be produced almost as easily as square ones. Furthermore, their self-similar shapes are fractals, and in that way closer to nature's forms. What made them eminently buildable in 1958 was the organizing form: a hyperbolic-parabola is made by joining skewed lines with easy-to-connect straight ones. That LC loved the grid and Euclidean architecture is beyond dispute, and his *Poème de l'Angle Droit*, a philosophical poem and set of lithographs produced in 1953, proves that love. Yet the swooping forms, the staccato ornament that moves around like a flock of birds, and the tensegrity structure at the entrance all show that a non-Euclidean geometry was being developed here. If Ronchamp opened up the first stage of Post-Modernism, then this building opened up its second—which is not to say LC would have approved of either.

If the handling of exterior form was brilliant—no architect since Gaudí had distorted mathematical and structural curves in such an expressive way—the combination of existing sensory tech-

204. Philips Pavilion, Electronic Poem (FLC). The human, the natural, and the cosmic dramatized and made into a light and sound *Gesamtkunstwerk*.

nologies in a new art form was equally significant. Four hundred amplifiers distributed sound around the interior shells to create, along with the projected images, an intense spatial movement [fig. 204]. These images, following each other in rapid succession, were projected all around the spectators much as later light and sound shows were to do at World's Fairs in Montreal and Tokyo. Le Corbusier spent most of his design time at various museums collecting these images. They varied in sequence from the terrifying to the harmonious, from photos of concentration camps to popular monsters to Le Corbusier's designs for communal living. It is rather as if the enameled doors of the General Assembly were animated as moving images: the content connects man to nature, society, and the cosmos.

The music, or rather three-dimensional sound arrangement, was conceived by Edgar Varèse as well as Xenakis. The total effect, a bombarding of several senses by sound, color, light, and moving images, was both backward-looking to the *Gesamtkunstwerk* of the opera, and forward-looking to the electronic media environments which Marshall McLuhan was to analyze. It did achieve the simultaneous involvement of almost all the senses and forced the spectators to participate in integrating and interpreting the evidence "all at once," rather than in a controlled, linear sequence. The experience was analogous to seeing the stained glass of a cathedral and hearing a ritual mass, except that the five hundred listener-spectators had to move on every ten minutes, as the stomach expelled them. In any case, it was quasi-religious, certainly meant to be spiritual and definitely entertaining. One million two hundred fifty thousand visitors experienced the pavilion, a testimony to LC's ability to reach mass culture when he got the right support. The Electronic Poem, however, was the single excursion of Le Corbusier into this new medium, and afterwards he returned to painting, writing, and architecture.

Le Corbusier's last exhibition structure and, also, the last significant building under construction at the time of his death, was his most developed essay in lightweight technology. It is a mark of his creative strength that he could produce in his middle seventies such an original and, in the context of his total oeuvre, unusual building. In many ways the Centre Le Corbusier in Zurich is a new departure, the opening up of a new steel aesthetic [fig. 205]. In fact it does hark back to previous exhibition schemes and

Following pages:
205. Centre Le Corbusier, Zurich, 1963–67. A gray steel roof, a giant *brise-soleil,* hovers over a light steel cage filled with colored enamel panels and clear glass.

Le Corbusier: Monumental and Symbolic Architecture 1946–65

206. Centre Le Corbusier, various views.

the pervasive ocean-liner metaphor, but in terms of its lightness and the erector-set aesthetic, it is a gem. Its thin, bolted steel sections and crisp infill panels represent quite an alternative to the concrete aesthetic of massive volumes set in opposition.

That this building was completed was due to the perseverance of Heidi Weber, an energetic and idealistic Swiss woman. A typical Corbu client, she is also in some ways a precursor of the Women's Movement, fighting a series of battles with the male authorities of Zurich. A self-made woman who started off selling modern furniture, she had to fight an assorted package of male prejudices: the Zurich planning officials, the local engineers who thought the building unsafe, and even the "so-called Zurich Le Corbusier friends" who, she said, "have harmed my activities during the realization of this Center by uttering envious calumnies." Apparently, these last named speculated immodestly on her relation with Le Corbusier (whose wife had just died) and questioned her motives for building such a monument with which she was so closely identified in the inception and daily running. The battle continued. In 1971, she threatened to unbolt this "flexible" building and

reerect it in another city where it was wanted, because the town council of Zurich would not help pay expenses for the exhibitions and were only interested in obtaining the building, at its original cost, as a tourist monument for the city. The building today is an elegant, wiry masterpiece, a sharp, witty instrument strung as tight as a harp and as light as a bow.

The two sheet-metal parasols hover over the steel cage with a certain tautness, being supported only at their midpoints and having expanding and diminishing sections which answer each other in antiphony: one rises, the other falls [fig. 206]. Below this basic overall theme, there is a staccato of colored panels, steel sections, and bolts. This flexible cage is constructed on Le Corbusier's favorite Modulor dimension of 226 centimeters, the height of a man's outstretched arm. The grid of space is carried throughout, even where there is double-height space, and constructed from four steel L sections, which are bolted together to form a cruciform column. This method of construction allows a great flexibility in exhibition use, the partitions and space being malleable for each new show. Twenty thousand screws were used

207. Centre Le Corbusier, main exhibition space.

to obtain this flexibility, and as Heidi Weber said, "All these numerous screws created a great problem, particularly in the mind of some Swiss engineers."

The overpowering feeling is of being on a beached ship. The steel roof is painted battleship gray. The metal doors have semicircular openings like the hatches of a ship; the "top deck" of the Centre is punctuated by steel ladders and periscope holes. Finally, the main double-height exhibition space with its open staircase, metal decking, and funnel is very much like the boiler room of an ocean liner [fig. 207]. On the exterior, the brightly colored panels, alternating like semaphore flags, complete the metaphor, and all

208. Richard Rogers and Renzo Piano, Pompidou Center, Paris, 1971–77. High-Tech architecture was initially highly polychromatic and like oil refineries color-coded to separate services. LC's last essay in steel opened the door to this expressive poetics, if not the later gray aesthetic.

one has to do is change the surrounding verdure to blue in order to see this building as some unusual vessel plowing over the water. As at Ronchamp, the suggested images seem appropriate to the function. An exhibition pavilion is plausibly "pure, neat, clear, clean, and healthy," the way Le Corbusier celebrated the qualities of ocean liners. The High-Tech aesthetic was born, several years before Richard Rogers and Norman Foster turned it into the reigning mode of British architecture [fig. 208].

PART V

Who Was
Le Corbusier?

209. *Mains croisées sur la tête*,
1928–1939–1940, oil on canvas,
100 x 81 cm (FLC).

Various Birds

In trying to sum up and evaluate Le Corbusier's contribution to architecture, not to mention city planning, painting, and writing, we are faced with an obvious conundrum. There is more than one Corbu, just as there were many different bird portraits, the *corbeaux* that appeared in his paintings, and plans, as signatures or self-portraits. Quizzical, enigmatic, and fleeting some may be, while others are serious, profound, and occasionally predatory, like vultures. If the architect were alive to study the recent avian portraits produced by scholars, he would be pleased because they also show the open nature of his imaginative works, the different ways they can be interpreted.

This multivalence is a property of his best work, as I have continually stressed, as it is of all engaging art in general. The several architectural languages that Le Corbusier developed are, in a way, as disarming for the historian as the various messages he communicated with them. One is bound to be wrong, or at least too limited, in any attempt to fix his essential contribution. The interpretations that are usually made are either contradicted by Le Corbusier's supremely dialectical development, or they pale beside the creative wealth of his output.

Several critics, and detractors, have tried to fix his message by excluding its richness. For instance, the psychoanalyst Gaston Bardot, and also the critics Paul and Percival Goodman, argue that Le Corbusier was a Calvinist, a Puritan, who took too narrow a view of man and was unconcerned with the sexual dimension. This interpretation is only plausible if one concentrates on the "sterile, white boxes," and dissolves on familiarity with the painting, Ronchamp, and his sensual formalism (to say nothing of his private life). Perhaps a sensual Calvinist, or passionate Puritan, would be adequate labels, but this again shows his dialectical richness. Other critics, especially city planning theorists such as Jane Jacobs, have faulted Le Corbusier for taking an overly simplistic view of the way the city functions, dividing it up into rigid statistical categories and paying no attention to complex, individual processes. This is a telling criticism, as I will argue shortly, but it does miss the variety of functions he would include when actually executing a project.

In brief, his dialectical method and dualistic personality pushed him continuously forward. Le Corbusier had the unusual ability of staying in touch with creative ideas and, judging by his

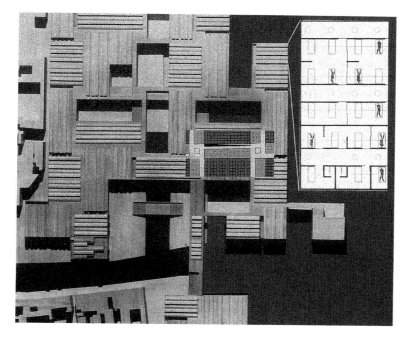

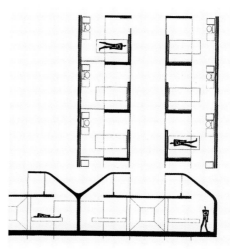

210. Venice Hospital, 1965 proposal, collage (FLC). A three-story grid, with patients on the top floor, is nestled into the Venice fabric. This contextual response with a low network building corresponds to the New Urbanism that was being worked out by Team X and Shadrach Woods at the time.

Venice Hospital scheme, which he was working on when he died and which has many of the complex, urban aspects which his critics were asking for, he would have changed tack once more [fig. 210]. His ability to respond to new situations was shown when he sided with the younger generation of ClAM against the older, his own generation. The younger group of Team X, he wrote to ClAM in 1956, were "the only ones capable of feeling actual problems, personally, profoundly . . . They are in the know. Their predecessors no longer are, they are out, they are no longer subject to the direct impact of the situation."

This cutting away of friendships, and previous ideological commitments, in favor of creativity and relevance was typical. The moment he felt the ideals he had fought for were anachronistic, or that his followers had betrayed him by imitation, or that other Modern architects were becoming slack, he would disown them just as he had rejected his teacher L'Eplattenier or his cohort Ozenfant. The ability to burn what he loved in order to start afresh remained to the end, and it is this flexibility which makes one believe that, given time, he would have answered most criticism with new developments. Indeed it is this flexibility which makes most criticisms rebound on the critic. Lewis Mumford, every so often, attacked him as a "crippled genius" who had "warped the work of a whole generation, giving it arbitrary directives, superficial slogans, and sterile goals." But the accusation refused to stick and implicitly questioned Mumford's own values. Were the British New Towns much better than the Radiant City? Only insofar as they were smaller in scale.

No doubt the Greenwich Village of Jane Jacobs and the "organic" city of Christopher Alexander *are* better alternatives, but neither Jacobs nor Alexander is a fully committed architect, nor have they built their ideal cities and tested their faults. Moreover, it is possible LC would have come round to their views had he lived. As to his city planning, it was undoubtedly flawed in several basic ways: in the assumption that one could build massive urban areas, at a stroke, without entailing the equivalent of a dictatorship; in the assumption that a city is a total work of art and not a piecemeal growth responding to countless economic forces and decisions; and finally the aesthetic and organizational point, something discovered in the 1990s, that a growing city *does* have a geometrical order, but not the Euclidean one LC favored. *The Fractal City* was published only in 1994, and it is unfair to blame him for not having preempted this innovation, as he did others, but it would have spared him a thousand misfortunes had he done so. Basically, the *bitter* part of his fight with society was over his misguided ideas of city living.

But what about the pleasurable part of the struggle? From what we have seen of his life there seems to be a deep connection between his combative personality and his overpowering creative drive. If we look at the sixty years of work, a dialectical, even spiral, pattern appears. Solution types are reached, then put aside for ten years, then reinvented in a new manner. What drives this dialectic from stage to stage? Many things—internal discoveries, external pressures, deep dissatisfactions with current architecture, but also the encounter with women. His travels, drawing, and painting also pushed him beyond a previous synthesis to a new level. These are the engines behind his protean drive, and, of course, on a conscious level, there was the Nietzschean philosophy, the belief in this creative drive, not to mention the example of other Modern creators. It is these creators, above all Picasso, who LC resembles both in general and in the continual revolutionizing of his work.

Howard Gardner, the Harvard cognitive psychologist, has shown the archetypal patterns behind some major figures of the

twentieth century: Freud, Einstein, Picasso, Stravinsky, T. S. Eliot,
Martha Graham, and Gandhi. His book *Creating Minds* shows how
these protean creators developed from childhood, revealing several archetypal situations, and in appendix II I argue that Le
Corbusier fits the pattern: he was the "Normal Genius of the
Twentieth Century," very much like the others. Continual revolution in style and approach, about every ten years, characterizes all
of their lives.

Beyond valuing creativity, what were his other strong beliefs,
his orientation toward the world? If one is to get close to an
answer, the first way will be through a metaphorical analysis of his
buildings, since some were so personally conceived as to be self-
portraits; the second way will be by looking at the metaphors he
applied to himself.

La Tourette as a Self-Portrait

The building that typifies what LC was looking for most of his life is
the monastery of La Tourette, located near Lyon on a sloping hill at
the edge of a small forest. He received this commission in 1953
from the Dominicans, a teaching order that believes in openness
toward the world. When they asked him to design their monastery,
they were looking for a Modern architect dedicated to "truth and
purity." Hence the commission suited Le Corbusier's character
and his belief that we are all essentially students of the cosmos
dedicated to finding the austere beauty of truth. Before designing
the building he visited the ruined abbey of Le Thoronet, near
Toulon, and was greatly impressed by what he called the Cistercian
"architecture of truth" (the subject of yet another booklet). So several old ideas come together: living like an impoverished student,
as he did in Paris, "who will fight with truth itself"; the idea, from
the Charterhouse of Ema, of the ideal relationship between the
individual cell and communal life; and the direct contrast with an
idyllic nature that is hidden, framed, and celebrated in opposite
ways. The violent, almost hostile, forms of one hundred monks'
cells perched above a chaotic nature, are defensive, aloof, and
withdrawn. Yet their unequivocal boldness and the musical play-
fulness give a contrast that recalls the photographic portraits of
Le Corbusier in the 1920s: implacable and still sensual [fig. 66].

This building teeters on the side of a hill and the edge of

verdure. It stands awkwardly and heroically apart from nature much as a Greek temple proclaiming man's loneliness and independence from the cosmos—the discontinuity with nature. One should see La Tourette as the antithesis of organic architecture and its metaphors of growth, reconciliation, and picturesque compromise. The tone is set by the blank wall of the church and the provocative forms that stem from it [fig. 211]. This invites exploration even as it stands aloof, a good illustration of Le Corbusier's

211. Monastery of La Tourette, Eveux-sur-l'Arbresle, 1953–57. Views from the approach, the north, with the blank facade of the church, the skewed "light cannons," and defensive-looking bell tower perched quizzically.

Le Corbusier: Who Was Le Corbusier?

theory that views should be withheld at the same time as they are implied. Suggestion and resistance are best when used together. Most mysterious are the strange ovoid forms that look out like periscopes, or flowers, reaching for the light. They spark curiosity, as do the other odd forms and slight deviations, such as the tilt of the parapet off the horizontal that squeezes the perspective toward the viewer. Why? Since everything looks functional and minimal, on this first view, one wants to know what possible use the protrusions and quizzical shapes might serve.

Thus one may pass the entrance gate, and bridge, into the monastery to investigate its opposite side. Here the basic decision, to place the building half up the hill on the slope, makes for a very dramatic contradiction: horizontal planes perch above a cliff face of *ondulatoires*, the very image that young Jeanneret admired and drew on Mount Athos [fig. 212]. Monks look out from these dark cave cells, like so many birds in their aeries, while below the legs of the building lean into the hill. This opposition between rectilinear building and curving meadow which spills in underneath becomes the main drama—one feels it everywhere.

The supreme, stunning view is just past the rectangular gate. Here one sees, between a violent polyphony of forms, the glimpse of a peaceful landscape. "Light cannons," pentagonal weapons tilted to let in direct light during the equinox, point to the left, and light reflectors above point to the right, while a vertical stack and horizontal walkway add to the drama of light and shadow. It is a cataclysmic struggle between sharp, pure forms that reminds one of Jeanneret's description of seeing the Acropolis for the first time—"the Parthenon, terrible machine, pulverizes and dominates everything for miles around."

Even in the refectory, the heart of the monastery where the monks take part in the good, simple life, which the young Jeanneret so much admired at Mount Athos, the view over nature is disturbing and awe-inspiring, not peaceful [fig. 214]. However, one does find in this room the feeling of a simple harmony, which Le Corbusier believed was the "heroism of everyday life." Simple, mass-produced objects, a wine flask and plates on a table, good basic food, shelter with a view of greenery and the syncopated rhythm of the *ondulatoires*—does one really need more, when these essential qualities are provided so straightforwardly?

Le Corbusier spent his summer months at his hermit retreat,

212. La Tourette, from the southwest. Horizontal layers (containing an open roof cloister, monks' cells, classrooms, library, and refectory) spill down the side of the slope.

213. La Tourette, view of distant landscape between a blank wall, bridge, smokestack, and "light cannons."

214. La Tourette, refectory. Brutally clear forms in precise relation. The monks eat in silence; otherwise these sharp, reflective surfaces would be impossibly reverberent. Note the floor-to-ceiling *ondulatoires*, arranged in musical syncopation.

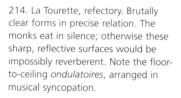

the *Petit Cabanon* on the Mediterranean, and lived much of his life like a monk [fig. 23]. He could see the poetry inherent in such simple objects, long after they had lost their charm for other Modern architects and, for that matter, the public. What had been largely a matter of taste and sophisticated fashion, the Spartan aesthetic of the Heroic Period, was for Le Corbusier a metaphysical principle based on the universal and archetypal. Hence while some people might see this architecture and equipment as empty and impoverished, he would see them as full-blown and evocative. This ambivalence is nowhere more striking than in the long, empty corridors containing just radiators, doors, and brightly painted water pipes. They are both banal and extraordinarily dramatic [fig. 215]. The Dominican monks took me through these corridors, pointing out the changes in light, the sudden glimpses of nature, and the way all the forms move in relationship as one walks. They were not preconditioned guides, but simply perfect Corb clients responding as he would.

The interior of the church, which to a layman might be a roughly constructed, blank box, is to the monks and LC the essence of "ineffable space": light, calm, proportion, and stark forms in tight relation [fig. 216]. He spoke about "a total poverty" to be sought here, no explicit icons, not even the tapestries that he used on similar blank concrete walls at the High Court in Chandigarh to soften the sound. The whole monastery is meant to ensure silence, every cell is acoustically isolated as at the *Unité*, and the church interior is where quiet isolation is most ensured. "I tried to make a place of meditation, research, and prayer for the preaching brothers . . . The brief was to house monks while trying to give them what people of today need more than anything: silence and peace . . . It is the interior which lives. The essential goes on in the interior." The only contact of this interior with the exterior are a few shafts of light, and a blazing vertical of brightness on the end wall, behind the high altar on the right. What sort of spirituality is being celebrated? That of denial, the *via negativa*, the Existentialist and Buddhist passion for the void, absence as a sign of fullness? The boxiness of this rectangle is awe-inspiring in its finality; it reminds one of LC's other *boîte à miracles* projected as a storehouse of inventions, except here there are only choir stalls, an altar, and the presence of light. True it is reflected through light cannons to become colored, or seen on the equinox, or seen as an explosion of

215. La Tourette, corridor with bare pipes. Ducts, radiators, and the musical alteration of void and solid, light and dark. The austerity was both chosen and a result of the budget being cut in half.

energy behind the altar, but in the end it is light. "Man the son of the sun" is the ultimate content of this architecture of meditation either here or up on the rooftop cloister where monks are in direct contact with only the sky. Like so much of his late work, the monastery is a monument to cosmic symbolism.

The building as self-portrait? One can see La Tourette as befitting a monk and a hero, a misanthrope and a prophet, and it is not surprising that Le Corbusier often characterized himself as both outcast and genius. What is surprising is the occasion on which he would use these self-deprecating and mixed metaphors.

216. La Tourette, "light cannons" above the altars, in different colors, create a mysterious still life in brightly reflected red, black, blue, and yellow.

Don Quixote, Panurge, Ubu Roi

On March 31, 1953, LC received the Gold Medal of the Royal Institute of British Architects in London. Nominally awarded in the name of the Queen, it was the most coveted architectural award in the world at that time, for its longevity and for the quality of those who received it, a true gold standard in the architectural world. The encomiums that LC received were fulsome, as usual for this ceremony. The president of the RIBA referred to Le Corbusier as a household name around the world, Sir Herbert Read praised him as a poet of life, Walter Gropius—the most extravagant—said he was "the Leonardo of our times," and others amplified the same message. When Le Corbusier finally got up to speak, he took a different tack. He thanked the Queen, the Institute, and his peers for the kindness they showed in honoring him and then, somewhat surprisingly, said that although a discoverer, he was "also a traditionalist . . . with his head, feet . . . and roots in the past."

But the really surprising message, at least a shock for the British and those who expected the ceremony to be the usual recital of triumphs, was his concentration on failure. He spent his entire address recounting one bitter defeat after another—sixteen catastrophes were reeled off—and referred to himself as an abject animal: "a true cab-horse who had received many blows with a whip." When he received the Gold Medal of the American Institute of Architects in 1961, his acceptance speech was even more terse and testing for the occasion, as he turned the famous Winged Victory in the Louvre on its head: "There is no 'wing of victory' in this room. There is no 'wing of victory' in life . . . It is Le Corbusier who cleans the toilet of 35 rue de Sèvres, and that's why he's the boss." At almost every award ceremony of this period, whether academic, professional, or national—and there were many—he took the opportunity to exact revenge. He had never been commissioned to build by the State or Power, he had suffered a life of insults, and now they were going to have their noses rubbed in it—hypocrites!

Or is he making another point? Some bitterness was there, surely, but perhaps the deeper point was a description of life's struggles and what any architect, of reasonable integrity and creativity, has to face. At these moments LC was speaking as a witness. He had been whipped as a cab-horse. In other contexts, he referred to himself as a rat, a person who had led a dog's life, an acrobat, and a clown. The image of a beaten, yet spirited, animal obsessed him. When one of the CIAM architects called him a genius, he made a drawing of a bird on the back of an ass and vice versa, saying, "Does the genius support the ass or does the ass support the genius?" Here one finds the implacable gaze, usually aimed at the world, turned in on itself in lacerating doubt.

According to friend and fellow architect Pierre Emery, he always carried around with him a well-worn copy of one of his favorite books, *Don Quixote*. Le Corbusier's brother, Albert Jeanneret, later sought out this copy in revealing words: "I discovered Christ late in life; for Le Corbusier, Don Quixote was a Christlike figure. He noted his reactions in the margins. By reading *Don Quixote* and his annotations, I, his brother, would be able to follow confidently and in a deeply intimate way, this legacy from one departed, and yet still present to one who is still alive." Le Corbusier often saw himself and Pierre Jeanneret as this knight-errant and Sancho Panza, tilting away at windmills in a comically noble light. This is clear from drawings of himself as Don Quixote and, as Ivan Zaknic has pointed out, the last testament he made weeks before he died, *Mise au point*. At the end of this key text, written in July 1965, Le Corbusier summarizes his debts to two literary figures and, significantly, they are seen as quasi-*spiritual* guides.

> Here, at this point, I must thank two men: Cervantes and Rabelais. The most beautiful reading for a man engaged in battle is the admirable Don Quixote of La Mancha. And life among these three companions, between Don Quixote and Sancho Panza, finds its explanation, if not its justification . . . [They] show us man hammering away with the persistence of the

tides, in the most optimistic outbursts: confidence, faith, love, a giving, a blossoming, a flowering, and an ecstasy, and their most precipitous falls clean and indisputable: punches in the nose preceded by spankings. Panza gets through, always survives it, and thinks of eating. He is always right. He knows how to accept (to offer or to thrash out a compromise). He lands on his feet. All this is extraordinarily true. At the other end, Panurge and Friar John carry on their discussions and commentaries beyond the limit of politeness, and rise above everything in the name of the wisest points of view, through the most laughable coarseness which welcomes them into the highest levels of the nobility. Shit, shit! . . . *braguette et balletron*, old whores beautiful as goddesses, dypsode and werewolf, Homer and Pliny. Homeric, above and below, outside of pettiness, of the great words, the clash of battles and the cutlasses. One takes cover from the brutishness, one laughs. Thank you, Rabelais and Cervantes.

"One laughs." One recalls the deep impact that his maiden aunt, Pauline, made on the young Jeanneret brothers when they were children, and how strange it was that she combined a high church morality with a love of Rabelais. She also used the funny made-up words of this earthy Renaissance author to chide the boys: "braggart, gasbag, blow mouth, proud as a peacock, empty pot . . . etc." These deflating characterizations were meant also, of course, affectionately. Like his aunt, Charles-Edouard Jeanneret could not stand pomp and pretentiousness, but at the same time he knew that Le Corbusier sometimes fell prey to these failings.

Here is a clue to an enigma. If we read Rabelais, and look at the character of Panurge, we find someone who takes great pleasure in outwitting the pretentious and conceited members of the establishment. Panurge has moments of great wisdom and guile and an absolute wit for the cunning trick that will expose hypocrisy. At the same time, in both Rabelais and Cervantes, there is the deep appreciation for daily life and muddling through. As LC writes, "Sancho Panza gets through, always survives [the falls] and thinks of eating. He is always right." Here we are reminded of Le Corbusier's paradoxical statements on visiting Pessac near the end of his life, to confront the way people had changed his architecture out of all recognition: "Life is right, the architect wrong."

Life is right, Panza is right, Charles-Edouard Jeanneret is right—therefore, horrible conclusion, Le Corbusier is wrong? In a series of lithographs called *Panurge*, completed in August 1961, we find some familiar themes that illuminate this dialectic. The frontispiece is a still life with the bottle, glass, and what appears to be a wedge of yellow cheese and a saddle of red beef, or ham. The five prints show the pleasures of Panza and Panurge, the wine, music, moon goddess, bull, interlocking hands, and architecture—the usual icons, but particularly those dedicated to the body and everyday life [fig. 217]. The Dionysian side to LC is honored here, the one that, through drinking too much pastis, perhaps shortened his life (or so he said his doctor warned). That this side is accepted *and* resisted is clear from the Ubu series of paintings and sculpture that is quoted within *Panurge*. Ubu, we remember, is that farcical king, the personification of greed, ignorance, and hallucination that so fascinated LC when he was mixed up with Vichy. Could it be that Charles-Edouard Jeanneret saw himself, or his other half, in this light—if only fleetingly?

217. *Ubu le Panurge*, August 18, 1961, lithograph. Ubu, to the right, distorts the right-angled world, a door and window.

The evidence for this is varied. There are the occasional jibes at his own self-importance, the buffoonery, and the quotes from his aunt, all directed at pretentiousness. Second is the fact that otherwise sympathetic clients, such as the mayor of Algiers, could point out the folly in his grandiose city planning. The mayor, remember, wrote him that in order to realize his plans "it would be necessary to have an absolute dictator." Perhaps Jeanneret grasped this truth; he certainly heard it often enough and even quotes it from time to time. Does this mean that the double entity, Jeanneret–Le Corbusier, was schizophrenic?

A surprising aspect of his writings is that they often refer to Le Corbusier in the third person singular, as "our man," or "he," rather than "I," as if Jeanneret's personal life and opinions were being hidden behind a mask. A revealing episode recounted to me by Jullian de la Fuente brings this out. As this architect, key in the atelier after 1961, was getting on a plane to go to Venice, LC said: "We are both working for Le Corbusier, eh?" Precisely. Charles-Edouard Jeanneret was always building up this persona, which does not mean he always agreed with it. The painter, poet, and modest friend in him—the Panurge, Rabelais, Cervantes—could see the other, humorous and ridiculous side. Cervantes has Don Quixote recant on his deathbed all the stupidities brought about by reading too much romantic nonsense: "Those profane stories dealing with knight-errantry," the Don says as he lays dying, "are odious to me." Is there a parallel, with the architect reading too much heroic literature when he was young, too much about the great prophets, *Les grand initiés*? And would this mean that LC also was recanting, through his painting and ironic comments, for having followed the idealism of Schuré and Nietzsche?

Probably not: it is more complex for both the knight and Père Corbu. Rather, idealism is being asserted and skeptically questioned at the same time. If "a world which has no place for utopia is not worth inhabiting," as Oscar Wilde said, and if all utopias forced on people are a folly, then the idealistic architect who is honest has only one choice. Like Don Quixote, he must keep tilting at his and society's ideals, but be prepared for shocks and the admission that they are also windmills. This dualism is what so many drawings and paintings show—that is, LC as the genius *and* the ass, Apollo *and* Dionysus, the geometer *and* the pack-donkey. But, does this opposition between Jeanneret and Le Corbusier mean that the combination was schizophrenic? Not in the technical sense, because if there was one thing he could do, and believed in doing, it was acting and thinking decisively. There was not the indecision and dithering of the schizoid personality. But it does show that Jeanneret knew how stupid and arrogant LC could be—at times—and that we must take the rhetoric, while deliberate, as partly ironic.

This is suggested by the self-portrait of LC with his cohorts at Chandigarh—Max Fry, Jane Drew, and Pierre Jeanneret [fig. 218]. Here they are all barnyard animals, the kind that one would see in many Indian backyards, strutting, showing off, questioning, nurturing, some trying to be the alpha male, or big mother, others placid and content. The implications are not only cosmic, comparing humans to eternal natural types, but satiric, in the manner of *Animal Farm*. The fact that Le Corbusier could synthesize a combination of local imagery, political critique, and natural metaphor shows, again, how he could turn signs into resonant symbols. It is this ability to synthesize contrary meanings that helps explain how, and why, LC himself could be so manifold and contradictory. He must have felt that, at a deep level, this complexity was truer to life than his own dogma: "life is right, the architect wrong."

218. Chandigarh, Assembly, detail of enamel door, 1962. "Family portrait of those responsible for the success of the enterprise." Pierre is the proud cock with his head pecking at the ground, Max is feeding from the she-goat, always a dominant earth goddess, in this case Jane Drew, and the quizzical Corbeau turns away from the family.

The Tragic View

Le Corbusier inspired devotion and love among his close friends, his cohorts in arms at rue de Sevres, the CIAM group of Modern architects, much of the public that heard him lecture, and a series of admirers such as Jane Drew. He got on with ordinary people, local workmen such as the Rebutato family who helped construct his *Petit Cabanon* at Cap Martin, or the man who served him pastis at the local bar. The modest, agreeable side to his character, the Jeanneret in him, was the attractive traveling companion, the humorous and affable man of the people. At the end of the life he often spoke about this humble or modest streak in his character. He said he did "not give a damn for honors," that there are no "glorious signs in heaven," nor did he really think of himself as an important person:

> . . . [When young I had] the feeling that I was a nobody . . . Not for a minute did I have the idea that I was worth anything . . . This I insist on saying here, because this is something crucial to my character . . . those who are not born with the idea of being somebody become so unintentionally, and by their work alone. To become somebody is indeed the Paris struggle . . .

It is clear from statements like these that LC was a persona to be constructed, and valued, through his good works alone. They, not success or money, he keeps saying, were to be the testimony, to be judged by one's conscience alone, not by opinion polls or politicians or the establishment. And the converse of this was true. Since Jeanneret thought of Le Corbusier as a kind of noble construction, he could throw himself into the Paris struggle with a certain disinterest and zest. This is dramatized again and again. "If you wish to do battle," he tells idealistic students about to become architects, "take up you lances and set off for Jerusalem, but you will probably die en route"; or, "Go ahead, kid; you'll get plenty of kicks in the butt to tell you that you're doing well . . ." Every good work achieved is seen as the result of a struggle and overcoming, either the outside world or the internal world of creation.

> Painting is a bitter struggle, terrifying, pitiless, unseen: a duel between the artist and himself. The struggle goes on inside, hidden on the surface. If the artist tells, he is betraying himself!

There is a curiosity involved in this presentation of struggle that should not escape notice. An architect by professional necessity has to inspire confidence in his clients and appear as a reasonable mediator who can get along with all sorts of people. When architects write about their work, they usually suppress any signs of conflict and try to appear as easygoing as your friendly bank manager. The reverse is true of Le Corbusier. Often he would erode confidence and increase conflict, from presenting his plans in an unconventional way to insulting his client. The logic behind this was twofold. It would disqualify, at an early stage, all clients who were unwilling to accept his genius and, more important, allow him to present conflict as the essential quality to creative life. How else to explain the fact that he would publish his unrealized projects with the condemnation of the enemy alongside them, *where they would do the greatest damage.* His rejected Paris plans of 1937 had the following caption:

> "A megalomania worse than Ledoux's, a vandalism unique in history, the dreary uniformity, vanity and monotony of these skyscrapers . . . have been proved spiritually and materially injurious, a contempt for historic and artistic tradition." (The author forgot to sign himself! . . .)

In a subconscious sense he might have felt these strictures were true—which they were to an extent. In any case the truth of conflict was as important as the truth of his projects, and one can get an idea of the joyful bitterness with which he relates his sufferings. The following quotes are taken from various sources, but they give an idea of the pleasure he got from dramatizing struggle (including even the pleasure of identifying himself with Hamlet).

> Mr Lemaresquier points out, "This scheme [for the League of Nations] has not been drawn in Indian Ink. It breaks the rules. I insist that it should be disqualified . . ." and it was . . . seven schemes for Algiers rejected, unpaid . . . Plans for Algiers, Stockholm, Moscow, Buenos Aires, Montevideo, Rio de Janeiro, Paris (without a break between 1912–1960), Zurich, Antwerp, Barcelona, New York, Bogotá, Saint-Dié, La Rochelle Pallice, Marseille up to (but excluding) Chandigarh . . . 1932–1935 and 1937, years of misery and of abject, blind folly

by the profession and officials responsible . . . But, by the autumn of 1939, Adolf Hitler was threatening Paris. The rest is silence . . . Unite, 1945. Five years of storm, spite and uproar followed, despicable, ugly . . . [Chandigarh 1951] is a contribution adjusted to human scale—to human size and dignity—by the efforts of a few men of character, worn, chafed and buffeted by the shocks and frictions of human relations, by the clash of individual personalities and temperaments. So be it! . . . In 1956 L-C was asked to accept membership of the Institut de France [Academie des Beaux-Arts] in Paris: "Thank you, never! . . . my name would serve as a banner to conceal the present evolution of the Ecole des Beaux Arts towards a superficial modernism."

This triumphant exhilaration in defeat brings up the odd comment that it would have been a disaster had Le Corbusier always been accepted by society and been cheated of the tragic role. "'Mon blason vers 1920: La vie est sans pitié'—My motto since 1920: Life is without pity" was the way he summarized it in 1952 [fig. 219].

This tragic view challenges the major, if unconscious, assumption today that positive human values are realizable without internal struggle and external attack. Le Corbusier accepted conflict as the essence of men's plurality and, except that he considered warfare as barbaric, admired the courage of warriors in a way that was common in the ancient world. It is worth recalling his Nietzschean rhetoric, as in an important letter of 1908, written at the age of twenty-one.

219. "La vie est sans pitié," redrawn comparison (from *L'Art Décoratif d'aujourd'hui*, 123; and the book's dedication to Madame Lucio Costa, May 17, 1952). LC's motto for his coat of arms, with a red sword above a blue body/cloud and yellow star. This inscription made for the Brazilian Lucio Costa, "never a pessimist," was similar to the drawing of a Greek medal made when LC was a youth. The latter also shows similar emblems, and LC comments on "the convulsion and emotion which flows from the perception of a relationship . . . between certain human emotions: the crescent moon, the star, the sword blade."

> I want to fight with truth itself. It will surely torment me. But I am not looking for quietude, or recognition from the world. I will live in sincerity, happy to undergo abuse . . . Thought is uncovered and one must fight with it. And to find it before fighting it, you must seek it in solitude.

In short, he brought about in his life the very bittersweet, tragic struggle he was seeking, and predicted, from the start. Judged by worldly standards his life was anything but a failure, even including the rejected schemes. But judged, as he often did, in larger terms, it was not a success. He did not realize his major goal, "to bring harmony to a machine civilization out of gear," nor complete one city plan, even Chandigarh, the way he wanted. He did not see one of his five plans for Paris even acknowledged by the authorities, and he saw Paris, as all the other major capitals, falling apart in a suburban sprawl of rapacious development—just as he had predicted. His city planning ideas may have been dictatorial and wrongheaded, and this is surely a reason they were continuously rejected. Yet there is another important point to be raised. If Le Corbusier's prescriptions for the future city were misplaced, nevertheless, like Karl Marx's analysis of what was wrong with capitalism, his critique of the modern city was profound. Both Marx and LC were good at seeing failures of the prevailing systems they studied, and predicting further problems, but they were equally bad at giving blueprints of what should be done.

The well-analyzed failure of urbanism was what LC called the tentacular city, the hundred-mile sprawl that has made the Edge City or Exopolis the major type of our time. LC fought against this for fifty years with his high-density city in the park and then the Radiant City. These countless city plans, which were never asked for and never paid for, finally ended up, after World War II, as proposals for dividing urban areas into three main types, *The Three Human Establishments*. This grandiose title, and idea, was simply a historical division of the city into evolutionary stages: the agricultural unit, the linear industrial city, and the radio-concentric city of exchange. That such analysis can masquerade as synthesis, or that cities can intelligently be frozen into such categories, is as laughable as the idea that the proletariat and the ruling class are frozen categories. What starts off as scientific analysis ends up as reified dogma, with the consequences everyone knows today, to their regret.

Hence in terms of city planning Le Corbusier's life really was a failure, and judging by many bitter comments he knew it. Yet even granting this major setback of his hopes, there remains the tone of indestructible joy bursting through the bitterness. Again it was probably Nietzsche who helped explain this aspect of tragedy.

In *The Birth of Tragedy*, Nietzsche focuses on the strange fact that the heroes' suffering and pain are depicted with relish and consumed by the audience with delight. Why could Le Corbusier get such pleasure from his conflict and even provoke it again? Because, according to Nietzsche, the commerce with pain is metaphysical and aesthetic, not moral: it is the Dionysian ecstasy best conveyed in music and dance which asserts itself in the midst of Apollonian cerebration and reason. Whereas a reasonable approach in the face of disaster is, in the words of the engineer, "back to the drawing board," the tragic approach is both more physical and metaphysical. On a bodily plane it is simply the resurgence of physical energy, the power of being alive, the animal optimism that LC had to an exceptional degree. This reasserts itself independently of the mind and its worries, while on a philosophical level it grants the possibly disastrous consequences of human action, no matter how well thought out and rational. The tragic view accepts and embraces this outcome with indestructible joy.

How far did Le Corbusier present a tragic view through his life and work? On an existential level, he seems to have continually cut himself away from his friends and society, rejecting them much as a figure in tragic drama, in order to realize his own individualized view of truth. He would periodically fire members of his atelier, he would attack and leave his closest teachers such as L'Eplattenier and Ozenfant, he would say "burn what you loved and love what you burned." He would constantly battle with the authorities as well as with his comrades in arms such as Gropius. Why all this struggle? First, because it was exhilarating, and second, because, as with Nietzsche's superman, the creator had to master his opponents' power, their ideas, before he would go on to destroy them in order to re-create them in a new synthesis. This destructive-constructive pattern is perhaps as common to the creative temperament as it is to the tragic figure in Western drama, and Nietzsche's superman is in part like the archetypal scientist as much as the tragic hero trying to restructure social values. But whereas the scientist reexamines and reconstitutes existing patterns to build new theories, the tragic hero also reinvents them in order to present a truth about the world and about the individual's suffering in solitude.

> . . . Art is a deep love of one's ego, which one seeks in retreat and solitude, this divine ego which can be a terrestrial ego when it is forced by a struggle to become so . . . It is in solitude that one can struggle with one's ego, that one punishes and encourages oneself.

Here the young Jeanneret of twenty-one sounds like both the prophet in the wilderness and the typical figure of modern

220. La Tourette, church interior, with center line focusing on the High Altar. Individual altars are under the "light cannons" to the left, balanced by the shaft of light spilling through the end wall to the right. Minimalist concrete chapels, with a single light source, were developed further as a sign of ascetic spirituality by Tadao Ando in Japan.

tragedy, Hamlet, dramatizing his doubts and sufferings—even his loneliness. Again this loneliness may be common to both creator and tragic hero since they both have to abandon the ordinary conventions of society. But the tragic hero accentuates his loneliness as a main theme in the drama: we attend his soliloquies, his tortured, inward questionings, as much as the unfolding of events.

Le Corbusier's writings and architecture also dramatize this loneliness and suffering. For instance, the church and corridors of La Tourette [fig. 220] are positively empty. The blank surfaces are not just an absence of conventional symbolism, but a very strong symbol in their own right. The feeling one has in much of Le Corbusier's architecture is of being dramatically isolated in a beautiful, but hostile, cosmos—like walking on a desolate Greek mountain range without the comforts, noise, or familiarity of daily life. The forms are brutal and harsh, sometimes even tortured—the bell "tower" of La Tourette [fig. 221] perches anxiously, even

221. La Tourette, bell tower. A head twice deflected, strong, awkward, defiant, and boldly sculptural.

awkwardly, over the church, at once a metaphor for the Church's insecurity and Le Corbusier's loneliness. Most bell towers are proud, vertical, and strong. This one is twice deflected, on a diagonal, and it is defiant rather than secure. It is stretching a point, but again Le Corbusier's physiognomy is there. The implacable stare of the genius combined with the bent body of the cab-horse or ass.

It is just as hard, however, with Le Corbusier's architecture, as it is with tragedy, to decide ultimately whether it is suffering and loneliness that triumph, or exhilaration. Is one depressed at the end of a tragedy? If so it is a strange kind of depression which seems robbed of its finality. Somehow the idealistic action of the tragic hero cheats his defeat of its ultimate pain. Le Corbusier continually tried to realize his goal of "harmony" for an industrial civilization, but was repulsed so often that his incessant efforts appear to be literally mad, insane, pragmatically futile. What was the meaning of an idealism which would only fail again? Perhaps symbolic. Perhaps Le Corbusier, like the tragic hero, saw the conflict between his ideals and society as being of equal importance as the attainment of these ideals. He certainly enjoyed these conflicts. And he presented "joy" in many key parts of a building: the "three essential joys," sun, space, and greenery, the color and crisp materials that would contrast with brutal concrete.

Everywhere the message is mixed, just as the meaning of tragedy is dualistic. One can see this dualism in a drawing that Le Corbusier produced at the end of the war as he was contemplating reconstruction. It is a double portrait, perhaps of himself: part Apollo, part Medusa, part the smiling sun god of reason, part the Dionysian, sensual figure of the underworld—a dark bitterness just barely balanced by joy and light [fig. 2]. It is a theme he came back to in different ways, as if he could solve the conundrum of dualism by continuously reworking it. One painting, *Mains croisées sur la tête*, actually was taken up at three points, 1928, 1939, and 1940, at the start of the war [fig. 209]. Here echoes of Picasso, and the bull of war, are superimposed on a Janus face. Flat graphics and bright colors are often at odds with the linear outlines and suggestion of depth, as if two languages of art were competing, one optimistic, the other agitated, while clasped hands, often a sign of reconciliation, are squeezed down on top of the combined heads. Metaphorically, opposites are being pushed together, harmony is forced, composition compacted—an effort of willpower—drives the contorted meanings into unity. Many of Le Corbusier's late works have this forced harmonization, as if he were determined to acknowledge the plurality of the world while jamming it into a whole. It is this plurality, and his fecundity, which are impressive and daunting at the same time. A world always changing, and LC always trying to stay ahead of this evolution by internalizing its variety.

The Continual Revolution

Le Corbusier threw himself continually into the architectural turmoil; in Rem Koolhaas's words, he surfed the ever-breaking edge of the zeitgeist. Excitement, conflict, commitment to the Modern NOW, but from the perspective of two thousand years of architectural history. Is there some deeper pattern to Le Corbusier's life and work as a whole—does he reveal something about the world of architecture that is normal, yet not sufficiently acknowledged by historians or critics? We have seen how internal struggle with his ego, and his art, were so central to his approach since the age of twenty-one, and how he internalized the battles of architecture as he saw them: technological, social, and cultural. We have seen how he changed style and approach six times, forging new versions of old ideas, while continuing some basic themes. The question arises, was this demonic creativity something generated from within, or more simply a response to a changing evolution of architecture and cities? Was he, like Picasso, following an internally generated program—the future he predicted with uncanny accuracy—or simply, like Bill Gates, trying to keep up with a changing market?

Put this way the answer is an obvious "both/and"—he adopted the Futurist or Nietzschean view of demonic change and he believed in continual creativity, reinventing himself every ten years or so. Stick and carrot, in common parlance, were equally important. One has to remember what appears to be such a strange fact: that although Le Corbusier was a household name, and a world-famous architect twice in the twentieth century—the 1920s and 1960s—like his father he was often out of work. It is this last truth, summarized in his personal motto, "Life is without pity," that relates to his notion, expressed so often, of Darwinian evolution. In one of his semiautobiographies, *Le Corbusier lui-Même*, he narrates his life starting off each year with a picture of that year's motorcar and a description of the latest technical, social, and political development: "1922 Fascist march on Rome. Mussolini takes power in Italy. Gandhi imprisoned in India by the English. Establishment of the International Court in the Hague . . . Les chenillettes Citroën cross the Sahara."

Here he typically projects himself into the stream of historical events, like a war reporter, coolly describing action on the front. His architecture is part of this global zeitgeist, and so naturally his accomplishments for the year—the Maison Citrohan and City for Three Million among other things—are put on the same level as the world-shattering events. "Stop Press! 1923. German revolution, earthquake in Japan. Le Corbusier writes *Vers une architecture*!" This, with only slight exaggeration, is how he presents the next year. It's breathtaking, laughably mad, pure Don Quixote, and interesting (since his book *has* had more influence on world events than many other things more widely reported). It makes one think: How many other epochal events are reported as news flashes? Almost none. For instance, the news of Einstein's new theory of a curved space-time universe, that was proven correct in 1919, was tucked away in the London *Times* on page nineteen. This, the usual relationship between daily and significant news, LC inverted as he continuously narrated his work, and made it more important than the sensationalist ephemera that always grabs the headlines.

Thus he acted on a world stage, and the demon of change in social evolution was always internalized, becoming the background for his creativity. He begins many justifications of his action with the words "a page turns," by which he means a progressive development or inexorable shift in the market has happened, like it or not.

This idea of quick evolution leads to certain questions, among which two stand out. First, most architects who are successful, such as Richard Meier or Richard Rogers, seem to do rather well by sticking with their identifiable style, their brand image, and sail over the ups and downs in the sea-change of architecture that goes on continuously. Second, Darwinian evolution is based on gradual, piecemeal improvement, competition within a standard, not revolutionary shifts between paradigms. These two points raise the twin questions: If Darwinian social change is gradual, how can there be continual revolution in architecture; and, if change is not gradual but sudden, how can the architect cope with it? The two issues illuminate Le Corbusier's life, just as it casts light on his changing work.

During the sixty years of LC's architectural life, there were many movements and trends, some short and others long in duration. These movements can be conceived as evolutionary species that wax and wane, with the proviso that the architect can jump from one to another, unlike a species that must propagate within its own genome. Together they create an evolutionary tree of competing movements. For instance, within LC's first twenty years of work there was the ten-year flourishing of Art Nouveau, from 1895 to 1905, the dominant Beaux-Arts tradition that waned in the 1920s, the rise of functionalism in the 1920s, and a host of competing movements: Expressionism, Constructivism, Dadism, de Stijl, Neue Sachlichkeit, Garden City Design, Neo-Folk, organic architecture, and his own Purism. This is only a partial list of competing options and it leaves out the largest group, the mainstream, and a host of regional schools of architecture. But it does suggest the plurality of approach, and one that only became much more varied as the century progressed—the New Empiricism, Brutalism, Metabolism, etc.

During the twentieth century there have been about forty or so such movements. As one wit put the demonic change, all the "isms became wasms." Looked at as evolving species, and Darwinian change, these movements can be seen as developments in knowledge, as new understandings of architecture and cities, as shifts in style and ideology, and as innovations in society and technology. All of that together. "The demon of change" in architectural reality is much more real than it is in the fields that gave birth to the phrase, painting and literature. Compared to architecture, they are creeping glaciers. The twentieth century saw architecture in continual revolution, if by revolution we mean the shifts in mental orientation and taste. One is reminded of the young Jeanneret's Darwinian expostulations to his master at the age of twenty: "Paris is the crack of the whip at every moment, death for dreamers." Just substitute "architecture" for "Paris" and one has the history of the twentieth century.

How did LC engage this demon with the whip? Not only through the constant revolution of his work, the reinvention, but also the writing, and rewriting. Remember, in his 1930s passport he called himself not an architect but a man of letters, and he produced some fifty-seven books. These books were often best-sellers, and some, like *Towards a New Architecture*, remain so. What they did *to* Le Corbusier was force him to reconsider the philosophical and polemical basis of his architecture; what they did *for* him was to publicize his work and turn him into the prophet of twentieth-century architecture. Unless they were of another persuasion, no student of architecture, no professor, no practitioner could afford to miss the almost annual message. A story about James Stirling, perhaps apocryphal, is that during the D-Day landings his cherished copy of the *Oeuvre complète*, brought along for spiritual guidance, came between him and a German bullet. Whatever the truth of that, Big Jim, as he was known, did model his own work and published architectural works directly on the master, so much so that they looked like posthumous volumes eight and nine of the *Oeuvre*. He and the English architect Tom Ellis were said to have "pored over the latest volume of Corb like Talmudic scholars analysing plans and sections." Similar stories could be told of architects in America, Italy, Japan, Brazil, Switzerland—indeed every part of the globe where Modern and Post-Modern architecture were to take root. In effect, the doctrine of Père Corbu replaced the teaching of the École des Beaux-Arts, the Modern academy destroyed the Ancient.

And here is one of the supreme ironies that would have amused and enraged our Don Quixote. LC said on many occasions he did not welcome followers, copycats, acolytes—and yet he did everything in his ability to create them. The result is that *Le Style Corbu* has become, like the Classicism before it, one of the stable traditions in a sea of turbulence. From the 1950s to the year 2000 the white International Style, and more particularly the Corbusian variations of it, have become the lingua franca of our time, and this has slowed down historical change. A simplified evolutionary tree of the twentieth century makes this point [fig. 222].

It also makes the point that there are a few long, and many short, waves, some piecemeal change, and lots of mini-revolutions. In effect, the same duality of natural evolution is operative, that is, one comprised of uniform evolution and cataclysmic jumps. This diagram and Le Corbusier's six languages, or types, of architecture show similar oscillations, some continuity amid incessant change. The forty movements and trends were the

222. Evolutionary tree of twentieth-century architecture. This simplified diagram is based on six major types of architecture (far left) that oscillate with respect to each other, rather like species. Like "strange attractors," they remain coherent even though they are loose or fuzzy categories. About forty explicit movements, or schools, emerged in the twentieth century, and Le Corbusier more than any other architect jumped from one to another, often leading them forward. As the diagram shows, his influence occurred four times, more than any other architect. The competitive pluralism—four to five movements at any one time and a new movement or trend every five years—is the engine of continual revolution. The International Style, or what is sometimes known as Conventional Modernism, or Corporate Modernism, is the stabilizing tradition. The paradox is that LC managed to occupy a revolutionary position while advocating a stable unchanging language. (The diagram should be in three dimensions, to show more complex interactions.)

background against which the architect of the twentieth century acted and reacted. It was a period of frenetic creativity and fashionable change driven by technical and stylistic innovation and the desire of countless architects to make their name. External pressure and internal motivation are, of course, the forces that drive any period of history, but the twentieth century was more hard driven than any other hundred years. Part of the reason for this was globalization, accelerating technical change, and rapid urbanization. But the ideologies of Modernism and social progress were also strong engines. The extraordinary thing about the protean LC is that, more than other architects, he responded to the situation as he found it and, because of his character and philosophy of struggle, stayed with, or led, the change. Writing, painting, women, Nietzsche—a full response to life—kept him sharp and, if he did cause a lot of trouble and pain in city building, his optimism and occasionally brilliant architecture more than make up for the damage.

Among all his uncanny predictions, perhaps that of his death is the most unusual. According to one account, he told a cohort, André Maisonnier, "how nice it would be to die swimming for the sun." Water, which recirculates and balances elements in both an alchemical and ecological sense, was always a great natural symbol for LC, one that he represented in countless painting with a strong horizontal—sign of peace and death. The sun was *the* symbol overarching everything with its twenty-four-hour cycle. So his many thoughts on death, put down in the summer of 1965 and earlier, refer to the beautiful silence and harmony that comes from being alone with oneself and the cosmos. "Finding myself alone again, I thought of that wonderful phrase from the Apocalypse: 'There was silence in heaven for about half an hour' . . . We must rediscover man. We must rediscover the straight line that joins the axis of fundamental laws; biology, nature, the cosmos. A straight line unbending like the horizon of the sea." On August 27, 1965, he left his *Petit Cabanon*, where he had been sequestered for several weeks alone, went down to the sea, and, as far as we know, swam for the sun.

Nietzsche and Le Corbusier

To understand Nietzsche's influence on Le Corbusier it is worth recounting the parts of *Zarathustra* with which the young Jeanneret must have identified. It was written in 1883 in Sils-Maria, a Swiss mountainscape that is even more dramatic than the Swiss village of Jeanneret's youth. Zarathustra, a visionary modeled on the Persian seer Zoroaster, comes down from his mountain exile to preach to a crowd. The assembled people, however, turn from him to see a ropewalker, performing an acrobatic feat, slip and kill himself (Le Corbusier was later to identify himself with an acrobat). Zarathustra buries this performer and preaches an agonistic message: "Live dangerously. Erect your cities beside Vesuvius. Send out your ships to unexplored seas. Live in a state of war." Question everything, including the Supreme Being. "'Is godliness not just that there are Gods, but no God?' Whoever hath ears let him hear . . ." Le Corbusier later borrowed this phraseology and changed the meaning to "eyes which do not see"—the terrible beauty inherent in the new machine age.

Zarathustra, like a good anarchist or member of the avant-garde, preaches the creative powers of destruction: "He who must be a creator in good and evil verily, he must first be a destroyer, and break values into pieces." For Jeanneret the big destroyer had already started to wreck its havoc: industrialization had broken up the home-based production units of La Chaux-de-Fonds, putting his father out of work several times and threatening cousins involved in the watchmaking profession.

For Nietzsche, if God were dead, and if this bitter truth were fully realized, then a new breed of supermen would emerge. They would "sacrifice themselves to earth in order that earth may some day become superman's." For Jeanneret this new breed would be a self-chosen elite of artists, architects, and industrialists who had the vision to see the new, beautiful order growing amid the destruction. Nietzsche warns that the superman is an ever-distant goal, someone who can be imagined but not attained, someone in the future for whom one should sacrifice oneself through tireless work and proclamation. It is not hard to find the parallel in Le Corbusier's career: his self-denying labor for the future, twelve hours a day for fifty years, a constant battle of toil for which he sacrificed a home life and the possibility of bringing up children.

The passages of the prologue that Jeanneret marked include

the revealing parts where Zarathustra goes down to the people to preach the message of overcoming.

"What is great in man is that he is a bridge and not a goal: what is loveable in man is that he is an *over-going* and a *down-going*. I love those that know not how to live except as the down-goers, for they are the over-goers. I love the great despisers, because they are the great adorers, and arrows of longing for the other shore. I love those who do not first seek a reason beyond the stars for going down and being sacrifices, but sacrifice themselves to the earth, that the earth of the Superman may hereafter arrive. I love him who liveth in order to know, and seeketh to know in order that the Superman may hereafter live . . ."(8–9); "When Zarathustra had spoken these words, he again looked at the people, and was silent. 'There they stand,' said he to his heart; 'there they laugh: they understand me not; I am not the mouth for these ears. Must one first batter their ears, that they may learn to hear with their eyes?'" (10); "Behold the good and the just! Whom do they hate most? Him who breaketh up their tables of values, the breaker, the law-breaker:—he, however, is the creator. Companions, the creator seeketh, not corpses—and not herds or believers either. Fellow-creators the creator seeketh—those who grave new values on new tables" (18); "More dangerous have I found it among men than among animals; in dangerous paths goeth Zarathustra. Let mine animals lead me!" (19); "To gain the right to create new values—that is the most terrible of conquests for a patient and respectful person" (35). In 1961 Le Corbusier reread these pages, annotated them again, writing "*la main ouverte*" opposite the lines "I would fain bestow and distribute, until the wise have become joyous in their folly, and the poor happy in their riches." Although Allen Brooks translates these words more straightforwardly, I have used the 1927 translation of Thomas Common, which keeps the biblical phraseology. Zarathustra is clearly writing the new Bible.

NB. H. Allen Brooks has discussed these markings in Charles Edouard Jeanneret's copy of *Ainsi parlait Zarathoustra*, Paris, 1908. See *Le Corbusier's Formative Years*, op. cit., pp. 174–75. The copy still exists at the Fondation Le Corbusier, and the above passages are marked with little pencil lines. Another discussion of the influence of Nietzsche can be found in Jean-Louis Cohen, "Le Corbusier's Nietzschean Metaphors," *Nietzsche and "An Architecture of Our Minds,"* edited by Alexandre Kostka and Irving Wohlfarth, The Getty Research Institute Publications and Exhibitions Program, Los Angeles, 1999, pp. 311–32.

Le Corbusier the Normal Genius of the Twentieth Century

In summarizing Le Corbusier's life and contribution it is necessary, like a sailor heading into the wind, to tack in opposite directions. One line of investigation must stress the archetypal nature of
his character, show how he was, in the odd formulation of this
appendix, a normal sort of great man, a typical genius, a standard
deviant from the average. The other line must stress his particular
and contingent contributions, those that were made by a Swiss
Calvinist who longed to be a painter and, after two great wars,
change the way we live. The universal and the historical are equally
determinant lines of development which intertwine richly, yet they
need different tools for analysis. Here I am concerned with the
first, the way he fits some general patterns shared with other
artists, scientists, and writers.

Le Corbusier's life follows, to an uncanny degree, that of the
great creators of the early part of the century, those early Modern
masters who each developed an aspect of Modernism in their field:
Freud, Picasso, Stravinsky, T. S. Eliot, and Martha Graham.
Furthermore, as the cognitive scientist and historian Howard
Gardner has shown, the developmental pattern of these protean
creators is shared by others who were making important breakthroughs at the beginning of this century, Einstein and Gandhi.
These seven, a representative sample of heroically productive
titans who overturned their fields, evince a similar line of development. Gardner outlines the basic protean type in *Creating Minds.* It
has the long subtitle *An Anatomy of Creativity Seen Through the Lives
of Freud, Einstein, Picasso, Stravinsky, Eliot, Graham, and Gandhi*,
(New York: Basic Books, 1993). Gardner shows how these creators
also follow particular paths, according to the field of the creator. At
the end of his investigation, he summarizes a composite portrait of
the Modern master, one I will paraphrase directly to bring out the
way Le Corbusier is like the others. Gardner calls this composite
the Exemplary Creator, EC, a phrase I will follow, except that I will
change the sex he uses to male, corresponding to Le Corbusier's.

Gardner's typical Exemplary Creator, the seven from whom
he extracts an ideal type, comes from a locale somewhat distant
from the center of power—the major city—and its culture that
asserts a pull on the province. To compare with Le Corbusier, LC
migrated from the semiprovincial town of La Chaux-de-Fonds to

APPENDIX II

Paris, just as Picasso was attracted from a lesser to a greater capital. The other six protean figures followed similar paths from periphery to center.

The Exemplary Creator comes from a family neither too wealthy nor too poor, neither highly educated nor undereducated, but a family with a great respect for, and expectation of, education. LC's father was educated at the local school and self-taught, and his mother and brother were teachers. Le Corbusier was a lifelong autodidact with a fanatical respect for education, as long as it came from books, museums, and travel, not the schoolroom.

The Big Seven were all bourgeois and valued hard work to the point of being proverbial workaholics. Picasso painted, on average, one work per day; Einstein never stopped work, and the other five were equally addicted. Dogged determination and strenuous work are the sine qua non of anyone who is going to make a significant breakthrough. LC was proud to admit that, like Marx's well-rounded socialist of the future, he was a painter in the morning, an architect and planner in the afternoon, and a critic and writer in the evening. Whenever traveling or looking at architecture, he would pull out his sketchbook, his thinking machine, and draw out the meanings so they would be engraved in his memory. As a young man he spent most of his free time in museums and libraries, noting the lesson of this and that. He also lived like a student-hermit until he was forty-two, in the relatively cramped Parisian garret of 20 rue Jacob, near the student quarters on the Left Bank of the Seine.

The EC's interests and strengths typically emerged at a relatively young age and were encouraged by the family, although the father and mother were ambivalent about a career that fell outside of the established professions. LC was encouraged by his father to develop his visual and manual skills, partly in order to go into the family business of watch engraving. But, after his first trip abroad at twenty, Le Corbusier's father constantly worried that the young man might become an impecunious artist, or Parisian Bohemian. The early years, from twenty to thirty, were a tortuous search for a new vision. This vision, the Purist/engineering/geometric synthesis, did not come fully formed until 1920, when he was thirty-three. Thus compared to the typical EC, he arrived at his first breakthrough rather late. However, it is possible to see two minor breakthroughs before this date: his

Jura Regionalism and Dom-ino system, so in these respects he again fits the pattern.

The atmosphere in the house of the EC is highly moral, if not always religious, and this inculcates a strict conscience within the EC that can be turned, like a searchlight, outward on society, or inward for self-examination. This upbringing leads the EC through many periods of religiosity, some of which are rejected, some of which are transformed. The young Jeanneret read Renan's *The Life of Jesus* and Nietzsche's *Thus Spake Zarathustra* and saw himself in the role of the prophet. After the collapse of his father's hand-crafted watchmaking business, which gave in to mass-produced watches in 1918, he saw his moral duty as bringing harmony to "a new machine civilization profoundly out of gear." Sometimes his implacable moral gaze would be turned inward, and he would see his own mistakes, apologize, and write in the manner of Augustine a section called *Confessions*. By the end of his life his "religious" message was codified in terms of a cosmic iconography and applied to churches, a monastery, and the city of Chandigarh.

After a decade of self-preparation the adolescent or young EC leaves home for the big city in order to test himself against the other leading lights of the profession, master his chosen domain, and challenge orthodoxy. LC fits this pattern well except that he leaves home for Paris twice, once at twenty for a year's stay and then at thirty to remain permanently. So, as mentioned, he makes the complete transition rather late. With surprising speed the Exemplary Creator discovers in the metropolis his mentor, and other peers, and together they explore the terrain, organize insti-tutions, write manifestos, and stimulate each other to new heights. LC fits the bill exactly. Once in Paris he goes to one peer, Auguste Perret, who introduces him to his mentor, Amédée Ozenfant, and together with Paul Dermée they found an institution, *L'Esprit Nouveau*, write manifestos such as *Aprés le Cubisme*, take part in joint Purist exhibitions, and work with other peers such as Fernand Léger. Painting now at night, Ozenfant and Jeanneret push each other, as did Braque and Picasso, to new heights of Purist painting which are sometimes so close to each other in style that it takes an expert to distinguish them—just as it did with the Cubist duo.

During this highly creative moment, one of tension and ques-tioning, of doubt and anxiety, the EC discovers a problem situation that promises to revolutionize the reigning paradigm of his chosen domain. He becomes isolated, seeks cognitive and affective support, and makes the first major breakthroughs of his career. These are quickly acknowledged by the field. Here again the developmental stages are on schedule, but not exactly parallel with the other seven. Instead of a short period of breakthrough—Picasso's *Les demoiselles d'Avignon* was 1907 and his analytical Cubist paintings were 1910—Le Corbusier's breakthroughs stretch over six or more years: Maison Citrohan (1920) and the villas La Roche (1923), Garches (1926), and Savoye (1928) epitomize the new white architecture, while his revolutionary city plans (1923, 1925) are at the center of this creative explosion. However, like the other seven, LC is both quickly acknowledged by society and the media and, at the same time, isolated and in need of affective and cognitive support. Ozenfant gives him this until 1924 when, much in the manner of the other Big Seven, he cuts off the hand that helped lift him up.

During this creative struggle, and success, the EC begins to fall under the sway of his own myth, or rather the feeling that his powers of invention are titanic, superhuman, something that must be propitiated. He enters into what Howard Gardner calls a Faustian bargain with this force, and makes an unconscious pact with the demonic god of creativity. This pact will sustain the flow of innovative work. Soon it becomes all-consuming; friends, lovers, family are sacrificed to the idol, to the career or Movement or Mission. Here I am exaggerating Gardner's analysis somewhat in order to fit Le Corbusier's development without, I think, betraying its basic spirit. By 1927 and LC's loss of the League of Nations project to the reactionaries, he is *the* prophet of the Modern Movement, well armed for warfare and disdainful of those who don't support the crusade. Indeed, by 1930 he writes *Croisade* (subtitled "the twilight of the academies") and at a furious pace churns out one polemic after another. He jettisons Ozenfant, marries Yvonne Gallis, has affairs with Josephine Baker and others, attacks the profession of architecture, acts with disdain to all who hold opposite opinions, and, importantly, produces "perfect" buildings—Garches and Savoye. Gardner, quoting Yeats, points out that the EC "chooses the perfection of the work over the perfection of life." This is true of Le Corbusier from the late 1920s into the future. However, it has to be said, there were moments of extreme anguish, when he recognizes how arrogant and limited he has become.

Because of the EC's enormous creative energy, and struggle, he is led on to another major breakthrough about ten years after the first one (what Garner calls the ten-year rule). This second great contribution is less radical than the first and more integrated with his oeuvre as a whole. Once again there are fairly precise analogies between the other seven and LC. By 1933 Le Corbusier has recast his 1923 City of Three Million and turned it into the *Ville Radieuse*, and by 1934 he has reinvented his white architecture as his second great style in the Weekend House: the strong, robust, concrete Brutalism that dominates the next sixty years of world architecture. The way this ten-year rule does not fit is that it has to be stretched to fit the lapse in realization and dissemination, for it is not until the *Unité* at Marseilles (1947–52) and Ronchamp, La Tourette, and Chandigarh, all in the 1950s, that the Brutalism is fully realized. There must be some latitude in interpreting the ten-year rule, which accounts for the difference in the domain. With Picasso the summation of his second major contribution is clearly *Guernica*, and, also with Picasso, it is arguable that there are further seminal contributions—for instance, those of the 1950s and 1960s. But Le Corbusier fits the main lines of the composite portrait: his second (and third?) breakthroughs are dialectical modifications of his oeuvre, not radical breaks with the tradition he has established.

Finally, as the EC reaches old age and his powers start to wane, in an attempt to retain his creativity he will seek previous marginal states, or heighten what Gardner calls his asynchrony (the out-of-step nature of the domain, the judges of that, and his particular cognitive talents). In order to stay fresh, Picasso, as he said, always raced ahead of beauty, always transcended the stereotypes when they caught up with him, and the typical EC makes a virtue of his relative inadequacies (paints like a child, exploits the awkward, finds the creativity in the mistake). Another method of staying young, Gardner points out, is by siding with, or exploiting, the young. Or, a variant on this, a way of growing old *ungracefully*, at which Picasso excelled, is to become lecherous, cruel, and perfectly unsavory (extreme Modernist tactics, which are conventional by the 1990s, as demonstrated by the "Sensation" show at London's Royal Academy). Other failing titans become elder statesmen (T. S. Eliot) or social and political commentators (Einstein). Here Le Corbusier both fits, and varies from, the construct. To stay fresh and rejuvenate himself he does side with the young; in fact, he supports the growing revolution within the official organ of the Modern Movement he helped create, that is, CIAM—the Congress of International Modern Architecture. He says at a meeting of CIAM in the 1950s that the "young are in the know"—referring to Team X—and that the old guard are no longer relevant. This authoritative declaration made to revise the body of Modern Architecture has the effect, like Gorbachev's revisionism of Lenin thirty years later, of actually destroying the body it was meant to rejuvenate. Unlike most of the Big Seven LC remains throughout the last twenty years of his life highly active and creative, only beginning to slow down a bit, because of heart trouble, in his last two years. He did not, in his seventies, become so much an elder statesman, as did another great Modernist, Walter Gropius, so much as an old warhorse, attempting once or twice to charge into a new battle. To the end he was a fighter and, as he knew, a Don Quixote.

From this brief comparison of EC and LC, we can see that Le Corbusier fits Gardner's construct to an extraordinary degree. He *is* a normal Exemplary Creator; I suppose now one should call it the Big Eight (if we can expand this Virtual Academy of Great Moderns). To see him as a type, and like the other seven, would not diminish him in the least—in his own eyes. Quite the contrary; as we have seen, he always wanted to be the Picasso of architecture, and he admired Einstein. These were the two titans he wished to be, and was, photographed with. He loved the idea of standardization and the type: "type needs," "type functions," "*objet-types*." So he would have liked to be considered a *normal* genius, warts and all, with all the nasty and cruel truths revealed in the end. If there is one obvious lacunae in the way I have laid out the comparison of EC and LC, and perhaps in Gardner's model itself, it concerns the empowering vision of the Protean Creator. Without emphasizing that mission, or all-consuming drive, one cannot understand what was at stake, what it was all about, for great creators are always, in the end, vehicles of their vision. They are not so much seeking to get into the Pantheon of Great Masters. Vision comes first, and so we turn to what LC wanted, to accomplish, in the end, and why he saw his life as a failure, perhaps even a tragedy.

PART I

NOTES

18   **"braggart, gas bag"**—*Le Corbusier, My Work*, trans. James Palmes, with an introduction by Maurice Jardot (London, 1960), p. 19. It appears from LC's 1948 copy of *Don Quixote* at the Fondation Le Corbusier (FLC) that he took most of these words from Cervantes in 1959: see annotations in frontispiece to that book.

22   **The historian Allen Brooks**—For Jeanneret's father and his journal, and the most thorough and best scholarship on the early years, see H. Allen Brooks, *Le Corbusier's Formative Years: Charles-Edouard Jeanneret at La Chaux-de-Fonds* (Chicago and London, 1997).

22   **"Froebel School"**—Ibid., p. 10.

23   **Architectural historians have often**—Marc Solitaire, "Le Corbusier et l'urbain: La rectification du damier Froebelian," in *La Ville et l'urbanisme après LC* (La Chaux-de-Fonds, 1987), ed. E. Tripet and I. A. Humair (La Chaux-de-Fonds, 1993), pp. 93–117; see also Adolf Max Vogt, *Le Corbusier, the Noble Savage: Toward an Archaeology of Modernism* (Cambridge, Mass., and London: MIT Press, 1998), pp. 286–99.

23   **"February 6, 1893"**—For journal entries see Brooks, pp. 12, 13, 15.

24   **"I remember seeing"**—Ibid., p. 18.

25   **Groups of workmen**—For LC's ideal society, a representational system having parallels with the watchmaking industry of the Swiss Jura, see *The Radiant City* (New York, 1967), pp. 192–93; first published as *La Ville radieuse* (Paris, 1935).

26   **"Sometimes I despair"**—Quoted in Geoffrey Hellman, "From Within to Without," in *The New Yorker*, April 26 and May 3, 1947.

27   **"'Only nature is inspiring"**—*L'Art décoratif d'aujourd'hui* (Paris, 1925), p. 198. The early buildings have been published by Etienne Chavanne and Michel Laville in *Werk*, December 1965, pp. 483–88.

29   **local architect, René Chapallaz**—The discussion of the Villa Fallet is based partly on material in Brooks, pp. 71–84. The letter is to Albert, December 15, 1907 (Ibid., p. 128).

33   **"Architecture is the masterly"**—*Towards a New Architecture*, trans. from the French by Frederick Etchells. First published in England 1927 by John Rodker. The Architectural Press facsimile edition 1946, 1948, 1952, 1956, 1959, 1963, and 1965. First paperback edition 1970. Etchells's translation of 1927 made from 13th French edition. Book originally published in Paris in 1923 by Editions Crès under the title *Vers une architecture*, from articles appearing in *L'Esprit Nouveau* since October 1920.

33   **Froebel Blocks are also**—Paul Turner, "The Education of Le Corbusier: A Study of the Development of Le Corbusier's Thought, 1900–1920," Ph.D. thesis, Harvard University, April 1971; Henry Provensal, *L'Art de demain* (Paris, 1904), p. 145. The quote is taken from Paul Turner, "The Beginnings of Le Corbusier's Education, 1902–07," *Art Bulletin* 53 (June 1971): 221. The notion of ideal beauty Provensal probably got from Julien Guadet's *Elements et theories de l'architecture*, pp. 1, 99, as Turner points out.

33   **The other aspect**—For Lalique, Galle, Guimard, and the Nancy School, see Turner, "The Beginnings," p. 215, which shows the influence of the French Art Nouveau designers on Jeanneret at this time.

34 **"the History of Art"**—See ibid., p. 128; the letter is to Albert, December 15, 1907.

34 **"so our task"**—Le Corbusier, *The Decorative Art of Today*, trans. James I. Dunnett (London, 1987), pp. 194–95. For a description of the watchcase, see Jean Petit, *Le Corbusier Lui-Même* (Geneva, 1970), p. 27.

36 **"the finished cost"**—Tim Benton, "Six Houses," in *Le Corbusier: Architect of the Century* (catalog to the exhibition at the Hayward Gallery, Arts Council of Great Britain, London, March 5–June 7, 1987), p. 50. This catalog is one of the key documents on Le Corbusier.

37 **"When one travels and works"**—This passage shows LC's confusion between the reader and himself. Le Corbusier, *My Work*, p. 37.

38 **"The city appears to me"**—Of Florence, see Brooks, pp. 96, 101, 109ff. for these letters and his translation.

40 **"I am coming home for a few days"**—Letter from Charles-Edouard Jeanneret to Charles L'Eplattenier, Paris, November 22, 1908, *Aujourd'hui Art et Architecture*, November 1965, p. 10.

41 **Later in life**—See Le Corbusier, *Précisions sur un état present et de l'architecture et de l'urbanisme* (Paris, 1930), pp. 17–18.

42 **In fact, the conflict**—Regarding LC and Zarathustra, see Turner, "The Education of Le Corbusier." Turner has looked very closely at the books Jeanneret collected and annotated up to 1930 and has established that Jeanneret read *Zarathustra* about 1908. My own previous research had established a general link between Nietzsche and Le Corbusier and also his dualism based on this link. See my "Charles Jeanneret—Le Corbusier," *Arena*, May 1967, in its revised form as part of my Ph.D. thesis "Modern Architecture since 1945," London University, 1970. There I discuss the influence of Hegel and Nietzsche's *Birth of Tragedy*. It seems to me he understood Nietzsche's ideas, as I argue in conclusion.

46 **Some of the passages**—Ibid., pp. 172–73; see also Turner, *The Education of Le Corbusier: A Study of the Development of Le Corbusier's Thought, 1900–1920* (New York, 1977), p. 63.

46 **"strike hard roots"**—Walter Kauffmann, *The Portable Nietzsche* (New York, 1954), p. 283.

49 **"The man of initiative"**—Le Corbusier, *Towards a New Architecture*, p. 24.

49 **As the historian**—Peter Serenyi, "Le Corbusier, Fourier, and the Monastery of Ema," *Art Bulletin* 49 (1967): 277–86; reprinted in *Le Corbusier in Perspective*, ed. Peter Serenyi (Englewood Cliffs, N.J., 1975), quote from p. 113.

49 **"I would like to live"**—See Brooks, p. 106n, and, for translation, p. 301.

50 **"my battles between rationalism"**—Letter from Jeanneret to his parents, January 1908, ibid., pp. 123–24n.

51 **"The greatest evil of our times"**—Edouard Schuré, *The Great Initiates*, Vol.1 (London, 1913), p. ix; other quotes from pp. xi, xvi, xxii, xxxv, xxxvi.

53 **"Jeanneret is tormented"**—For young Jeanneret's concept of idealism and ideals, see Brooks, p. 152.

54 **This ultimately leads to the persona**–Regarding the "Nietzschean Corbusier," see Stanislaus von Moos, *Le Corbusier: Elements of a Synthesis* (Cambridge, Mass., 1979), pp. 291–92, 364 n43; Patricia May Sekler, "Ruskin, the Tree, and the Open Hand," in Walden, ed., *The Open Hand: Essays on Le Corbusier*, ed. Russell Walden (Cambridge, Mass., and London, 1977), p. 92 n86; Kurt W. Forster, "Antiquity and Modernity in the La Roche–Jeanneret Houses of 1923," *Oppositions* 15/16: 143. Allen Brooks in conversation agreed with my assessment that Nietzsche had an influence on the young Jeanneret. Paul Turner ("The Education of Le Corbusier," p. 56) has discovered the passages of Le Corbusier's 1908 edition of *Ainsi parlait Zarathoustra* in which the artist noted in 1961 passages speaking of Zarathustra as a "Christ-like figure." Turner comments elsewhere: "And in some of these books (including Friedrich Nietzsche's *Zarathustra* and Ernest Renan's *Life of Jesus*) Jeanneret's annotations suggest that he had begun to identify with these figures and to think of himself as a kind of prophet too, in the realm of art and architecture." That this is in fact the case is apparent from his letters to the art critic (and his confidant) William Ritter in 1911–13. The Nietzschean tone is unmistakable. For a fuller treatment see Eleanor Gregh, "The Dom-ino Idea," in *Oppositions* 15/16: 75–79, 81, 83–87.

54 **As well as the many Nietzschean phrases**–Regarding the Nietzschean drawings, see Turner, "The Education of Le Corbusier"; and Gregh, "The Dom-ino Idea."

57 **"I have Viollet-le-Duc"**–Jeanneret is starting to reject Ruskin's Gothic for Classicism. Brooks, p. 171.

60 **The Ateliers d'art is descibed**–Le Corbusier, *Ouevre complète 1, 1910–1929*, ed. W. Boesiger and O. Stonorow (Zurich, 1964; and London, 1966), p. 22.

61 **The most extraordinary invention**–For "La Construction des Villes," a manuscript unearthed by Allen Brooks, see Brooks, pp. 201–8.

64 **"As French"**–Regarding the opposition of art and industry in national terms between France and Germany, see Charles-Edouard Jeanneret, *Etude sur le mouvement d'art décoratif en Allemagne* (La Chaux-de-Fonds, 1912). The influence of the Garden City movement on Le Corbusier can be found in Brian B. Taylor, *Le Corbusier et Pessac 1914–1928*, Vols. 1 and 2 (Paris, 1972).

65 **"autocratic and tyrannical"**–For this and further quotes relating to Behrens, see Letter from Jeanneret to L'Eplattenier, January 16, 1911, in Brooks, pp. 238–39.

66 **This was Cingria-Vaneyre's**–See Turner, "The Education of Le Corbusier," p. 80.

66 **These sets of conjoined ideas**–Regarding Jeanneret's "Voyage to the Orient," see ibid., p. 237.

68 **"When one travels and works"**–See Maurice Besset, *Who Was Le Corbusier?* (Geneva, 1968), p. 11; and Le Corbusier, *My Work*, (London, 1960), p. 37.

69 **"I practiced architecture without professional lectures"**–See Letter from LC to Jean-Pierre de Montmollin, March 15, 1965 (FLC, Dossier U3 9, 214).

69 **This Le Corbusier had trouble doing**–Regarding LC's regret of his form of self-education, see Le Corbusier, *Entretien avec les étudiants des écoles d'architecture* (Paris, 1943); translated as *Talks with Students* (New York, 1961), p. 77.

70 **"We defend beautiful modern technology"**—Charles Jeanneret, *Le Voyage d'Orient*, written 1911–14, reedited by Le Corbusier on July 7, 1965 (Meaux, 1966), p. 38.

71 **"We visited rooms"**—Jeanneret, *Journey to the East*, ed., annotated, and trans. Ivan Zaknic with Nicole Pertuiset (Cambridge, Mass., and London, 1989), quotes from pp. 22–23.

74 **"See what confirms"**—Jeanneret, *Le Voyage d'Orient*, p. 38.

75 **"the undeniable Master"**—See Jeanneret, *Journey to the East*, quotes from pp. 30, 184, 234, 220, 226, 226, 216, 264 n10, 217, 263 n2.

75 **"the harsh, tyrannical sway"**—Letter from LC to William Ritter from Athens dated either September 8 or 18, 1911; quoted in an excellent article on this period, Gregh, "The Dom-ino Idea," pp. 76, 86 n102, n107.

76 **"in this town"**—Ibid., pp. 77, 87 n115.

76 **"imagination and cold reason"**—See Le Corbusier, *Towards a New Architecture*, p. 190.

76 **The idea of the Parthenon**—Ibid., pp. 195, 197, 201.

77 **"It is a question of pure invention"**—Ibid., pp. 202–4.

79 **"You recognize these joys"**—Jeanneret, *Journey to the East*, pp. 14, 15, 16, 18, 24.

82 **"The obsession for symbols"**—Regarding LC's Purist theories of communication, 1921, see ibid., pp. 176–77.

83 **"Sensations, manifold and extreme"**—Ibid., pp. 174, 179.

83 **"The table is set"**—Ibid., p. 188.

84 **"The Obsession"**—Letter from LC to Ritter, April 6, 1913, Brooks, p. 375.

86 **"Wait 10 years"**—See Jeanneret, *Sketchbook A2, 1915–16*, with a preface by André Wogensky, introduction by Maurice Besset, notes by Francoise de Franclieu (London, 1981), p. 97.

88 **"It is the ruin of all my teaching"**—See Jean Petit, *Le Corbusier Lui-Même* (Geneva, 1970), p. 4. The source and date of this quote are not given by Petit.

88 **"Italy is a graveyard"**—Jeanneret predicts conflicts and broken friendships *before* they occur, *as a consequence* of his will to impose his vision of the new truth. See Gregh, "The Dom-ino Idea," pp. 76, 86 n109.

89 **When sold, in 1919**—This sad tale is masterfully set out in Brooks, pp. 310–29.

98 **Jeanneret virtually stole the design**—Brooks, pp. 414–15.

100 **This sort of simplicity**—Regarding LC's La Scala Cinema under attack, see Petit, pp. 48–49, quote from *La Sentinelle*, La Chaux-de Fonds, December 1916.

104 **But several unfortunate events**—Regarding the Villa Schwob project's cost overruns and lack of supervision, see Letter from Jeanneret to Anatole Schwob, April 24, 1917. Ibid., p. 427.

104 **"It seems to me"**—Letter from Jeanneret (La Chaux-de-Fonds), October 28, 1915. Ibid., p. 46.

PART II

110 **"A swamp"**—*L'Art décoratif d'aujourd'hui*, p. 217.

111 **"A conviction"**—Ibid.

112 **"In May 1917"**—Amédée Ozenfant, *Mémoirs 1886–1962* (Paris, 1968), quoted in *Aujourd'hui Art et Architcture*, November 1965, pp. 14–15. The first date of meeting is disputed. Le Corbusier claimed it was a year later, in the spring of 1918.

113 **"The war is over"**—Behind Purism was a notion of Darwinian evolution. Charles Jeanneret and Amédée Ozenfant, *Après le Cubisme* (Paris, 1918), p. 27.

114 **"Decadence is produced by facility in making"**—Quoted in ibid.

114 **"a magnificent epoch"**—Jeanneret's reference to the Parthenon shows how intent he was on making new architecture an equivalent of ancient virtues. Ibid.; also in *Aujourd'hui Art et Architecture*, November 1965, pp. 14–15.

114 **In the second chapter**—The first chapter was written by Ozenfant. Turner ("The Education of Le Corbusier") comes to much the same conclusions on who wrote most of which chapters, from the internal evidence and style. The interest in comparing the "rigor" of the Parthenon with that of the machine was more Le Corbusier's than Ozenfant's.

116 **"A great epoch has begun"**—On LC's Calvinistic strain—a form of economic determinism appeals to him—see *Towards a New Architecture*, p. 210.

116 **"1. Primary sensations"**—Ozenfant and Jeanneret distinguished two types of formal sensation. See "Le Purisme," *L'Esprit Nouveau* 4 (1921): 369–86, quoted in Robert L Herbert, *Modern Artists on Art* (Englewood Cliffs, N.J., 1964), pp. 61–62.

118 **Ozenfant described the genesis of Jeanneret's persona**—See *Aujourd'hui Art et Architecture*, November, 1965, p. 15.

119 **"L'Esprit Nouveau, which had such an attractive title"**—For LC's last interview and the revolutionary persona see interview with Huges Desalle in Ivan Zaknic, *The Final Testament of Père Corbu* (New Haven and London, 1977), pp. 110–11.

120 **Also "Saugnier" was getting too much credit**—In the second edition of *Towards a New Architecture*, Le Corbusier omitted the name Saugnier and dedicated the book to Ozenfant. Quoted in Hellman.

123 **"This is a successful achievment"**—Le Corbusier, *The Four Routes* (London, 1947), p. 103; first published in French as *Sur Ies 4 Routes* (Paris, 1941).

124 **"A thousand excuses"**—See *L'Art décoratif d'aujourd'hui*. The apology was written at the reedition of the book in 1959, p. xv.

124 **"He loves to have adversaries"**—For the writings in LC's father's journal, on Corbusier's combative character, see Brooks, p. 493.

124 **"In architecture such an error is fatal"**—For Le Corbusier's condemnation of German architecture, see Le Corbusier–Saugnier, *L'Esprit Nouveau* 9 (1922).

125 **This attack on Peter Behrens**—Ibid.

125 **"But what saddens us"**—LC (or Paul Boulard) continues to bring against the Germans their lack of technical rationality. See *L'Espirit Nouveau* 19 (1923).

125 **"In the depths of our being"**—For Paul Boulard's thoughts on German Expressionism, see Paul Boulard, *L'Esprit Nouveau* 25 (1925).

126 **"Here is the mirage"**—Ibid.

127 **"The realist, useful object is beautiful"**—LC moves from one attack to the next. See *L'Art décoratif d'aujourd'hui*, p. 17.

131 **"A QUESTION of morality"**—For Le Corbusier's mechanical idea, concerning the engineer's aesthetic and morality of unblinkered truth, as opposed to deceits of the then current architecture, see *Towards a New Architecture*, p. 17.

131 **"We throw the out-of-date tool on the scrap heap"**—LC had come to the important conclusion that one of the truths that the engineer, as opposed to the architect, upholds was that of preserving only useful tools and scrapping all others. Ibid., p. 17.

132 **"We claim in the name of the steamship"**—More qualities that some engineers may strive after. Ibid., p. 23.

132 **"The purpose of construction"**—LC formulates the tuning-fork theory of cosmic communication. Ibid., p. 23.

132 **"This sounding-board"**—LC interrogated science and mathematics for their hints of a universal language in accord with our "axis." Ibid., pp. 192–96.

133 **"We are all acquainted"**—For Plato's elite of philosopher kings we get a modern substitute of enlightened businessmen. Ibid., p. 22.

134 **"The art of our period"**—The William Morris idea of Modernism. Ibid., p. 96.

134 **"The social contract which has evolved"**—Ibid., p. 126.

134 **"Rome's business was to conquer the world"**—Ibid., p. 142.

134 **Ernest Mercier**—See Robert Fishman, *Urban Utopias in the Twentieth Century: Ebenezer Howard, Frank Lloyd Wright, Le Corbusier* (Cambridge, Mass., and London, 1982), p. 195.

134 **"The magnificent flowering"**—For LC's interest in Taylorism, see ibid., pp. 258–59.

135 **"But what especially moves me"**—For Max Du Bois's conviction that LC's architecture and paintings were the best, see William Curtis, *Le Corbusier: Ideas and Forms* (London, p. 74); Russell Walden, "Le Corbusier's Early Years," in *The Open Hand*, p. 153.

136 **"Ah! Those prisms"**—Max Du Bois, in answer to Jeanneret's "What Architecture Is"; see Curtis, p. 74.

136 **Or, when Le Corbusier was hanging the collection**—This story is told several times by Le Corbusier; see, for instance, *My Work*, pp. 62–63; or for a good discussion of the story, see Fishman, *Urban Utopias in the Twentieth Century*, pp. 188ff.

140 **"Man walks in a straight line"**—Le Corbusier, *The City of Tomorrow*, trans. Frederick Etchells (London, 1929), p. 7; from *Urbanisme* (Paris, 1925). As Reyner Banham has pointed out, the pack-donkey also walks in a straight line—if given a flat surface and a big push.

140 **"This modern sentiment is a spirit of geometry"**—For LC's Purist concept and Classicism, a result of modern industry, see ibid., p. 38.

141 **"Thus a street"**—Ibid., p. 74. This idea of LC's was dropped by the end of *Urbanisme*.

141 **"My role has been a technical one"**—*Ibid.*, pp. 298–301.

143 **"I am going to enable you to realize your theories in practice"**—See Le Corbusier and Pierre Jeanneret, *Oeuvre complète, vol. 1, 1910–1929*, ed. W. Boesiger and O. Stonorov (Geneva, 1929), p. 78.

143 **"explorer, multivalent artist"**—Quoted in Philippe Boudon's excellent sociological study, *Pessac de le Corbusier* (Paris, 1969), p. 11.

143 **"1. Chaos, disorder"**—LC quoting the eighteenth-century French Classicist Abbé Laugier in *The City of Tomorrow*, p. 72.

144 **Indeed, judging by the sociological study**—Boudon.

147 **"This redistribution of the land"**—For one of CIAM's main points of theory, see Ulrich Conrads, *Programmes and Manifesto on 20th Century Architecture* (London, 1970), p. iii. The statement comes from the CIAM foundation manifesto of 1928.

148 **For the next several months**—*The Contemporary City for Three Million* was conceived overnight as an accident. See *My Work* (London, 1960), p. 62; *Oeuvre complète, vol. 1, 1910–1929* (Zurich, 1930), p. 34.

153 **"There already exists"**—For the idea that "the machine inevitably leads to a more egalitarian society," LC followed Adolf Loos and the Modernists. See *L'Art décoratif d'aujourd'hui*, pp. 39, 42.

154 **"Decorative art is an imprecise term"**—LC's ideal of social liberation, obtained through the machine, was shared by others such as de Stijl. Ibid., p. 67.

154 **In all his four revolutionary tracts**—For the silent-butler view of functioning objects, as proposed by Loos, see *Towards a New Architecture*, p. 89.

154 **"When the typewriter was invented"**—See *L'Art décoratif d'aujourd'hui*, p. 76 n1.

155 **"Useful objects in our lives"**—Another aspect of morality, scrapping objects when they cease to function, as in LC's *Towards A New Architecture*. See quote in ibid., p. 1.

155 **"Lenin was seated in the Café Rotunda"**—Ibid., p. 8.

155 **"The all-naked man"**—Ibid., p. 24.

156 **"We are at the dawn of the machine age"**—LC brings together the mechanical and cultural evolution. See *The Decorative Art of Today* (London, 1987), p. 126. James I. Dunnett has provided a skillful translation that keeps the layout and character of the original, and a good introduction.

156 **"Cinema, books"**—Ibid., p. 128.

157 **"The machine is conceived within the spiritual framework"**—In this parable of Le Corbusier's, one can hear the echo of Zarathustra, preaching the superman, the machine as the enabling god. Ibid., p. 106.

158 "His enthusiasm overflowed"—Ibid., p. 106–7.

158 "**Ordered! Let us reflect**"—LC has transferred his previous love of nature to the machine. Ibid., p. 112.

159 "**Art has no business resembling a machine**"—Ibid., p. 114.

161 "**Demand bare walls in your bedroom**"—See quote in *Towards a New Architecture*, pp. 114–15.

162 "**His spirit has created the geometry**"—LC's previous arguments of Purism are extended—man is a geometrical animal. See *La Peinture Moderne* (Paris, 1925), p. 37.

162 "**The spirit of man and nature**"—Ibid., p. 138.

163 "**We understand for want of a better word**"—Ibid., pp. 153–54.

164 "**as it was put, the problem of beauty was insoluble**"—Ibid., pp. 170–72.

164 "**[Modern man] has need of the ideal certainties**"—Ibid., p. 10.

165 "**The Five Points of a New Architecture**"—*Oeuvre complète, vol. I, 1910–1929*, pp. 128–29.

179 "**Demand a bathroom looking south**"—The bathroom: the first demand of LC's "Manual of the Dwelling," *Towards a New Architecture*, p. 114.

184 "**Arab architecture gives us a precious example**"—*Oeuvre complète, vol. 2, 1929–1934* (London, 1964), p. 24.

PART III

191 "**When I was married**"—Quoted from memory by Kunio Maekawa, the Japanese architect who worked with Le Corbusier, in *Aujourd'hui Art et Architecture*, November, 1965, p. 109.

192 "**A great event today**"—Yvonne Gallis quoted in Petit, p. 77.

192 "**He spent the evening discussing women**"—Taya Zinkin, "No Compromise with Corbusier," *Guardian*, September 11, 1965.

194 "**Yvonne died yesterday morning**"—See Petit, pp. 120–21; and *My Work*, p. 199.

196 "**In a stupid variety show**"—Petit, p. 68.

198 "**1. Entrance**"—For ballet designed by LC for Josephine Baker, see Richard A. Moore, "Alchemical and Mythical Themes in the Poem of the Right Angle 1947–1965," *Oppositions* 19/20: 118.

199 **There are countless sketches**—See the letter from Jean de Maisonseul to Samir Rafi, in Stanislaus von Moos, "Le Corbusier as Painter," *Oppositions* 19/20: 89. This article of von Moos makes telling and important connections between the art and architecture of LC.

200 "**Our wanderings through the side streets**"—Zinkin.

202 **"As we were getting off the plane"**—Zinkin. For quote, see Le Corbusier, *When the Cathedrals Were White: A Journey to the Country of Timid People* (New York, 1947 [written in 1935 and 1945]), pp. 135–36.

203 **"I made a trip to Vassar"**—Ibid., p. 137.

203 **"A piece for each Amazon"**—Ibid., p. 145.

204 **"You women are also interested in Caravaggio?"**—Ibid., pp. 146–47.

204 **"The perpetuation of the species"**—A series of antitheses between Cubism and Surrealism. Ibid., pp. 150–51.

206 **"As the painting is"**—Ibid., p. 151.

207 **"I was neither mad nor clownish"**—For LC's rejection of cosmopolitan life and urbane sophistication see *The Radiant City*, p. 6.

207 **"I am attracted to a natural order of things"**—*My Work*, p. 146.

212 **But just as Le Corbusier produced**—*Oeuvre complète, vol. 1, 1910–1929*, p. 190.

215 **"The goal of the Mundaneum"**—*The Radiant City*, p. 200.

221 **"In the very first pages of this book I have warned you"**—A new tone is discernible in LC's writings. For this metaphor in city planning see Anthony Sutcliffe, "A Vision of Utopia," in *The Open Hand*, p. 227.

221 **"in a new slavery"**—Ibid., p. 186.

221 **"Rome meant enterprise"**—*When the Cathedrals Were White*, pp. 5, 4.

221 **"When the cathedrals were white"**—The Age of Faith. See *The Radiant City*, p. 177–79.

222 **"The Van Nelle tobacco factory in Rotterdam"**—*When the Cathedrals Were White*, p. 168.

223 **"In the Ford factory"**—Quoted by Lionel March in a review of Norma Evenson's book *Le Corbusier, the Machine, and the Grand Design*, in *Design* magazine, 1970, p. 70.

228 **Walter Gropius wrote compromising letters**—For the Modern Movement see Petit, p. 75; and *Oeuvre complète, vol. 11, 1929–1934*, pp. 17–18. Some of this material I covered in *Architecture 2000: Predictions and Methods* (London, 1971), in the section called "La Trahison Perpetuelle des clercs," which was slightly expanded in *Archithese* 11 (Zurich, fall 1971). Further references can be found there, although the overall problem has not been adequately dealt with anywhere.

228 **"M. de Senger published his second book"**—Petit, p. 81.

230 **"From my point of view"**—See ibid., p. 78. The "other story" was told to me by M. Andrieni at the Fondation Le Corbusier.

231 **"In Rome, 1934"**—See Robert Fishman, "From the Radiant City to Vichy: Le Corbusier's Plan and Politics, 1928–1942," in *The Open Hand*, pp. 245–83; see also his *Urban Utopias in the Twentieth Century*, pp. 213–51.

231 **"good people"**–Quoted from a letter from M. Brunel to LC, December 26, 1932, in Mary McLeod, "Le Corbusier and Algiers," *Oppositions* 19/20: 82 n10.

232 **Robert Fishman has clarified many of the issues**–See Petit, p. 86.

234 **Settling into an abandoned farm**–Ibid.

234 **Here he goes against many of his previous ideas**–McLeod, pp. 55–85, quotes from pp. 74, 79.

234 **"Thus at the time of defeat"**–For the Ubus after Alfred Jarry, see Le Corbusier, *The New World of Space*, ed. Reynal and Hitchcock (New York and Boston, 1948), p. 21.

236 **Because, he implies**–Regarding the Vichy bandwagon, see Petit, p. 86.

237 **"The minister Peyrouton"**–For Le Corbusier's early part of his story, *Poesie sur Alger*, see Petit, p. 87.

238 **Already he had changed his Syndicalist slogans**–McLeod, pp. 74–80.

240 **"Town planning"**–*My Work*, p. 147.

240 **"I told them it was they who ought to join me"**–For LC's words, see Hellman.

241 **This old idea is at least arguable**–See Hannah Arendt, "Bertolt Brecht," in *Men in Dark Times* (London, 1970), pp. 207–50.

PART IV

246 **"A French aperitif"**–*When the Cathedrals Were White*, pp. 103–4.

248 **"it is an architectural melody"**–LC's plans of Saint-Dié were rejected by all sides. Quoted in Petit, p. 94.

248 **It synthesizes ideas**–For these ideas see Serenyi; see also Le Corbusier, *The Marseilles Block* (London, 1953).

252 **"The spirit of power triumphs"**–Again LC compares the Marseillian Block with his idea of the Parthenon. *Le Voyage d'Orient*, p. 154.

253 **Thus the Unité is seen, metaphorically**–Peter Blake, *Le Corbusier* (London, 1963), p. 123.

254 **"The defects shout at one"**–Regarding New Brutalism and postwar architecture, see *Oeuvre complète, vol. 5, 1946–1952*, p. 191.

254 **"I have decided to make beauty by contrast"**–Ibid., p. 191.

255 **He spent a day with Picasso**–Petit, p. 122.

258 **"Five years of storm, spite and uproar"**–See *My Work*, p. 138.

259 **While Le Corbusier was in the States**–Regarding his time with Nivola, see *Architectural Forum*, December 1969, p. 60.

261 **"inevitable space"**–*The New World of Space*, p. 8.

262 **The architect's words at the dedication**–*Oeuvre complète, vol. 5, 1946–1952*, p. 190.

262 **Father Couturier, editor of <u>L'Art Sacré</u>**—For this and a good discussion, see Timothy Benton, "Notre-Dame du Haut, Ronchamp," in *Le Corbusier: Architect of the Century*, pp. 247–49.

263 **"given free rein"**—Quoted in the best critical source on Ronchamp, Danièle Pauly, *Le Corbusier: The Chapel at Ronchamp* (Basel, Boston, and Berlin, 1997), p. 59.

263 **"I can remember so well"**—Ibid., p. 63.

265 **"the work (architecture, statue or painting)"**—"L'Espace indicible," *L'Architecture d'aujourd'hui* (1946), p. 9. Translated in Pauly, p. 111.

267 **This shift from Classical and Modern geometries**—In the first and subsequent editions of my *The Language of Post-Modern Architecture*, 1977, I featured Ronchamp for its metaphorical emphasis and multiple meanings; at the time I was unaware of Benoit Mandelbrot's *The Fractal Geometry of Nature*, published the same year, a book I did not read, alas, until 1991.

269 **The architect James Stirling and the critic Nikolaus Pevsner**—The two main attacks were James Stirling's "Le Corbusier's Chapel and the Crisis of Rationalism," *Architectural Review*, March 1956, pp. 155–61; and Nikolaus Pevsner's *An Outline of European Architecture* (London, 1963), p. 429. There were other attacks, by critics such as G. C. Argan, that typified the attitude of a whole generation of architects brought up on the tenets of rationalism.

270 **Yet Le Corbusier, the pantheist and nonconformist**—Regarding metaphorical analysis, see *Oeuvre complète, vol. 5, 1946–1952*, p. 72.

272 **"[Journalists at Ronchamp] virtually machine-gunned me"**—See Le Corbusier, *The Chapel at Ronchamp* (London, 1957), p. 7.

272 **At the same time, he was here experimenting**—Moore, pp. 109–39.

272 **So, here is the problem**—For enigmatic Symbolism and suggestive narratives as a typical Post-Modern genre, see my *Post-Modernism: The New Classicism in Art and Architecture* (London, 1987), pp. 52–65, 67–98, 101–24.

276 **"an ecclesiastical garage"**—For these epithets, see Pauly, p. 97.

277 **"In 1956 L-C was asked to accept membership"**—*My Work*, p. 141.

277 **His most bittersweet moments**—For a description of his success as an artist, and the quotes, see Petit, pp. 112, 118.

277 **"It is there [in creating art]"**—Ibid., p. 112.

278 **Major French art critics**—For the art critics against Corbu see the very good discussion in Christopher Green's "The Architect as Artist," in *Le Corbusier: Architect of the Century*, pp. 111–18.

280 **"I was, I think, his first encounter with 'India'"**—All quotes of Minnette De Silva are from Minnette De Silva, *Minnette De Silva: The Life and Work of an Asian Architect* (Orugodawatte, Sri Lanka [private printing], 1998), pp. 92, 100, 100, 147, 156, 343.

285 **Pandit Nehru, the leader committed to realizing Chandigarh**—Nehru quote is from one of the best books on LC and a good discussion of Chandigarh, von Moos, *Le Corbusier*, p. 261.

286 **Indeed, at the conference**–"Celebrating Chandigarh–50 Years," organized by the city and Jagdish Sagar among others, created a website after the conference, where its conclusions were aired; my summary of the consensus over what should be done was, apparently, included though I never did check to see. Some very good papers were given by Beinart, Sarin, Frampton, Sorkin, Safdie, Correa, Rewel, Wilson, Curtis, Doshi, Khosla, and many others.

290 **"This 'cap' . . . will become a true physics laboratory"**–*Oeuvre complète, 1952–1957*, p. 94. Quoted in von Moos, *Le Corbusier*.

295 **"open to receive newly created wealth"**–LC's justifications for the Open Hand are discussed in von Moos, *Le Corbusier*, p. 447, 456, and the symbolism is also analyzed in Sekler, pp. 43–95.

296 **"This, in fact, is the hardest task of all"**–For Nietzsche's references to the Open Hand marked by LC, see von Moos, *Le Corbusier*, p. 292.

296 **"sign of our epic"**–André Malraux letter quoted in Sekler.

300 **The linguist Noam Chomsky**–See Noam Chomsky, *Syntactic Structures* (The Hague, 1957); and his *Language and Mind* (New York, 1968).

300 **"It seemed to me that I was at the end of the road of logic"**–Regrettably I have lost the source of this quote.

300 **His "Five Points of a New Architecture"**–*Oeuvre complète, 1910–1929*, p. 26.

301 **"It is necessary to start at zero"**–Said often by Le Corbusier, for instance in *L'Art décoratif d'aujourd'hui*, p. 217.

302 **Balkrishna V. Doshi**–Doshi described the changes on the Secretariat at "Celebrating Chandigarh–50 Years," 1999.

302 **"I think if one accords some significance to my architecture"**–The "secret labor" of painting was mentioned several times as the source, for instance, in 1948 at the exhibition in Boston. See *My Work*, p. 197.

303 **"I adopted a technique of my own"**–For improvisation see Zaknic, pp. 111–13. This and the next quote were made in an interview in May 1965.

303 **"And it turned out later"**–Ibid., p. 117.

310 **He consciously promoted the transposition of concepts**–Stanislaus von Moos shows the transposition of forms from one function to another in *Le Corbusier: L'Architecte et son Mythe* (Paris, 1971), pp. 132–35.

311 **I have found more than fifty**–A list of LC's neologisms constitute his basic contribution to architectural language. These "words" or grammatical units he either transformed from others or invented, and they became his fundamental architectural concepts: 1. architectural promenade or Arab architecture seen in movement; 2. Domino structure; 3. *pilotis*; 4. roof garden; 5. free plan; 6. ribbon window; 7. free facade; 8. cell-box; 9. empty or blank wall at Schwob and La Tourette; 10. slab block; 11. zigzag blocks or blocks *à redents*; 12. serpentine slab; 13. loggia niche; 14. picture wall; 15. movable partitions; 16. curved wall or piano curve; 17. interior ramps; 18. pivoting doors; 19. neutralizing wall or respiration exact; 20. double-height space; 21. studio

space and interlocking section; 22. up axonometric and frontality; 23. marriage of contours; 24. flat shallow layered space; 25. spatial ambiguity, transparency; 26. compaction composition; 27. undulating roof; 28. independent or parasol roof; 29. sculpture on the roof; 30. exhaust stacks; 31. rain spouts; 32. periscope skylights, 33. light cannons; 34. spiral stair; 35. bare stair; 36. *ondulatoires*; 37. *brises-soleil*; 38. bottle rack; 39. cooling towers; 40. Spiral Museum; 41. light catchers; 42. tapering *pilotis*; 43. *béton brut*; 44. Four Functions; 45. Three Essential Joys; 46. Seven V's—Circulation Separation; 47. Six Types of Shade; 48. regulating lines and Modulor; 49. tension cants at Firminy; 50. cellular housing.

313 **"I shall not give your pavilion a facade"**—for the Electronic Poem, see *My Work*, p. 186.

315 **Le Corbusier's last exhibition structure**—The Centre Le Corbusier was the final work that he saw through to the working drawing stage; there were other works, completed after his death, in Chandigarh, Firminy, and elsewhere. The projects that influenced the Zurich Pavilion were his Nestle building of 1928 and pavilions for Liege, 1937, and Tokyo, 1957.

318 **"so-called Zurich Le Corbusier friends"**—Heidi Weber, *Documentation of the Centre Le Corbusier* (Zurich, 1967), p. 7.

PART V

324 **For instance, the psychoanalyst** — For the attacks on Le Corbusier as a sexual puritan see Gaston Bardot, "Charles-Edouard contre Le Corbusier: Essai de Psychoanalyse," in *Revue de Mediterranée*, September–December 1947, pp. 513–30, 682–96; and Paul and Percival Goodman, *Communitas* (New York, 1960), p. 49.

324 **Other critics** — Jane Jacobs, *The Death and Life of Great American Cities* (New York, 1960), esp. chaps. 1, 2.

325 **"The only ones capable"** — Jurgen Joedicke, *CIAM '59 in Otterlo* (London, 1961), p. 16.

325 **Lewis Mumford, every so often, attacked him** — See Lewis Mumford, *Progressive Architecture*, October 1965, p. 236; and his "The Case against Modern Architecture" and "The Marseilles Folly," in *The Highway and the City* (New York, 1963).

332 **"I tried to make a place of meditation"** — Quoted in Boit and Perrot, *Le Corbusier et L'Art Sacré: Sainte-Marie de la Tourette Eveux* (Lyon, 1985), p. 9.

333 **The encomiums that LC received were fulsome** — For the Gold Medal praise and LC's speech, see *RIBA Journal*, April 1953, pp. 215–18.

333 **"There is no 'wing of victory'"** — quoted in Zaknic, p. 51 caption.

334 **When one of the CIAM architects called him a genius** — Sigfried Giedion, *Space, Time, and Architecture*, 5th ed. (Cambridge, Mass., 1967), pp. 568–69.

334 **According to a friend** — Letter from Pierre Emery to Russell Walden, in Walden, *The Open Hand*, p. 158 n46.

334 **"I discovered Christ late in life"** — Albert Jeanneret's letter is quoted in Zaknic, p. 21. Zaknic, I think, concurs with the emphasis I placed on *Don Quixote*, suffering, and the tragic view in the first edition of this book.

334 **"Here, at this point, I must thank two men"** — See Zaknic, p. 99.

339 **"[When young I had] the feeling that I was a nobody"** — Zaknic, p. 110.

339 **"Painting is a bitter struggle"** — *My Work*, p. 219.

340 **"A megalomania worse than Ledoux's"** — Ibid., p. 131.

340 **"Mr Lemaresquier points out"** — Ibid., pp. 49, 50, 51, 52, 138, 140, 141.

343 **"burn what you loved and love what you burned"** — this phrase, written when Jeanneret was twenty-one, is from the letter discussed on pp. 40ff.

343 **"Art is a deep love of one's ego"** — Ibid.

349 **"pored over the latest volume of Corb"** — Mark Girouard, *Big Jim: The Life and Work of James Stirling* (London, 1998), p. 87.

352 **"Finding myself alone again"** — Quoted in Zaknic, p. 100.

INDEX

Photography

Courtesy of the Architectural Association: 112

The Architectural Press, London: 123, 124

Archizoom: 96

Artemis Verlag, Zurich: 2, 7, 8, 9, 20, 67, 68, 74, 78, 84, 87, 121, 126, 127, 128, 131, 132, 136, 138, 139, 140, 141, 142, 143, 146, 148, 159

Tim Benton: frontispiece, 17, 98, 99, 171, 205

Alan Blanc (Courtesy of the Architectural Association): 58

Bibliothèque de la Ville, La Chaux-de-Fonds: 3, 6, 11, 34, 47, 48, 50, 54, 56, 57, 63

City of Chandigarh: 175

Collection Ahrenberg: 115, 117, 118, 119

Dokumentation Le Corbusier, Stiftung Heidi Weber, Zurich: 23, 66, 114, 116, 120, 122, 125, 133, 135, 149, 202

Dunod, Paris, by Philippe Boudon, © Dunod: 86 b.

Editions Crès, Paris: 35, 40, 55, 72, 75, 77, 79, 80, 90, 91, 92, 103

Fondation Le Corbusier, Paris: 1, 10, 31, 36, 37, 38, 39, 41, 42, 43, 44, 45, 69, 71, 93, 95, 137, 147, 150, 166, 173, 204, 209, 217

French Government Tourist Office: 167, 168, 169

Lucien Hervé, Paris: 134

Information Service of India, London: 191

Charles Jencks: 4, 5, 12, 13, 14, 15, 16, 18, 19, 21, 22, 24, 26, 27, 28, 29, 30, 32, 33, 46, 49, 51, 52, 53, 59, 60, 61, 62, 64, 65, 70, 76, 81, 82, 83, 88, 89, 105, 106, 107, 108, 109, 110, 129, 130, 144, 145, 152, 153, 154, 155, 156, 157, 158, 161, 172, 176, 177, 178, 179, 180, 181, 182, 183, 186, 187, 188, 189, 190, 192, 193, 194, 195, 196, 197, 198, 199, 200, 201, 203, 206, 207, 208, 210, 211, 212, 213, 214, 215, 216, 218, 219, 220, 221, 222

Rhomi Khosla: 184

Paul J. Mitarachi: 165

Tino Nivola: 162, 163, 164

Rodrigo Perez de Arce: 185

Jean Petit: 25

Hillel Schocken: 170

Victoria and Albert Museum, London: 94

Ken Yeang: 97

F. R. Yerbury (Courtesy of the Architectural Association): 86 a., 100, 101, 102, 104